Lacan and Klein, Creation and Discovery

Lacan and Klein, Creation and Discovery

An Essay of Reintroduction

ADAM ROSEN-CAROLE

LEXINGTON BOOKS
A division of
ROWMAN & LITTLEFIELD PUBLISHERS, INC.
Lanham • Boulder • New York • Toronto • Plymouth, UK

Published by Lexington Books
A division of Rowman & Littlefield Publishers, Inc.
A wholly owned subsidiary of The Rowman & Littlefield Publishing Group, Inc.
4501 Forbes Boulevard, Suite 200, Lanham, Maryland 20706
www.lexingtonbooks.com

Estover Road, Plymouth PL6 7PY, United Kingdom

British Library Cataloguing in Publication Information Available

Library of Congress Cataloging-in-Publication Data

Rosen-Carole, Adam, 1979–
Lacan and Klein : creation and discovery : an essay of reintroduction / Adam Rosen-Carole.
p. cm.
Includes bibliographical references and index.
ISBN 978-0-7391-6456-3 (cloth : alk. paper) -- ISBN 978-0-7391-6458-7 (electronic)
1. Psychoanalysis. 2. Lacan, Jacques, 1901–1981. 3. Klein, Melanie. I. Title.
BF175.R66 2011
150.19'50922--dc22 2010037458

∞™ The paper used in this publication meets the minimum requirements of American National Standard for Information Sciences—Permanence of Paper for Printed Library Materials, ANSI/NISO Z39.48-1992. Printed in the United States of America

For Todd Kesselman, in appreciation for the provocation

Contents

Preface

Many are convinced that theoretical divergences in psychoanalysis would be resolved, or at least sapped of their significance, would partisans of different schools attend more closely to the relative uniformity that prevails when it comes to handling particular clinical phenomena. The hunch is that though experience-far concepts, e.g., metapsychological concepts, may vary considerably, there cannot be *that much* difference in how analysts interpret particular clinical phenomena, at least when such interpreting is phrased in experience-near, low-level terms. Wishing to bring the unseemly rancor of psychoanalytic polemicism to a halt, wanting psychoanalysts to acknowledge their common identity and pursue a common good, adherents of this position suggest that it would be best to put theoretical disagreements on the backburner and focus on how much analysts have in common when it comes to "on the ground" clinical work.

One influential exponent of this view is Robert Wallerstein. The core of Wallerstein's highly influential argument in "One Psychoanalysis or Many"[1] is that a uniform observation language—e.g., "the patient was acutely distressed over the coming cancellation and was reacting unhappily and resentfully to that announcement" (51)—can be, if it is not already, consensually established and that

> [w]hen we reach beyond the interactions of the analytic consulting room, beyond the elucidation of the present unconscious, beyond, that is, the clinical phenomena captured in and explained by our *clinical* theory, to a more encompassing, more generally explanatory, more causally developmental accounting of mental life from its earliest fathomable origins, we are getting into the other realm that George Klein called the unnecessary *general* theory that we should sever and cast out by an action dubbed "theorectomy, the realm that the Sandlers call the *reconstructed* past unconscious,

> the realm of our pluralistic theoretical perspectives in psychoanalysis." (51–52)

This strategy is tempting. It would at least explain why the outcome rates of practitioners who vary considerably on theoretical and technical issues are more or less identical: no one does what they think they are doing (i.e., pursuing some unique range of goals in some specific manner), rather, they are all doing something sufficiently identical under a broad enough description.[2] But there are a number of difficulties with this position. For instance, one might think that Wallerstein overestimates the consensus "that unites us all as psychoanalysts," namely, the understanding that clinical theory is necessarily a theory "of transference and resistance, of conflict and defense" and is concerned primarily with "the present unconscious" (52). Or one might think Wallerstein naïve in casting "our pluralism of theoretical perspectives" in terms of "the various scientific *metaphors* that we have created in order to satisfy our variously conditioned needs for closure and coherence and overall theoretical understanding" (52–53). One need not be a sophisticated philosopher of science to suspect that Wallerstein's understanding of the work and status of observation language and theoretical language leaves much to be desired; and one need not be Derrida to have a reasonable suspicion about the facility with which Wallerstein distinguishes metaphor from literal meaning.[3] Or one might worry that the ascetic restriction of psychoanalytic knowledge claims to low-level, experience-near terms would mean forfeiting the claims of psychoanalysis to cultural interest as a hermeneutic apparatus without which various cultural objects and political scenarios would remain persistently unintelligible or insufficiently understood. Or one might worry that Wallerstein's defense of the amenability of psychoanalysis to scientific testing and thus its claim to scientific status—"[i]n regard to clinical theory, I view the theory formation, aided though it is in its conceptualization by the symbolisms of our metaphoric constructions, as nonetheless sufficiently experience-near, anchored directly enough in observables, to the data of our consulting rooms, that it is amenable to the self-same process of hypothesis formation, testing, and validation as any other scientific enterprise" (56)—falls short, that excising metapsychology would render the hypotheses formulated too vague to be of interest and value (e.g., except at the most superficial level, pursuing such hypotheses would not help to adjudicate between competing interpretations).

But the real problem is that the orientation Wallerstein advocates will not solve the plurality "problem," i.e., those problems pertaining to insular dogmatism, partisan polemicism, and widespread failure to learn from one another, *and he knows this*: "each of these theoretical explanatory contexts . . . will be persuasive indeed to the adherents of that viewpoint, who in fact will look at it as *the* useful and natural way in which to understand the . . . clinical interaction," (52) who assume their partisan commitments as "articles of faith" (56). The orientation he advocates would only prompt us to ignore, or, more precisely, disavow, the plurality "problem." Wallerstein's program for one psychoanalysis at the level of clinical theory and toleration for many metaphors at the level of metapsychology is both too weak and, though perhaps not too strong, problematic in its inability to acknowledge its normative force. It would yield a superficial and largely irrelevant unity and covertly suppress psychoanalytic plurality through the norms operative in its understanding of what counts as the basic data of psychoanalysis and the observation language in which this data must be couched: a formula for the return of the repressed if ever there was one.

Seeking along with Wallerstein's to intervene in the dogmatic gridlock of contemporary psychoanalytic polemicism, the following text rebukes his claims that attending to concrete clinical phenomena resolves or moots formal differences and that these differences are, inevitably, the expression of firmly established partisan convictions that take concrete clinical phenomena as mere occasions for their rehearsal. Although differences in the interpretation and treatment of clinical particulars express differences in perspective that run much deeper than even proponents of the "common ground" approach care to acknowledge—the number of theoretical, clinical, epistemological, and ethico-political questions implicitly involved in seemingly local questions of interpretation are immense—acknowledging the depth and significance of the pluralistic and perspectival character of psychoanalytic knowing may be a more effective manner of intervening in the impasse of stalemated polemics to which much psychoanalytic theorizing has succumbed, and it may yield new insights into the nature of the particular objects with which psychoanalytic theorizing is concerned: such objects are ontologically indeterminate, both discovered and created in the course of their investigation. Specifically, through a reading of the engagement of a psychoanalytic theorist widely considered to be one of the most dogmatic, namely, Jacques Lacan, with the work of another theorist considered to be at least equally dogmatic, namely, Melanie Klein, the following text seeks to retrieve the cognitive and ethico-therapeutic value of the exaggerated, perspectival, and endlessly pluralistic character of psychoanalytic knowing.

The ambition to retrieve the value of perspective and plurality from Lacan's engagement with Klein will no doubt strike many readers as paradoxical. In *Seminar I*, Lacan provides what seems to be a rather arrogant and mean-spirited commentary on Klein's famous "Dick" case (elaborated in "The Importance of Symbol-Formation in the Development of the Ego"). And throughout Lacan's corpus, it seems that Klein is dismissed on the grounds that she is theoretically naïve, therapeutically dangerous, and, due to the import she places on the ego, collusive with repressive ideologies. Returning the favor, many Kleinians either ignore or dismiss Lacan, especially on the ground of his nonacknowledgment of the pervasiveness and clinical-theoretical significance of phantasy. If Lacanians and Kleinians do not simply ignore each other, their "dialogues" quickly devolve into heated yet stalemated polemics.

My contention is that both Lacanians and Kleinians have failed to appreciate crucial aspects of Lacan's engagement with Klein and this has lead to (1) a false polarization and (2) a wild deformation of Lacan's teachings. Returning to the text of *Seminar I*, we will see how Lacan subtly displays a deep intimacy with Klein and thereby challenges us to read both Klein and himself in new ways. This text in which Lacan is so manifestly embroiled in a scathing assault on Klein will bear out the claims that on Lacanian grounds Klein's reading must be taken seriously, and only by taking Klein's perspective seriously can Lacan bring his claims to their truth. It brings them to their truth as limited and provisional articulations of the phenomena with which they are concerned and thus as opened onto the continuing need for other perspectives, for ongoing dialogue in the psychoanalytic field. What Lacan allows to be seen in his engagement with Klein is that truth emerges in psychoanalytic thinking in and through the taught dialectical tension of mutually qualifying and mutually challenging perspectives. Specifically, Lacan shows that truth transpires in a field of exaggerations and that only caught up in the currents of exaggeration and counter-exaggeration does truth emerge in its withdrawing fullness. If the following can render Lacan's manner of engaging Klein compelling, psychoanalytic plurality may finally become something other than a cantankerous chorus of partisan self-assertion or a target primed for scientific reduction.

Notes

1. Robert Wallerstein ed., *The Common Ground of Psychoanalysis* (Northvale, N.J.: Aronson, 1992).
2. Ibid., 55.
3. Jacques Derrida, "White Mythology: Metaphor in the Text of Philosophy," in *Margins of Philosophy*, trans. Alan Bass (Chicago: University of Chicago Press, 1985), 207–72.

Lacan and Klein, Creation and Discovery

> To bring the subject to recognize and to name his desire, this is the nature of the efficacious action of psychoanalysis. But it is not a question of recognizing something that would already have been there—a given—ready to be captured. In naming it, the subject creates, gives rise to something new, makes something new present in the world.
>
> —Lacan, *Seminar II*, 267

I. A Rebeginning through Logos

In "The Importance of Symbol-Formation in the Development of the Ego," Melanie Klein presents the case of Dick. What immediately captures Klein's attention is Dick's lack of ordinary, expectable anxiety. Strikingly, it was as if anxiety—the affective registration and psychic elaboration of the potential diminishment or dissipation of some good (and so of the destitution, even destruction, of the self committed to that good[1]) or of the intrusion of some injurious force—had been foreclosed by Dick's imperviousness to the compelling claims of the world, even to the simple sweetness of life. It was as if Dick was altogether untouched by the claim of the good, indeed as if he were functioning outside the parameters of normative expectation altogether. It was as if Dick had no stake in the world, no feel for the world as a source of joy and a site of self-realization, thus no need for anxiety over loss, frustration, lack, or injury. Abject, worldless, as if anxiety-free, Dick suffered immensely. Here is Klein's summary of the clinical picture: Dick was "characterized by an almost complete absence of affect and anxiety, a very considerable degree of withdrawal from reality, and of inaccessibility, a lack of emotional *rapport*, negativistic behavior alternating with signs of automatic obedience, indifference to pain, preservation."[2]

Of course, Klein would never concede that anxiety is altogether lacking. The key word here is "almost." Dick was surely not immune to anxiety, the claims of self-preservation, etc. Quite to the contrary, he was so racked by latent anxiety that, at times, he became excessively cold, detached, uninterested in the world around him and his place in it. Nor was Dick impervious to the demands of self-preservation. Again, quite to the contrary, he at times became mechanically oppositional, seeking to secure his faltering sense of self through rigid negativity—much like Dostoyevsky's narrator in *Notes from Underground* but without the conflicted pathos and manifest aggressiveness. In Dick's massive affective nonpresence, Klein discerns a fragile thread of subjectivity that she will seek to support and enhance. Suffering under a diffuse aura of unbearable anxiety, Dick could not respond to features of the world that ordinarily compel attention and interest, in response to which, ordinarily, horizons gradually expand and subjectivity develops. Or more precisely, Dick was minimally responsive to the goodness of the world but was so overwhelmed by latent anxiety that his engagements with the world were bereft of affective intensity, the weight of significance, implied commitment to the world being one way rather than another. The preponderance of diffuse anxiety established a bulwark against which efforts to connect with others and articulate his desire crashed and crumbled.

Although Klein for the most part presents Dick as suffering from impeded ego development consequent upon extreme paranoid anxiety, whether or not Dick had yet developed into the paranoid-schizoid position is somewhat ambiguous in Klein's presentation. In her account there are two main threads of description that are not easily reconcilable.

(1) It was not that connections with others were too risky for Dick—the problem was not guilt and phantasized fear of retribution for his aggression—but rather that such connections had no claim upon him, whirling as he was in a vortex of undifferentiated, terrible weightiness. Dick was a subject of suffering, a "subject" only in the sense of being thrown under an all-too-homogenous field of anxiety. He was overwhelmed, benumbed by terrors that knew no name, had no place—terrors that articulated the minimal contours of the hazy whole that was his horrifying universe. When presented in this light, Dick seems to be the poster child for Kristeva's account of abjection, or at least for the particularly torrid dimensions thereof.[3] Dick, it seems, had not yet developed the structure of paranoid-schizoid anxiety wherein projection and introjection lead to the development and specification of an originally nonobjectal, global anxiety that, for Klein, is the affective correlate of original "self"-directed sadism (viz., sadism directed at the very life of the being who is not yet distinguished from an object

world, who has not yet developed a sense of self through identifications with others or via other means).

(2) It was an aura of catastrophic danger looming over his relations with others, specifically with his mother, that fundamentally impeded Dick's development. In this vein, which is pursued more explicitly than the former, Klein claims that "Dick's further development had come to grief because he could not bring into phantasy the sadistic relation to the mother's body" (1975: 224). With inimitable boldness—yet a boldness that is in part tempered by and in tension with the previous description—Klein asserts that Dick's "interest in [trains, stations, doors, etc.] had a common source: it *really* had to do with the penetration of the penis into the mother's body. Door and locks stood for the ways in and out of her body, while door handles represented the father's penis and his own. Thus, what had brought symbol-formation to a standstill was the dread of what would be done to him (particularly by the father's penis) after he had penetrated into the mother's body" (1975: 224; emphasis added).[4] Unable to bear his sadistic impulses—which were manifest in his aversion to any act of aggression, e.g., his refusal to bite food and extreme awkwardness with scissors, knives, and tools—and fearing what would ensue if these impulses were unleashed (retribution, guilt, etc.), Dick abandoned the world. "The genital had begun to play its part very early; this caused a premature and exaggerated identification with the object attacked and had contributed to an equally premature defense against sadism. The ego had ceased to develop phantasy life and to establish a relation with reality. After a feeble beginning, symbol formation in this child came to a standstill" (1975: 223–24). In other words, Dick suffered from an extremely early and exaggerated sadism-infused and genitalized desire for his mother—and vicariously, as a resident in the mother's body, for his father and/or his father's penis. This desire promoted identification, an early form of satisfaction, but since Dick had not yet developed firm boundaries between inside and outside, the identification with the object of desire was simultaneously an identification with the object of assault. Desire and aggression thus succumbed to the same fate: near total repression.

Perhaps the former was a result of the latter; perhaps the two were somehow conjoined and overlaid; perhaps the radical indiscernability of Dick's affective life is registered in the tension between the two accounts. What is important to underscore for our purposes at the moment is that (1) as a result of being submerged in an all-too-consistent field of anxiety and/or (2) fearing his potentially self-and-world-annihilating sadism and its projected consequences, when Klein met Dick, he bore but a fragile attachment to his life. And it was precisely this fragile self-attachment that Klein was able to exploit in order to initiate him into a more complex relational field—into a world of symbolism, connection, and desire.

In a miraculous feat of therapy, Klein regulated Dick's anxiety sufficiently to initiate him into a world of differences and desires. The effect was truly transubstantiating. Through Klein's interventions, a resonance was struck that under her care gradually permuted into the full-fledged tones and motifs of (desirous, anxious) subjectivity. Dick was gifted with a world, bequeathed with psychic life (understood as the space of anxious and desirous representation). Klein's extraordinary achievement with Dick was, in her terms, to reinitiate his faltering development by facilitating the transformation of latent anxiety into manifest anxieties. In the course of the treatment, as particular objects were marked (by or as an indirect result of Klein's interpretations) by anxiety, new objects were turned to, explored, and connected with, and as these new objects became suffused with anxiety, Dick turned to ever-new objects, gradually configuring a world. Klein's achievement with Dick was nothing less than provoking the phobic construction of a world.

Concomitant with the worlding of and by anxiety, dependencies were fostered that allowed Dick's world exploration to develop according to a less-anxious rhythm. Though initially objects and others were sought only to alleviate anxiety, eventually more secure attachments were forged whereupon relations could be enjoyed (1) for their own sake, (2) insofar as they satisfied newly emerging desires, (3) insofar as they allowed new desires to emerge (the promise of desire is itself desirable), and, of course, (4) insofar as they continued to provide solace from his still extraordinarily gripping anxiety. Eventually, in the context of his newly achieved dependencies and object attachments, Dick's epistemophilic impulse (which is on Klein's account arguably innate, or, if not, surely primordial) gained sufficient momentum to liberate itself (to a significant extent) from the anxieties that were its initial condition. Whereas, previously, Dick was exclusively interested in objects only in virtue of their neutrality or distracting power, that is, only insofar as attending to them afforded a brief respite from the terrors of his anxiety-saturated existence, in the course of therapy he learned how to love the world, how to appreciate life amid objects and others, how to affirm and take root in his exposure and permeability, how to revel in the delights of development enabled by relational dependency.

Through her interpretations, Klein initiated Dick into a world of relations in which his place and status mattered, in which his questions and concerns were of pressing relevance, in which others' care was genuinely sought, and in which the possibility of possibility could be enjoyed. In Klein's words, "It has been possible to get into contact with him with the help of quite a few words, to activate anxiety in a child in whom interest and affect were wholly lacking, and it has further been possible gradually to resolve and to regulate the anxiety released" (1975: 228). Klein specifies that she "succeeded in causing the anxiety to become manifest by diminishing it in its latent state. When it did manifest itself, [Klein reports, she] . . . was able to resolve part of it by interpretation. At the same time, however, it became possible for it to be worked over in a better way, namely, by its distribution amongst new things and interests; in this manner it became so far mitigated as to be tolerable for the ego" (1975: 229).

Through but a few acts of *naming* or *symbolizing* that disclosed the world as comprised of concrete anxieties and latent desires, that is, by showing the world to be composed by somewhat enigmatic yet ultimately specific enough triggers of anxiety (specific enough to be at least temporarily avoided or negotiated with) underneath which trembled his own longings, Klein facilitated the distribution, and thereby the partial dissipation, of Dick's unbearable anxiety and the release of his desirous subjectivity. Through the work of symbolization, through the work, we might say, of Klein's interpretive metaphorics, Dick was conveyed (meta-phorized: carried across) to a world hospitable to the feeble resources of his fledgling ego. She provoked and allowed to unfurl an image of worldliness that Dick could assume as his own. Presumably, this image-world appealed to Dick, in addition to the reasons elaborated above, insofar as its assumption allowed for (1) enhanced connectedness with others, (2) the pleasures of development, i.e., experiences of the goodness of human nature in its developmental unfolding and of all the satisfactions associated therewith, and (3) a discovery of and investment in the unsuspected pleasures of life, an immersion in the exquisitely compelling character of spontaneous and passionate living (i.e., play). In sum, the image-world that Klein created/allowed Dick to discover significantly diminished his latent anxiety and thereby allowed him to experience, most broadly, the pleasures of being in the world and the solicitation of desire by which life is, at least at moments, enchanted.

The specific mechanism that promoted these felicitous developments was, strikingly, a quite heavy-handed Oedipal interpretation: "In this case . . . where the capacity to represent . . . was almost entirely lacking, I found myself obliged to make my interpretations on the basis of my general knowledge, the representations in Dick's behavior being relatively vague. Finding access in this way to his unconscious, I succeeded in activating anxiety and other affects. The representations then became fuller and I soon acquired a more solid foundation for the analysis, and so was able gradually to pass over to the technique that I generally employ in analyzing children" (1975: 228–29).

II. Controversy: Creation or Discovery

Lacan comments on Dick's case in *Seminar I*.[5] A major point of contention between Klein and Lacan is that Klein insists that her technique affords *access* to Dick's unconscious, while Lacan insists that Klein *produces* what she claims to find or facilitate. For Lacan, Klein's *speech* gives birth to Dick as a subject of the unconscious. By this he means that her desirous discourse impacts Dick in ways that completely obviate his conceptual comprehension and give rise to the psychic metabolism through which the unconscious is born. For Klein, on the other hand, it is because her interpretations are sufficiently *correct* that they resonate with Dick's unconscious—only thus can her therapeutic achievements be explained.[6] If Dick were not always already a subject or at least a proto-subject of the unconscious, and if her interpretations did not resonate with his unconscious, how could she have released the aggressive and epistemophilic impulses under the sway of which he became ever more prone to turn away from anxiety-suffused objects and toward other objects and persons, thereby developing new interests and eventually a livable world? How could it be that objects once turned from are not psychically abolished but persist sufficiently for him to return to them with augmented aggression, concern, and curiosity, that is, sufficiently for him to envelop these objects in various play activities, if the interpretations that she offered of Dick's relations with these objects did not, in some sense, resonate with elements that already had a place in his unconscious phantasy life?

Lacan, however, will remain skeptical about these lines of inference. Indeed, as we will see, he will problematize these claims along with the most crucial terms of Klein's treatment (such as projection, introjection, and ego development).

Klein and Lacan agree on the import of much of the case material (i.e., *that* the material is significant) as well as on the import of the results of Klein's interventions, e.g., Dick's burgeoning interest in and adeptness with words, his investments in objects and others, the massive diminution of his anxiety, and so on. But the significance of what transpires in the analysis differs radically for the two. As we will see, Klein's accent continually falls on *discovery*, while Lacan continually emphasizes *creation*. To be sure, by contacting the "rudiments of phantasy-life and symbol-formation," Klein believes she is able, by way of interpretation, to metaphorize, to carry and transform, latent anxieties into manifest anxieties and so she by no means wholly neglects the creative dimension of her therapy. However, Lacan will emphasize the dimension of creativity to a much greater extent than she, even to the point of suggesting that Klein creates the problems she solves, somewhat analogously to what happens with the development of transference neurosis in ordinary adult analysis.

In order to prepare the confrontation between Klein and Lacan concerning the meaning of the case material and what is at stake therein, let us first recap in a bit more detail exactly what Klein does in Dick's treatment.

III. The Treatment

In the first session, Dick was undisturbed by his nurse turning him over to a stranger, i.e., Klein. This strikes Klein as highly unusual. After Dick shows no interest in the toys set up for him, Klein "took a big train and put it beside a smaller one and called them 'daddy train' and 'Dick train.'" Thereupon, Dick picked up the "Dick train," rolled it to the window, and said "Station." Immediately, Klein "explained" (her term): "'The station is mummy; Dick is going into mummy.' He left the train, ran into the space between the outer and inner doors of the room, shut himself in, saying 'dark' and ran out again directly."[7] After allowing Dick to repeat this performance several times, Klein intervenes (again, in her terms, "explains"): "It is dark inside mummy. Dick is inside dark mummy." Following that, Dick "picked up the train again but soon ran back into the space between the doors." Then, astonishingly, in the midst of Klein's repetition of her initial "explanation" that Dick was "going into dark mummy," he "said twice in a questioning way: 'Nurse?'" Klein responds: "'Nurse is soon coming.'" Later, Dick, who suffered serious difficulties with language acquisition, used these words correctly (1975: 225).

In this session, it seems that Klein's goal is to provoke Dick's anxiety, to bring it onto the therapeutic stage, and, what's more, to provoke it into latching onto a few objects and/or the relations obtaining between them. This, she hopes, will both partially diminish Dick's latent anxiety by making it more ego-syntonic (because manifest and object-related) and allow the newly concretized anxiety to serve as the kernel around which symbolic play will develop. Fortunately for Dick, her intuition is a fruitful one. As a result of her astonishingly simple initial intervention (this is "Dick train," that is "daddy train"), a new motility is produced that provides further material for interpretation.[8]

In the very first session, an aura of hope, a sense of futurity, begins to settle in. Dick, responding to Klein's provocation, seems to be attempting to crawl out from his entombment in unnamable dread. It is unclear whether his amenability to play results from an intrinsic desire for development (he is just waiting for the opportunity to localize his anxieties and develop warning signals against overwhelming, i.e., traumatogenic, objects, events, etc.), from a desire to revive memories of the satisfactions of development (the play is an occasion to recall the goodness of life unfolding outside the constrictive parameters of his cavernous entombment), from a mimesis of Klein's desire for his play (Klein's solicitation to play or perhaps the solicitous or simply desirous quality of her voice through which the interpretation is articulated cuts through the thickness of his anxiety and strikes Dick as a faint glimmering, an opaque image, of desirous play), or from some other source. But play he does. Somehow, Klein's acts of naming resonate with Dick. Presumably, they resonate with his desires and anxieties, provoking them and encouraging their further articulation.

Regardless of exactly what precipitates Dick's rolling the train to the window or his enunciation of the word "station," once he does so, Klein takes the opportunity to "explain" that the station is "mummy," that Dick is going into mummy. Although Klein seems to be grasping at straws here, even creating by sheer interpretive willpower a symbolic relation between "station" and "mummy," this comment clearly strikes a chord with the child, who, in running to the space between the doors and then saying "dark" and running out again, is, as far as Klein is concerned, associating to station/mummy. Even if "station" did not yet represent "mummy" at the time of her enunciation of this word, Klein cannot ignore that once mummy and station are connected, Dick runs to the space between the doors and says "dark." Contiguity for Klein indicates unconscious association. Mummy is this dark place, Dick is in dark mummy. Klein tells him this explicitly after allowing him to repeat the performance several times.[9] Allowing the game to go on uninterruptedly for awhile allows Dick's anxiety (indicated by the repetitiveness of the play) to increase to the point where, just on the brink of becoming overwhelmed, he is open to the soothing function of Klein's words. *A new association is forged between interpretation and the abatement of anxiety*. Conveyed through the interpretation is a sense that repetition need not go on forever, that an *other* can provide solace, that dependency need not mean (only) overwhelming anxiety. The evidence for this, it seems, is that as Klein is in the midst of repeating her interpretation, Dick feels safe enough to announce a desire, specifically, a desire for further relief, a desire for an other, for an exit from dark mummy: "Nurse" he says twice, questioningly. Maybe Dick is calling out for the nurse. Maybe he is asking if there is a difference between mummy and nurse or between dark mummy and mummy-nurse. But perhaps even more important than the meaning of this word ("nurse") is Dick's questioning attitude and the implicit articulation of desire with which it is enunciated. Dick wants something . . . is it coming? Dick recalls something in its absence, represents it through speech, uses words both to soothe himself (by projecting a future, through words, in which the nurse would arrive) and to acknowledge his dependency on others.

Klein's therapeutic work at this point is organized around the following terms:

1. *The Ego*: Dick's ego is fragile but develops as his anxiety is regulated for him.
2. *Anxiety*: Klein sees in every move an expression of and/or an attempt to quell overburdening anxiety.
3. *Projection*: Klein reads Dick's play as projecting his internal objects (dark mummy, daddy, etc.) onto objects or spaces.
4. *Introjection*: Dick is able to introject Klein's words sufficiently for his anxiety to be at times provoked and at other times partially diminished by them.

5. *Phantasy*: For Klein, there are preexisting phantasmatic contents (daddy, mummy) and relations (sadistic, retaliatory, etc.) that are deployed in Dick's play projections.

In the next session, we witness something of a repeat performance. Dick "ran right out of the room into the dark entrance hall. He put the 'Dick' train there too and insisted on its staying there. He repeatedly asked: 'Nurse coming?'" (1975: 225). Some sort of symbolic play seems to be developing. The quick return to play suggests that Dick is beginning to symbolize more freely. Though ordinarily he is so hemmed in by diffuse anxiety that he cannot generate or accede to interest in the world around him, here he allows himself to be swept up by his desires and anxieties. He allows his desires and anxieties to come to the fore and carry his play. As anxious as this play may be, it indicates a certain relaxation, an amenability to being swept up and moved by his feelings. Dick even expresses an interest in the structure of his world. The train must remain in the entranceway. The nurse is continually called for. She isn't here; that shouldn't be. Dick seems to have internalized the possibility that anxiety can be met by pacifying care. The analytic scene is becoming for him the model of a universe in which his desires matter and his dependencies yield relief.

The rest of Klein's report on this session emphasizes the gradual unfolding of symbolization and play. In this session there is a bit of variation on the established routine. This time, in addition to running into the hall between the doors, Dick runs behind a chest of drawers, is overcome with profound anxiety, and calls out for Klein. Also, he begins to show an interest in the toys in the room, and through his interaction with them he is able to tentatively release a bit of his buried aggression: "He pointed to a little coal-cart and said 'Cut.' [Klein] gave him a pair of scissors" with which he attempted to scratch the toy coal (1975: 226). However, his efforts somewhat unavailing, he glances at Klein in a way that prompts her to join in. After she cuts out the pieces of coal for him, he "threw the damaged cart and its contents into the drawer and said, 'Gone'" (1975: 226). Klein then tells him that he is cutting feces out of his mother, whereupon Dick runs into the space between the doors, begins to scratch them, and then rushes over to the cupboard and steals away into it. For Klein, this indicates that his symbolic universe is gradually expanding, that "he identified the space with the cart and both with the mother's body, which he was attacking," and, presumably, that he fears massive retaliation for his violation of the maternal body (1975: 226).

In this third session, Klein notes an appreciable apprehensiveness in the repeated calling out for his nurse, who, at the end of the session, is welcomed with atypical delight. Klein draws a link between the specification of Dick's anxieties (want of the nurse, fear of the specific place behind the chest of drawers, etc.) and his expression of dependence on both herself and the nurse. Manifest anxiety propels Dick into the care of others upon whom he can depend. Also of note is that localizing anxiety renders Dick receptive to the soothing words "Nurse is coming soon."

The organizing terms of this session are:

1. *Repetition*: Dick runs into the entranceway again, repeats his call for the nurse, etc.
2. *Verbalization*: The anxiety provoked by the entranceway (dark mummy) provokes Dick to verbalize his desire for a consoling other.
3. *Anxiety*: Latent anxiety gradually modulates into manifest anxiety as it is soldered onto particular, new objects (the chest of drawers, different toys).
4. *Sadism*: Dick for the first time expresses aggression against the coal cart.
5. *Phantasy*: Klein reads Dick's play as drawing on contents and processes that dwell in his unconscious (feces, retaliation).
6. *Dependency*: Dick calls out for the nurse, who is warmly welcomed at the end of the session, and, for the first time, Klein. Perhaps a certain transference to Klein is gradually becoming established. Dick also involves Klein in his anxious affective life, allowing her to be the proxy for his aggression. Perhaps a certain identification with Klein is taking hold.
7. *Symbolization*: whether Dick is relating symbolically to new objects or is open to Klein's interpretive overlaying of his play with Oedipal meanings, Dick's symbolic horizon is slowly expanding.

By the start of the fourth hour, Dick's dependence on his nurse had intensified: he cries when she drops him off. His expression of discontent is perhaps enabled by his deepening belief in the possibility of consolation. His dependence on Klein is growing too, thus he soon becomes calm in her presence. This time, his inquisitiveness is piqued by the various toys in the room, which he duly examines. In the process, he comes across the coal cart and its dismembered contents, which are pushed aside and covered with other toys, perhaps indicating guilt or at least a localization of anxiety and symbolic resilience (the coal pieces from the last session have left an impression; they *still* indicate aggression and perhaps evoke guilt). Klein takes Dick's expulsion of the cart from the scene of play as a cue to intervene. She tells him that the damaged cart represents mother, whereupon he retrieves the cart and scattered coal and conveys them to the space between the doors—a first reparative offering?

Klein claims, in light of what transpires in the further course of the analysis, which is to say, in a moment of retrospective clarification, "that in thus throwing them out of the room he was indicating an expulsion, both of the damaged object and of his own sadism (or the means employed by it)" (1975: 226). Here we witness the development of projection.[10]

The new terms relevant to Klein in this session are:

1. *The Epistemophilic Impulse*: Although this impulse may have been suppressed by Dick's early "theorizations"/phantasies about his mother's body—his mother's body may have been phantasized as a vengeful, retaliatory force that would annihilate Dick in consequence of his sadistic desires—now, with the partial alleviation of anxiety and more secure dependencies on others (cohorts who would protect him?), the impulse is released. Dick becomes curious.
2. *Guilt*: Covering the dismembered coal cart suggests guilt over the aggressive act.
3. *Reparation*: By placing the dismembered cart (which Klein has told him is associated with his mother) in the entranceway (dark mummy), Dick may be attempting to repair aggressed-against mummy, to make her whole again by returning her dismembered parts to her, or simply offering an object of his enjoyment to her (a sacrifice to the dark maternal lord?).
4. *Expulsive Projection*: Dick, bothered by the coal cart, pushes it aside. Expulsion functions as defense; Dick not only turns to new objects and others to quell his anxieties, he takes direct action to get rid of anxiety-provoking objects.

From this point on, Klein's case report focuses predominantly on the slow expansion of Dick's symbolic universe, his attachments to others, and the relation between his sadism and paranoid anxieties. The wash basin becomes a focal site for anxiety (specifically through a fear of wetting), which Klein interprets as relating to his mother's body. Dick wipes water off of Klein's hands, which Klein takes as evidence that dependencies on and concern for others are enhancing. Anxiety is further particularized and associated with ever-new objects and processes: there is anxiety about urinating, feces, his penis, etc. Klein continues to interpret Dick as bringing into the open his aggression against his mother's body and the relation between this aggression and his paranoid anxieties: she commandingly asserts that "Urine and feces [and soon penis] represented to him injurious and dangerous substances," objects with which he might attack his mother's body and that, in the wake of their destructiveness, put him in jeopardy (1975: 226). Introjection and destruction become linked: Klein interprets Dick's phantasies of a penis in mother's womb and growing feeling of aggression against it, specifically feelings of aggression that are related to the desire to eat and thereby destroy it.

IV. How to Read Melanie Klein (A Few Comments)

Before proceeding to Lacan's understanding of what happened in the course of Dick's therapy and what is at stake therein, let us not forget that Lacan was, as we are, working with Klein's case construction, with a text that was written to demonstrate the validity and efficacy of her theories of psychosexual development. But the text is no mere illustration of an established doctrine, nor is it a knock-down demonstration of the validity and efficacy of her approach. Rather, the case unfolds, uneasily, as a series of rigorously conditional claims about the *plausibility*, the persuasive yet ever-questionable standing, of Klein's theories and technique. Klein is by no means the brute beast of theory she is often made out to be. Unfortunately, however, her critical scrupulousness has its limits—it never prompts her to thematize or, in her practice, really try to take account of the nature and status of psychoanalytic knowing. Vexingly, Klein continually acknowledges the problematic nature of theory forged by speculating and generalizing from finite clinical experiences, yet she fails to make anything of it. On occasion Klein even explicitly acknowledges the perspectival quality of her thinking but fails to explore what this might entail.[11] Klein's texts tend toward yet regularly refuse dogmatic self-certainty. They strive toward nomothetic universality while tenaciously clinging to idiographic specificity. The tension between the two is precisely the taught space of Kleinian thinking.

Klein's explicit and continual acknowledgments of the assumptions informing her work will bear significantly on how we understand the differences between her position and Lacan's and on our assessment of Lacan's reading of her text. As much as Klein leverages Dick's case to shore up her grand claims about psychosexual development—the major claim of the article is that "Since the child desires to destroy the organs (penis, vagina, breasts) which stand for the objects, he conceives a dread of the latter. This anxiety contributes to make him equate the organs in question with other things; owing to this equation these in their turn become objects of anxiety, and so he is impelled constantly to make other and new equations, which form the basis of his interest in the new objects and of symbolism" (1975: 220)—she will not let us forget that she is working with a number of assumptions and hypotheses that are, to a degree, but only to a degree, borne out in their plausibility by the case at hand. This marks a decided departure from her mission in the 1920s to corroborate Freud's reconstructions with direct observations of children's play. Though these assumptions and hypotheses are, Klein insists, "confirmed in a remarkably striking way by a case in which there was an unusual inhibition in ego development," they are continually, if not always as explicitly as one might like, marked *as* assumptions and hypotheses and thereby sustained in their questionability (1975: 221).

Klein begins "The Importance of Symbol-Formation" by foregrounding her assumptions about the psychosexual development of children. The argument of the paper, she says at the very beginning, "is *based on the assumption* that there is an early stage of mental development at which sadism becomes active at all the various sources of libidinal pleasure" (1975: 219; emphasis added). This "assumption" is a condensed statement of a complex position, the broad outline of which can be articulated as follows. Sadism is an element of the paranoid-schizoid position in which, at this early stage, the child's "dominant aim is to possess himself of the contents of the mother's body and to destroy her by means of every weapon which sadism can command" in order to defend himself from aggression which was originally aimed at his very being and subsequently projected onto (and/or attended to as it manifests in) the external world (1975: 219). Sadism is a primary mode or mood of infantile eroticism. The erotogenetic zones of the body ("all the various sources of libidinal pleasure") give rise to phantasies of self-preservation and pleasure in which both are attained through violent incorporations and expulsions. The phantasmatic operations of taking in and expelling facilitate a sense of secure self-attachment, the originary rudiments of which Klein assumes to be primordial and of primary import.

This means that, for Klein, Dick is aware, even if unconsciously and incompletely, of the difference between internal and external, which is for Klein equivalent to the distinction between self and world. From the beginning, and necessarily so, Dick is projecting and introjecting. There is always already categorical differentiation in the Kleinian cosmos—an assumption that is not shared by Lacan, indeed an assumption around which a great amount of their disagreement turns.

Moreover, in Klein's understanding of infantile sadism, as implied in the passage cited above and in what follows in the course of her text, the life of the body translates into the life of the mind. In a certain sense, for Klein, *anatomy destines*. The sensitivities of the various erotogenic zones activate phantasies of consumption and expulsion, phantasies that, more precisely, involve taking in and throwing out particular contents. Such contents are the in-built correlates of these phantasies.[12] Klein specifies the contents of phantasies as follows: "The child expects to find within the mother (a) the father's penis, (b) excrement, and (c) children, and these things it equates with edible substances. . . . Thus the child's sadistic attacks have for their object both father and mother, who are in phantasy bitten, torn, cut, or stamped to bits. These attacks give rise to anxiety lest the subject should be punished by the united parents, and this anxiety also becomes internalized in consequence of the oral-sadistic introjection of the objects" (1975: 219).[13] Said otherwise, the infant imagines, or acts as if s/he imagines, that there are certain "objects" in the mother's body: the father's penis, excrement, children, etc. On the one hand, these part-objects are "good" in that their incorporation promises pleasure and with them defenses against aggressive, persecuting objects can be mounted. On the other hand, these are "bad" objects in the sense that, when introjected in order to access their good qualities, they are threatening. Such objects either are or are related to (i.e., are emissaries of) the very persecuting objects that motivated the acts of incorporation in the first place. The tragic conundrums of infantile phantasy are (1) that the appeal to or incorporation of the good object brings with it, unwittingly, the bad, and (2) that expulsion of the bad provokes, in phantasy, the risk of catastrophic retribution by the parents ostensibly injured thereby.

These are bold claims, to be sure. But notice the recurrence throughout the article of the rhetoric of experience: "I have found . . ." "It is my experience . . ." "According to what I have found in analysis . . ." "I have arrived at these conclusions from my general analytical experience." As if supposing that we are forever on the verge of forgetting it, Klein continually returns her addressees to the clinical realm from which her speculations arise. Strikingly, the second sentence of the article not only situates the particular developmental claim that "sadism reaches its height . . . [when] ushered in by the oral-sadistic desire to devour the mother's breast (or the mother herself)" under the qualifying rhetoric of "In my experience" but also implicitly situates the quintessentially Kleinian claim that the desire of the infant is "to devour the mother's breast (or the mother herself)" and thus, implicitly, the claim that the breast is an object of which the child is intrinsically, unconsciously aware, within this tentative ambiance. To be sure, the strength of the qualification falls on the former claim, but it does seep into and partially sap the bold extravagance of the latter claims. The qualified mode of claiming implied by "In my experience" extends, albeit surreptitiously, throughout the first section. For instance, when Klein asserts in the next sentence that "At the period of which I am speaking, *the subject's dominant aim* is to possess himself of the contents of the mother's body and to destroy her by means of every weapon which sadism can command," her tone is ambitiously universalizing (*the subject*, i.e., all of us, has *the* dominant aim, which, more than any other, motivates him/us at this phase) (1975: 219; emphasis added). Klein is offering an interpretive template through which the primary tendencies of infants at a particular age can be clearly discerned. However, the universalizing thrust of the claim is met and tempered, indeed contradicted, by the qualifying rhetoric of "In my experience" that is only one sentence removed from this grandiose assertion.[14]

Subsequent claims about what the child expects to find in the mother's body, about what the child phantasizes as the meaning of parental coitus, about originary sadism and the proportionality of violent defense to the violence of originary sadism, about the various objects of the child's sadistic attack (and so about projection and expulsion), about the anxieties to which such sadistic attacks give rise, and about the fate of such anxieties as they are metabolized in phantasy (more precisely, in phantasy presumably governed by talionic codes of retaliation), and so, implicitly, the whole of the Kleinian theory of the paranoid-schizoid position (which elaborates the fate of this anxiety and the defensive formations and subject positions to which it gives rise), indeed the whole of the Kleinian understanding of child development and the theory of pathogenesis it implies, should be understood as qualified by the appeal to finite clinical experience—more precisely, to a particular perspective, its informing assumptions, and its material conditions—that establishes the rhetorical frame.

Klein's strong claims about anxiety, defense, introjection, the early development of the superego, and so on, all located within the scope of this first section, are significantly tempered by the soft-lit ambiance emanating from her explicit "In my experience" and so must be read in their tentativeness and questionability, read, that is, as articulations of and from a certain perspective motivated by but not reducible to limited case material.[15] Klein is given to neither positivism nor groundless speculation but rather to *thinking*, which hangs tensely between but at an infinite distance from its twin poles of corruption . . . though she does lean toward one pole or the other rather often. Hence the difficulty and necessity of *reading* her.

It is not incidental that when Klein cites Freud to support her claim that "The excess of sadism gives rise to anxiety and sets in motion the ego's earliest modes of defense" the line she cites (1) is marked by the self-qualification that is so prominent in her own work and (2) does not exactly support her claim so much as it acknowledges that something like her account is possible, or, at best, plausible: "Freud . . . writes: '*It may well be* that before its sharp cleavage into an ego and an id, and before the formation of a super-ego, the mental apparatus makes use of *different methods of defense* [not necessarily the methods Klein adumbrates] from those which it employs after it has reached these stages of organization'" (1975: 220; emphases added). Likewise, it is not incidental that shortly after citing this line of Freud's Klein recalls the opinions of Ferenczi and Jones about the development of symbolism against which her own takes a stand. Even if she proves convincing, her position will have been marked in advance as an opinion among others. Moreover, the phrasing of the recollections foregrounds the perspectival quality of each position, and by implication Klein's own: "Ferenczi *holds that* identification, the forerunner of symbolism, arises out of the baby's endeavor to rediscover in every object his own organs and their functioning. *In Jones' view* the pleasure-principle makes it possible for two quite different things to be equated because of a similarity marked by pleasure or interest" (1975: 220; emphasis added). There is no reason to believe that Klein's opinion will be other than a holding, a view. Not a grasping at thin air, but a holding. Not a view from nowhere, but a view informed by experience and reflection. Further, nothing in Klein's essay suggests that she is attempting to demonstrate that Ferenczi and Jones are simply wrong and that she is unimpeachably in the right. Quite to the contrary, read closely, Ferenczi and Jones's positions are, as elaborated by Klein, fully compatible with her own. Thus the effect of the citation of her predecessors is not simply to situate her work as an authoritative overcoming of prior prejudices and mistakes and a legitimate extension of Freudian thinking but, rather, in something of a counter-stroke, to disclose the work of her predecessors, as well as her own, as plausible yet questionable, as perspectives worthy of remembrance and consideration. Klein, sometimes despite herself, leaves us not with a secure conviction but with a memorable, engaging interpretation. The authority of her interpretations resides in their exemplary force, not their demonstrated validity.

As much as the contingency and inescapable insecurity of her claims are unthematized and undeveloped, and this is surely lamentable, the continual explication of her claims as conditioned by finite clinical experiences and as opinions among others of interest should punctuate the boldness of her claims with a prominent question mark and inscribe a critical hesitancy with respect to their generalizability and adequateness to the matters under consideration. In other words, from Klein's perspective, the meaning of feces etc. slowly crystallized, came into the open, emerged from out of concealedness and into view. It became clear. Through the regular recurrence of the rhetoric of experience and other self-qualifying techniques, Klein's exceedingly strong claims take upon a more nuanced quality. Framed as emerging from her limited field of clinical experience and as intelligible through assumptions, hypotheses, and interpretive templates drawn from elsewhere, Klein's bold assertions are simultaneously tempered and provocative.

And yet, Klein is nothing if not bold. However much on the basis of a certain limited experience and prior speculation, Klein puts forward the astonishing claim that "I have found these anxiety situations of the early phases of mental development to be *the most profound and overwhelming*" (1975: 219). The tension between "I have found" and "the most profound and overwhelming" perfectly emblematizes the difficult terrain of Klein's thinking.

On the one hand, this bold assertion is explicitly predicated on rather limited clinical experiences ("I have found"), and so the claim to the ultimate import in infantile life of these anxiety situations is fully conditioned by the variable quality of Klein's reconstructions as manifest in her published and unpublished work to date. Situating this claim as emergent from out of a vast field of publications, and, what's more, from out of the broad scope of clinical experiences that never made their way into the published works, Klein keeps this bold claim moored to the unfathomable depths of her thinking and experience. By explicitly predicating the claim on experiences and reflections to which, in principle, our access is limited, the claim is sustained in its fundamental and inescapable opacity, and, thereby, in its eminent questionability.

On the other hand, Klein's claim is that more than anything else, and certainly more than any anxiety generated by later Oedipal conflicts, these pre-Oedipal "anxiety situations . . . [are] *the* most profound and overwhelming." These anxieties are the "deepest" and most devastating. Period. In a quasi-theological tone, Klein professes these anxieties to be that than which something more terrible than cannot be understood. By predicating the claim on experiences and reflections to which our access is limited, Klein grounds them in her personal authority.

And yet—to read Klein is to regularly find oneself between one "and yet" and another—in the very next sentence Klein returns to the rhetoric of experience, which to a degree reinforces the qualified status of the former claim. The boldness of the former claim, as if threatening to overwhelm its qualified presentation, to annul the hesitation inscribed at the beginning of the sentence, is met with a redoubled effort to explicate the finite realm of experience from which it emerges. The effect is a redoubled hesitancy that generates a great tension between the assertive and tentative qualities of Klein's writing. In the subsequent sentence, Klein states that "*It is my experience* that in the phantasied attack on the mother's body a considerable part is played by the urethral and anal sadism which is very soon added to the oral and muscular sadism" (1975: 219). Can we hear an echo of Freud's implicit "it is my experience" that is both the springboard and yet, at least sometimes, the tempering agent of so many of the theses of which he became convinced as a result of his self-analysis? Can we hear the strain of the simultaneously universalizing and particularizing ambitions of psychoanalytic knowledge?[16] Here, not only do we encounter a return to the qualifying rhetoric of experience, to a domain of experience that Klein marks as emphatically her own (well, maybe not all that emphatically), we also encounter, albeit in token form, an explicit acknowledgement that Klein's developmental theory (oral and muscular sadism is followed by urethral and anal sadism, etc.) is predicated on her limited clinical experiences. That developmental theory emerges from clinical reconstructions should be no surprise. What is nonetheless striking is that Klein so consistently reigns in her generalizations by keeping them explicitly within the framework of clinical construction. Klein is unwilling to forego either authoritative universalization or the critical scrupulousness that reigns it in. Unfortunately, though, she is willing to forgo (or is simply oblivious to the need for) discussion of what this means for psychoanalytic knowing. She fails to thematize her writerly practice.

In what follows from this claim, the tension between self-consciously limited and daringly universal claiming is significantly intensified. Klein continues,

"In phantasy the excreta are transformed into dangerous weapons: wetting is regarded as cutting, stabbing, burning, drowning, while the fecal mass is equated with weapons and missiles" (1975: 219–20). Within its immediate context, it is clear that Klein is recalling a certain set of experiences on the basis of which her speculations ensue. Yet even within the generally tentative scope of her claiming, Klein here speaks in a masterly voice. She speaks of what seem to be the utterly mechanical and predictable operations of the psyche and of her unqualified access to them. Her claim is that the work of phantasy translates excreta into dangerous weapons, wetting into stabbing, and so on, as if in a regular and altogether transparent fashion. Klein's phrases "regarded as" and "equated with" imply that the phantasy takes bits of both external and phastmastic reality and translates them, as if according to textbook rules. Is this claim not as dubious as the most outrageous of Jung's archetypal posits or the claims made by Freud about phylogenetically inherited universal symbolism? The audaciousness of the claim is that the unconscious, ordinarily considered a principle of opacity, distortion, and displacement, can be *known* in its most intimate operations and that it is Klein who is in possession of the secret decoder ring that unlocks their hidden meaning. Klein here, as much as she bases her claims on a certain set of experiences, assumptions, and hypotheses, is acting as if she can speak the truth of infantile phantasy once and for all. Wetting means this, excreta mean that. And insofar as such proficiency in speaking the truth of the unconscious is predicated on the system of equations *actually operating* in the unconscious, Klein is implicitly claiming that speculative, reconstructive analytic discourse can be—and that in fact hers is—entirely adequate to, indeed interpretively exhaustive of, the reality of unconscious life.

But, then again, the claim may not be as bold as all that. To be sure, Klein clearly implies that the unconscious translates ("regards as" or "equates with") certain terms into other terms. But the details of the translation she offers, whether or not intentionally, put us on guard against any notion of the unconscious operating as a programmed translation machine. It's ever a rollercoaster ride when reading Klein. When she asserts that "In phantasy the excreta are transformed into dangerous weapons," are we not compelled to query, even if there is innate knowledge of, say, the breast, is there innate knowledge of dangerous weapons? This question takes on greater significance as we follow through Klein's summary of what is "regarded as" or "equated with" what in phantasy life. To cite her again, "wetting is regarded as cutting, stabbing, burning, drowning, while the fecal mass is equated with weapons and missiles" (1975: 219–20). If nothing else, the claim about "missiles" should give away the bluff behind the bombast. Surely (one certainly hopes), there is no innate, unconscious knowledge of "missiles." Maybe there is a plausible story to be told, whether in phylogenetic, neuroscientific, or other terms, about the propensity of infants to recognize the breast and weave fantasies around it. But to assume innate knowledge of missiles, poisons, etc. seems much less plausible. Could this have escaped Klein? From this detail, two interpretations of Klein's manner of interpretation should be considered.

(1) It may be that, for Klein, the unconscious is to some extent culturally particular. By this I mean that on this point Klein may be considered a strict Freudian. For Freud, a traumatogenic event is, initially, an overwhelming intrusion—whether empirical or phantasmatic—that outstrips an individual's capacity to make sense of it, to bind it in the order of meaning. Like a contagion, a personal epidemic, the force of trauma unsettles the very order of intelligibility that is insufficiently resilient and/or adaptive to accommodate it. Unbinding past, present, and future through the intrusiveness of its overwhelming, inescapable presence (facticity without meaning), trauma's impact is such that if *it* cannot be assimilated, the whole of the individual's psychic structure, sense of identity, and worldly bearings become imperiled. The *eventfulness* of the traumatogenic event signifies its excessiveness or abrasiveness with respect to the self-image(s) and related order of intelligibility of the one who suffers such impingement. Trauma thus names the faltering of self-representation and the unworlding of the subject whose meaning-making resources are significantly disrupted or even put out of play by an unmetabolizable impingement.

Subsequently, the overwhelmingly agitating *presence* of the trauma compels various efforts of symbolization or narrativization whereby one attempts to integrate the inchoate traumatic kernel into the framework of intelligibility made available by one's sociosymbolic resources, and, more specifically, dictated by one's prevalent or newly expanded self-images. Trauma names a rupture, an unsettling irritant that rifts the fabric of meaning within which, ordinarily, the subject makes sense of herself and her world and thereby compels the often compulsive work of symbolization (which may involve symptom formation) through which the excessiveness of the trauma is to some extent contained and metabolized.[17]

This means that, to a certain extent, trauma is culturally specific: it is a violation of a cultural order of intelligibility. Of course, it is more than likely that certain terrible events cannot be integrated into the life of anyone, anywhere. But insofar as trauma is measured, indeed defined, by the breakdown of a sociosymbolic order (as it has been internalized by a particular individual), it seems fair to say that at least certain traumas mark the limits of a particular cultural order of intelligibility. Moreover, the process of containing and metabolizing, of narrativizing, or, more broadly, form-giving, through which trauma is sapped of its devastating force of disruption, will inevitably draw upon the symbolic resources of a particular culture. The attempted metabolization of trauma involves the overlaying of the traumatic event—perhaps only ever partially and incompletely—with cultural coding such that a general sense of meaningfulness is restored. Of course, the resources of a particular sociosymbolic order may not be up to the task, and thus trauma may motivate either symptom formation as an idiosyncratic mechanism of meaning making or, hopefully, the expansion and development of the sociosymbolic order. In the latter case, trauma sparks the creative work of those who struggle in the want of available cultural resources to give form or meaning to their suffering.[18]

One can thus read the equation of the fecal mass with weapons and missiles as an indication that a certain relatively inchoate experience of aggressiveness was traumatically registered and thus set into motion processes of symbolization wherein the relatively amorphous aggressiveness became culturally coded as an attack with missiles on a parental target (one cannot forget that "The Importance of Symbol-Formation" was published in 1930). So when Klein claims that, for instance, the fecal mass is phantasized as or unconsciously equated with missiles or that urine is equated with poison, this may be read as a description of *the fate* of an initial and to some extent irreducibly obscure aggressiveness. The steadfast conviction that fecal masses *are* missiles might thus conceal and defend against the inchoate, unmetabolizable traumatic impingement that underlies it. Such concreteness (fecal mass = missile) might thus serve as a defense against the limits to intelligibility and/or utter permeability of the human suggested by trauma or that with which they are associated.

If Klein is read this way, her interpretation would neither presume to speak the transhistorical, transcultural truth of unconscious systems of equation nor presume that there is, in fact, a naturally programmed system of phantasmatic equivalence. Rather, Klein's interpretation would amount to uncovering what a certain traumatic aggressiveness *will have meant*, either in a particular case or, tendentially, in the phantasy life of in a particular cultural-historical formation.

(2) It may be that, for Klein, analytic reconstruction supports the work of symbolization that has not yet sufficiently metabolized various traumata. In other words, it may be that analysands generally are, and Dick more than most is, not yet sufficiently able symbolize traumatic aggressiveness. If so, Klein's interpretations *create* for Dick the meaning for which he is longing. In this case, her interpretation would not be of a preexisting system of unconscious equivalences but rather would record the fate of ineliminably opaque traumatic aggressiveness as it has been modified in the course of therapy.

Of course, these two lines of interpretations are far from incompatible. Also, neither puts out of question the possibility that Klein conceives the unconscious as a transparent translation machine. But, though Klein is inimitably bold, can we assume that she is simply convinced of something as implausible as innate unconscious knowledge of missiles, poisons, etc.?

Finally, before we turn to the differences between Lacan and Klein, one more point about the perspectival quality of Klein's discussion is in order. On the one hand, with astounding self-assurance, Klein claims that as aberrant as Dick may be, he manifests—albeit in an exaggerated fashion, in a manner exaggerated enough to bring into fine relief what is otherwise obscured by its transformation in the course of human development—the most ordinary features of early development. In fine, Dick manifests (1) the phase of development in which pregenital organizations gradually issue into genital and Oedipal configurations that are colored by their predecessors, (2) the oral-sadistic aggressiveness that tends to express itself in desires to bite and devour the mother's body, and (3) the utterly foundational role of symbolism in the development of interest and investment in the world as well as the way in which the development of symbolism turns on the "optimum balance" of anxiety. In Klein's words, what the case demonstrates is that "not only does symbolism come to be the foundation of all phantasy and sublimation, but, more than that, it is the basis of the subject's relation to the outside world and to reality in general" (1975: 221). Symbolism serves its foundational role, though, only if there is a "sufficient quantity" of manifest anxiety and a strong-enough ego—both of which are lacking in Dick. Thus, on the other hand, and here is the twist, Dick manifests these "natural" phenomena *only as a result of Klein's intervention*. These "natural," ostensibly ubiquitous phenomena emerge conspicuously only as *constructed in the space of analysis*, through what we might call analytic prosthetics.

The point is certainly not to discount, let alone dismiss, Klein's claimed discovery on the basis of the "artificial" conditions of her observations. Likewise, the point is not to discredit Klein's contributions by pointing out that she has constructed precisely what she claims to be a feat of nature. Rather, the point is that the supplementary work of analysis needed to actualize latent trends in Dick's development indicates a limit to the generalizing of findings based on this case. In the end, Klein gives us two "proofs" of her thesis. One is an appeal to clinical experiences other than those presented in the article that presumably instance the work of symbolism in regulating anxiety and thereby expanding interest and investment in the world. "I have arrived at these conclusions from my general analytical experience," she says (1975: 221). But these experiences are never elaborated in any detail, and so the thesis, on this basis, is *manifestly* underwarranted. Is Klein here too self-assured to provide anything like sufficient warrant for her claims? Or is she, as with the example of the implausible, maybe even ludicrous, statement about missiles above, allowing a *manifestly* contentious, even outrageous claim to capture our attention and motivate reflection? The other "proof" is the case of Dick, in which, as we have seen, Klein creates the developments that are claimed as regular features of natural growth. Here too, the thesis is *manifestly* underwarranted. Even if Klein is not remarkably adept at highlighting the questionable, provocative status of her insights, is this not what she is *trying* to do?

Toward the closing of this opening section, Klein states that "these conclusions are confirmed in a remarkably striking way by a case in which there was an unusual inhibition of ego development" (1975: 221). In part, what is "remarkably striking" about this confirmation is its ability to claim us, to call upon our conviction, to solicit a "yes, this sounds right," to refuse to let us think about early development, pathogenesis, or other related matters—in the clinic or elsewhere—in a way that would simply ignore or sidestep Klein's contributions. What is striking, then, is the authority of the claim despite, or, better, in virtue of, its ultimately nondemonstrable character. Whether intentionally or not, Klein's text elaborates its key claims as no more and no less than *plausible and fecund*, as developments of a perspective eminently worthy of consideration, as claims that need to be taken seriously but that are by no means apodictically certain or even all that well grounded. Perhaps the cavalier boldness and inimitable self-assurance of Klein's ever-authoritative writing solicits in us a certain susceptibility or even submissiveness to her claims; questions concerning unacknowledged transference, exploited guilt or masochism, etc., cannot be simply tossed aside when accounting for the compelling force of Klein's contributions. But is not part of the extraordinary achievement of Klein's writings to open us to and sustain this exposure to the authority of her voice, this exposure without which, perhaps, convictions could not be formed, without suppressing, and perhaps even while everywhere soliciting, our critical vigilance? Is not one of Klein's globally unappreciated achievements—an achievement of which, perhaps, even she was unaware—to have developed a style of psychoanalytic claiming that is at once incredibly forceful and convincing while simultaneously self-questioning and critically hesitant?

Let us conclude with one final example. Klein is surely bold when she emphasizes that "Urine [penis] and feces represented to [Dick] injurious and dangerous substances" with which to attack the mother's body (1975: 226). Although one could read this as a typical, dogmatic imposition of a preestablished understanding of the phantasy life of infants onto the case at hand, notice that Klein states "*It became clear* that in Dick's phantasy feces, urine and penis stood for objects with which to attack the mother's body" (1975: 226). On the one hand, it is not immediately evident that such-and-such behaviors correspond to such-and-such unconscious meanings. Unconscious meanings do not just jump out and grab hold of us. Psychoanalysis requires opining, reflecting, supposing, comparing initial interpretations to what subsequently unfolds, etc. On the other hand, feces, urine, and penis stand for objects with which to attack the mother's body. It became clear.

V. Lacan Visits the Butcher

Lacan's and Klein's understandings of Dick's case differ starkly. Though there are certainly points of confluence, there are manifest tensions between the terms and structures they emphasize, the accounts of therapeutic success they put forward, and the theoretical and practical conclusions they draw from the case material. Specifying the precise character of these tensions will allow us to explore (1) the singularity of each perspective, (2) the inevitable underdetermination of theory by evidence in psychoanalysis, (3) the exaggerated quality of psychoanalytic knowledge entailed by its underdetermination, and (4) the perspectival status of each approach. This last task is particularly important since Klein and Lacan are widely considered to be among the most dogmatic of psychoanalytic theorists. If the presumption of *their* dogmatism can be debunked, the claim that psychoanalytic knowing is emphatically yet differentially perspectival will be significantly bolstered.

Lacan's disagreements with Klein over how to understanding what transpired in Dick's case and what we should learn from it are elaborated, as noted above, in *Seminar I*. However, since Lacan's thinking subsequently underwent many important developments, in the following I will attempt to present both the disagreements with Klein detailed in *Seminar I* as well as disagreements pertinent to this case that follow from his later teachings. This way, at the risk of importing later Lacan into early Lacan and thereby obscuring the great many shifts and developments in his thinking—both inconsistencies and new approaches to old topics—a more profound and pronounced disagreement between "Lacan" (the Lacan that will have been . . . of course, from a certain point of view) and "Klein" (the Klein who, of course, was to develop in her own right and who will likewise be presented through a retrospective reading that uses later developments to explain and explore this instance of her earlier work) will come into view.[19] This account will be an exaggeration, a distortion. It will not be a simple exegesis of *Seminar I*'s commentary on Klein's famous case study. Rather, this will be a little drama, a staged confrontation between what I take to be a *Kleinian perspective* and a *Lacanian perspective* that takes off from *Seminar I* but does not stay within its orbit. To the extent that it is successful, though, it will stay within its gravitational field.

In Klein's case presentation, quite characteristically, some of the most relevant terms are anxiety, projection, introjection, and the ego. Through a mapping of and intervention into scenes of projection and introjection, Klein claims, she is able to regulate Dick's anxiety sufficiently for his budding ego to tolerate the complex claims, the pleasures and pains, of life with objects and others. Lacan will have none of this—or at least his attention is directed decidedly elsewhere.

In Lacan's reading, quite characteristically, the most relevant terms are speech, lack (and the lack of lack, i.e., the Real), the Imaginary, and the Symbolic. While for Klein the case is a demonstration of the mutually implicated development of symbolization, worldliness, and the ego, for Lacan the case is a demonstration of his claim that the unconscious is the discourse of the Other. However adept our egos become, Lacan insists, we are constitutively unsettled by the radically inassimilable discourse of the Other, indeed so much so that mapping the structure of address—who is speaking to whom, who is speaking through whom, whose desire resonates in the affective life that, at first glance, seems to be the patient's "own"—is as important for him as mapping projection and introjection are for Klein.[20] While Klein stresses the miraculous flowering of worldliness that follows from sufficient ego strength and diminished anxiety, Lacan stresses the unsymbolizable remnants (e.g., products of primal repression) that incessantly perturb our involvements with objects and others, that cannot but be misrecognized, and on account of which our self-awareness is irrevocably distorted and self-formation implacably troubled. While Klein focuses on the projective and introjective mechanisms through which Dick is already responding to phantasized relations to others, Lacan focuses on the power of Klein's speech to initiate relations to others and the Other. While for Klein Dick exemplifies the aggressivity of early oral-sadistic tendencies to bite and devour the mother's body, for Lacan Dick's treatment exemplifies the hazards of developmental theory guiding clinical practice.

These differential emphases are more than two sides of the same story; they are fundamentally different approaches to the case at hand and carry widely disparate values and implications for psychoanalytic theory and practice. When Lacan says that the case material shows that the unconscious is the discourse of the Other, he means in part that despite her claims to the contrary Klein did not access Dick's unconscious phantasies (as if they were simply his "own," i.e., autochthonous) and on that basis induce modifications that promoted ego strength sufficient to tolerate the complex claims of his proto-world. For, Lacan suggests, there was no unconscious to access prior to Klein's interventions: "In this subject [Dick] there is no unconscious whatsoever. It is Klein's discourse which brutally grafts upon the initial egotistic inertia of the child the first symbolizations of the Oedipal situation" (*Seminar I*: 100). While for Klein unconscious phantasies and anxieties are there from the beginning (or perhaps nearly so, perhaps they quickly follow from the need to negotiate with unbearable self-directed sadism and/or early object relations), for Lacan the unconscious, properly speaking, emerges from the need to metabolize the desire, and especially the desirous speech, of the Other. Insofar as Dick was unimpacted by the speech (the desirous address) of others and did not speak to others (for the most part, he did not address them—"the child does not address any call to anybody" [*Seminar I*: 98]—at most he used words negativistically, e.g., to refuse the demands of others to use language in a consistent and intelligible way), he was relatively immune to, insulated from, the desire of the other—the psychic metabolization of which, for Lacan, gives rise to the unconscious. The unconscious, for Lacan, is social through and through; it is a consequence of exposure to others and, through them, the Other (the Symbolic order). This is one reason Lacan speaks of the unconscious as "transindividual." More precisely, for Lacan, the unconscious emerges from our responses to the desire-suffused, affectively impacting, and irrecusably enigmatic *enunciations* of an Other. Speech, for Lacan, is where it's at—this is his exaggeration, the one-sidedness that conditions his insight. In short, from Lacan's perspective, while it may be true that Klein's interventions regulated Dick's anxiety sufficiently for his ego to develop and his object relations to obtain a greater resiliency and personal import, such extraordinary efficacy by no means proves that Klein was intervening in Dick's *unconscious*. For Lacan, there is psychic life prior to the institution of the unconscious.

Already we can catch a glimpse of the radically exaggerated status of Lacan's claims. Even within the parameters of Lacanian theory, it is highly dubious that Dick did not yet have an unconscious, or at least elements thereof. No matter how overburdened with anxiety, no matter how insular he may have been, did not Dick's vulnerability to and dependence on his primary caregivers expose him to the intrusion of signifiers from their desirous discourse[21] that he could not make sense of yet felt as somehow important, as addressing or at least having to do with him? If not, how can one explain his availability to Klein's interpretive suggestions? It is highly unlikely that Dick was *more* dependent on, thus vulnerable to, Klein than he was on his primary caregivers. But in the context of Lacanian theory, that would have to be the case if Klein created his unconscious *ex nihilo*. However muted their impact may have been, Dick must have been exposed to signifiers emanating from his primary caregivers, and such signifiers, for Lacan, are the seeds of the unconscious. To be sure, as a result of his massive anxiety (which must have emerged from somewhere—perhaps from the overwhelming force of desire conveyed in the speech and/or behavior of his primary caregivers?), Dick's symbolic capacities were so greatly diminished and his concern with others so minimal that it may well be that the implanted signifiers took on terribly little importance for him and failed to connect in the ways that ordinarily give rise to the associational webbing of the unconscious. Be that as it may, Lacan's suggestion that Klein's discourse, and her discourse *alone*, created Dick's unconscious is, on his own terms, exaggerated. It is as if Lacan figures Klein as a parodic incarnation of his metapsychology.

It seems much more likely that, in Lacanian terms, Klein's ability to induce the development of Dick's unconscious was predicated on the resonance of her speech with the signifiers already implanted in him. Lacan indeed admits in

Seminar I that Klein's interpretations are effective only because they resonate with the symbolic elements, the signifiers, already pertinent to Dick (Lacan specifically marks out "dark" and "void" as signifiers that must have already been implanted in and were already somehow meaningful for Dick). Was Dick really, originarily and altogether, deaf to the desirous discourse of his primary caregivers? Was he really so overburdened by anxiety from the beginning that he was wholly oblivious to the desire of the other? To a certain degree, Dick was closed off from the world, but within the parameters of Lacan's metapsychology *absolute* insularity is impossible. An infant is never a monad; some measure of exposure to the desire of the other is inescapable.

As I read it, the point of Lacan's claim that Klein created Dick's unconscious is to focus our attention on the ways in which the discourse of others, especially under conditions of heightened vulnerability and dependency, contributes to the genesis and development of the unconscious. The point is not so much that *Melanie Klein's* discourse, and this alone, unwittingly gave rise to Dick's unconscious. The point is rather that the discourse of the Other produces the unconscious and that Klein's blindness to this detrimentally impacts her theory and practice. Sometimes Lacan was too much of a polemicist to make his point clear. The function of Lacan's exaggeration is to (1) focus our attention on what our entrenched beliefs cannot admit, say, that the unconscious is produced and socially mediated rather than simply given and the guarantor of some measure of externality from the social, and to (2) encourage us to draw the consequences of these tendentially neglected or repudiated claims.

And already we can catch a glimpse of some of the most crucial differences between a Lacanian and a Kleinian perspective. While Klein focuses on *meaning* or *content*, e.g., on the phantasmatic meanings of urine, feces, penis, etc. in Dick's overwhelmingly anxious psychic life,[22] Lacan focuses on (1) the *nonsensical*, that which forever eludes—and in eluding, mobilizes—meaning,[23] and (2) the enunciative—bodily and relational—dimension of speech and its effects. Klein focuses on content, Lacan on speech.[24] Broadly speaking, Klein's interpretations seek to discover and create *meaning* and thereby to initiate Dick into a more hospitable world. Her interpretations both clarify and, by way of her symbolic graft, focalize—and even to a certain extent construct—the meaning of Dick's play and other behavior. In contrast, Lacan attempts to draw attention to that which persists in and through, and ultimately beyond, meaning. He cautions us again and again to avoid *understanding* at all costs.[25] Understanding, Lacan contends, proceeds through the projection and reification of meaning and is thus the work of the ego, which, as we will see, is often for Lacan a pathogenic agency. So while Klein attends to narratives or proto-narratives that, from her perspective, already structure Dick's experience and inform his play (Oedipal narratives in particular), Lacan homes in on disruptions and fractures, on the unreadable, the ex-timate core of the individual implanted by the Other that renders the individual forever foreign to herself. Lacan is more interested in the effects of speech, especially its unintended effects, than in the presumptive content of speech. He is interested in that which will have been initiated, in excess of any intention, through the embodied interaction, especially the vocal interaction, of desirous subjects.[26] From Lacan's perspective, Klein is mesmerized by meaning. One final way of glossing this would be to say that whereas Klein's privileged framework is the ego (the ego of the analyst speaks to the besieged ego of the analysand, supports it, allows it to develop to the point where it can entertain more robust relationships with other parts of herself, objects, and others), Lacan's privileged framework is the unconscious, understood as that which resides beneath and throws off-kilter ego-to-ego and ego-to-object relations. Lacan is attentive to disruption and disorganization as much as Klein is keyed to subjective and intersubjective narrative coherence.

While Lacan and Klein agree that developing a sense world-orientation and certain significant cognitive developments (in the expansive sense of phantasy, conceptual schematization, practical coping habits, etc.) run together, they disagree about the motivators and significance of these developments, thus about the proper therapeutic responses to them. For Klein, the impulse to know is both an expression of libidinal attachment to the mother—a natural vicissitude of attachment—and a mechanism through which anxiety is regulated via dispersion. On this account, the initial cognitive mapping and phantasizing[27] through which incipient forms of world-orientation are established are compelled by nature: by the nature of attachment, of love seeking to elaborate itself, and by the nature of anxiety's averseness. The analyst's task is to facilitate self-and-world-consolidation by supporting these natural trends.

In fine, a world inceptively opens on the condition that various phenomena appear mommy-like or mommy-related, i.e., attract interest and compel exploration due to their relation to the maternal presence. But the interlocking forms of world-orientation and cognitive development that can be achieved as expressions of libidinal attachment to the mother are limited—imagine a world *exclusively* elaborated on the model of amorous connection to the maternal body. More refined forms of world-orientation and cognitive developments require an alternative motivational force. On Klein's account, this motivational force is anxiety aversion. Fortuitously, Klein claims, our natural impulse to know is a readymade mechanism to alleviate natural anxiety via dispersion. In flight from our anxious condition, we are propelled into explorations of our environments. That is, the elaboration of our innate epistemophilic impulse becomes the stage for the projection of anxiety onto each new site we are prompted to explore, thus for the qualitative diminishment of anxiety via its quantitative dispersal. As we saw above, through repeated projections of anxiety, a world is gradually configured.

The details of this account need not be rehashed here. What is significant in this context is that (1) world-orientation and cognitive development run together (absorbing attraction to the mother-world and repulsion from projected anxiety establish the rhythm of world-exploration/cognitive development), (2) it is the analyst's task to support such developments, and, (3) though when isolated (as it often is due to its striking features) Klein's account of the anxieties of infantile life and her discussions of what emerges in their wake may make it seem as if prospects for being at home in the world are dashed from the beginning and become increasingly less tenable over time, when contextualized by her accounts of primordial and insuperable object attachment, specifically of the world-forging fate of maternal attachment and of the anxiety-abating elaboration of the epistemophilic impulse, it becomes clear that as given to anxiety as we may be, we are, on Klein's account, naturally disposed and possessed of the resources to find ourselves at home in the world.

For Lacan, the impulse toward knowledge may be motivated by lack of *jouissance*,[28] that is, by dissatisfactions that compel one to explore a world of objects and relations that promise greater satisfactions than obtain in her psycho-relational status quo. The desire to know is not given by nature, at least not in the way Klein suggests, but rather emerges in response to the failure of the world to sufficiently satisfy; it signals our nonreconciliation with the world in which we find ourselves. Or, Lacan more frequently suggests, the impulse toward knowledge (and so expansions of and alterations to our world-horizon, even the very birth of a world) may be motivated by the need to subdue the disturbing excess of the other's desire. Knowledge (in the expansive sense) elaborates and through elaborating binds and contains the enigmatic indeterminacy of the affectively freighted, disturbingly present desire of the other. In both cases, Lacan's focus is on estrangement. The analyst's task (at least initially) is to underscore and amplify estrangement, to resist its tendency to dissipate as we gain our bearing in the world into which it incites us or to become converted into our attachment that world.

Let us not allow the glaring obviousness of the contrasting therapeutic consequences drawn to overshadow the perhaps slight but highly significant differences between Lacan's and Klein's respective accounts of the interlocking developments of cognition and world-orientation. Klein stresses love and anxiety as the core motivators of worldliness and cognitive development, while Lacan most often stresses the relation to the desirous discourse of the other as their motivator. There may well be anxiety in the relation to the desirous discourse of the other, but Lacan stresses that the desire to develop an image of oneself as coherent and lovable, or in any case as the transfixing and fulfilling object of the other's desire, the pursuit of which is, on his account, one of the primary ways in which we become determinately located in the world, is motivated by a need to metabolize the disconcerting excess of the desire of the other. For Lacan, the real issue is not anxiety abatement but the urgency of negotiating with the desirous discourse of the other.[29]

With this in view, the contrasting therapeutic orientations can be concretized. A Lacanian would likely focus on Dick's wondering about his place in the desire of his significant others, especially insofar as this contributes to his striving to consolidate an image of himself as lovable (which would amount to a repudiation of his wondrous condition, of the being-in-question, the essential estrangement, of self and world), with the aim of sapping the captivating force of these questions and pursuits or at least shifting their shape, while a Kleinian would likely focus on Dick's anxiety and its phantasmatic fate, with the aim of sponsoring mutually implicated developments of cognition and world-orientation.

A final difference between Lacan and Klein concerns their broader clinical ambitions. Klein's basic goal is to facilitate Dick's entry into a world of meaning. She aspires to situate him in a world of which he would feel a part, a world whose compelling structures of significance would envelop him, giving him place and role, thus practico-cognitive orientation. To be sure, Klein seeks to deliver Dick to a world in which he can feel himself to be a source of meaningful change, an agent, but her primary emphasis is on his becoming rooted, immediately implicated in structures of significance. She aims to provision Dick with the capacity to experience his life as intimately and meaningfully bound to objects and others. Though she seeks to facilitate the experience of this binding as a negotiable interface of significance, authoritative binding more than susceptibility to reworking is of primary import. Klein seeks a complex balancing of stability of placement and security of subjecthood, but first and foremost she seeks Dick's conviction in, indeed immersion in, a world of sufficiently stable and well-contoured meanings.

Lacan's clinical effort is directed toward destabilization. He aims to render the subject a question to herself, not exactly for its own sake but in order to provoke the incessant work of reconstructing—personalizing and assuming—the meaning(s) of one's history, desires, actions, etc. The attention Lacan doles upon the unintelligible, his persistent highlighting of the enigmatic, his oracular speech, and so forth are designed to shake up his analysands' complacencies with the narratives, the schemas of self- and world-interpretation, to which they are committed. He aims to destabilize our ever-congealing sense of self, to introduce tremors and disturbances into our well-wrought worlds.

On Lacan's account, it is often prevailing interpretations of events, and especially fantasies of self-consistency, from which we suffer (though relieving his analysands' sufferings is not his only, perhaps not even his most-pressing, motive[30]). People in very similar circumstances bear them quite differently, Lacan contends, because, to put it very roughly, they attribute different meanings to the events undergone. Thus learning to acknowledge oneself as a source of meaning—learning that meaning, though hardly an effect of sovereign positing, is something for which one is somehow responsible; learning that meaning, in order to take hold, must be acknowledged, assumed; thus learning to acknowledge oneself as a source of meaning in the sense of a necessary but insufficient condition—is often a condition for the abatement of suffering. Lacan's foregrounding of the nonsensical, his resolute attending to the obscure and enigmatic, to the cracks and fissures in our dominant self-images and interpretations of significant life events is part of a larger effort to renew, or, better, remobilize, personal efforts of meaning-making. His aim is to provoke the analysand to continually create—both to associationally/speculatively enhance and expand and to assume and in a certain sense become responsible for—the meaning of what s/he has undergone until s/he has reached a point where s/he no longer needs to do so, i.e., the point where s/he has arrived at a sufficiently satisfactory interpretation of, say, her/his freighted past or conflicted present to move on and concern her/himself otherwise, to make her/himself available to desires that could not come to the fore so long as s/he was suffering in the way s/he had been.

The Lacanian ambition, broadly speaking, is the release of *desire*. But in order to promote the release of desire, Lacan, in what seems to be a paradoxical gesture, seeks to cultivate in his analysands a sense of responsible agency. An absolutely encompassing responsibility is, for Lacan, freedom from *ressentiment* and from the ideals against which we measure ourselves only to find ourselves forever wanting. Agency to say "yes" to all we are and have been is freedom from the imperious demand for meaning, specifically from the demand to remain consistent with a privileged self-interpretation.[31] It is freedom to be and become otherwise. The exaggerated attention to enigma and obscurity, to disruption and dislocatedness, is not meant to induce the analysand to wallow in her ineffability but rather to incite her to renewed efforts of narrativization. Ideally, the goal is for ongoing (re)narrativization and associational expansion to substantially mitigate, perhaps even at the limit cancel, the need for narrative consistency. Lacan seeks to traumatize his analysands in order to provoke their creative efforts of meaning-making, of self-fashioning, or, more precisely, of becoming subjects. The effort is to provoke a different mode of narrativization, one that (1) would not seem so external (i.e., dictated solely by the events themselves; Lacan is deeply averse to positivism, both theoretically and clinically) and (2) would not figure itself as the full and final account, the sole and emphatically correct account, of, say, one's history or traumatic experiences. Though Lacan is emphatically attentive to and prone to amplify disruption and disorganization, he is not simply dismissive of the need for narrative coherence manifest in Klein's work. Rather, he seeks to manipulate the desire for narrative coherence in a manner that turns it against itself.

As we will see later in greater detail, these differential foci respond, in part, to different conceptions of psychic signification and of the unconscious, and they imply manifestly different orientations toward and interpretations of "truth." For now, let us anticipate by noting that, for Klein, unconscious signification is composed of phantasmatic contents amenable to analytic deciphering, the corollary of which is some version of a correspondence theory of truth: X behavior or affect corresponds to Y phantasmatic meaning. Even if it is acknowledged that Y unconscious meaning is partially constituted by its interpretation and is perhaps to some extent culturally contingent, this is still what the behavior or affect *means*, or perhaps *will have meant*. Even if one reads Klein as less interested in the veracity of her interpretations than in the efficacy of her technique, likely it will still be admitted that she is eminently interested in the effects of the *meanings* she discovers and/or creates. The Kleinian accent is placed on meaning, specifically, on its ubiquity and therapeutically beneficial decipherability.

In contrast, Lacan stresses that the order of the unconscious is not—or is not simply—the order meaning. For him, the unconscious is composed of *signifiers* implanted by the discourse of significant others (who often inherit these signifiers through their relations, especially their early, formative relations, to their significant others, who in turn inherit signifiers in the course of their formative relationships, and so on). Consequently, Lacan is more interested in the *effective implantation* of signifiers, and therewith the institution of subjectivity, by Klein's interpretations and in Klein's authoritative, stabilizing identification of the signifiers she implants with various signifieds than in the veracity of these interpretations. While it is true that, for Lacan, signifiers are the terms in relation to which, indeed out of which, fantasies and unconscious narratives—generally, meanings—are composed, signifiers are irreducibly excessive of any such meaningful compositions.[32] Through innumerable associative links, signifiers are built up into complex formations that may be deciphered in analysis, but in a very different manner and with very different aims in mind than Klein's deciphering of phantasmatic contents or narratives. Lacanian signifiers do not "have" referents or even meanings (in the sense of firm possession) so much as they will have come to have provocative effects: they both provoke and undermine meaning-making. Keeping this dynamic alive is crucial for Lacan. Part of his worry about Klein's theory and practice is that by promoting security in the horizon of meaning it saps the dialectical tension between meaning and nonmeaning and thereby undermines prospects for therapeutic success, even puts the very futurity of the analysand in jeopardy.

Signifiers are conditions for the (im)possibility of meaning. They are the nonsensical par excellence, the pulsating kernels around which socially mediated yet idiosyncratic psychic meanings will form but that remain forever irreducible to the order of meaning they provoke, thus remaining a constant snare to meaning's consistency and coherence.[33] Rather than *referring to* phantasmatic meanings, signifiers *index* emotionally charged, inescapable questions: questions that hover, at least initially, on the outskirts of lucidity, inchoate and more or less ineffable questions, "questions" that indicate more a mood of questioning, a freighted sense of insecurity or befallen-ness, than a specific question that can be put to rest by some answer. Such a diffuse mood of questioning in which our existential exposure is registered[34] is later elaborated through more determinate questions, questions that channel our existential quandaries into determinate concerns about our place in the world, i.e., our relations to significant others and the Big Other (the social order). More precisely, this diffuse mood of questioning is channeled into concerns about the place of the individual in others' desires, in the world their attention articulates, and, later, into concerns about the place of the individual in the Symbolic order (i.e., culture, or, more broadly, human community). These questions, for Lacan, are fundamental questions, questions as fundamental as those concerning the quality of our relations to internal and external objects are for Klein.

Signifiers, in other words, even when they come to compose more determinate questions, pertain more to the interrogative mode or mood of subjectivity than to the constative order of clear and certain meaning or to the order of intersubjective relations within which meaningful communication transpires. Signifiers inscribe subjectivity with a question mark, a hesitation, a trembling uncertainty. The Lacanian emphasis embedded in the concept of the signifier is placed on perturbation, on the incessant and ultimately uncapturable movements of significance (both "within" and between individuals—though even the language of individuality is certainly strained here, perhaps to the breaking point). Signifiers, then, do not correspond to unconscious meanings so much as they incite interminable and unsteady processes of meaning-making; their truth is the truth of the emphatic undecidability of meaning, the truth of our symbolic limitations, our want-of-meaning, lack, or "castration." With the concept of the signifier, Lacan stresses radical polysemy, polyvalency, and ultimate illegibility. In his writings, his seminars, and his clinic, Lacan extends the assumption of meaning, only to revoke it . . . again, at least in part in order to provoke his addressees to make meanings they can assume, to become responsible for their meanings. Though much more needs to be said about these matters, let this suffice for the initial establishment of a contrast between Klein's focus on meaning and Lacan's emphasis on the nonsensical elements of meaning.

Having cast some light on some of the prominent terms of Lacan's theory and practice, we can now approach the question of what Lacan means by the thesis—crucial to his engagement with Klein's case study—that the unconscious is the discourse of the Other. *Lacan's claim is that the unintended and unacknowl-*

edged effect of Klein's speech is to create an unconscious for Dick. From this perspective, Klein may be right that transforming latent anxiety into manifest—thus bearable, negotiable—anxieties allows Dick's interest to expand and his ego to develop. However, averse as he is to efforts to strengthen the ego, Lacan is less concerned with what allows Dick's ego to develop than he is with what attention to the development of the ego and object relations systematically obscures, e.g., the incoherent pulsation of bodily life prior to and forever in excess of Oedipal normalization; the absolute exposure of the infant to the ministrations of his or her caregivers that is subsequently buried by the development of various proficiencies, self-images, and forms of social immersion; the flight and force of *desire* beyond the bounds of object relatedness and identity; the inassimilable Real; the transindividual status of the unconscious; the persistent enigma of others' desires and the psychic, significatory momentum to which this irritating enigma gives rise; and the irreducible polysemy and indefinite deferral of psychic significance that we recurrently attempt to domesticate by narration and other manners of interpretive overlay, that is, the essentially nonsensical and abyssal "ground" of meaning (the troublesome persistence of the signifier).[35]

Related to this is Lacan's framing of Klein's interpretations as less Oedipal (at the level of content) than Oedipalizing (at the level of function). From Lacan's vantage point, Klein's interpretations do not access Oedipal meanings inhering in Dick's phantasy life. Or if they do, this is of secondary importance insofar as they "only" impact his simultaneously over- and underdeveloped ego. Her interpretations are not Oedipal interpretations in the conventional sense because they do not speak to—clarify and modify—a prevailing Oedipal narrative structuring Dick's experience and behavior. If anything, Lacan claims, Klein's interpretations construct and impose that narrative. For Lacan, Klein's interpretations are Oedipalizing both in the sense of overlaying Dick's experience with an Oedipal frame and, more importantly, of *initiating, by way of their perlocutionary effects,* (1) a sense of connection to and separation from others and (2) affective investment in the Symbolic order (connection to and separateness from the Other). On Lacan's reading, Klein's speech initiates Dick into the Symbolic order, and on the ground that this initiation is ordinarily associated with the resolution of the (male) Oedipal crisis Lacan intimates that Klein's interpretations have an Oedipalizing effect. For Lacan, it is ultimately unimportant—or at least far less important—*what* Klein says; what is important is *that* she speaks and that Dick feels touched by, implicated in, her speech. And even more important for Lacan is that *Dick responds*, that he not only feels implicated in her speech, in her desire, in a world irreducible to himself—both outside the parameters of his omnipotent narcissism and outside the deadening hold of his anxiety—he attempts to assume a place in this world (as indicated by his responsiveness and subsequent attempts to address himself to others). Dick, who was once for the most part unimpacted by the presence or absence of his primary caregivers, now calls out to them and to Klein; he addresses others and feels himself addressed by them. A major change has taken place: now others and objects have a *significant place* in Dick's psychic life; their claims, desires, compelling and repulsive characteristics, etc. can be ignored or denied but only subsequent to their recognition, subsequent to what is now an initial, inescapable affirmation. From here on, Lacan suggests, Dick cannot but be radically open to objects and others. His is now an emphatically expositive and relational horizon. Through his assumption of speech, Dick becomes part of the human horizon: a horizon of mutual dependency and exposure, of the affective and significant presence of oneself to others and others to oneself, a horizon from which there is no shelter (at most, there may be evasion and distraction). As Aristotle knew well, the human is *in between*: always in the midst of others, constitutively communal, i.e., political. Only beasts and gods are, if anyone or anything is, radically alone and self-sufficient.

Lacan and Klein further differ in their interpretations of the "key" to the case. For Klein, the key is the accuracy of her Oedipal interpretations, specifically, their ability to modulate Dick's anxiety and thereby unlock his ego development, object relations, and symbolic capacities. For Lacan, the key is Klein's *speech*, more specifically, her implanting within Dick a condensed symbolic order via her Oedipal(izing) interpretations: "The myth enables us to collate a series of relations between subjects, in comparison with whose complexity and wealth the Oedipus appears to be such an abridged edition that, in the final analysis, it is not always utilizable" (*Seminar I*: 101). For Lacan, Klein's "key"—accurate Oedipal interpretations—is a "reduced key" (ibid.).

As we have seen, Lacan is interested in the Oedipalizing *effects* of Klein's momentous interpellation. He is interested in the effective subjectivization of Dick, in Dick becoming a subject who can, indeed must, express his desires and call upon others to facilitate his satisfactions; indeed a subject whose very survival depends on felicitous recognition of his needs; a subject who must assume, or at least negotiate with, his dependency, his humanimality, his subjection to both the sustaining function and the affective presence and significance of others, their call, and eventually to the symbolic norms and structures of attention their speech conveys. On Lacan's reading, Klein's interpretations are Oedipalizing not in the sense of coordinating currents of pre-Oedipal sexuality into genitalized sexuality (though they may do this too) but rather in the sense of opening a rift in the unbearably homogenous anxiety in which Dick was subsumed. They perform a cut; their effect is one of "castration." Klein's interpretations do not tear Dick away from symbiotic fusion with the Bountiful Mother by positioning the mother as the father's property. They do not threaten castration if Dick trespasses upon the rights of the father. The typical Freudian narrative of the

Oedipus complex has no purchase here. Klein's interpretations are Oedipalizing precisely in virtue of their effective opening of Dick onto his lack, onto his need for others, and onto the lack in others. That is, they open Dick onto others' desire (their lack) insofar as it is both directed at and beyond him, insofar as it weighs upon yet is relatively independent of him. Klein's interpretations are Oedipalizing in that they bring Dick into a relation of connection to and separateness from the Other—this, for Lacan, is the Oedipal structure reduced to its basic formal elements.[36]

Through Klein's speech, Dick is "cut-into," inscribed in, a world where others figure an outside to his anxiety-suffused ambience of existence. He is opened onto a dimension of radical exteriority and yet simultaneously inscribed in a world where help may be forthcoming, where his needs may be caringly tended. Quite precisely, Klein's interpretations are Oedipalizing in the sense of bearing the paternal function; they "castrate" Dick by imparting to him and inscribing in him an inescapable and affectively significant *question* about his place within a symbolic and relational horizon that irreducibly exceeds him yet to which he is irrevocably bound. On Lacan's reading, it is not or not just the accuracy of Klein's interpretations that modulate Dick's unbearable latent anxiety into manifest anxieties; Dick's binding to this symbolic and relational horizon *is his release from his unbearable anxiety.* The opening of this new perspective closes down or at least substantially mitigates the pressures of his prior horizon. It is the disclosure of a human world, a world of mutual dependence and concern, that releases Dick from submersion in a sea of stubbornly diffuse anxiety. Klein's speech, which is Imaginary at the level of content (she speaks of his identifications and fantasies, particularly of his Oedipal identifications and fantasies), initiates Dick into the Symbolic and is thus Oedipalizing on account of its form.[37] Klein's speech is *formally* Oedipalizing even if Dick does not, either on its basis or prior to it, desire to sleep with one parent and kill the other.

In order to attain a better, albeit still provisional, understanding of what Lacan is saying here, let us elaborate upon some of the terms relevant to this discussion (e.g., the Imaginary, the Symbolic, the Real, lack, signifier, and desire) and upon the relations that obtain between them.

THE IMAGINARY

The Imaginary names a form of experience or a series of categorical and morphological commitments that obscure the originary and persistent sense of one's body and world as eruptive, unconsolidated. Imaginary relations are thus self- and object-relations through which self, others, and objects reciprocally acquire an illusory sense of consistency, stability, and symmetry. To be immersed in the Imaginary is to be captivated by the seeming coherence of self and world, both independently and together; say, to be ensnared by a fantasy of the absolute identity of personal integrity and social integration, of the absolute identity of autonomous, authentic, conscientious individuality and unbreakable social belonging, a fantasy of the We having become I, and the I, We. Imaginary relations are dominated by the impulse to flee from experiences of one's body-world horizon as irredeemably incoherent and inconsistent—unruly and even when rule-ish, subject to ongoing processual differentiation that defers the closure and so the intelligibility of the rule.[38] This is to say, Imaginary relations are forms of flight from experience itself as relentlessly temporalized, i.e., irremediably fractured into bits and pieces, inassimilable or at least incompletely assimilable to static and discrete forms. More precisely, the impulse is too flee from experiences wherein the unity of body and self, as well as the differences between body/self and world, are not yet—and anticipatorily may never be—firmly established. These are experiences wherein, say, many differences obtain between body, self, other, and object, though they are too multiplicitous, too unruly and indistinct, to articulate a consistently contoured world within which a body/self might find a place, path, or position that can be either assumed or disclaimed as one's own. Imaginary relations take flight from the insuperable inauthenticity of saying "I," from our existential homelessness. Or, to take a slightly different tack, the Imaginary is a form of flight from experiences in which phenomena are possessed of an overproximous, sublime might that overburdens our capacity to orient ourselves.

Initially and to some extent persistently, we experience our body-world horizon as an aggregation of sensations, impulses, and zones lighting up sometimes rhythmically, sometimes erratically, and in any case well beyond the framework of subjective unity. This state of differentiation without clear-cut differences is what Lacan sometimes calls symbiosis: a term that stresses merger, indistinctness, and envelopment. Contrary to mainstream Lacanian doxa, however, symbiosis does not refer to an originary experience of unencumbered Oneness with the world/mother that is later cut through by the law of the father.[39] For Lacan, a sense of Oneness is a retrospective illusion that attempts to cover over multiplicitous differentiations and ongoing differentiation. It comes on the scene too late to be altogether convincing. A great many differentiations between body/self and world are already incumbent to the structure of infantile experience, though these differentiations fail to cohere into the sort of distinct, determinate differences requisite for later forms of practical life. A sense of subjective coherence (and all the more so, subject-world coherence) remains dubious *because* it comes as such a relief. Properly speaking, then, symbiosis names those experiences characterized by hazy indistinction (distinctions without a Big Difference) between self and other, body and object, body and self.[40] It names a form of experience characterized not so much by being *split* (this form of experience will develop later with the institution of the unconscious) as by being *radically riven*. The paintings of Hieronymus Bosch, Lacan suggests, can be viewed as illustrations of this state, or, better, this form of experience.[41]

The Imaginary names the orientation of desire toward objectification, toward static images of ourselves, others, objects, and the relations obtaining between them. For instance, guided by Imaginary proclivities, a diverse series of injuries suffered are brought back to and "explained" by an image of oneself as, fundamentally, a victim. However distressing it may be to sustain an identification as essentially a victim, this self-image is in certain respects deeply satisfying. (1) The coherence of this self-image is formally desirable; (2) insofar as it facilitates a stable world-orientation, it becomes all the more desirable; and (3) it may become even more desirable as it accrues a number of secondary investments from the specific path it projects through the world. For example, on the premise that I am fundamentally a victim, I may feel justified, even righteous, in alleviating my pain through acts of retribution, manipulation, or even capricious cruelty. Holding myself to be exempt from the forms of moral evaluation appropriate for those who have not had to bear such irreparable—perhaps early and abrupt, perhaps systematic—injuries, believing myself to be paid up in advance or as it were ontologically exonerated from whatever infractions of civility, sociability, or morality I may commit, I allow myself the base pleasures of viciousness and so forth that consolidate my identification with the jealously guarded victim stance that affords me the comforts of a stable self-image. As creatures of the Imaginary, we are gluttons for form.

The Imaginary names a pronounced interest in script, character, and narrative—more precisely, the Imaginary resonates with the manner of redeeming contingency, facticity, and ephemerality constitutive of narrative but only as one moment of its dialectic. Though certain forms of Imaginary captivation may issue in profound hostility to the world, as in the previous example, at another level, Imaginary captivation always promotes illusory reconciliation: both within the self and between self and world. It is an ideological impulsion pressing implacably for affirmation of the basic patterns of meaning of status quo, however difficult to bear they may be. Feeling myself to be essentially a victim may be terribly painful, but it provides the Imaginary consolation of coherent identity. The Imaginary names our efforts to bring an end to the difficulty of negotiating with our status as problematic subjects, subjects of desire.[42] It is an eminently anti-modern orientation.

As we have begun to see, identification is central to the Imaginary. Broadly, the Imaginary names our insuperable penchant to identify with various images that figure our desired cohesion and consistency. Slightly more specifically, the

Imaginary names our insistent predilection for (1) relationships wherein we feel recognized as possessed of an object-like integrity and (2) objects (images, communities, relationships, principles of governance, etc.) whose clear-cut contours and veneer of organic integrity or mechanically forged totality inspire narcissistically gratifying identifications. As beings of the Imaginary, we crave stable relations, a determinate and recognized place in the familial, social, and even metaphysical, religious, or cosmic orders. As beings of the Imaginary, we solicit recognition from others as discrete and, ideally, constitutive elements of a close-knit social fabric, a national or religious community, or perhaps just as coparticipants in a shared lifestyle. We solicit recognition from others whom we invest with the authority to define us, to establish us as the bearers of definite roles and thus as entitled to expect definite forms of treatment, others before whom we are willing, perhaps all too willing, to sacrifice—or at least suppress and keep under wraps—much of our raging and far-ranging desire, our polymorphous potential, for the sake of objectifying recognition. (Viewed politically, the Imaginary is a perversion of egalitarian recognition; and due to its basis in a willful or extorted, i.e., unearned and irrational, investiture of authority—authority is invested, not acknowledged—Imaginary recognition is prone to skeptical collapse, or what amounts to the same, unsatisfiable, voracious demand.) As beings of the Imaginary, we seek role models after whom we can pattern our lives. These role models are at first, ordinarily, our primary caregivers. Later, they are often those who impress us as "characters": personality types that manifest a determinate and recognizable—even if caricatured—style. The culture industry feeds on the desire for Imaginary (mis)recognition. As creatures of the Imaginary, we crave recognition and will cast ourselves in molds that are our inroads to social intelligibility, even if the cost is much suffering and self-suppression.[43] Through his elaboration of the Imaginary, Lacan seeks to register a fundamental human tendency to assume a passive stance, to repudiate our self- and world-transforming desire, to disavow our possibilities and desire for becoming ever otherwise. For the sake of a comforting sense of static integrity and finality—that is, death—we are willing to abandon much of our ownmost potential, to abdicate the truth of our in(de)finite *desire*.

Our identifications, Lacan stresses, are less propelled by an intrinsic desire for connection (as Fairbairn and others claim), by the need to reduce tension (as certain classical Freudians claim), or by the natural momentum that paves the way for symbolism (as Klein claims in "The Importance of Symbol Formation" and elsewhere)—though all this may well be—than by an imposing demand to experience ourselves as stable, unified, and bound-up in firmly fixed relations with coherent objects and others.[44] Thus the tragic paradox: via identification we strive for self-coherence and -consistency, yet identification is the mechanism through which we incessantly become other to ourselves. As we identify with various images or imagoes[45] throughout the course of our lives, we become a multilayered precipitate, a composite of identifications that do not neatly cohere as a unified, harmonious self. Having mimetically incorporated, e.g., the diverse modes and tendencies of desire, evaluation, object-relation, and so on of those with whom we identify, we become profoundly inconsistent. Identification may, in any given instance, confer the desired *form* of self-cohesion, but the outcome of identification is flimsy, and thus its work incessant, because it is too *formalistic*. In order to access the integral form of the objects with which we identify, we are bound to take on various aspects of their contents. These contents, once internalized, persist in tension with one another; we become a matrix of irreconcilable self-images, a locus of conflicting desires, orientations, sensibilities, and value orderings—hardly a self at all. In short, we get more than we bargained for. Through our identificatory efforts to achieve a stable sense of self-integrity, we become ever more tension-ridden and inconsistent. Lured by the fantasy of finally achieving an inviolable integrity, though, we tend to chalk up our inconsistency (our confusion and disorientation) and our suffering under the conflictuality of our desires to any number of causes. Just about anything will do—hence the penchant to assign the blame for our suffering or discomposure to anything external (or available for expulsion) that can be coded as the cause of our "insecurity."

The Imaginary is marked by what Lacan terms *alientation*. Though this term, as per usual with Lacan, has an extensive polysemic range, suffice it to say that, minimally, alienation refers to the ways in which Imaginary identifications overlay and suppress the fragmentary form of experience with which we started (the Real).[46] However, Lacan insists, this primordial form of experience can never be altogether overwritten: alienation, like repression, is highly permeable. Thus we are set on an interminable path of covering over, by way of ever new identifications and other means by which we assure ourselves of our subjective consistency and world-integration (familial, professional, or social recognition, etc.), the fragmentary form of experience that is identity's irrepressible, abyssal underside and the tragic consequence of our efforts to surmount it. Captivation by the Imaginary imposes severe limits on our ability to avow our constitutive and unending exposedness, thus on our self-conscious self-formation. Our proneness to become ensnared by rigid regimes of narcissistic duality (I am this, you are that, we relate as discrete and determinate, complementary entities on a well-contoured social landscape; or, to highlight the rivalrous dimension of Imaginary duality, you are X, but I want to be X, so you must be my persecutor who must be destroyed so that I can unproblematically recognize myself as X) suggests the ineradicable incoherence festering beneath—and partially motivating—such relations. While the compelling qualities of various objects and their seductively integral form may partially account for our incessant penchant for identification, Lacan insists that accounting for the massively energetic propulsion of identification requires us to assume more than the *pull* of objects—i.e., their alluring charms. We must also assume an urgency to *push away* from an unbearable state of fragmentation and all that comes to be associated with it in the symbiotic matrix: preemptory neediness, the inevitable frustrations of infancy, overwhelming stimulation, the overproximity of caregivers or even of phenomena as such, etc.

Imaginary identification is thus defensive, a large-scale defense against the residual form of experience in which the self and the relations between body/self and object/other are registered as incoherent, irredeemably inassimilable to prevailing forms of understanding, tactics of manipulation, or relational habits. According to Lacan, we cannot bear the inescapable sense of self, body, object, and other as fundamentally excessive of our regimes of intelligibility and relationality. Beneath defensive identifications is buried a pulsating and disjointed wanting that exceeds any determinate configuration and thus cannot be satisfied by any particular object or quality of object relation. Beneath identification is entombed a sense of ourselves as forever incomplete (*manque-à-être*): lacking, disjointed, out of place. For Lacan, the subject is a void of *desire*.

To clarify and preempt a common misunderstanding, though Lacan's emphasis is surely on the defensive character of identification, and, more broadly, the Imaginary, identification and the Imaginary are not, on his account, exclusively defensive. Identification may be prompted by or come into the service of psychic pressures and activities other than the suppression of the fragmentary form of experience, but it will at least *always also* be used for this. From this angle, it is clear why Lacan continually emphasizes the link between the Imaginary and defensive ego functioning.[47] Lacan stresses again and again that the ego—developed as a precipitate of identifications—is a citadel of defense. On his account, the ego is less the seat of reality testing or compromise between various psychic agencies than a composite of identifications, a forum for Otherness that is mistaken as the inviolable and distinctive core of the self. What we take to be our uniqueness is our alienation in Otherness. For Lacan, it is more or less inevitable, and not always undesirable, that we (mis)take ourselves this way, but this does not dull the critical edge of his claim that this is a mode of *alienation*. As we come to privilege and assume certain self-images, as we come to take a fundamental and recognizable stance in the world, and as this stance and these images are reflected back to us in social interaction, we come to believe that *this* (character reflected) is who we truly are. For Lacan, though, the sense of personal distinctiveness attained in such a manner is the epitome of conformity, a marker of unacknowledged assimilation to the values, desires, behavioral norms, sensibilities, and senses of "reality" that we have picked up from others. The ego is a defense that bolsters the disavowal of our interminable, unfathomable, in(de)finitely shifting *desire* and the experience of the body-world horizon as riven by it. Under the sway of *desire*, our bodies, our worlds, are endlessly unsettled, indeed threaten to be torn apart, to open onto the nothingness, the void upon which they are precariously constructed.

As noted above, Lacan's use of the term alienation is complex. The ego, though alienating, protects us from more direct exposure to our radical self-alienation, from a more direct encounter with our insuperable alienation from ourselves, objects, and others, that is, from our constitutive *riven-ness*, our *desire*. Identifications are thus defensive insofar as they cover over the truth of the subject, the truth of desire, the truth that at bottom, or perhaps alongside our privileged self-images and sense of cohesive selfhood, we are a diffuse jumble of inchoate longings, or, more accurately, a pure, non-objectal longing or wanting, an insistent force of desirous negativity, and, as such, cut off from replete, finally pacifying satisfaction and from a secure sense of belonging in and to the world.[48] By focusing—or, better, as the focusing of—our attention on discrete and determinable objects with whom or with which stable relations can be established, the ego insulates us from the dimension of sublime rupture, from the register of *desire*, and thereby allows for a great many significant developments, indeed allows a life to be lead. But at a price. It is Klein's failure to worry about the price paid for the development of Dick's ego that so distresses Lacan.

We will return to this concern shortly. For now, let us elaborate a few of Lacan's worries that proceed from a suspicion that Klein is beholden to another crucial feature of the Imaginary: symmetry. From Lacan's perspective, Klein's theory and technique manifest uninterrogated and problematic commitments to Imaginary symmetry. Notice that the terms of Kleinian theory—good object and bad object, part-object and whole object, projection and introjection, inside and outside, phantasy and reality, ego and object, persecutory anxiety and idealization, etc.—are strikingly dyadic, even for the most part symmetrically oppositional. This leads Lacan to suspect that Klein's metapsychology and theory of technique reflect her captivation by the Imaginary. His question would be: Might the symmetrical oppositionality of the major terms of Klein's theory and technique indicate her desire for a manageable intellectual architecture even if this comes at the expense of significant injustice to the experiences with which she is concerned?

Of course, especially compared to her predecessors, Klein is emphatically attuned to the labile madness of both ordinary and pathological psychic states, specifically to the disruptions and discontinuities that psychotic anxieties continually provoke. But despite Klein's attention to, say, the incessant fluctuation between paranoid-schizoid and depressive anxieties, the highly unsettling phantasies that result from this, the continual upsurge of fragmenting aggression, and the various other motivators of dissociation—anxiety always interrupts reparation; no whole is ever finally consolidated—the terms through which she conceptualizes these destabilizing forces manifest a striking symmetry: projection and introjection, part and whole object, good and bad, mother and infant.

But this is just the beginning of a suspicion. The suspicion is deepened when we consider that good and bad part-objects are eventually integrated into a whole object that Klein explicitly deems "real."[49] Even though she underlines that the "real," "whole" object will eventually split into good and bad part-objects due to the recurrence of paranoid-schizoid anxiety, she specifies that the experience of such diremption is phantasmatic. For Klein, even if it is incompletely attainable, reality is defined as the successful integration of good and bad,[50] i.e., wholeness, while for Lacan reality is closer to the experience of uncoordinated fragmentation that, on Klein's account, is to a large extent overcome via the internalization of the good object and depressive integration.

Further amplifying the suspiciously Imaginary character of Kleinian theory are the following considerations. First, Klein's theory of early development seems to be the story of how the infant transitions from a state in which patterns of relatively stable, though highly unsettling, relations (projection and avoidance) obtain with relatively discrete and determinable entities (part-objects, that is, internal or external objects that function as repositories of the infant's constitutional sadism) to a state in which different but still relatively stable relational patterns (introjection and projection) obtain with both part-objects and whole objects (which are even more discrete and determinable).[51] Klein seems to be narrating development from the perspective of the ego, articulating the desire of the ego for integrity[52] and determinate, intelligible object relations as the truth of subjective development. If this is correct, one might then suspect that the entirety of Klein's developmental theory, even the entirety of her metapsychology, enacts a defense against the primordial and persistent experience of self and world as tumultuously rent, irremediably fractured into bits and pieces. Further, one might suspect that Klein's therapeutic technique, by enjoining the analyst to transition from being a part object to a whole object with whom the analysand can identify, may likewise collude with defenses against experiences of self and others/objects as inconsistent, lacking, etc. In Lacanian terms, her technique would conspire with defenses against *desire*, "castration," separation, and the Real. If Kleinian therapy is as hospitable to the ego's desire for stable images of and relations between self and other/object as it seems, this means that, in Lacanian parlance, it will likely result in a reinforcement of alienation.

Second, Klein's theory of permanent oscillation between the paranoid/schizoid and depressive positions implies that we will forever feel ourselves to be subject to others' retributions and they to ours, thus that we will endlessly seek compensation/reparation for assaults waged on us and offer compensation/

reparation for assaults we have waged on others. Does this deadlock of retribution and compensation/reparation not itself bespeak a belief in an all-powerful other who can deeply damage or deeply satisfy? Is it not a theoretical reification of Imaginary trends? Even if depressive integration involves recognition of self and other as both good and bad, limited, and so forth, does not the theory of oscillation between the paranoid/schizoid and depressive positions presuppose, and in practice effect, limits to separation individuation?

Though Klein rejects the romantic allure of construing relations between infant and mother or self and other as placid and harmonious, oddly, the terms through which she characterizes the instability of object relations are themselves rather neat and symmetrical. Might the self-assured composure of Klein's theory suggest a disavowal of, even a manic defense against, the unsettling force of the experiences theorized? Though she pays keen attention to the unending difficulty of consolidating a border between inside and outside, self and other, she never calls into question the guiding metaphor of inside/outside. In fact, she naturalizes the metaphor: phantasmatic "internal reality," or, in her terms, "unreal reality" (1975: 221), is neatly distinguished from "external reality," which she identifies with the experience of the whole object. It is as if Cartesian axiomatic dualism is displaced into the sphere of the mental. At this point, Lacan might well ask: Why is wholeness indicative of reality rather than, say, a fantasy that oscillates with the fantasy of good and bad part-objects? Is not the whole object a fantastically idealized antidote to part-object anxieties that are themselves equally fantasmatic?[53] And might not both fantasies register and repudiate the primary and persistent experience of oneself/the world as fundamentally rent, inconsistent, non-whole?[54] (Recall that one of the major charges Kleinians level against Lacan is that he is insufficiently concerned with fantasy.) As much as Klein pursues theoretical symmetry and technical procedures that promote the concomitant cohesion of ego and object, Lacan pursues asymmetry, both theoretically and technically. As much as Klein works under the banner of reparative integration, the dominant emblems on Lacan's family crest are the Möbius strip and the Klein bottle.[55] Of course, the characterization of Klein as unwittingly and all-consumingly beholden to the ego-imperatives of symmetry and integrity involves a profound exaggeration of what may be little more than a vague and subdued undercurrent of her thinking. But perhaps such exaggeration is necessary to bring it into the open.

All we have done so far is articulate a suspicion (and a few clinical worries) which is itself rather suspect given Klein's ample attention to (1) the various factors that impede the integration of the ego and the object and (2) the forces that work against pacified, normalized relations between ego and object. Klein is nothing if not a thinker of dynamism and disruption. She could not insist more clearly or adamantly that depressive reparation and integration are continually unraveled by the upsurge of sadistic impulses and various anxieties. What has been mended is sundered once more. This suspicion will prove worth considering only if it can help us see certain problems in Klein's theory and technique to which she was blind. In order to get there, a bit of backtracking is in order.

Recall that in Klein's account of the concomitant development of symbolization and the ego, sadistic phantasies motivated by the death drive initially overcode reality via identification: the infant identifies/equates her "internal," sadism-ridden reality with various objects (assumed at the level of phantasy to reside in the mother's body) in a self-preservative effort to rid herself of her innate sadism. Consequently, the child will turn from one object to another, attempting to avoid the sadism she has implanted in the objects previously encountered. Eventually, and rather miraculously, the good part-object makes its presence felt, after which the projection of bad part objects and introjection of good part-objects proceeds cyclically, and it would seem endlessly. Yet however deadlocked the infant seems to be in the cycle of projection and introjection, the recognition and internalization of the good part-object paves the way, once again rather miraculously, for reality, in the form of the whole object (sometimes described as just good and sometimes as both good and bad) to make itself known, thereby initiating the transition from the paranoid-schizoid to the depressive position, from splitting to reparation. The "beautiful and 'perfect'" image of the whole object is the antidote to paranoid/schizoid disintegration. Klein specifies that the whole object makes its presence felt via the conduits of libidinal attachment that assure (1) Eros a certain triumph over the death drive and/or (2) reality testing through which the differences between inner and outer worlds are established. But this begs the question. The inexplicability of these transitions, from Lacan's perspective, suggests that something is amiss.

Might it be, Lacan might well ask, that these transitions are inexplicable within Klein's theory because that theory is governed by a force to which it is blind, namely, the Imaginary desire for personal stability and relational symmetry? Might another term, the Symbolic, be required to account for both the desire for and initiation of a transition from a state of riven-ness to one of personal and intersubjective stability? And by seeking to facilitate such a transition, might Klein's therapeutic technique unwittingly conspire with the ego, the Imaginary, and so with normalization and alienation? Might it be that, generally, Klein's theory and technique are beholden to the desire of the ego and thus the Imaginary? It is these suspicions that are at the center of Lacan's worries about Klein. And it is these suspicions that lead him to conceptualize projection and the relation between projection and introjection in a manner that differs radically from Klein. Lacan queries,

> [H]ow should we indicate the correlative of projection? It is necessary to find another term than introjection [presumably, because the simplistic symmetry of the dyadic structure of projection/introjec-

tion is suspicious and because introjection assumes a relatively well-contoured self into which projected part-objects can be absorbed]. In the way we use it in analysis [that is, Lacanian analysis], introjection is not the opposite of projection. It is practically employed [Here Lacan is characteristically equivocal. When he says that introjection is "practically employed," he seems to mean both that the term is employed in his theoretical-therapeutic practice, thereby acknowledging his inheritance of Kleinian thought, and that the term is nearly employed, not quite wholeheartedly employed, employed but with a critical hesitation or ironic attitude because the term "introjection" risks suggesting an Imaginary unity of inside and outside, thereby marking his distance from Klein] . . . only when what is at stake is symbolic introjection. [Now Lacan clarifies that not only is he hesitant when using the term, but he will use it only if it is understood as a very different concept than Kleinian introjection. For Lacan, it is not as if, as Klein seems to suggest, part-objects are *literally* taken in—into where?—via introjection and expelled via projection. Part of what is at stake here is Lacan's profession of commitment to a modified Heideggerian notion of being-in-the-world, as opposed to what he presumably takes to be Klein's quasi-Cartesian dualism.] It is always accompanied by a symbolic denomination. [What is taken in is always a symbol, a differential element, an element of meaning, thus something mediated by the desire of the other and the Big Other/Symbolic Order. But if what is taken "in" is so mediated, in what respect can the internal be said to be strictly opposed to the external? Further, if what is taken "in" always bears social symbolism, can Klein's account of the infant as initially ensnared in wholly phantasmatic, "unreal reality" and only progressively able to accommodate meanings that it does not project onto its experience of proto-objects hold up?] *Introjection is always the introjection of the discourse [or speech] of the Other* [the desirous discourse of the other, manifest both in the speech of the other and in the experience of objects as such, cannot fail to make an impact on the infant, who is thus not nearly as monadic as Klein assumes. Is not the Kleinian infant who projects its self-directed death drive onto various part-objects, who *identifies* them with its own sadism through its "symbolic equations," essentially a solipsistic monad? Does Lacan then mean to be redeeming Klein's intuitions concerning primary relationality? Further, what is taken "in" is always already *mediated*, thus one must wonder if there can ever be a clean-cut distinction between reality and phantasy, as Klein maintains.], and this fact [Lacan is by no means averse to bold statements of his insights, to a boldness that mirrors what he later characterizes as Klein's violent boldness. More on this later.] introduces a dimension altogether different from the dimension of projection. [*What is taken in is not symmetrical with what is projected.*] It is around this distinction that you can separate, and see

> the difference, between the function of the ego, which is of the order of the dual register, and the function of the superego [pertaining to the triangular register. In other words, Lacan seems to suggest that Klein's theory unwittingly gives voice to the perspective of the ego and thus naturalizes the Imaginary. The import placed on projecting the bad (or the imperiled good) and taking in the good (or the bad that threatens to consume the goodness of the good that has been projected) such that ego and object integrity can eventually obtain is, perhaps, the *projected desire of the ego*, not the truth of early infantile experience.]. (*Seminar I*: 97)

According to Lacan, Klein accurately describes projection when she speaks of the infant's identification/equation of its sadistic phantasies with "reality," though she fails to consider that projection, and so "reality," may indicate an effort of de-differentiation, an effort to (perhaps sadistically) abolish the (both intrinsically and because always already mediated by the Other) impinging and uncertain dimension of experience. Projective identification, by concealing the disorganized or at least unsettled, processually differentiated character of experience, establishes "reality" as a comforting veil of illusion. Klein fails to consider that projection is Imaginary and the interplay of projection and introjection (in her sense) even more so. Further, she misunderstands introjection as the symmetrical correlate of projection and mischaracterizes the dynamic of projection and introjection as naturally leading to the consolidation of a relatively stable self and object, and thus the possibility of relatively stable object relations. Is this not the dream of the ego fulfilled?

Klein fails to consider that underlying her account of the concomitant development of the ego, symbolism, and worldliness may be a demand for Imaginary symmetry and cohesion. Thus she fails to ask after the conditions of this demand and whether or not, clinically, there is reason to disrupt it. In order to give an account of this demand, Lacan is compelled to assume that the Symbolic is primordial, that significance always already saturates the field of experience. Specifically, in order to give an account of the demand mobilizing Kleinian theory and practice, Lacan is compelled to assume the infant's originary exposure to the increasingly intelligible yet originarily and to some extent persistently enigmatic meanings of the Other. And in order to disrupt this demand as it manifests in the clinic, Lacan is compelled to develop a number of practices that lead the analysand from alienation to separation, from identification to de-subjectification, from Imaginary fixation to freedom.

Seeking to gain some distance from the perspective of the ego and thereby put himself in a position to account for its demands, Lacan insists that introjection be understood as Symbolic in two senses. First, as the taking "in," or, more precisely, the exposure to, the initially and to a degree persistently indecipherable meaningfulness of every object of experience, i.e., to the pre-conceptual, pre-practical significance of phenomena. Second, as the taking "in" of the social significance of objects and of the field of relations in which various objects are located (i.e., the Symbolic, understood on a basically Saussurian model). On the basis of his claim that introjection is an exposure to, a registration of, the initially and persistently indecipherable meaningfulness of objects of experience, Lacan can offer an account of the Imaginary proclivities that Klein's theory and practice reify: perhaps only because the infant is exposed to and troubled by the enigmatic meaningfulness of the world (and the enigmatic significance of the desire of the other that alights various aspects of the world, that carves out and foregrounds various objects through her streams of attention) does Imaginary de-differentiation/identification come into play; for what is Imaginary identification if not a way of generating the parameters within which a relatively stable world-orientation can develop? On the basis of his claim that introjection is a registration of (1) the pre-conceptual and pre-practical significance of objects, (2) the uncircumventable presence of the desire of the Other and the quandaries it generates, (3) the social significance of objects, and (4) the field of relations in which objects are located, Lacan develops what he takes to be a richer account of development than Klein in a way that directly pertains to Dick's case and provides a more full account of Klein's impact on Dick than she can offer, specifically, an account that can identify the dangers and unthematized—thus underdeveloped—advantages of Klein's work with Dick.

For Lacan, there is never simply an object, part or whole. Objects are not discrete monads; they are constituted, at least in part, by their location within an evolving matrix of relations. It is these relations that are "taken in" via introjection. Though objects may later appear as discrete monads, this is, on Lacan's account, a reflection of the projected desire of the ego: a paradoxical form of self-absorption. As much as Klein emphasizes that introjection is the introjection of a good or bad part-object, Lacan emphasizes that introjection is the introjection of a relation: in/out, it/in, it/me, desire/addressee, etc. As we will see in much greater detail below, for Lacan the infant comes to distinguish interiority from exteriority, fantasy from reality, and so on only because her significant others do so and because she seeks to secure their affection via mimesis (or at least Lacan will stress that the institution of such distinctions is secured by their place in tactics of mimetic ingratiation).[56] Considering the case at hand, we can witness this happening as Dick identifies himself with a signifier, a name ("Dick"), at the behest of Klein's solicitous nomination of one train as "Dick train" and the other as "daddy train." Dick introjects not—or not just—part-objects but relations, proportions (*logos*, "language," the Symbolic). And he does so at Klein's provocation. Picking up on Klein's desire that he recognize a certain relation, Dick comes to see that he is to little train as daddy is to big train, and so on. What

Lacan seeks to underscore is that, though surely not without their advantages, Klein's solicitations to see things this way conspire with Dick's Imaginary proclivities toward identificatory de-differentiation. The space between the doors *is* dark mummy; Dick's anxiety when between the doors *is* his anxiety about being in dark mummy. Complex relations obtain between Dick, Klein, mummy, daddy, nurse, trains, coal, various sorts of play, desire, anxiety, etc., and Dick slowly absorbs their significance as articulated by Klein.

From Lacan's perspective, Klein fails to understand her therapeutic achievement on two counts. First, it is not that Klein simply regulates Dick's anxiety sufficiently for the auto-activation of natural mechanisms of ego development and symbolization. Rather, magnificently, she initiates Dick into forms of relation that constitute a (proto-)world, helps him understand himself as, fundamentally, part of this relational (proto-)world, and introduces him to what she deems some of the more important relations structuring that (proto-)world. Second, by introducing differences/relations, call it a basic grammar, Klein introduces Dick to substitutability and so paves the way for (or perhaps thereby institutes) the metonymy of desire. "The Kleinian school . . . has failed to even glimpse the category of the signifier" (*E*: 532/637).

Further, from Lacan's perspective, Klein's avoidance or neglect of the Symbolic may have caused her to fail to understand an important dimension of Dick's anxiety. Might a crucial dimension of Dick's anxiety have arisen from his introjection of Symbolic relations? Might a significant portion of his anxiety pertain to his induced exposure to Symbolic differences/relations, whether because this exposure implies the partial loss of the de-differentiated reality in which he had been immersed (or the fantasy thereof) and all of the investments (narcissistic, secondary, etc.) it was able to accrue; because the differences/relations are clearly important but do not as yet make much sense, i.e., are bewildering and partially disorganizing; and/or because the differences/relations are perceived as important, even imperative to understand, though he feels largely unable to understand them, to fulfill the imperative of understanding (and whatever it resonates with)? This in turn provides reason to question whether or not the epistemophilic impulse that Klein considers innate is, rather, in this case, an effect of her implicit demand to understand, and, generally, of the implicit demand to understand articulated by caregivers as they socialize their children.[57]

It would be tempting at this point to further discuss the points of convergence and divergence between Klein and Lacan, but let us be patient. Recall that this foray into the Imaginary (and eventually the Symbolic, the Real, and other related concepts) is motivated by a need to better understand what Lacan means when he claims that Klein's interpretations are Oedipalizing and that the unconscious is the discourse of the other. To this end, before continuing to elucidate the Imaginary, let alone proceeding to discuss the Symbolic and the Real, a few terms we just encountered need to be fleshed out: the ego, desire, the subject, and truth (as in the truth of the subject and the truth of desire). Understanding these terms, their relation to the Imaginary, and what is generally at stake in them will be crucial for clarifying the differences between Lacan and Klein.

THE EGO (AND THE OBJECT)

Lacan stresses that the ego is an agglomerated precipitate of various and varied identifications. Its illusory unity, reflected in privileged self-images, is an effect of idealization and selective attention. The unity of the ego is a dream we share and support in one another. That is, the idealized integrity of the ego is supported by the reflections of subjective consistency we receive from one another in ordinary social interaction. Though recognition reifies, our sense of subjective integrity is always on credit and, as such, ever precarious. Due to an opaque—unconscious?—recognition of this precariousness, or, more precisely, due to our difficulty avowing and assuming our ineradicable multiplicity and relentless motility, the all-too-human temporality of our ever-shifting *desire*, unity (competence, mastery, security of place, clarity of identity) is sought after with ever-renewed vigor. Incessantly renewed vigilance will be required to (re) secure a sense of oneself as whole—self-contained, complete—yet the paradox, perhaps the tragedy, is that this vigilance renders us extremely brittle, perhaps even paranoiac about threats to our integrity.

Not despite but in virtue of its impossibility, ego idealization is, for Lacan, nearly inescapable. It will take the long and arduous work of a specific sort of analysis, or perhaps social crisis, to disrupt the self-consolidating identifications we hold most dear. And even exposure to disruptions may not unsettle our cherished sense of coherent selfhood, quick as we are to find new identity coordinates. In moments of crisis we tend to reconsolidate a sense of coherent identity rather than work through, find ways to affirm and live out, our multidimensionality, our inconsistency, our in(de)finite *desire*. Hence Lacan's admonishment to the revolutionaries of '68 was that they were unwittingly seeking a new master, and this they will get. His worry was that the revolutionaries were dancing with the architecture: rearranging the structures of power but, despite their claims about this being a "cultural revolution," neglecting to work out ways of distancing themselves from the regime of social normativity that would inevitably supplant that of the status quo. After the revolution much may change but commitments to stable identity and social integrity will remain unperturbed; perhaps these commitments will even be invigorated once the dissatisfactions with the social order are allayed by the institutionalization of the revolutionary program. That is, Lacan's worry was that once the revolutionaries come to feel comfortable in the new power structures, what were once insurrectionary principles will serve as supports for a renewed conservatism.

Although Lacan never quite put it in these terms, it is consistent with his thinking to say that commitment to the idealized unity of the ego points to our failure to develop a fully secular culture, a culture that can sustain an explicit and continual acknowledgement of—to put it in Castoriadis's terms—its self-institution. A fully secular culture would be without transcendental ground or guarantee. It would be a culture to which we are committed not because it offers the rituals and recognitive regimes through which an illusory and narcissistically gratifying sense of personal unity and social cohesion are sustained but because it allows our ownmost potential (better, our potentiality) to flourish; because in it we can be most truly ourselves, give ourselves over to unbounded, spontaneous play and thus accommodate ourselves most fully to our truth, the truth of in(de)finitely desirous subjectivity. Lacan, like Rosa Luxemburg, wants no part in the revolution if he can't dance. And like Nietzsche (to a point), he measures the value of social values by their felicity for the expression of "noble" natures.

Of course, immersion in the Symbolic order (language games, forms of life) of a more fully secular culture would be both inevitable and clearly of vital import. But it would not be the ground of our commitments to such a culture. From a Lacanian standpoint, a fully secular culture would be one to which we are committed, not because it allows us to defend against the void of our desire (let's say, for now, against the anxiety of freedom), and not even because its mechanisms of distribution and recognition are maximally satisfying or ethically praiseworthy, but because it supports forms of separateness and connection through which our *desire* can be in(de)finitely explored, lived out, discovered, and created.[58] Lacan would stress that if recognition and redistribution are important, it is because they contribute to *this*.[59]

Back to the exposition of the ego. Lacan's characterization of the ego as a static, reified locus of alienation is a hyperbolic corrective to the dominant trend of situating the ego as a seat of agency, adaptation, freedom, and the like. Lacan's elaboration of the ego is also set in opposition to those who describe it as an arbiter between reality, the id, and superego demands, that is, as a function that brings us into harmony with ourselves, our history, and our world. This, Lacan insists, is yet another version of the fundamental fantasy of symmetry from which we suffer. *We suffer from ideals of absolute satisfaction, harmoniousness, and self-possession against which our partial satisfactions, compromised competencies, and ongoing passivity are found forever wanting and in view of which we pathologize, or at least debase and deny, our in(de)finitely shifting desire.*[60] In the framework of this fundamental fantasy, we take a stand against ourselves: against ourselves as lacking, wanting, forever incomplete and unreconciled. We take a stand against ourselves as subjects of the unconscious, as beings who *are* our bodies, saying No! to our constitutive dependencies.

For Lacan, the ego cannot serve as a neutral mediator that maximizes the satisfaction of id-impulses while appeasing the needs for constraint issuing from the superego and the dictates of reality. And even if it could, characterizing its primary role as that of securing such an ideal balance would deny the *suffering* of symptomatic life. As much as we enjoy our symptoms for the compromise satisfactions they broker, they are nonetheless sources of torment, bespeaking our profound dissatisfaction with the forms of life we have so far cultivated or could plausibly imagine cultivating. A symptom is a vigorous rejection of the livability of our consciously pursued impulses and courses of life (and of those we sense as genuinely available to us). Symptoms are the best compromises we have been able to come up with given our conflicting desires, internalized structures of prohibition, etc., but they fail to sufficiently satisfy the desires out of which they are composed. Symptoms bespeak contradictions at the level of desire that cannot be resolved (a symptom is a fragile compromise, not a resolution, hence its susceptibility to mutation) and manifest structures of prohibition that condemn us to repudiate our own longings. The picture of harmonious balance often figured in accounts of the ego is, for Lacan, implicated in the illusion of the ego as a seat of mastery and the fantasy of harmonious symmetry from which we so often suffer.

Over and against the emphasis that many analysts put on the ego as an agency of reality testing, Lacan insists that (1) the ego's so-called reality testing is an ideological cover for complicity in regimes of social normativity and (2) the ego condemns us to repeated acts of *misrecognition*.[61] Concerning the former claim, Lacan contends that our sense of "reality" is pilfered from others whose import to us makes accommodation to their value-laden, perspective-governed senses of reality nearly inescapable.[62] Reality, Lacan emphasizes, is that to which we should *really* pay attention. The essential exposedness of the human—the exposedness registered when, as infants, we sense that we cannot provide for ourselves in the least—renders us prone to accommodate ourselves to others, to solicit their care by showing ourselves to be fundamentally like them. Unlike Winnicott, who views such conformity as a response to infelicitous caregiving (this would be the path to a "false self"), Lacan suggests that the infant, or the infantile register of experience in the adolescent and adult, is quick to pick up on the nearly fathomless narcissism of its caregivers or significant others and feels compelled to ingratiate him- or herself into this narcissism in order to secure their needed affection and ministrations. Through this register of experience we are attuned to others' emphatic self-concern[63]; in seeking to please them, we identify with them, showing ourselves to be loveable within the terms of their narcissism.

This strategy of ingratiating identification has a variety of permutations. We may show ourselves to be what the other desires or what the other has yet to recognize as the object of her desire. We may display ourselves as desiring what the other desires, becoming the vicarious embodiment of the other's desire, and thereby, we hope, motivate their identification with us or at least secure a sense of connectedness. Or we may become the principle of the other's desire itself, less its intentional object than that which sustains its momentum and/or sharpens its edge. But our various frustrations and the inevitable directedness-elsewhere of the other's desire suggest that our work has been (yet) insufficient: neither they nor we are ever fully satisfied. As much as we insist ourselves into the orbit of the other's narcissism, no matter what we do, the other is still somehow closed to us, insuperably self-interested, or, more precisely, interested in what she must become in order to secure the love of *her* significant others. The other's self-centrism is as illusory as our own. The other's desire directs her elsewhere; she is an independent vortex of desire around whom a world, *her world*, turns.[64] In Lacanian terms, the mystery of feminine desire that plays such a prominent role in the films of David Lynch—in *Blue Velvet*, Jeffrey Beaumont says to Sandy Williams that, yeah, he likes a mystery *that* much, and she is a mystery. What does Dorothy Vallens want from Frank Booth in the infamous chair scene? Why does she comply with his brutal desire rather than turning him over to the police? Of course she is terrified for herself, her husband, and her child, but . . . And why is Renee Madison so closed off from her husband, Fred Madison, in *Lost Highway*?—is a structural feature of subjectivity.

But unable to acknowledge or just forget the necessity of defeat and the vulnerability this entails, that is, neither able to acknowledge nor forget the depths of human separateness and the ongoing risk of this separateness being bridged in threatening ways, we incessantly question what we must become in order to secure the other's love. Crucially, this is a form of questioning that we often misrecognize as we come to experience it as the question of what *we* want. We forget the initial question (*che vuoi*?), and so our primordial heteroplasticity, as we learn, in the course of attempting to satisfy the desire of the other, to view ourselves as independent seats of desire, as autonomous individuals. Our allo-centrism gives over into, or, more accurately, is filtered through, a newly dominant self-centrism. Consequent upon the transformations of the mirror stage (to be discussed below) and supported by experiences of oneself as the perpetual accompaniment of desire and satisfaction, the question seems to become less what the other wants than what *I* want (or what there is to satisfy my wanting). But, Lacan insists, this question can sustain our attention only insofar as the responses to it implicitly respond to the inescapable, primordial question of the desire of the other.[65]

The infant (or the infantile in the adult) senses that its caregivers (or significant others and social cohorts) are creatures of want, that their wanting exceeds anything it might become, that such wanting is never satisfied by any particular object or form of relation but rather indefinitely circulates around them. Others' desire is displaced from object to object, from relation to relation. Yet we continually attempt to assume ourselves into the place of their wanting, figuring ourselves as the coveted object that will finally satisfy.[66] In what seems to be our ownmost wanting, at what seems to be the peak of our self-interest, we are eminently concerned with and implicitly seeking to satisfy the other. Our desire is thereby alienated, caught up in the quagmire of the desire of the other, which is as much an enigma to the other as it is to us.

This should shed some light on what Lacan means when he says that desire is the desire *of* the Other: desire is directed toward the other (subjective genitive), comes from the other (objective genitive), is Other to the other (the other's desire is unconsciously structured, i.e., nontransparent to her), and, as we will see, is filtered through and interpreted by the Other qua Symbolic order, and as such is indeterminate and polyvalent, ever other to fixed and final configurations (other to itself). Further, desire is always the desire of the other in the sense that it emerges from the other-in-ourselves (from "the other scene," the unconscious), emerges, that is, from our unfathomable recesses and in excess of any formulations we might give to it. The desire of the other in this sense names the resistance of desire to placation by this or that particular satisfaction, its irreducibility to concrete demands, its inchoate or drive-like character.

To put the point directly, one's sense of reality is mimetically acquired from and in the service of conformity to the Other's desire. The ego does not innately posses the magical power to differentiate reality from misleading appearance. Rather, Lacan insists, what passes for reality is what the ego learns to countenance *as* real. What passes the test for reality is, proximally and for the most part, that which important figures in our lives or a significant sector of society tend to consider worthy of attention, what they tend to become absorbed by, what for them has the *weight of reality*. Reality is, from this perspective, a matter of gravity, of attraction. More precisely, reality concerns the structuring of attention by phenomena that claim us and so by those who mediate such claiming by lighting up the significance of phenomena through the structure of their attention. This is what Lacan is getting at when he says that "feelings are always mutual" (*Seminar I*: 43/32). When the ego tests for reality, it employs the perspectives, the interpretive and evaluative stances, of others (or what these perspectives are imagined to be), perhaps singularly rearranged consequent upon their internalization but nonetheless indicative of the nearly unbreakable hold that our significant others' perspectives have on us. To rearrange others' perspectives into one that is uniquely one's own is, from Lacan's perspective, still to be ensnared in otherness. Originality and mimesis are not contraries. What is often discussed as reality testing is thus more accurately described as a testing of the continued viability of structures of socially and personally prized attention and evaluation, a testing not so much of their validity or viability in securing objectivity or successful world-orientation—at least, this is not where Lacan's emphasis falls—so much as it is a testing of their continued efficacy in securing needed recognition from or a sense of identification with significant others. For Lacan, the sense of what's real and what's right (as in the socially or personally imperative perspective to take on the matter) can never be altogether dissociated. From this vantage point, the distinctions between the ego, ego ideal, and superego are quite hazy.

To summarize: the ego is an ideological cover for complicity in regimes of social normativity, itself in the service of a fantasy of completion. The ego is inevitably an ideal ego, an ideal of self-coherence, of mastery and competence, by which we are mastered and managed, an illusion of unfettered autonomy in the pursuit of which we are integrated into the familial and social orders. The ego names our radical heteronomy in the moments we seem to be functioning with the utmost autonomy, the ways in which we are oriented by and toward others even when we seem to be guided most implacably by self-interest. The ego is faintly if at all distinct from the ego ideal qua seat of social normativity. The ego, as a precipitate of identifications, is the effective, workable answer to the question What does the other want? or What am I for the other? In other words, the ego quells the more troublesome, indeed abyssal, question of what one *can be*—a question rife with sociopolitical implications coursing through the subtext of Lacan's thinking—by answering the question as if it were a question of what one *should be*, specifically, of what one should or *must be*, in order to secure the love of significant others, social recognition, and/or a narcissistically gratifying sense of autonomous integrity.[67] As the seat of reality testing, the ego deludes us time and again: non-dupes err. One can now see how easily ego functions are co-opted by the superego's imperative to enjoy: *one must* enjoy one's identifications, *one must* enjoy the question of what the other wants, *one must* enjoy one's symptom in the sense of enjoying the compromise formations out of which our privileged self-images are forged, *one must* enjoy the self-images that keep our radical self-discontinuity at bay, that is, *one must* enjoy one's narcissism.[68] Otherwise, one risks opening onto the jouissance, the shattering pleasure-in-pain, of in(de)finite *desire*.

Concerning the latter claim about structural misrecognition, Lacan contends that the ego *is* our propensity to misrecognize ourselves, objects, and others as more determinate, stable, and unified then we and they truly are.[69] For instance, in *Seminar VII* Lacan suggests that the ego is a mirage concealing the subject's (and implicitly, the object's) *manque-à-être*.[70] In order to stress his point that the ego should not be ascribed the power of reality testing, Lacan goes so far as to say that "the essential function of the ego is very nearly that systematic refusal of reality which French analysts refer to in talking about the psychoses" (1953: 12).[71]

Misrecognition here names attention predominantly or exclusively lavished upon the (relatively) determinate qualities and (relatively) coherent aspects of ourselves, objects, and others: though distorting, misrecognition is of course a form of recognition. Under the sway of misrecognition, the world conforms to an *imaginal consistency.* (Mis)recognizing ourselves, others, and objects as wholes, as discrete and determinate entities with whom or with which predicable, systematizable, or otherwise calculable relations obtain or may obtain, we misrecognize—become myopic to—the flux over which images of wholeness are but a thin veneer. This flux is *desire* from the side of the subject and the Real (or phenomenal excess) from the side of the object: the ego is maintained by "its essential resistance to the elusive process of Becoming, to the variations of Desire."[72] Glossing over this flux, we misrecognize a fundamental propensity of ourselves, others, and objects for in(de)finite self-differentiation, for becoming and appearing otherwise, perhaps altogether otherwise[73]: that is, for becoming or appearing otherwise in so radical a fashion that it is no longer clear whether differentiation can be retrospectively comprehended as the self-unfolding of a prior unity or even comprehended within the various schemas—the regimes of intelligibility—we have heretofore developed. And in a way, misrecognition is always mutual: misrecognizing objects as unified and self-identical naturalizes the interpretive framework that supports our propensity to misrecognize ourselves as unified and self-identical, and vice versa. Tendential misrecognition naturalizes patterns of attention according to which self-cohesion (classically, substantiality) is the quintessential feature of being. Consistent and manageable "reality," then, is precisely fantasy.

Lacan's understanding of the ego and his understanding of the object are intimately intertwined. First, the object is modeled on the ideal integrity of the ego. What counts as an object, and what attention tends to gravitate toward, is what appears as self-identical, as whole, as the ideal ego. Second, the ego's coherent self-image is supported by immersion in a world of presumptively self-identical, determinate objects.[74] Habituation to the experience of objects as self-identical supports the forms of attention through which we come to view ourselves as self-identical subjects. As we have seen, recognition of the object is necessarily misrecognition of its instability, its excessive phenomenality, its irreducibility to our conceptual schemes. Likewise, recognition of the object as *the* object or cause of our desire is a misrecognition of our desire, of our truth, insofar as (1) desire exceeds any object-cause or object-orientation (desire is forever unsatisfied by even the objects and others we cherish most dearly or covet most intensely[75]) and (2) desire is implanted by and issues from the Other at least as much as it is solicited by various concrete objects. Desire, while drawing us *toward* various objects, is not exactly directed *at* them. Rather, desire loops around or brushes off objects—if only to preserve the object from immediate consumption, thereby preserving desire itself, or to avoid direct contact, since this would reveal the object as quite distinct from the ideal shimmering through it. Desire is vectored beyond objects, aimed at something presumably in them that they do not in fact possess (the promise of satisfaction is always a manipulation). This "something" at which desire aims is opaque, utterly indeterminate—and, precisely for that reason given symbolic form by fantasy.

What desire aims at, prior to and forever in excess of its fantasmatic structuration, is irreducible to the objective, assessable properties of the object. And only on this condition can the object stand for the promise of ultimate satisfaction. Lacan calls this opaque something at which desire aims *objet a* (sometimes also "lamella"). Because it can never be directly perceived, because it does not in fact exist, *objet a* can never disappoint. *It* cannot disappoint, but of course we are regularly disappointed because *objet a* does not exist: "Object *a* is no being. Object *a* is the void presupposed by a demand. . . . '*That's not it*' means that, in the desire of every demand, there is but the request for *object a*" (*Seminar XX*: 126/114). (Getting over the expectation of absolute satisfaction, and so becoming unavailable to this disappointment, is a primary goal of the Lacanian clinic.) Immured in the Imaginary, *objet a* is a placeholder and support for the fantasy of full and final satisfaction; it is that which promises a simultaneous, mutually coordinated, and absolute satisfaction of our desire and/as the desire of the Other. *Objet a* will be discussed further in the course of the discussion of the Symbolic. It has been introduced now only to focus attention on the ways in which the object, like the ego, may be a lure, an element of a fantasy of completeness, of fullness, of the termination of desire, that tempts us to misrecognize the labile, in(de)finite dimensions of our *desire*.

Finally, the object is akin to the ego *in its truth*. The object, like the ego, is composed of a great many, often irreconcilable, perspective- and environment-mediated impressions. If not necessarily incorrigibly tension-ridden, as is the ego, the object is akin to the ego insofar as it is fundamentally incoherent, i.e., ever-amenable to becoming and/or becoming disclosed otherwise. If its unity is not necessarily illusory, as is the ego's, it is at least idealized. The object, like the ego, is essentially indeterminate: excessive with respect to the uses to which it may be put or the forms of attention through which it may be experienced. The object fails to be fully assimilated to the designs into which it is nonetheless integrated. When Lacan claims that "[t]he essence of the object is failure," in part what he means is that (1) the object perpetually fails to complete us, that it fails to yield final satisfaction, and (2) the object will never unconditionally conform to our schematizing grids or privileged patterns of object relation; it will always fail to be perfectly subsumed, will never be fully objectified (*Seminar XX*: 58/55). The object in its truth is a principle of *resistance*: though it is not simply other to our regimes of intelligibility, it resists our comprehension, our patterns of use, our efforts to assimilate it to our various projects and schemas. The object essentially resists—herein lies Lacan's moment of materialism.[76]

The ego, then, is a *schemer* in two senses: (1) it is an agency that dupes us into believing in the integrity and conceptual-practical assimilability of objects; (2) it ties us to various schematizations of ourselves, objects, and others. Or, to put the point in terms of our registers of experience, through the ego we misrecognize—in the sense of failing to invest with significance or pay sufficient attention to—the ways in which self, objects, and others are registered—*sensed*—as unconsolidated, as constellated fragments processively emerging and evolving rather than finished products standing steadily forth, thus as suffused with possibilities for being (minimally, being understood and related to) otherwise. If impression is mediated by but irreducible to historically and culturally constituted categories of experience (concepts of an object, relational and cognitive schemas, etc.), then there remains a primacy of the object, or, we might say, of phenomenality, and of sensibility over intersubjectively constituted forms of comprehension. The object maintains primacy over the ego.

This is to say, the ego is a *principle of selection*; it names our penchant to home in on stability, determinacy, and integrity—generally, on that which is unproblematically assimilable to the horizons of instrumentalization and systematic elaboration (whether such horizons are ultimately one cannot be addressed here). The ego names our proneness to shy away from phenomena as they impose upon us—impress us with—more than our privileged frames of experience can assimilate, as they insist themselves into our attention as possessed of a dimension of indeterminacy. What the ego cannot bear is the register of experience attuned to objects as heterogeneous series of sensory impressions that have yet to consolidate into familiar patterns or yet remain irreducible to them. The ego names our resistance to confusion, ambiguity, disruption, and dispersal—to anything that throws us off-kilter or strikes us as out of joint. The ego is a principle of resistance to temporalization.

In Lacanian terminology, the ego names our reticence to acknowledge the Real, a concept that will be elaborated further below but that for now we can associate with the excessiveness of phenomena understood in the following way: phenomena fracture—and thereby call forth—our engrained forms of attention and understanding; the upsurge of phenomena is in excess of immediate recognition and unsettles—both undermines and enjoins—our horizons of competence, our desire for mastery. Of course, depending on our disposition when encountering various phenomena, and perhaps depending on the specificity of the phenomena and their contexts of emergence, imaginative capacities through which we rework our frames of attention and forms of understanding may be called forth as well. But in the end, some determinacy will have been yielded, and what Lacan seeks to emphasize is that the—perhaps newfound—determinacy will be our primary focus when the ego dominates.

The ego thus names a form of belated attention to phenomenalization (the coming into being of phenomenal determinacy), a neglect of the wresting forth of phenomenal determinacy from out of an essential concealedness that remains as its perpetual lining in favor of attention to what various phenomena will have been grasped *as* once they are reduced to our habitual—or newly refashioned—forms of understanding and relationality. The product is favored over its processual emergence. The ego glosses over the facture and lingers with the form. Insofar as the ego names the *inadmissibility* of the registers of experience and dimensions of phenomena (i.e., the dimension of the Real) that threaten our comfortable sense of belonging and orientation in social regimes of intelligibility and relationality, our boundedness to culture, the ego, even prior to its differentiation into the superego, is always already moralized. The ego is a structure of prohibition, a principle of resistance to the Real.

On this basis we can better appreciate many of Lacan's comments about Klein in *Seminar I.* There, Lacan maligns Klein's interpretations as "symbolic extrapolations," accusing her of unwarranted speculation (if ever there were a case of the pot calling the kettle black!). The claim is that Klein mechanically forges from a minimum of raw material just what she is looking for: Oedipal dynamics, sadism, persecutory anxieties, and the like. "She has applied—indeed mechanically imposed—the symbolization of the Oedipus myth" (*Seminar I*: 85).[77] Like Captain Hank Quinlan from Orson Wells's *Touch of Evil,* Klein always finds exactly what she expects, even if she has to put it there herself. Is it so clear that in the infamous "Tea daddy" incident "[t]he introjection of the father's penis *proved to be* associated with the dread both of it, as of a primitive, harm-inflicting superego, and of being punished by the mother thus robbed: dread, that is, of the external and introjected objects" (1975: 227; emphasis added)? Or have Klein's theories colored her perceptions to the point where she can no longer see beyond her expectations? What is the "proof" that Dick's father's penis is associated with the dread of it and of the mother thus robbed (and of all of the introjected and external objects with which the father's penis and mother's vengeance have come to be associated)? On Klein's account,

> On one occasion Dick lifted a little toy man to his mouth, gnashed his teeth and said "Tea daddy," by which he meant "Eat daddy." He then asked for a drink of water. The introjection of the father's penis proved to be associated with the dread both of it, as of a primitive, harm-inflicting super-ego, and of being punished by the mother thus robbed: dread, that is, of the external and introjected objects. . . . At this point the genital phase had become active in Dick prematurely

> . . . [as indicated by the fact] that such representations . . . were followed not by anxiety only, but by remorse, pity, and a feeling that he must make restitution. (1975: 227)

Must Dick's asking for a drink of water mean that he has introjected his father's penis? And that this introjection is associated with the dread of it as a harm-inflicting superego and of the retributive vengeance of his mother? What makes Klein so certain that "Tea daddy" *means* "Eat daddy"? Is there a one-to-one correspondence between speech/behavior ("representations") and unconscious meaning? What warrants Klein's conviction that introjection and projection are universal psychic mechanisms, let alone the keys to unlocking the significance of this scene? Is she just seeing what *she* projects? Is the following scene where Dick proceeds to place the little toy men on Klein's lap and hand, put everything back in the drawer, and so on, knock-down evidence that Dick is expressing reparative tendencies, that he has already acceded to the depressive position, and thus that, as a result of his inhibited ego development, he is bound to frenetically oscillate between the depressive and paranoid/schizoid positions, as Klein intimates (1975: 227)? Is Klein's reading of this scene—and might the import she places on the concept of reparation be—an indication that she is ensnared by the Imaginary, that *she* desires to see everything repaired, made whole? When Dick throws objects out of the room, is this clear evidence of projection, specifically of "an expulsion, both of the damaged object and of his own sadism" (1975: 226)? Are similar scenes always to be read in these terms? Is it so clear from this (or similar) behavior that constitutional sadism as well as the phantasmatically damaged—thus retaliatory—objects that bear the brunt of this sadism are pro-jected, thrown out as a basic defense mechanism?

Part of what worries Lacan is that both in her early interventions and later on Klein schematizes, or, more precisely, mythologizes: she anxiously foists a rigid narrative frame onto a deeply ambiguous series of events. Klein contends, plausibly, that because initially Dick does not verbally free associate, play, or even make a distinction between herself and the room's furniture, she has to fall back on assumptions about what happens at various developmental stages; she has to treat Dick as an indifferent instance of a developmental stage in order to make any sense of him. But even if this gesture is, at the initial moments of therapy, quite savvy, and even if reliance on developmental schemas is at times inescapable, later, when Dick's play is freer, Klein is equally schematic and doesn't realize it. She still heavily relies on developmental narratives and broad conceptual frameworks to explain, organize, and justify her interventions into her client's suffering. And, to be sure, this practice is by no means confined to her interaction with Dick; it is a hallmark of Kleinian practice.

One way to get at Lacan's worry is this: If a skeptical moment or dimension of theorizing is an acknowledgment of, perhaps better, a dramatization of the indeterminacy of the matter theorized, and of human finitude generally, its intermittent evaporation in Klein's work may signal a failure to engage appropriately with her client both as agent and patient. Specifically, this may signal a failure to attend appropriately to Dick's capacity to give and receive form and so to support the development of Dick's subjectivity, i.e., to encourage the endless work of wording the world. Or to put Lacan's worry in Kantian terms, Klein systematically substitutes false and facile determinative judgments for the more taxing yet therapeutically and theoretically fecund work of reflective judgment and risks having this substitution mimed by her patients. Both in Klein and in Dick, "What doesn't happen is the free play, the conjunction between the different forms, imaginary and real, of objects" (*Seminar I*: 82). What is shut down, again in Kantian terms, is "free play" between imagination and understanding, i.e., ongoing, creative self- and world-schematization. What is shut down is spontaneity, creativity, subjectivity.

From Lacan's vantage point, Klein's heavy-handed schematization both represents and reinforces the tendencies of the ego and, through them, her client's susceptibility to the claims of dominant culture. To put it bluntly, and Lacan *does* put it this bluntly, Klein does not know what she is saying; she is unaware of the effects of her *speech*. In calling her interpretations "symbolic extrapolations" and "symbolic equations," Lacan suggests that Klein's material does not mean to Dick what it does to Klein—at least not prior to the interpretations. She is ill-attuned to Dick's psychic reality, anxious as she is to show that her privileged interpretive apparatus is applicable even to Dick, that is, anxious as she is to show that in fundamental ways she shares a world with him, that the human condition is susceptible to theoretical generalizations. From where Lacan stands, Klein is inducing Dick into *her* sense of psychic "reality"; she is acting as an auxiliary ego and thereby covertly doing violence to his spontaneity, his form-giving impulse, indeed to his *desire*. Klein is preemptively limiting Dick's *desire* by dictating it to him in the form of standard (Oedipal) narratives. To put it a bit extremely, Klein is preempting the emergence of Dick as a modern subject, microcosmically undoing the achievement of modernity. She is his own personal culture industry.

For Lacan, Klein's interpretations say more about the content of *her* phantasies and fixations than they do about Dick's *desire*.[78] If the claim is that Klein reproduces her fixations in Dick, then the charge is of illicit "suggestion" and the implication is that Klein's practice is in some respect pre-analytic.

Further, if we recall that the ego, for Lacan, is primarily defensive, then the point is also that Klein's interpretations, even if they modify the patient's anxiety or defenses, are themselves defensive and, accordingly, generative of new forms of anxiety to which she, and her patients, will be blind.

Ever prone to polemics, or, more generously, ever-concerned with keeping alive the dialectical tension of thought, Lacan seeks to counterbalance Klein's ego-centrism by writing in a way that both performatively elaborates and thematically foregrounds what cannot—*will not*—be seen from the standpoint of the ego: unremitting polysemy, ongoing indeterminacy, ultimate ambiguity, deep voids of meaninglessness, shifting and variable meanings and relations, the indefinite effects of speech, etc. To be sure, this is not altogether clear in Lacan's engagement with Klein in *Seminar I*, hence the need for this mildly reconstructive effort, but I take it that, though undeveloped, this is the principle organizing Lacan's confrontation with Klein both in *Seminar I* and elsewhere. His ambition is to direct our attention to what remains and resists, to what cannot be finally contained or subsumed by concepts and narratives, and to the singular efforts of each analysand to metabolize this resistant, excessive material. What Lacan insists upon and calls upon analysts to support and encourage is precisely what Klein's theory and practice detract attention from: the analysand's ongoing efforts to re-symbolize her world and the urgency of *desire* subtending this.[79] The presumptive automaticity and established terms of Klein's theory of symbolism are the foil against which Lacan's perspective brings itself into focus.

Clinically, through his focus on the need for personal (re)symbolization Lacan hopes to give freer reign to the analysand's form-giving impulse and to help her take responsibility for her symbolizations: "[t]hat the subject should come to recognize and name his desire, that is the efficacious action of analysis" (*Seminar II*: 228–29/267).[80] Thereby, he hopes to habituate the analysand to the intimate admixture of the intelligible and the unintelligible and thus to help her become less prone to suffer from want of meaning and less likely to become stuck in rigid and uncomfortable meanings: (re)symbolization is binding that unbinds, i.e., diminishes fixations. The clear implication of Lacan's style, an implication that is supported by the thrust of his thinking throughout *Seminar I* and elsewhere, is that attention must be turned away from the Imaginary, away from the ego, away from the determinate object (breast, dark void/mother, etc.), *because there will be plenty of attention paid to them anyway* and toward the unconscious, the Symbolic, and the Real, which seem ever on the verge of oblivion. Lacan's claim is that we need to attend to (1) the excess of phenomenalization over its predigested, schematic representation and (2) the responsiveness—or lack of responsiveness—of singular subjects to this. Lacan both embodies and thematizes unintelligibility, or, better, undecidability, in order to unsettle Kleinian and any other sedimented and all-too-plausible schematizations and thereby displace the centrality of the ego. Though Klein considers herself to be giving priority to the Other (the breast, the mother, etc.), Lacan claims that she is in fact prioritizing the Same: namely, the ego. With Klein, the framework within which relations to the other are assessed is the development of the ego, or, more precisely, the concomitant development of the ego and worldliness (object relations). Object-relations theory is yet another ego psychology.

To draw out one more clinical implication, it is on the basis of these sorts of concerns that Lacan is generally averse to working with the countertransference and specifically averse to working with it in the Kleinian fashion. Note, however, that Lacan agrees with the Kleinians who insist that countertransference is inescapable. As he says in *Seminar I*, "feelings are always mutual" (43/32). The analyst can never rigorously assume the position of a blank slate upon which transferentially motivated desires, etc., are projected and then objectively reflected back to the client through the analyst's interpretations.[81] Furthermore, Lacan agrees with the Kleinians who contend that through countertransference and empathy the analyst can discern the affective states of the analysand and how the analyst is positioned in the analysand's fantasies (and vice versa). He even agrees that through the countertransference the analyst can anticipate the reemergence of repressed material on the side of the analysand.[82] Nonetheless, Lacan strongly cautions against disclosing countertransference when this might suggest to the analysand what the analyst wants—which is, on Lacan's account, how countertransference disclosures are usually received (or manipulated), especially in the earlier stages of analysis. *The* question the Lacanian analyst seeks to demotivate is the question of what the analyst (generally, the other) wants.

Countertransference disclosures risk drawing too much attention to the person of the analyst and thereby impeding analytic progress. On Lacan's account, effective analysis requires that the analyst disappear as a concrete person and embody the Otherness of the unconscious.[83] To the extent that s/he appears as a distinct person, the analyst risks not just encouraging the question of what s/he wants but provoking competition and rivalry, i.e., Imaginary deadlock. As one prominent Lacanian commentator puts it, "the analyst must endeavor to embody desirousness, revealing as few personal likes and dislikes, ideals and opinions as possible, providing the analysand as little concrete information about his or her character, aspirations, and tastes as possible, as they all furnish such fertile ground in which identification can take root" (Fink 1996: 88).[84] Aside from the fact that to focus on countertransference is to focus on the level of meaning, content, and object relations, the level of the Imaginary, disclosing countertransference, whether directly or via interpretation, risks inhibiting the analysand's ability to relate to the analyst as Other, i.e., as enigmatic, inassimilable to the analysand's desires and conceptual schemes, as forever incapable of being satisfied by anything the analysand may say or do or become, and ultimately as no more (and no less) than the *cause* of her *desire*, which, on Lacan's account, is crucial for therapeutic progress. To disclose countertransference, let alone to dwell on it, is to risk mitigating the resurgence of the analysand's *desire*.

Counter to the Kleinian trend and in line with the early Freud, Lacan urges analysts to put their feelings aside as much as possible. This is not a matter of denying one's emotional embroilment with the analysand and feigning a haughty stoicism[85]; it is a matter of urging analysts to neither affirm nor deny the veracity of their interpretations (e.g., countertransferentially motivated interpretations) or of their client's interpretations and to instead use these interpretations as material for association, indefinite interpretation, and resymbolization. What must be suppressed is not emotional engagement but the tendency of emotional resonance to issue in interpretive overconfidence and, consequently, rigidity. The risk of working with countertransference, Lacan intimates, is that the analyst who believes herself to be "well analyzed" and on this basis believes that she *knows* what certain countertransferential feelings, impressions, fantasies, etc. mean for her, and so for her client, is a lure to assume an all-too-knowing stance and thereby impede the work of analysis.

Finally, to draw out one last clinical implication, it is again on the basis of these sorts of concerns that the Lacanian clinic focuses on symbolic transference as opposed to imaginary transference. "[T]ransference occurs essentially at the level of symbolic articulations" (*Seminar IV*: 135). To work with imaginary transference, as Klein does, is to focus on how the analyst is positioned by the analysand, e.g., as a good or bad object. The aim is to highlight the discrepancy between how the analyst is being treated and the grounds for so treating her. Drawing this distinction, the analyst seeks to disclose the phantasmatic coordinates in which the analysand cannot help but position herself and others and thereby assist the analysand in her quest for self-awareness. To listen for imaginary transference, then, is to listen for the anxieties, desires, and phantasies that mediate the analysand's perceptions of and responses to the analyst. From Lacan's perspective, the focus on imaginary transference and the interpretations that follow therefrom will bind the analysand to the order of meaning, to the Imaginary, too tightly. What's more, privileging imaginary transference suggests a questionable self-aggrandizement or self-centrism, even a certain dimension of paranoia, on the part of the analyst who remains unshakably convinced that the analysand's unconscious messages are directed to *her*.[86] Hence Lacan insists that "there is no other resistance to analysis [i.e., to the Symbolic orientation] that of the analyst himself" (*E*: 497/595).

To listen from the position of the symbolic transference, on the other hand, is to listen for the analysand's slips (not insofar as they bespeak a deeper meaning but insofar as they suggest something rumbling on the Other Scene: a noise, a turbulence), the polysemic range and enigmatic underside of terms employed, the analysand's idiomatic language use, for fleeting thoughts that open new vistas for exploration, and so forth. It is to listen for all that might disclose the enigmatic multiplicity of the analysand's meanings and for the moments of nonmeaning that punctuate her discourse. Here, the analyst positions herself not as the one (the ego) who is sufficiently self-aware to know when she is being treated inappropriately, in a way uncalled for by the context (e.g., in a way that signals that the analysand's ego is responding to a conflict or upsurge of sadism by defensively projecting libidinal or sadistic impulses that s/he cannot abide onto others or responding to previous projections of this sort), but as the Other, the register of multiple meanings, indefinite significance, and ultimate opacity. What the analyst returns to the analysand are not the phantasies, anxieties, and desires that underlie her perceptions and responses but the enigma of her over-teeming meaning, her self-strangeness, and, ultimately, the irreducible, nonsensical signifiers to which she is subjected: "Interpretation is a signification that is not just any signification. . . . It has the effect of bringing out an irreducible signifier. . . . What is there is rich and complex, when it is a question of the unconscious of the subject, and intended to bring out irreducible, *nonsensical*—composed of non meanings—signifying elements" (*Seminar XI*: 250).

While imaginary transference is ego-to-ego transference, symbolic transference is unconscious-to-unconscious transference. In the former, what the analysand's ego cannot abide is defended against via enactment, which the analyst's ego registers as an inappropriate response in need of clarification. In the latter, the analysand's unconscious material resonates with the analyst's unconscious material, assuming unforeseen shapes and significances to which the analyst attempts to draw attention, aiming generally to disclose the unanticipatable fate and imperfectly legible character of unconscious material. In symbolic transference, the analyst embodies, indeed dramatizes, the radical strangeness of the Other. The interventions that elaborate symbolic transference are not interpretations of role positioning ("you are treating me as your persecuting mother," etc.) but efforts designed to disclose the strangeness of the material encountered, the uncanny dimensions of oneself and others. They aim to make plain that others always elude capture by the phantasy frameworks or patterns of object relation into which they are corralled, just as one's phantasies and patterns of object relation always involve more than one has yet to uncover. They draw attention to excess. For instance, this means showing, contra Klein, that no matter how effectively one is able to subsume one's client's experiences into narrative form, addressing this narrative or aspects thereof to the client means exposing it to mediation by the client's unconscious, and so in effect saying, and doing, something quite other than what one intended. Relations between ego and object/other are mutually transformative, thus never subject to final decoding. They can *only* be re-symbolized (in a lively or mortifying manner); and the analysand is encouraged to make the most of this.[87]

Elaborations of symbolic transference aim to disclose that both self and other are inconsistent, non-whole; they aim to render conspicuous the asymmetry between and split in the ego and the object/other. Basically, the analyst aims to expose and underline the limits of understanding and relational manipulation. On this basis, she will be able to more effectively urge the analysand to explore ever-new forms of relation and develop ever-new symbolizations.

When Klein claims that she can access the most significant structures of the analysand's unconscious via transference interpretation, Lacan worries both about the value of her ambition and about her presumption. With regard to the latter, he worries that her "access" to these structures is but a projection: a projection of her assumption that there are standard components of a generic psychic apparatus elaborated in recognizable yet somewhat idiosyncratic permutations within each individual, just laying in wait to be uncovered. Against this impulse to stampede to the familiar, Lacan councils patience. He urges analysts to suspend what they think they know (the standpoint of the ego), to help the analysand do likewise, and thereby to allow an analytic encounter to unfold in which, perhaps, the most relevant terms and structures will gradually reveal themselves, and in which, whether or not they do so, the analysand will become more hospitable to the strangeness of her-/himself and others/objects.[88] Though this may not be apparent at first blush, and though Lacan is keenly aware of the aporias involved, the Lacanian clinic is meant to be a deeply ethical enterprise.

To be sure, Lacan's strategy is "polemical" or better, "dialectical"; the point is not to supplant or simply shut down concern with the ego and object relations but to undermine the prevailing hegemonic import of the ego and object relations, to supplement, challenge, and render more complex the current analytic scene.

Lacan was so intent on emphasizing the defensiveness of the ego, both in his considerations of Klein and elsewhere,[89] that he risked telling a developmental story, or, rather, what was bound to be heard as one, in order to underscore this point. This story, the story of the mirror stage, makes it seem as if the ego is *genetically* defensive and thus makes it seem as if Lacan has fallen prey to a simple genetic fallacy: because the ego arises as a defense, it will forever function as nothing but a defense.

Certain ego psychologists have leveled the charge of succumbing to the genetic fallacy against Lacan in order to liberate Lacanian theory from its founder's logical misstep and therewith to put themselves in a position to demonstrate the ultimate confluence of (slightly reconstructed) Lacanian and ego-psychological perspectives. Specifically, they focus on the logically possible coordination of these perspectives, claiming that the Lacanian account of the ego in no way rules out conflict-free, autonomous ego functioning.[90]

In one respect, these ego psychologists are undoubtedly right: the two perspectives are in some respects *logically* compatible. Accordingly, they are to be complemented for their attention to the one-sided, hyperbolically exaggerated character of Lacan's teachings. However, there are a number of problems with their strategy. First, locating excess on the side of their adversary or newfound ally, these ego psychologists fail to appreciate the insuperably one-sided character of their own program. Ego psychology is ego psychology only insofar as it attributes an excessive import to and harbors a profound optimism about the development of autonomy, rationality, and successful social integration. It is at this level that the two perspectives are irreconcilable. Second, these ego psychologists regularly refuse to allow Lacan's emphasis on the ego's defensiveness to influence their clinical practices and theoretical trajectories. In short, their concessions to Lacan are superficial. Attention to the logical confluence of the Lacanian and ego-psychological positions tends to gloss over the significance of Lacan's urge to suppress this rather obvious formal compatibility. Through an emphatically one-sided account of the ego's defensiveness, Lacan seeks to call into question any wholistic approach that, in its all-encompassing theoretical splendor, would suppress or insufficiently acknowledge precisely what the ego suppresses and insufficiently acknowledges: our condemnation to misrecognition, heteronomy, and superficial social integration (within foreseeable social forms). Although ego psychologists recognize that the ego *may* operate defensively (the jumping-off point of ego psychology was Anna Freud's *Ego and the Mechanisms of Defense*), this in no way unsettles their conviction that we can achieve nondefensive, adaptive ego functioning, at least proximally and for the most part, or perhaps "at worst" with a bit of therapeutic assistance (Hartmann's *Ego Psychology and the Problem of Adaptation* was published three years after Anna Freud's book and was conceived as its complement). These claims Lacan vehemently denies.

The risk of a more comprehensive and balanced approach, then, is that one loses sight of the significance of Lacan's insistence on the insuperability of misrecognition, the value-laden and normalizing features of reality testing, the ways in which the ego suppresses the truth of *desire* and generates large-scale resistances to the Real . . . not here and there or only in moments of weakness, but structurally. From a Lacanian perspective, the integrating ethos of ego psychology manifest in their insistence on the logical compatibility of their position with Lacan's *enacts the misrecognition and the fantasy of symmetry they are wont to thematize, explore, or allow to influence their clinical ambitions.* By excising the abrasive pathos of Lacan's discussions of the ego, ego psychologists transform Lacan's polemical emphasis on the ego's defensiveness into a series of qualified propositions (e.g., the ego may operate defensively) that are all too easily assimilable to their own projects, profoundly deforming Lacan's insight. By way of a facile and abstract admission of the defensive character of the ego, more specifically, by "acknowledging" the defensiveness of the ego as a pathological defect or instance of immaturity that can be eventually overcome or at least sufficiently surmounted for the attainment of rational and autonomous, well-adjusted and largely conflict-free cultural life, the reign of ego psychology is retrenched. That the ego may err when overwhelmed by instinctual conflict and that the ego binds us to misrecognition are not the same point.

In order to properly appreciate Lacan's discussion of the mirror stage, one must begin by appreciating how aberrant this foray into developmental theory is for him. Lacan's wariness about developmental theory stems from three related suspicions.

First, a suspicion about developmental theory's subsumptive machinery. Fitting individuals into pre-packaged developmental schemes is clinically dangerous insofar as it prompts analysts to overestimate their grasp on the material unfolding before them, to receive this material as a readily intelligible instance of a familiar story of development and developmental arrest, and thus to assume a certain *knowingness* that supports the analysands' transference illusion that the analyst, as the one who knows, will be their salvation, their new master.[91] What the analysand needs, Lacan insists, is not a new master but rather provocation and encouragement to divest from the framework of mastery and its attendant guarantees, to find ways of living without rigid reference to the question of what the other wants, of what will secure the other's identity-consolidating recognition, of what will complete the other, and so the self, etc. This would amount to an approximation to our *truth* as beings riven by far-ranging, ever-changing, never wholly intelligible *desire*. Lacan counsels that the analysand learn how to resist ceding on her desire, that is, learn how to not give herself over so readily to the question of what the other wants and thereby afford herself opportunities to explore—create and discover—the in(de)finite variations of *her* desire. The aim of Lacanian analysis is not so much awareness of repressed and conflicted desire per se so much as it is the cultivated affirmation of the in(de)finite desirousness of the subject.[92] Additionally, if leaning on developmental theory generates overconfidence that the material unfolding has been well understood, a particularly pernicious risk courted by this reliance is that, so emboldened, the analyst will seek to convey his understanding to the analysand rather than confront her with her nonsensical elements, with the ways in which her symptoms and sufferings arise from her fantasies of self-consistency and facile intelligibility and from the efforts by which she keeps these fantasies in place.

Second, a suspicion about developmental theory's occlusion of the singularity of each analysand and so of the fundamental goal of analysis. Rather than allying with the analysand to discover and describe afresh the sources and significance of her suffering, rather than allowing a personal history and its associational amplification to be elaborated in terms that are significant to and useful for *this* analysand, analysts who rely on theories of pathology guided by developmental theory risk silencing their analysands, and so conspiring with their symptoms and sufferings, by foisting upon them preconceived notions about and vocabularies for discussing such symptoms and sufferings. Even if they get it right, they do wrong. Of course, offering words to describe certain tormentingly unintelligible experiences may be, on occasion, an invaluable clinical gesture. But even so, and especially when such words are offered in early stages of the analysis, the risk is that such beneficence will block the development of a personal idiom (or idioms) through which the analysand discovers/creates a sense of herself that breaks free from her reigning self-conceptions—self-conceptions that are, in no small part, the source of her suffering. Developmental theory may provide useful guideposts to orient analytic listening, but if the terms of developmental theory are substituted for the process of creating/discovering one's own terms, the analysis fails to become sufficiently personalized, fails to acquire the affective traction that makes it such a powerful and transformative experience.

Third, a suspicion about the uses to which developmental narratives are put. All too often, developmental narratives are used—sometimes intentionally, sometimes not—to pathologize the unruly, non-adaptive, or "infantile," thereby underwrite the disciplinary operations of analyses guided by their terms. Also, developmental narratives are often complicit in projecting a state of fulfilled development, progress toward which, and all the more so, the ideal terminus of which operate as constrictive lures. Analysands are quick to pick up on what their analysts consider developmental achievements and ultimate developmental fulfillment, just as they are quick to pick up on their analysts' desires for their attainment. Assimilating these goals as their own, analysands may fail to make the most of analysis as a space in which to engage in sustained, intimate reflection on their desired ends, on what makes for a desirable end, on what constitutes achievement and accomplishment in various sectors of life. In both cases, rather than releasing the analysand from his constraining identifications and thus from the consuming question of the desire of the Other, analysis becomes silently normalizing, controlling and directive, as it substitutes the analyst's sense of what is developmentally appropriate for the patient's need to work through her fundamental fantasy of coherent identity, dislodge or at least sap the force of the question of the desire of the Other, and thereby open onto her freedom to explore her in(de)initely shifting *desire*.

With these criticisms in mind, we can appreciate why Lacan deems Freud's theory of developmental stages the "shakiest aspect" of his work (*Seminar II*: 211) and why Judith Feher Gurewich describes Lacan's mirror stage as "a sort of allegory that draws on developmental psychology yet is not itself a developmental theory" (21).[93] To be sure, in his discussion of the mirror stage, Lacan tells a tale of the infant's initiation into illusory self-identity and self-mastery from out of a state of motor incapacity, generalized uncoordination, subjective dehiscence (the experience of the body-world horizon as a loose aggregate of sensations, impulses, and zones), and radical dependency. However, the narrative form is a heuristic device, a bit of sugar coating that makes slightly more palatable the painful point of the story, namely, that this state of radical dependency and fractured experience, this state of floundering and ineptitude in the face of our wants and needs, is never completely surpassed.[94] The tale does not presume to be empirically verifiable, though Lacan draws on what his audience would likely recognize as empirically supported developmental theory.[95] Rather, the discussion of the mirror stage articulates in sequential terms a transmutation in the subject's dominant *form of experience* from one of symbiotic flux and fracturedness to one keyed to stability, consistency, and coherence.[96] It articulates in narrative terms the swaying of attention from powerlessness and ineptitude to moments and fantasized attainments of mastery. Both the narrative form and the feint of empirical credentialing are concessions to the ego, akin to analytic interventions that seek to avoid immediate repression or an onslaught of defenses by conducting themselves in an ego-syntonic manner.

Lacan's elaboration of the mirror stage aims to emphasize the radical rupture from the experience of oneself as more or less "spatially dislocated, positionless, timeless, perspectiveless" and immersed in the turmoil of insuperable frustration and its psychic consequences to the experience of oneself as possessed of a basically coherent perspective (coherent enough for inconsistency to stand out as a problem) and largely competent vis-à-vis the essential, that is, located within a horizon where most of life's problems can be, at least in principle, successfully met (Grosz 1990: 42).[97] But the point is also to underscore that this rupture is not a triumphal break that leaves its predecessor behind. Lacan's account of the mirror stage emphasizes the ways in which later developments—the formation of and attachment to the ego—constitute defenses against ongoing experiences of fractured, dislocated, unmastered life, against the depths of our vulnerability, against, we might say, the void of desirous negativity or (what may be the same) our openness to phenomena as they exceed, complicate, and at times utterly confound our conceptual schemes and relational horizons.

The original, fractured form of experience and the sense of oneself as fundamentally incompetent, fully dependent on the ministrations of others, Lacan suggests, becomes unbearable once another form of life is glimpsed. This unbearability motivates identification with an image of wholeness, self-possession, and sovereignty upon which the ego will be modeled—an image perceived in, through, or as the m/Other.[98] The image of sovereignty to which we become committed, and so the commitment itself, is infantile: extreme, immediate, and absolute in a way that resonates with the infantile situation. Whether the infant perceives the first instance of determinate Form in or as the m/Other, in the m/Other's image of the infant, or somehow in both is less important for Lacan than *that* the infant comes to sense that forms or shapes hold together, that certain wholes seem to be self-directed (or at least profoundly more powerful than the infant), and that the infant is compelled by this *form of life*. We are captivated by form, Lacan suggests, and thus bound to love objects as such. From this moment on, we are bound to love objects insofar as they recall the satisfying stability or powerful presence of the mother. That is, we are bound to be fascinated by objects and others in virtue of their formal unity because unity is forever associated with (1) the commanding presence of our primary caregivers who first figure wholeness, (2) the satisfactions with which these caregivers are associated, and (3) the images of ourselves to which we aspire. We are seduced by images of a lack of lack. To push the point a bit, the totalitarian temptation is structurally unsurpassable.

Of course, the infant's "identification" with unitary form or images of self-mastery is more of a longing than an accomplishment. The accomplishment of coherent selfhood and self-mastery will be always on the horizon. In Mikkel Borch-Jacobsen's apt phrasing, the ego

> can erect itself as a stable ego only through "precipitation," imaginary anticipation: the infant, delivered as he is into a sort of primordial "dehiscence" . . . anticipates his bodily unity and mastery in an image, whether his own specular image or that of some counterpart (*semblable*) whose stature or commanding presence happens to fascinate him. In this sense, the unity of the ego is fundamentally *imaginary*—that is, both fundamentally illusory (with respect to the chaotic reality of the body) and fundamentally visual. (1991, 48–49)

The ego arises as and forever remains an ideal—an ideal in the service of alienating us from our fundamental finitude.

This anticipation of self-identity and self-mastery is marked by an *affairement jubilatoire*, a sense of joyous escape from the fragmented body-world horizon and all the turmoil and frustrations with which it becomes associated. Narcissism, then, is fundamentally ek-static, keyed to an image of ourselves that we forever approximate, an image that our identifications are ever in the service of consolidating. Though never fully attained, this is an image that brings tears of joy to our eyes. Our commitments to our (ideal) ego cipher our fascination with a desired image, our enthrallment to an other. Narcissism is not exactly a form of self-love; it is not a love of ourselves as we actually are. Rather, it bespeaks an attachment to the (absolutely formal, impossible) self we are forever attempting to become. Through his elaboration of the mirror stage, Lacan seeks to make sense of our commitments to our alienation.

We are imperfect, dependent, and unable to secure the replete satisfaction we imagine we are due either through our own resources or via the ministrations of others. Rather than giving up on the image of complete and fully satisfied life against which our partial satisfactions, accomplishments, etc. are found wanting, rather than giving up on (i.e., betraying) the Ideal, we subject ourselves to continuous suffering that fuels a fantasy of "the end of days." The implacability of omnipotence and total fulfillment as standards against which we measure our lives condemns us to perpetual frustration, but even this frustration is enjoyed as it upholds a most-coveted image of ourselves in negative relief. That is, though the joy of imaginary self-anticipation is bound to fade somewhat as we are frustrated by our imperfect attempts to assume our desired self-image, with the fading of this joy arises an intense desire to become as self-sufficient and fully satisfied as we imagine we can be; hence arises once again the joy of imaginary self-anticipation. Frustration converts into and sustains the desire frustrated and upholds the self-image we can never attain and that will condemn us to suffer endlessly.

This jubilation is quickly thrown into the mix with another primary affect of the Imaginary: paranoid aggression. Lacan suggests that we displace onto others the hostility we feel toward or resulting from our various dissatisfactions and frustrations. Unable to assume our incompleteness and dependency, and committed to the intelligibility of our suffering, we tend to scapegoat. The paranoid aggression produced thereby is compounded by the fact that the identifications by which we seek to assume our desired self-image throw us into rivalry with those with whom we identify. What one loves in the other is what one would like to *be* more than—or at least as much as—what one would like to *have* because the identity of the other seems to be an answer to the pressing question, What does the Other want? But if the other *is* who one would like to be, the other's very existence blocks satisfaction. Love of the other transmutes into hatred, which we cannot bear—because we also love the other and fear the consequences of our aggression—and so motivates defensive feelings of persecution: I do not hate the other, she hates me. To know the other is to hate the other; this is what Lacan terms *connaissance paranoiaque*.

Identification and the knowledge of others it yields are suffused with aggression. To "know" (in the sense of familiarity with rather than cognition of, *connaître* rather than *savoir*) the other is to know what one would like to be, but it is also to know that the other stands in the way of my assumption of his or her place. This is manifest most clearly in paranoiac aggressivity. In the paranoiac horizon, the other is always in my place—the later, Lacan might add, enjoying in my place—the other's very existence threatens me with nonexistence, with the non-attainment of my desired self-image, with my nothingness (if I am not *that*, I am nothing), and so I become hostile. As much as we are bound to love objects and others, we are bound to hate them as well.[99] The infant, and the infantile in the adult, Lacan suggests, thinks in all-or-nothing, zero-sum terms (primary-process thinking): It's either you or me, there can be only one. Because I cannot—or cannot fully—assume my finitude, my lack, my incompleteness and inevitable failings, because I cannot assume my truth, the truth of my in(de)finite *desire* and all-too-human dependency, I ascribe the cause of my dissatisfaction to you, the other, who must then be destroyed . . . and yet the other is the object of my love and so must be preserved. Desire is structured by a tragic paradox.[100]

The point of this foray into the mirror stage is to show how, for Lacan, the development of the ego is coterminous with alienation. The more I identify with a particular image of my desired self-mastery, the more I am alienated from my status as lack, as pure deathly and vertiginous *desire*,[101] from the ek-static temporality of human life through which I forever become other to myself, a perpetually unfinished project. The ego functions as a defense against "castration," understood in the broadest sense. The image of self-coherence and self-mastery is an image of the repudiation of my desire, my truth. Thus the imaginary identifications by which I seek to consolidate my identity function as veils over "castration anxiety," over anxiety about finitude, incompleteness, humanimality. The human is such a strange creature, unable to abide itself, as if self-consciousness means self-contempt.

While for Freud imaginary wish-fulfillment (through identification, representation, fantasy, dreaming, etc.) speaks to the repressed truth of the subject's desire, for Lacan, Imaginary wish-fulfillment, that is, the illusory attainment of images of oneself as coherent and self-possessed, is a permanent impediment to the affirmation and exploration of the jouissance of drive life, of our incompleteness and thrownness into ever-new constellations of desire, and thus a hindrance to the avowal of our truth. The subject, for Lacan, is associated with death, irrevocable splitness, perpetual ek-stasis or negativity, with the void of *desire*.[102] The subject is less a substantial unity, more a tendency to ever become otherwise, to negate, i.e. divest from or allow to fall away, our current self-formations and most-cherished object relations for the sake of becoming otherwise. Thus the subject is never apparent as such but only in a compromised form; the subject is only apparent in and through the particular transformations or negations that, in their incessance, bespeak the subject as pure negation.[103]

This leads quite naturally to an exploration of the four final terms needed to attain an adequate sense of Lacan's notion of the Imaginary: the subject, desire, *objet a*, and truth.

THE SUBJECT

The ego and the subject are not synonymous in Lacan's lexicon. Quite to the contrary, the ego is what defends against the dimension of the subject. The ego is a source of resistance to assuming our status as unfulfillable voids of *desire*, a large-scale defense against our proneness to become dissatisfied with, or even if not, depart from our most cherished forms of life, self-images, patterns of object relation, etc., against our proneness to become ever-otherwise. The subject names the propensity of even those forms of life in which we are highly invested to die away as our desire and identifications take on new coordinates, only to die away once again. The subject names our persistent transitionality.

As subjects we are as if spontaneously self-differentiating, forever becoming other to ourselves, permanently unreconciled with ourselves and our worlds. As subjects we are creatures of ineffable want, propelled by a boundless, restless wanting, which is to say, *driven*. As subjects we are driven, but this does not mean that we are motivated by (1) discrete drives (libidinal or aggressive, self-preservative or anaclitic, eros or the death drive), (2) particular objects soldered onto the drives, or (3) fantasies within which such objects are enveloped. Though we are surely motivated in all these ways, such motivations do not speak to the pure drivenness, the protean pulsation of the subject. As subjects we are simply and purely driven, thrusting-thrusted forth, pulsating with an implacable (one might even say, in a certain manner, mechanical) *liveliness*. The subject is a primordial push into becoming—living, loving, relating, developing—otherwise, an insurgence of potentiality into the seemingly sutured totality of actuality. Lacan's notion of the subject emphasizes our irreducibility to any particular configuration of desire or conglomeration of identifications, our self-exceeding nature. The subject is a force of de-rigidification, of negativity, the element of our fundamental futurity. With the notion of the subject, we find ourselves on the threshold of the Real.

A few qualifications about what the Lacanian subject is *not* will bring this notion into finer relief. The subject is not the subject of representation, a theater for mental representations, the empirical-psychological correlate of Kant's transcendental unity of apperception.[104] Nor is the Lacanian subject the subject of self-awareness, what comes into view as we become more aware of our heretofore unnoticed or obscured desires, patterns of attachment, characterological structures, etc. The subject is not the personality. Least of all is the subject a core self hidden beneath social conformity. Though the subject is in a certain sense that which underlies culturally mediated identities (*sub-jectum*: thrown under), it is not an individual's essence or authentic identity if by these we understand something like a unique definition, the fully predicated statement of "what it is to be me," or what the individual would be if she could unburden herself of the totality of her social conditioning, extract herself from all social bonds and regulatory pressures, and "simply be herself."

Rather, the subject is the truth that gives the lie to socially mediated identity as the full and final statement of who I am. Yet it has no positive status: "The subject is . . . so to speak, a negative object."[105] The subject is less substance than principle of self-differentiation, of in(de)finite self-regeneration. The subject names our abyssal, evanescent character, our propensity to become yet otherwise. As should be evident, the subject is other to the order of identity: while, for Lacan, identity is a reified precipitate of identifications and thus associated with the ego, and, more broadly, the Imaginary, the subject is associated with the Real, with a fundamental inconsistency that is occluded as we become "self-aware," say, through the mediation of dominant forms of psychoanalysis: "the subject that [the signifier] represents is not univocal. It is represented, undoubtedly, but it is also not represented. . . . Something remains hidden in relation to this very signifier" (*Seminar XVII*: 101).

Linguistically or otherwise intersubjectively mediated categories *must be* the terms through which we recognize ourselves and others; there is no other way to attain coherent experiences of oneself or others than through the regimes of intelligibility available in one's socio-historical milieu, even if only at its outskirts. *Yet*, the self that becomes available in this way is not the full picture: the self is not the subject. The subject is the propulsion to become otherwise that is eclipsed by the framework of selfhood or identity. The subject is not what is yielded by social processes of subjectification; it is not a product of our subjection to symbolic norms or structures of interpellation through which we assume a recognizable social identity and acquire the capacity for coherent experience. Quite to the contrary, the subject is what fractures identity, keeps it in motion.

In passing, let me caution against too quickly latching onto the liberatory resonance of this notion of the subject. To keep identifications in motion is not to escape identification; and neither are always desirable, certainly not in an unqualified sense. The claims of the ego and the Imaginary are by no means easily sloughed off; and this is not necessarily cause for lament. We will return to this.

The subject names less a substance, an identity, or an effect of socialization than a temporal modality: the inherence of futurity. More concretely, the subject names the recurrent insistence of *desire*, the eruptive intrusion of yet another horizon that fractures open and juts us beyond whatever comforting, narcissistically (and otherwise) invested identity formations, stable patterns of object relation and attachment, etc., we have established. The subject, for Lacan, is remarkably proximate to—perhaps it *is*—the excessive, disruptive force of phenomenality.

As subjects we are prone to the dying away of our identities and symbolic coordinates. As subjects we are death-bearing, possessed of a force of negativity that devitalizes our commitments to whatever social bonds and personal orientations, projects, and value-horizons we have so far developed. As subjects, we are without bearings, vertiginous and adrift, radically forlorn. Sublime? The subject names our irreducibility to and noncomplacency with our most coveted patterns of attachment, self-images, and social arrangements. The subject is, for Lacan, a radical: a principle of contraction into the roots of *desire* out of which we surge into ever-new forms of life. When Lacan speaks of the subject, the accent is on ek-static temporality, on our implacable, world-negating agitatedness, on the pulsating and primordial force of *life*. Death-bearing to be sure, the subject is life—not quite life bereft of form, not quite "bare life,"[106] but life that insists *between* and motivates the perpetual undoing and transformation of its various determinations.[107]

The subject is a blade that cuts through various subjective determinations. It is not an entity; rather, it is more akin to the force, the incisive edge, of an insistent *question*: a question of what we are yet to become, a question of what horizons are yet to open before us, a question of—to risk a paradoxical formulation—our ownmost potentiality. "What constitutes me as subject is my question" (*E*: 247/299).[108] This is *the question* that, for Lacan, defines the human, and it is *the question* that is obscured by, or deformed as it is expressed through, the question of what we are or should be for the Other: the question that sustains the Imaginary. The subject is a question of possibilities beyond the horizons that can be foreseen from our current vantage points, a question of our in(de)finite futurity. It is thus linked to Lacan's notion of *passage à l'acte*. The subject is an ex-orbitant creature, an alien, a figure of excess, a boundless wellspring of futurity. The subject is a tremor, an insistence, a perturbation: the trembling of in(de)finite *desire*. The subject is *desire* as it will have been.

What then does it mean to affirm or accommodate ourselves to our truth as subjects? We affirm ourselves as subjects not by presuming to slough off the cultural detritus under which our "true selves" are buried but rather by discovering/creating ways to affirm and assume, to really live out, our abyssal, evanescent character, that is, by finding ways to accommodate ourselves to our in(de)finite *desire*. Like Hegel and the young Marx, Lacan wants to do justice to the infinite rights of subjectivity. To affirm ourselves as subjects is less a question of what we do than of how we do it. It is a question of our orientation toward, our manner of inhabiting, the identities and patterns of attachment we inevitability assume. To affirm ourselves as subjects involves keeping open a distance toward all subjective determinations and particular constellations of desire. However, this distance must not be an ironic or cynical detachment, e.g., the irony or cynicism embodied in the presumption that the socially mediated identities and desires that seem to be most "me" are but indications of my inability to extricate myself fully from social norms and obligations, that the "real me" will only see the light of day when all forms of social binding are successfully broken. Rather, it must be a joyous affirmation of one's in(de)finite futurity. Despite the Spinozistic-Deleuzian coloring of this claim, pursuing Lacan's notion of affirmation through that assemblage may be profoundly misleading. For this is where Lacan's thought manifestly resists metaphysical mania and overlaps with the utopian demands of Critical Theory, disclosing thereby its ethico-political charge: massive social change, social change on the scale of messianic redemption, would be needed to bring about a world in which one's uncertain futurity could be unconditionally affirmed rather than fretted about more or less constantly or energetically evaded.[109] Only in a messianic light does the subject appear in its social actuality, which is to say, under contemporary sociopolitical conditions, the subject appears for the most part in negative relief. For now, Lacan maintains, freedom is always our "scant freedom" (*E*: 213/257).

Though under contemporary conditions freedom appears primarily through the filter of the Imaginary—e.g., as the unsettling and provocation to reconsolidation of identity and symbolic coordinates or in the form of fantasies of individual autonomy—we do have some experiences of ourselves as subjects. In fact, the Lacanian clinic aims at precisely this experience, however mitigated it must be in a world such as our own.[110] To sense oneself as subject is to feel *fortunately, joyously* ever-incomplete, ever on the way, a work in perpetual process, irrevocably exposed to developments that will not have been anticipated. Might we call this a sense of ongoing adolescence? In any case, this is, for Lacan, a utopian vision, but a utopian vision unreconciled to merely prophetic status. Lacan's notion of the subject enjoins us to ask, What would it mean, in practical, everyday terms, to affirm my radical incompleteness, my constitutive exposure and dependency, my lack, my non-identity with the self-images and patterns of desire I feel to be most truly and authentically my own? What would these affirmations mean in the arenas of love and friendship, of politics and civic society? Generally, what would these affirmations mean for our social bonds? What are the limits of these affirmations under current social conditions? Might awareness of these limits help motivate various social and political transformations? How might a social order support our flourishing as subjects, as in(de)finitely desirous beings?[111] And, of course, given how terrifying it seems, upon reflection, to acknowledge one's absolute vulnerability,[112] given the manifestly good reasons we have to avoid it by immersing ourselves in social routine, what is the good in pursuing these developments? Whence the joyousness of becoming ever-otherwise? Is unlimited potential something that can be unconditionally affirmed? "At the end of a training analysis [which is, for Lacan, "pure analysis"] the subject should reach and *should know* the domain and the level of experience of absolute disarray" (*Seminar VII*: 304; emphasis added).

Still, Lacan's notion of the subject is bound to strike us as rather abstract, as if the subject is either (1) the subject of the Structuralist science of psychoanalysis, an academic postulate, or (2) a utopian dream. In a way, this is correct. In "Science and Truth," Lacan figures the subject as the subject of science, i.e., as the subject of tentative, hypothetical knowledge. In this moment of his work it is most clear that the subject is a construction; but Lacan's purpose is not to emphasize the subject's ideality. The subject is neither empirical nor ideal, neither a scientifically verifiable datum nor a strictly speculative postulate. Rather, precisely in its utopian or ideal dimension, the subject is what insists in and through the rubble of damaged life. The subject is known, tentatively, either by creative/speculative induction or as what impresses itself on us in certain limit experiences—say, when an apparently satisfactory form of life suddenly loses its compelling claim and begins to feel painfully mundane or somehow deeply disappointing.[113] Either way, the manner in which it can be known attests to the fugitive character of the subject.

Lacan's point in speaking of the subject as the subject of tentative, hypothetical (in this sense, "scientific") knowledge is to simultaneously emphasize the need for critical caution when making claims about it (discussing it as a persistent substance would be to efface it) and the need to bring to light its excessiveness, its disorienting urgency (which is most conspicuous in certain limit experiences but perhaps faintly insistent throughout life). A double bind, a double injunction. The notion of the subject requires clarification, yet we cannot but be hesitant when speaking of the subject insofar as the subject is for the most part conspicuous only at the limit, alienated or tendentially eclipsed by the categorical contours of everyday life and their reflective elaboration in conscious experience. The subject is alienated in the Imaginary, alienated in identification with an alter ego, alienated in symbolic interpellations through which one assumes a recognizable social identity (in Lacanese, alienated in the Big Other). The subject, proximally and for the most part, is alienated. Thus it needs to be elaborated in terms that are fundamentally abrasive with respect to the familiar: mimetically appropriate terms. The ineffable must find expression without reducing its strangeness, its liminality.

In other words, Lacan's point is not that the subject is an ideal-type construction extrapolated from analytic experience (though this is true) or a utopian posit (though this too is true) but that the dimension of the subject must find expression even though—or, better, precisely because—it is systematically obfuscated by the ego's penchant for stable self- and object representations and relations.[114] The subject is an excessiveness that the ego tends to shy away from; but in shying away from it, the ego articulates its negative contours.

As Real, the subject is a principle of interruption: it interrupts the orders of self- and object representation, knowledge, instrumental and relational facility, etc. It is the dialectical counterpoint of the ego as principle of selective self- and object representation. The subject, this excess, will only become apparent, at least under prevailing social conditions, in certain limit experiences—experiences of certain modernist works of art come to mind, as do certain features of analytic experience. Hence the temptation to be avoided is redescribing the subject in "experience-near" terms. Our descriptions of the subject need to keep front and center its remoteness from conscious experience, from our tendential forms of self- and object representation, from the categorical contours of the everyday. Our descriptions need to register the subject within yet in its excess of the order of representation.

Three final addendums are now in order. First, although the subject still sounds rather abstract, and though holding onto its abstractness is a crucial way of avoiding its falsification via reduction to "experience-near" terms, Lacan insists that "the subject" is always a singular subject. The ek-stasis of "the subject" is always a singular *ek-stasis*, *my* ek-stasis—however difficult it is to assume as mine.[115] Paradoxically, this ek-stasis is *mine* precisely insofar as it exceeds my cognitive grasp and instrumental hold, insofar as it disrupts my efforts of self-appropriation and self-determination, insofar as it responds to an insistent questioning lodged so deeply "within" that no effort of self-excavation will ever be up to the task of bringing "it" to the light of day. It is *mine* not in the sense of being under my control but of bearing singularly on *me*—on my ego, identifications, fundamental fantasies, etc. This urge to become ever-otherwise is *my* urge precisely insofar as it moves me in ways I cannot control, anticipate, or adequately account for, even retrospectively. The subject names an incessant interruption of my various projects that pro-jects me out, throws me out over myself onto ever-new horizons. Language is bound to be contorted here, but perhaps I can put it this way: the subject is what is in me, what *is* me, more than me qua composite of identifications, patterns of attachment, privileged self-images, etc.

To put one final spin on it: one can never quite point to any dimension of experience or pattern of behavior and confidently say, *This* is what I am qua subject, for the very gesture of (self-)appropriation effects the eclipse of the subject. First, the subject is eclipsed insofar as it is falsely rendered in substantial terms, as if it were an entity, a "this" that can be pointed to objectively. Second, the truth of the constative statement (This is what I am qua subject) is falsified by its enunciation. The "I am" gets in the way of a true articulation of my being qua subject. As subject, "I am" a movedness, a pulsation concerning which I can only ever offer an imperfect, retrospective account. Again, the subject is *desire as it will have been.* The subject is less an object of knowledge than an "acquired" sense of oneself as possessed of an insistent liveliness, an undead, quasi-mechanistic vitality. Thus, in a certain sense, the subject is an extrapolation, an inevitably retrospective construction, a dimension of our being whose comprehension is constitutively belated. But it is always the extrapolation from the ever-becoming-otherwise of a singular being, a subject stretched between this birth and this death; in this respect, the subject is always singular.

Second addendum: There is an enormous difference between the singular subject and the singular individual. When Lacan says, (in)famously, that there is no sexual relation,[116] part of what he means is that there is no ideal pattern of sexuality, no one satisfying form of relationship, that will appeal equally to all. Each individual has a singular approach to and stake in sexuality; each individual will be excited by persons, objects, and situations that no one else is excited by in quite the same way. Each individual's sexuality develops as an unique symptom, a unique compromise between an underlying unfulfillable wantingness (the dimension of the subject) and the particular forms of sexuality or attachment through which this wantingness will be given determinate form (the dimension of the individual).[117] There is a difference, then, between, on the one hand, the individual's singular orientation toward and relation to his or her body, sexuality, pleasures and pains, fundamental questions, significant others, and objects and, on the other, the insistence of pure want named by the subject. Subjectivity in this sense is not individuality but rather its ek-static principle. The distinctive organization of the individual responds to but does not fully overlap with the singular subject. As unique individuals, we are unique identificatory composites, unique assemblages of signifiers, and unique responses to the questions and provocations signifiers harbor. As unique individuals, we have unique relations to the sociosymbolic order. But, in part, what propels the incessant process of individualization (via identification, etc.) is the subject.

Third addendum: There are two or maybe three distinct phases of Lacan's exposition of the subject, but my sense is that what accounts for the differences between them is mostly a matter of strategic emphasis. From the 1950s to the late '60s, Lacan speaks of the subject of meaning or the subject of desire. When he discusses the subject of meaning the emphasis is on our alienation in meaning, in the desire/discourse of the Other. But the emphasis is also on the ways in which the subject, like meaning, is constantly emerging, as opposed to the inertia of the ego.[118] When he discusses the subject of desire, the emphasis is on our status as forever lacking, as voids of *desire* or wellsprings of negativity that cannot be constrained, let alone satisfied, either by analytically promoted personal growth and social adjustment or by foreseeable, however radical, political transformations and the more humane world they herald. Our *desire* outstrips the satisfactions onto which it opens us; it is the principle of nonassimilation to whatever cultural formations in which we find ourselves. The accent in this phase of Lacan's work is on our finitude, our incompleteness, our perpetually dissatisfied nature. Against false promises made by certain analysts and certain political revolutionaries that complete and harmonious satisfaction is just around the corner, that utopia can be realized here and now, Lacan emphasizes that our tension-ridden desirousness is inescapable, untamable, and bound to unsettle our commitments to any foreseeable social order. No matter how acclimated to social reality we become and no matter how hospitable society becomes to our needs and desires, we will be forever wanting, fundamentally unreconciled.

Subsequently, Lacan speaks of the subject of the drive. Here, the emphasis is on the repetitive pulsation of the drive, on the ways in which we are driven to seek after objects that forever fail to satisfy, perhaps enjoying the very pulsation of drive life as such but never sated. In this phase of his work, Lacan underlines our incorrigibility: we never quite seem to grasp that the objects toward which we are driven are not the harbingers of replete satisfaction they seem to be. Furthermore, Lacan underscores that there are dangers associated with the objects of our longing to which we blind ourselves even though we have encountered them time and again. We return to the same objects, the same types of relationship, the same fantasies, time and again. And time and again we are let down, if not worse. This pleasure-in-pain (jouissance) of missing the object is the register of the drive. The drive is "stupid," possessed of an insistent rhythmicity that propels us into situations we should know better than to get ourselves into. The accent is on our fixation, on the compulsive repetition of patterns of attachment, fantasies, etc. You've fallen for the same type of person so many times before, but "this time it will be different." Lacan insists that we must own up to this stupidity and learn how to enjoy the insistence of the drive as such; we must learn to assume the jouissance of the drive. Otherwise, to indicate only one consequence, we will measure our satisfactions against an impossible ideal of absolute fulfillment, converting partial pleasures into occasions for self-torment.

As much as this emphasis on repetition and fixation seems diametrically opposed to Lacan's earlier emphasis on the in(de)finiteness of desire, I take it that the difference in emphasis responds to only a difference in perspective; it is not as if the conception of the subject fundamentally changes. Under the heading of the subject of the drive, Lacan provides a close-up on our object relations. Bracketing the in(de)finite displacement of desire, he tarries with the subject as her wanting becomes fixated on a particular object or relational configuration. To be sure, the subject is still a pulsating vitality that drives her from object to object and unsettles her most cherished patterns of attachment and identifications (or at least threatens to, thereby provoking Imaginary reconsolidation). The subject is still characterized by a state of desirous unrest that moves her into ever-new forms of life and love. The discussion of the subject of the drive simply homes in on a particular moment of desire in order to explore it in greater detail. The mystery, then, is how our fixations give way to ever-new object attachments, how our captivation by particular forms of desire and attachment are unsettled such that we are thrown out onto ever-new horizons—this mystery is just the mystery of the subject. One way to translate "passage à l'acte" would be "it happens." The seeming contradiction between Lacan's earlier and later understandings of the subject registers the contradiction in the object (the subject) itself.

DESIRE

Much of Lacan's understanding of desire has been implied and partially discussed in the foregoing. However, a brief recapitulation of ground already covered will be of service in preparing the discussion of two topics central to the notion of desire that have not yet been adequately addressed: the peculiarly normative status of *desire* in Lacan's work and the various fates of desire to which he is superbly attentive. Addressing these topics is crucial for explicating the stakes and significance of Lacan's engagement with Klein.

Desire in the strict sense is basically synonymous with the notion of the subject elaborated above. *Desire is* our ek-stasis or ex-orbitance; more of a mode of ex-istence than a substance. This understanding of *desire* is starkly opposed to Klein's sometimes quite literalistic interpretation of the drives, specifically of the death drive in "The Importance of Symbol-Formation."[119] As many commentators have noted, Lacan's *désir* implies a more continuous force than the German *Wunsch* or the English *wish*. Wishes can be granted; *desire* is endless.

Tellingly, when Lacan speaks of desire, he most often speaks not about what it *is* but about how it becomes involved in a number of fantasy formations. Since desire "itself" is nothing that can be pinned down and pointed to, Lacan's discussion of desire is bound to focus for the most part on the shapes it assumes (and unsettles). Pure *desire* manifests, if anywhere, only in the incessant sliding, the processive unraveling, of its determinate shapes, i.e., obliquely.[120] To discern *desire's* operativity in oneself, one would need a keen sense of one's history, which is why Lacanian therapy, especially in its later stages, is not wholly averse to genetic reconstruction.[121] In most of Lacan's teachings, then, *desire* is discussed in terms of what it has become, what it has provisionally stabilized *as*. Notice the distinctively Heideggerian method of inquiry: if *desire* "as such" manifests only through its occlusion, if *desire* appears only in compromised form, then attending to *desire* as folded into and pressing out of a number of relatively determinate forms, i.e., crafting a history of desire, is the only way to inquire into *desire* "as such."

The first fate of *desire* is the desire to be the object of the other's desire.[122] This is manifest in the great many tactics of ingratiation through which we seek to insinuate ourselves into the other's narcissism, or at least the other's interest, and thereby secure his or her all-important care. Born premature—unable to provide for ourselves in the least, absolutely vulnerable—we are born sycophants. *Desire* initially manifests as the desire for recognition, specifically, for recognition as whatever the other might want, whatever the other would feel completed by, whatever would bring the other's distractedness and involvements elsewhere to an end (*E*: 285ff/343). The operative fantasy[123] is either (1) when the other is completed, s/he will then perfectly provide for me, provide in so preemptory a fashion that I will no longer suffer the pangs of need or want, or (2) the completion of the other *is* self-completion (since self and other are more or less indistinct in the infantile register of experience). The excessive, rupturing force of *desire* is quickly, almost immediately, harnessed into fantasies of completeness.[124] And with good reason: the extremity of our global vulnerability—to which *desire* may make no small contribution—cannot but be profoundly unsettling, all the more so as it becomes associated with a number of local instances of frustration, deprivation, pain, etc.[125] Caught within either fantasy frame, *desire* aspires to be self-canceling, to open onto a state of symbiosis in which the once desirous being fuses with the other, becoming a single, self-satisfied organism.[126] God, in other words. Even after we have achieved a certain physical and mental maturity, we cannot bear our exposure, Lacan contends, because it is too closely associated with—indeed, sometimes feels indistinct from—the tumult of infantile frustration, because it is marred by the terrors of infantile vulnerability. Our unremitting exposure—related but not reducible to our *desire*—is tendentially eclipsed as we project and become deeply invested in a horizon of symbiotic satiation. Corralled into this fantasy of symbiotic merger, *desire* leads us astray. Captivated by a fantasy of symbiotic omnipotence, we fail to heed the signs of and in various ways obscure the lacking, wanting, utterly exposed, and incomplete nature of ourselves and others. Harnessed in this way, *desire* tends toward the repudiation of finitude. We might even say that it gives rise to an ontological mistake, a misrecognition of the *manque-à-être* (lack of being, being as lack, or want to be) constitutive of the human (and perhaps not only the human).

Later, *desire* undergoes a transmutation as one learns to desire *desire* itself, that is, as one learns to appreciate the crisp edge of longing, the pulsating vitality of want, the paradoxical goodness of unfulfillment (whether as an intrinsically compelling affective state, an affective registration of freedom, or a provocation to encounter and engage, to passionately negotiate with, the unexpected).[127] Once preemptory neediness is sufficiently diminished and a sense of the world as hospitable enough is instituted by a good-enough caring environment, we learn to love, or at least enjoy, our longing itself and perhaps all that is associated with it: exposure, dependency, attachment, and so on.

The desire for *desire* is clamorously evident, albeit in distorted form, Lacan contends, in certain neuroses. The hysteric tends to tease, to keep the desire of her lover alive and on edge. She then keeps her own desire alive by identifying with her lover's unfulfilled desire. (Hence the aura of depressive withdrawal characteristic of the typical femme fatale; it is against the strong undertow of depression that her solicitations defend. Hysteria may even be an expression of melancholia: making the other into the loser, i.e., becoming what the other is doomed to lose or has already lost, the hysteric disavows her own loss.) Or she dismisses every satisfaction on offer, once it has been secured, as "not it."

The obsessive desires the impossible,[128] an ideal before which all real partners fall short. This is why the object of desire has to be kept at a distance through complex rituals and rigid behavioral regulations; it must be kept impossible, unconsumed thus alive. The obsessive cannot settle down with any one partner, or, if he does, he remains profoundly attached to something or someone else that epitomizes "real" satisfaction—something that or someone who, to be sure, will always be held at a distance, e.g., by idealization so intense that the object comes to appear unapproachable, or by making sure that, "inexplicably," there are always insurmountable difficulties involved in its pursuit. Thereby, the obsessive keeps his desire alive.[129]

The hysteric and the obsessive are to be understood as strategies of desire seeking to keep desire alive rather than pathological aberrations to a psychosexual norm. They are pervasive strategies of sexuality inherent in all of us to various degrees, not diagnostic categories—or at least this what Lacan tends to emphasize, even if he may on certain occasions use these terms as diagnostic tools.[130]

Cultivating, indeed purifying, the desire for *desire* itself, promoting the desire to live and be recognized as a void of *desire*—as fundamentally insatiable, a force of negativity abrasive to any particular configuration of identity, desire, or relationality—or, more precisely, promoting the desire for mutual recognition of *desire*,[131] is a paramount goal of Lacanian psychoanalysis. As death-bearing[132] and dismal as the desire of *desire* may seem, Lacan is committed to it as a regulatory ideal. To the extent that we do not desire to be recognized as voids of *desire*, Lacan insists, we have failed to accommodate ourselves to our truth, have succumbed to the corruption of comfort.[133] From Lacan's perspective, *we should* as much as possible conform to the truth of our in(de)finite *desire*. *We should* as much as possible develop ways of living out, of affirming and keeping in the fore, our abrasiveness with respect to any determinate configurations of desire and relationality, culturally facilitated satisfactions, etc. We must become who we are, namely, wellsprings of negativity, subjects in process.

Has Lacan given himself over to a moralized metaphysics of *desire*? His claim that "[t]he psychoanalytic goal is . . . to teach the subject to name, to articulate, to pass into existence, this desire which is, literally, beneath existence, and for that very reason, insists" both invites and resists this criticism (*Seminar II*: 266). If desire "insists" "beneath existence," it is because the fantasmatic consistency of "existence" cannot bear (yet feeds off, i.e., reconsolidates itself in the face of) the disruptiveness of *desire*. Thus to "teach the subject to name, to articulate, to pass into existence, this desire" is to encourage her to bring to bear a shattering force of negativity against all symbolic, subjective, and relational stabilities. It is to directly encourage a death-dealing disruptiveness, a disorienting disintegration of any and all settled forms of life. Profoundly impersonal, "this desire . . . beneath existence" into the emissaries of which Lacan seeks to turn his clients seems an apocalyptic force. Encouraging this direction because it would amount to accommodating one's truth would seem to be moralized metaphysics at its most vicious. But notice that desire, "which is, literally, beneath existence," is "to pass into existence," to be named and articulated, i.e., achieve determinacy, however provisional. Though in a way Lacan seeks to induce a repetitive, indeed death-driven, assault on determinacy, the rhythm of repetition and the vectors of assault will yield determinacy as if in spite of themselves. And recall that the fantasmatic consistency of "existence" reconsolidates itself in the face of the disruptiveness of *desire*; the urgency with which Lacan advocates destruction assumes the implacability of reconstruction. What Lacan seeks to instill in his analysands is hardly a penchant for anonymous, antinomian violence. Quite to the contrary, naming and articulating desire means personalizing it, symbolizing it, bringing it to bear in the world. Desire as named and articulated becomes public, singularly significant though socially recognizable. Better, desire as named and articulated is a principle of world-renewal. The furious release of desirous negativity transpires—"pass[es] into existence"—through the cultivation, the creation/discovery, of finite, determinate desires. Naming and articulating desire means subjective and symbolic recreation—becoming, like Joyce, a "saint homme/sinthome."[134]

What must be underscored is that Lacan's notion of *desire* is fundamentally normative.[135] As infants, and later to a great extent unconsciously, we tend to desire objectification, i.e., integration into the desire of the other (which we image—or, better, fantasize—to be determinate, if somewhat opaque to us). Though our insuperable permeability and the frustrations, deprivations, and terrors of infancy and later life with which this exposure becomes associated render unavoidable the desire for the desire of the other, still, Lacan insists, we *should not* desire the desire of the other. At least not in the ways we tend to, e.g., because we unconsciously believe (fantasize) that by fulfilling the desire of the other we will put an end to need and want. And at least not with the force with which we tend to. Rather, Lacan contends, we should seek *separateness* at the level of desire, cultivate a *relative independence* of desire. This means both (1) developing forms of desire less ensnared in the desires of others (thus less ensnared in the inherited desires obscurely resounding in and keeping fundamentally unsettled the desires of others), forms of desire that open us onto our ownmost possibilities, onto horizons of becoming that, perhaps, will have been very much our "own" though they cannot be unanticipated from our current vantage points, onto forms of life that, perhaps, will have allowed us to flourish to the greatest possible extent and in the broadest possible terms (in this respect, Lacan is a diehard pluralist),[136] and (2) developing forms of life that would be extensively mobile, thus well-suited for a continual affirmation of our desirous negativity.

Although, as indicated above, as if by nature we come to desire our *desire*, to desire recognition as voids of *desire*, as inassimilable to the desires and directives of others,[137] Lacan continually insists that *we have yet done so insufficiently*. Of course, desiring the desire of the other may facilitate pleasurable connections with others or various pleasures facilitated by these connections, thus it is not something we are likely to give up lightly and it is not immediately clear why Lacan would insist ever again on our so doing. Moreover, fantasizing replete and harmonious satiation may be psychologically necessary for the infant. Without this fantasy, could the infant bear dissatisfaction without utterly breaking down? And, later, this fantasy may provide great solace or even revolutionary momentum? Lacan is not cruelly insisting that we outright repudiate each incarnation of our desire to be the desire of the other or simply reject (as if this were so easy) our fantasies of symbiotic completion. He does insist, however, that we must not cede on our desire, that we ought not neglect our fathomless, in(de)finite *desire*. Were we to do so, not only would we condemn ourselves to domination by the question of the other's desire and the fundamental fantasies through which we respond to it, not only would the forms of suffering that result from Imaginary fixation remain steadily in place, what is *perhaps* worse on Lacan's account, we would stray from our truth or authenticity. From Lacan's perspective, the injunction not to cede on one's desire, that is, not to become ensnared in the desire of the other, articulates a goal both necessary and impossible.[138]

The idea of authenticity is surely cause for concern. Does it not seem that Lacan illicitly promotes a certain picture of desirous life to the status of authentic, ontological truth and moralizes this truth as the one to which we must conform? Is this not counterproductive given his broadly Nietzschian notion of pathology (ideals we cannot hope to satisfy turn into sources of endless self-torment)? Yet as questionable as the onto-moralization of a certain aspect or mode of human (only human?) life may be, there is a political and a clinical point to Lacan's insistence that must be considered.

The political point is both too obvious and too ambiguous to comment upon in any detail. Suffice it to say that if we understood ourselves and others (let alone phenomena as such) as primarily in(de)finite pulsations of *desire*, as wellsprings of longing who will not and *must not* be—or be seen as—encapsulated in any particular social or relational coordinates, if we learned how to experience ourselves and others as unstable, unobjectifiable urgencies of becoming otherwise, as invariably exceeding statistical enframing and efforts of external administration, life would be *very* different. Some such intuition, some such dream seems to be bound up with Lacan's onto-moralization of *desire*. But, again, the intuition or dream is vague.

The clinical point is that the desire to be the desire of the other all too easily becomes coextensive with a fantasy of replete, final satisfaction against which our partial satisfactions, the pleasure-in-pain of jouissance, are found wanting. Under the shadow of utopia, we come to despise our partial pleasures, become fundamentally self-loathing, cynically distant from our own pleasures and pursuits. We fail to appreciate, thus in a certain way fail to undergo, the pleasures we "experience" because they are not *that*, because they do not absolutely satiate. By keeping in place a fantasy of salvation in which some omnipotent other (divinity, romantic partner, political leader, economic guru, techno-scientific research program, etc.) will administer a fully satisfying existence and bring our longing to rest (or in which the completion of the other is at once our self-completion), we set ourselves up to degrade, to repudiate, to feel uncomfortable with or even somewhat ashamed of taking pleasure in the partial satisfactions available to us. Pleasure becomes betrayal of the Ideal.[139]

Strangely, though, the point of Lacan's distinction between demand and *desire* seems to be to unsettle our complacency with partial satisfactions (the satisfactions of discrete demands) in order to open us to the truth or authenticity of *desire* in excess of determinate demand. Is there not a fundamental tension between Lacan's insistence that we accommodate ourselves to our insistent negativity and his implicit advocacy that we learn how to enjoy the partial satisfactions available to us? Well, yes . . . of course there is. But this is not because Lacan is naïvely contradicting himself. Rather, it is because his thinking responds to the difficulties of robust self-affirmation.

We can start to work through this problem by clarifying the distinction between demand and *desire*. Though *desire* may, perhaps must, be interpreted by—channeled into—specific demands, it always exceeds these demands and thus the horizon of satisfaction. Our body lights up with inchoate neediness, and, later, guided by experiences of our neediness having been quelled by specific sorts of experiences facilitated by those who interpret our neediness in particular ways (originally, our primary caregivers), we develop particular need-interpretations. Some of these need-interpretations are for the most part inescapable, e.g., the need for food and water. Some are more malleable: experience with a range of satisfying objects and relations, along with the work of fantasy and the interpretations of our neediness by those who respond to it, will determine what we feel we need. When a general state of neediness, an ambience of ineffable want, is interpreted as a specific need or set of needs and this is conveyed to others as a claim upon them, we have a demand.[140] *Desire* is what is leftover when demand is subtracted from need. *Desire* is *residual*, an insistent remainder that is forgotten but not transcended in the development of need-interpretations and the self-images that accompany them. *Desire* is an "analytic" category.

Yet the difference between demand and *desire* is not as clear-cut as it may seem. While demands are need-interpretations addressed to a particular other, they always also encode a demand for unconditional love. "Demand in itself bears on something other than the satisfactions it calls for. It is demand for a presence or an absence. This is what the primordial relationship with the mother manifests, replete as it is with that Other who must be situated *shy of* the needs that Other can fulfill" (*E*: 579–80/690–91; also see *Seminar IV*: 101). Demands are addressed simultaneously to a specific other and to the Other of our fantasy of symbiotic completeness, the Other who can provide us with the unconditional love that would set our world aright by bringing our desirousness, our neediness, our exposure and dependency to an end (via her full presence or her removal of some contingent impediment—"the demand of an absence"). Demands are for specific sorts of satisfactions, but beyond this, "demand annuls the particularity of everything that can be granted, by transmuting it into a proof of love" (*E*: 580/691). Demands are never fully satisfied because the particular something we thought we were asking for never yields the replete satisfaction we unconsciously expect. And we will never obtain this satisfaction because it is strictly speaking fantasmatic. So we go on demanding, interminably. "[D]esire is situated in dependence on demand" (*Seminar XI*: 154). Because the world is forever out of joint, because we are yet unsatisfied, we unconsciously assume that we have yet to formulate the right demand or address it to the right person. We are condemned to litigate. The crucial point for our concerns is that in its intrinsic unsatisfiability demand is similar to *desire*.

Or we might put it this way: within the fantasy of symbiosis, desire can never be satisfied because it is oriented toward an impossible fulfillment; it aims at the absolutely secure attention of one's primary caregivers and the limitless satisfaction one unconsciously believes they can provide. Demand and *desire*, then, are not two discrete entities. Rather, demand is a species or fate of *desire*. As Lacan puts it in his typically over-the-top way, "desire is nothing other than that which supports an unconscious theme, the very articulation of that which roots us in a particular destiny, and that destiny demands insistently that the debt be paid, and desire keeps coming back, returning, and situates us once again in a given track, the track of something that is specifically our business" (*Seminar VII*: 319). Demand is what becomes of *desire* when it is harnessed to a particular fantasy formation. This is why, seeming to collapse the distinction between *desire* and demand, Lacan emphasizes that desire is tendentially compromised and object-oriented, rather than, as one would expect, "pure." Along these lines, Lacan speaks of desire as "a defense, a defense against going beyond a certain limit in jouissance" (*E*: 699/825). The limit desire will not surpass, *insofar as it is caught up in the fantasy of symbiotic completeness*, is the frame of the fantasy itself. The difference between demand and *desire* is ultimately that *desire* is what *may* carry us beyond—or at least generate interest in the beyond of, and so partially sap the force of—fantasies of final fulfillment.

To affirm ourselves as desiring subjects, then, we must cultivate ways to affirm both our in(de)finite desirousness and the determinate demands into which *desire* is channeled[141] without fetishizing the former or becoming complacent with the latter. In fetishizing the former, in affirming ourselves *only* as voids of desire, we would viciously repudiate the determinate configurations of our desire and the partial satisfactions they yield. We would, thereby, repudiate one dimension of our finitude. This would amount to a wild self-loathing. To affirm *desire* at the expense of demands and the qualified satisfactions they yield would be, paradoxically, *to fail to affirm desire* since demand is itself a species of *desire*, a distinctive fate of *desire* that cannot be simply brushed aside if we are to affirm *desire* in its fullness (what it will have become).

In becoming complacent with the latter, in resigning ourselves to affirm only this or that demand rather than the in(de)finite desirousness that we *are*, we would keep in place the fantasy of symbiotic completeness that, paradoxically, would prevent us from taking pleasure in the satisfactions with which our particular demands are met.

Further, to affirm only *desire* would require unremitting engagement in practices devoted to facilitating the assumption of castration and separation, sapping the force of fundamental fantasies and otherwise debilitating Imaginary captivations, and so forth. But if these practices substantially diminish expectations, as seems to be their stated goal, would they not bring those who too intensely engage in them perilously close to the adaptationist program of ego psychology? Would they not be structurally self-defeating?

To affirm only our demands and their associated partial satisfactions at the expense of our in(de)finite desirousness would be, paradoxically, to fail to affirm both our demand and our *desire*. To affirm our demands without affirming them *as* compromised instances of *desire* would not really be an affirmation of our demands, for it would not be an affirmation of our demands *as* compromised formations of an exorbitant *desire* that dwells within them and may yet fracture open these demands, the forms of life to which they contribute, and the fantasy in which demands as such are possible. And to affirm our specific demands and the partial satisfactions they yield as the be all and end all of human existence would be to deny the ways in which, possessed of *desire*, we always demand more and may even eventually learn to *desire* outside of the frame of symbiotic completeness.

The truth of the subject is a complicated, tension-ridden truth. We affirm ourselves most truly when the ways in which we do so are themselves suffused with tension. As Lacan puts it in *Seminar XX*, "in the desire of every demand, there is but the request for *object a*" (126).[142]

OBJET A

The difficult logic of self-affirmation outlined in the preceding section can be further elucidated by appeal to Lacan's notion of *objet a*. The ambiguity of what it means to affirm one's *desire*, to accommodate one's truth, responds to the ambiguity of the peculiar "object" toward which *desire* is directed and by which it is mobilized: *objet a* (understood as developed in Lacan's later work).

Before and beyond its captivation by fantasy, *desire* is evoked by and turns around *objet a*. *Objet a*, like a perfect—nonconflictual, totally satisfying—sexual relationship, does not exist. Rather, it insists as the ex-timate core of an object (person, part-object, form of relation, etc.) that provokes *desire* beyond any specific demand. The "trick" of *objet a* is that since it does not exist, it cannot be captured by any ploy of seduction it eludes us even when our strategies of seduction come to successful fruition; the impossibility of its consumption guarantees desire's incessance. In this sense, "the petit a is the cause of the subject" (*Seminar XXI*, Feb. 12, 1974). It is the cause that incessantly mobilizes the subject precisely because it is "never there . . . always situated elsewhere . . . always something else" (*Seminar V*: 19).

Objet a is what, *from the side of the object*, keeps desire in motion. With the notion of *objet a*, Lacan insists on the irreducibility of desire to demand *without intimating that individuals are driven by an ulterior internal agency* (the drive, desire, or the subject). With this notion, Lacan resists, or at least keeps in question, the primacy of the intrapsychic. Part of Lacan's motivation to develop the notion of *objet a*, it seems, was his awareness that his discussions of the subject, desire, and the drive risked making it seem as if the exorbitance of *desire* is an "inner force" or stems from an "inner me" unreconciled with the world. In other words, they risked the misleading intimation of a convergence between Lacanian theory and Romantic existentialism. Further, and more importantly, he seems to have been aware that his discussions of these topics risked making it seem as if *desire* is fundamentally "narcissistic" in the sense of self-enclosed, not *really* concerned with objects but only with its own incessant mobilization.[143] But this would risk denying the primordial and unending exposedness of psychic life, its "transindividuality" (call it the risk of crypto-Cartesianism). Thus, with the notion of *objet a*, Lacan insists on desire's irreducible excessiveness without appealing to the push of the drive or the pulsation of *desire*, that is, without suggesting that the drive or *desire* stem from "within."

Perhaps because much of Freud's reception had been dominated by a misplaced concreteness—motivation, and more broadly, the psychic, was taken to be located *in the head* or at least somehow *in* the individual—Lacan, with his notion of *objet a*, insists on the porosity of the human, on our constitutive openness to that which exceeds and fractures us, on the calling-forth of *desire*—our truth—by something that may not be quite "external" but is surely not simply "internal." With this notion, Lacan insists on the non-autochthony of the subject's truth, on its irrecuperability by introspection, or, in a more conventional Lacanian idiom, on the subject as split, ek-static.[144]

With the notion of *objet a*, Lacan keeps the metaphoricity of the distinction between "internal" and "external" conspicuous, resisting Klein's (and a great many others') tendency to literalize drives and part-objects. Perhaps an element of what is at stake here is keeping the speculative dimension of psychoanalytic knowing in the fore. Lacan's concepts tend to mark themselves as efforts—sometimes, as if in order to make the effort all the more evident, as rather torturous efforts—of knowing, of sense making, that may not be, perhaps cannot be, fully adequate to their objects. Lacan's concepts tend to mark themselves as efforts to discursively render the provocations and perturbations of phenomena that to a certain extent resist discursive recuperation. They attempt to call attention to themselves as points of crossing between the Imaginary and the Symbolic, as sites of a tension-ridden interface of the irreconcilable. As we will see, one of the major points of conflict between Klein and Lacan concerns the question of how concepts are to be understood: through a theory of truth as adequation (Klein) or otherwise (Lacan).[145]

Though Lacan develops the notion of *objet a* well after *Seminar I*, its service in refocusing the discussion and partially recasting the meaning of "object relations" suggests that he was, throughout his career, intimately engaged with Klein and her legacy. Through this notion, Lacan seems intent on turning attention away from an allegedly indigenous repository of phantasies that coordinate and partially motivate our object relations and toward the exorbitance of *desire*, i.e., the nonalignment of desire with a fully satisfying or all-consuming object or relation. The notion of *objet a* seems designed to direct attention toward our perpetual dislocatedness, toward the unremitting upsurge of natality, thus away from the stability and satisfactoriness of our object relations. Contra Klein's concern with the programmatic elaboration of phantasmatic object relations and impediments thereto, Lacan seeks to call attention to our primordial alloplasticity, our formative experiences with objects and others, or, more precisely, with what is "in" the object or other more than itself.

We are now in a position to see that self-affirmation is necessarily inconsistent, thus not something that Lacan *can* teach us to achieve. Because they cannot be consistently fulfilled, Lacan's injunctions to accommodate *desire* should not be received as intending to vanquish Imaginary captivation but rather to interrupt it, to underline and amplify dialectical tension between the Symbolic and the Imaginary. More precisely, what we are now in a position to see is that it is not just that the Imaginary and the Symbolic oscillate; they are not categorically distinct.

If *desire* outstrips demand, it is because of our *responsiveness* to *l'objet a* "in" the object. Thus to affirm our *desire*—to affirm ourselves as subjects, our truth—is to affirm our mobilization by that which radically exceeds us. It is to acknowledge—belatedly, searchingly, impossibly—our exposure to and provocation by that which cannot be brought back to us. Self-affirmation is at once an affirmation of the radically other. But if self-affirmation requires an affirmation of *objet a*, and *objet a* does not exist, what can self-affirmation amount to, practically speaking? We can begin to address this question by noting that *l'objet a* by which *desire* is evoked is both unrepresentable and always represented. Fantasmatic representation eclipses the essential indeterminacy of *objet a*, but *objet a* can exert its impact in no other way than through fantasmatic elaboration. *Objet a* (mis)directs desire: it both serves as the scaffolding of fantasy and impedes its consolidation. *Objet a* exceeds the order of representation—it is the Real lining the image that causes representation to tremble—yet it is what is figured in all determinations of the desirable. *Objet a* is (dis)figured by fantasy.

Concealed in the course of its unconcealment, eviscerated through its objectification, *objet a* is a paradoxical figure of the ineffable. Though it is often figured by a trait that elicits desire and around which fundamental fantasies are constructed, it is irreducible to its figural fate. Consequently, to affirm "it" is at once to affirm the fantasy-mediated desires it mobilizes and their proneness to give way; it is to affirm, simultaneously, our givenness to the Imaginary and our standing as subjects of in(de)finite *desire*. To affirm *objet a* is strictly speaking impossible, necessarily inconsistent. Such (self-)affirmation would have to affirm *l'objet a* as it appears and as that which cannot appear.

To affirm *objet a,* and thus ourselves as subjects of *desire*, is to affirm one of its manifold appearances and thus to fail to fully affirm it/our *desire* in its excessive unfigurability. "Object *a* can take on many different guises. It may be a certain kind of look someone gives you, the timber of someone's voice, the . . . feel, or smell, of someone's skin, the color of someone's eyes, the attitude someone manifests when he or she speaks—the list goes on and on" (Fink 1999: 52). But these are guises—guises by which *objet a* comes into view and claims us within the Imaginary. Within the Imaginary, understood as a form of attention structured by a fantasy of symbiotic completion, by a desire for the death of desirousness and the exposedness it implies, *objet a* appears, however much under the radar of conscious perception, as that which one cannot do without, that which one's very life can be staked upon, that ideal something that promises full and final satisfaction (or, from another angle, that which, capable yet refusing to provision absolute bliss, induces fits of rage). So represented, *objet a* appears not so ineffable after all. However hazily, we know it all too well: within the Imaginary, *objet a* is that image of lost jouissance we aim to recapture in each encounter with the object of desire. Thus, to affirm our *desire* in excess of its overdetermination by demand is paradoxically to affirm our desire as it has been determined by demand. Idealization—thus, demand—sustains *desire*: renders the object incorruptible, all-plentiful, and so unobtainable, ever on the horizon, faintly but insistently beckoning. Absent idealization, the desirous undoing of determinacy would collapse on itself, become a vortex of melancholy. Indeed, the proximity of *desire* to the death drive should indicate the immanent risk of desire devolving into depression, a self-stultifying fate. But, all the same, though *desire* appears as, and so can be affirmed in the form of, an idealized demand, it somehow eludes representation by even this demand. To affirm our *desire* is to say in a single breath, Yes, this is *it* and No, this won't do. Perhaps one can do no better than this: self-affirmation would be an affirmation of *desire's* disappearance.

Within the Symbolic, *objet a* may appear as "an 'embodiment' of the nonobjective object of desire, an 'image' of the unimaginable castrated phallus, a 'reflection' of the nonexistent vacuity of the subject—in short, an impossible image, a sort of ultimate limit of identification, a self-portrait in which the subject will see himself as he cannot see himself, a vision of horror in which his own nullity appears to him" (Borch-Jacobsen 1991: 237). Here, *objet a* is figured as the *subject of desire*, the pure negativity one desires to be recognized as. Here, *objet a* is figured as the proper object of Symbolic recognition. But here, too, *objet a* is *figured*—embodied, imaged, reflected, portrayed, no matter how strained these manners of objectification may be—and thereby misrepresented: misrepresented because represented. Were schematization to be altogether avoided, the pursuit of Symbolic recognition would be sheer self-defeating chaos. Self-affirmation is ineluctably inconsistent.

The primary conclusions to be reached are the following. (1) Efforts to affirm oneself exclusively as a being of the Symbolic (pure *desire*) or of the Imaginary (demand) are bound to fail. Such efforts always slide into one another, indeed sustain each other. Imaginary idealization is what presses *desire* onward; conversely, *desire's* nonfulfillment fuels Imaginary elaboration. To pursue either form of recognition at the expense of the other is to evade the complexity of the human predicament and thus to cede on the tension-ridden fullness of *desire*. (2) The concrete meaning of self-affirmation cannot be delivered by theory. Affirmation of one's *desire* is impossible, cannot be consistently realized, and it will take the full course of a Lacanian analysis in which we repeatedly confront our (in)consistency, our (in)determinacy, our dialectical complexity, or, even more, the full course of a life in which we utilize the forms of attention and insights acquired in such an analysis, to work out what this impossible affirmation will look like for us.

A final coda: As noted above, Lacan councils accommodation to our truth as subjects of *desire*, which involves at least intermittent exposure to the fracturing force of *objet a*. However, as indicated, he does not simply extol the virtues of abstract freedom or claim that the liberation of *desire* is an unproblematic good.[146] Lacan does not suggest that we unconditionally and interminably open ourselves to *whatever* befalls us, suspending judgment in order to explore all avenues opened by the dislocating efficacy of *objet a*.[147] Nor is he prone to wholeheartedly condemning refusals to sustain absolute vulnerability to or reticence in pursuing certain prospects opened by the fracturing force of *objet a* as an abdication of the onto-moralized task of assuming our truth. Though disclaiming or suppressing his onto-moralized invectives would be profoundly distorting, his subtle efforts to call attention to the difficulty, indeed the impossibility, of consistent self-affirmation is meant to mitigate the normative urgency of his cry to assume our status as subjects of *desire*. To be sure, Lacan's onto-moralization of *desire* manifests in vehement insistences on assuming the truth of *desire*, but his exaggerated prioritizing of the assumption of *desire* seems to be a polemical antidote to, a manner of counterbalancing, what he perceives as an all-too-consuming desire for conformity. The ambition, as per usual with Lacan, that committed contrarian, is to dialectically mobilize his addressees, not to dictate a determinate path of development. His direct (and practically, i.e., therapeutically, elaborated) admonishments not to cede on desire are meant to steal the stage, but only because the audience is nodding its heads in unison.

That Lacan does not fetishize freedom is most evident when, in his later work, he comes to conceptualize anxiety as overproximity to *objet a*. At this stage in his work, anxiety is precisely the registration of the void, the permanent ek-stasis, of the subject. By calling this registration of desirous subjectivity *anxiety*, Lacan attests to the significant unease it occasions, making it clear that he is by no means advocating a monofocal pursuit of pure *desire*. That would be an extreme form of moralized masochism he has no interest in underwriting. To be sure, there is a distinctly Heideggerian resonance to this notion of anxiety: the anxiety occasioned by overproximity to *objet a* seems, in part, purified of its negative affective valence through its ontological construal as exposure to unlimited possibility, specifically to possibilities beyond those that can be anticipated from within the horizon of the reigning actuality. But the anxiety elicited by overpromixity to *objet a* is still, for Lacan, a source of affective distress. As such, it is not something that can be unconditionally affirmed, and Lacan is certainly not in the business of condemning us for failing in the face of the impossible. Quite the contrary. When Lacan identifies overproximity to *objet a* as a source of anxiety, specifically as the anxiety of freedom, the pleasure-in-pain of the subject's liberation, it becomes evident that emancipation from our dominant desires, identifications, and object relations, the freedom of exposure to whatever comes,[148] is not and cannot be something we might wholeheartedly pursue. "[I]n my experience, it is necessary to canalize [anxiety] and, if I may say so, to take it in small doses, so that one is not overcome by it. This is similar to bringing the subject into contact with the real" (*Seminar XI*: 41). The self-preservative function of the defenses is not to be lightly dismissed, nor are the captivating qualities of our current configurations of desire, identification, object relation, etc. The Jacobin lesson was lost on Lacan; he is not looking for us to become purists of *desire*. He knows full well that to council the ruthless dissolution of symbolic, relational, and desirous determinacy in the name of instituting a life of pure *desire* would be to moralize melancholy, to condemn his clients to suicide.[149]

One may suspect that Lacan is something of an active nihilist or freedom fetishist from a highly selective reading of his early work on anxiety. However, this suspicion falls flat when his various notions of anxiety are situated in relation to one another. Lacan's later notion of anxiety, that connected with overproximity to *objet a*, seems diametrically opposed to his earlier conception of anxiety as occasioned by the threat of engulfment that arises from the overproximity, the intrusive and constitutively unbearable presence, of one's primary caregiver(s).[150] In early Lacan, anxiety results from the overintrusiveness of the desire of the other, from the crowding out of the subject by the other's desire. Anxiety, in other words, registers in the mode of distress, indeed horror, an encroachment upon or saturation of the individual's field of experience by the desire of the other. In *Seminar X*, for instance, in response to his query, "What provokes anxiety?" Lacan responds, "[c]ontrary to what people say [notice Lacan's typical counter excess], it is neither the rhythm nor the alternation of the mother's presence-absence [in brief, Lacan is distancing his conception of anxiety from the notion of signal anxiety, thus from the presumptive dominance of the pleasure principle as a homeostasis-inducing mechanism]. What proves this is that the child indulges in repeating presence-absence games: security of presence is found in the possibility of absence." In short, anxiety results from the overproximity of the other, from the threat of being overwhelmed. Lacan continues, "[w]hat is most anxiety producing for the child is when the relationship through which he comes to be—on the basis of lack which makes him desire—is most perturbed: when there is no possibility of lack, when his mother is constantly on his back" (Dec. 5, 1962). Within this context, desire, bearing one beyond the intrusive, potentially annihilating force of the desire of the other, or bearing the other beyond her consuming concern for you, emerges as a force of liberation. "Desire is a remedy for anxiety," Lacan states in *Seminar VIII* (430).

When isolated, this early notion of anxiety might suggest that Lacan is inclined to fetishize *desire*.[151] However, as we have indicated throughout and will explore later in greater detail, seeming opposition regularly signifies dialectical interimbrication throughout Lacan's work. In this context, this suggests that the later notion of anxiety may not be a dramatic change of course, i.e., meant to repudiate the earlier notion of anxiety, and thus that Lacan never for a moment believed that the relentless pursuit of lack, freedom, *desire*, etc. is the highest good.[152] Rather, the development of the later notion of anxiety seems designed to disclose the one-sided, limited character of *both* conceptions of anxiety and so of *both* notions of the good that they bring into negative relief (the earlier notion of anxiety implies the good of freedom, the later implies the good of enjoying those goods already available, even the good of some degree of stability and consistency). The development of the later notion of anxiety would be a way of keeping both figures of the good in play. If this is Lacan's intention when developing his later notion of anxiety, it would be not only methodologically consistent but also particularly apposite in regard to anxiety. The immediate distress of anxiety can make it seem as if identifying and removing its source would suffice for happiness. Thus by developing diametrically opposed conceptions of anxiety (one sourced in too little freedom, one in too much), Lacan suggests that neither a monomaniacal pursuit of freedom nor its rigid evasion will satisfy, ultimately that full satisfaction is not a viable ideal for the finite and complex creatures we are.[153]

Anticipating the dialectical mobilization he seeks to institute through his later notion of anxiety, Lacan actually provides two competing conceptions of anxiety in *Seminar X*. As we have seen, in *Seminar X* anxiety is described as the suffering of too little freedom, but it is also described as initiating a flight *from* freedom. At certain moments of *Seminar X*, anxiety is said to be elicited by the threat of the loss of an object that had been very present to us, this threat bringing the object into view as *the Thing*, the wondrous, utterly compelling *it* (July 3, 1963). So wondrous does this object seem under the threat of its loss that we are inclined to put everything else (our desires, self-images, moral commitments, plans and ideals, etc.) on the backburner for the sake of its pursuit. Strikingly, with this conception of anxiety Lacan suggests that we suffer under the threat of losing that which had, according to the other concept of anxiety operative in *Seminar X*, distressed us so severely. That which gave rise to the anxiety of annihilation is now subject to a melancholic hyperidealization, consequent upon which it becomes the stuff of rigid fixation. And, significantly, Lacan labels this manically idealized object "*objet a*." For instance, "the breast becomes an object *a* for an infant when weaning is initiated"; "[t]he parent, in making demands, lays down a law (of weaning or toilet training, for example) that isolates an object, cutting it away from its context or background, creating a foreground and a background: the breast is constituted as a separate object at the moment at which it is prohibited" (Fink 1999: 191). In this context, the pursuit of *objet a* involves a seeming repudiation of *desire*. Significantly, as described here, *objet a* is not a provocation to pursue the lability of *desire* for its own sake; rather, it induces us to narrow our focus and plot a course of pursuit to which we will remain true. *Objet a* here takes upon Imaginary dimensions.

Two points are to be underlined. First, were Lacan a purist of *desire*, it would be highly peculiar that the very term—*objet a*—that later will be associated with the fracturing force of freedom is presented here as the object of rigid fixation, the Imaginary object par excellence. Second, investing a single term—*objet a*—with seemingly contradictory dimensions would be a perfectly appropriate strategy if these two dimensions (the Symbolic and the Imaginary) are not polar opposites, in view of which it would be possible to opt for one rather than the other, but rather bound up with one another in complex ways. For instance, a fixated pursuit of an idealized object, insofar as this involves emancipation from one's habitual forms of object relations, transformations to one's self-image, substantial modifications of one's fantasies, structures of desire, and so on, seems to be an expression of *desire*. Is not the madness of love's pursuit resonant with the mobilization of *desire*? Would not the purist of *desire*, the one who repudiates all things Imaginary, be her own greatest impediment?

Finally, as if to make plain that anxiety can neither be simply construed as the registration of the overproximity of the desire of the other (thus that *desire* cannot be an absolute good) nor as the overproximity of *objet a* (thus that resolutely suppressing *desire* cannot be an absolute good), Lacan ends *Seminar IX* with a peculiar little story about himself and a praying mantis. The story marks a transitional moment in his conceptualization of anxiety, to be sure, but its transitional character may not be that of the neural medium providing a clear path between an origin and a destiny or that of a confused amalgam of what will need to be separated in work to come. Perhaps the transitional character of the story means to impact what precedes and what follows, specifically to show that they are involved with one another in ways that are more difficult to discern once they are analytically separated.

In the story, a praying mantis draws itself up to human height and faces Lacan, who cannot but feel anxious before the creature in want of any idea of what its intentions may be. The story seems to be an allegory for the fate of the subject consequent upon her heroic liberation by desire from the intrusive embrace of the other's desire. Thus it is appropriately situated between the earlier and later conceptions of anxiety. In this story, the subject no longer fears immediate annihilation by the desire of the other, though he is anxious, indeed terrified, when confronted by the other's uncanny and absorbing desire. But he is also attracted by this desire. He does not turn and flee. Nor does he seek to slay the creature. Moreover, the subject is not completely convinced that the other desires to do him harm. He is neither convinced that the desire of the other implies his effacement, that there can be only one desire, nor that what the other wants is or implies the subject's suffering, supplication, or annihilation. Perhaps the desire of the other is attracted to his own desirous subjectivity, hence the mimicry of the subject's stance (i.e., the subject's standing or status). Perhaps, given the uncanniness of the encounter, the allegory means to suggest that the subject is beginning to work out his desire for the desirousness of the other yet feels that this is something monstrous, dangerous yet attractive. Perhaps there is an intimation that the scene of desire is fraught with peril and uncertainty, dangers that would be amplified were the subject to become a purist of desire. In any case, what seems clear is that the other is interested in me and so powerful that I cannot dismiss the question of how I am implicated in his/her/its desire. Enclosure in the field of my own desire is not an option. Not knowing what the other really wants, if the other even knows what it wants (it is a preying mantis, after all), and how I might respond to this want are the fundamental sources of anxiety.

In this transitional moment, anxiety registers the intrusively persistent enigma of the other's desire, which is perhaps the enigma of my own desire, the enigma of desire as such. In the earlier conception of anxiety, the problem was that the other was too close, completely crowding me out. In the later conception of anxiety, the problem will be that the other is too distant, her loss already looming. Here, the problem is that the other—perhaps the other in myself, perhaps *desire* as such—is too much a mystery, intrinsically unsettling, something with regard to which there is no hope for reconciliation. Between the anxiety of annihilation and the anxiety of loss stands the anxiety of ambiguity, just as the story stands ambiguously between two conceptions of anxiety. Here, the other is present, in a way too present, but also too far away. The creature is figured as the site of an impenetrable interiority, as if another subject. To be a subject is to be *that.* Anxiety in the face of the creature, then, would figure the ongoing difficulty of affirming oneself as a subject of desire. Attraction to and repulsion by desirous subjectivity cannot be disentangled. Anxiety as occasioned by the enigma of desire figures the unending difficulty of self-affirmation.

TRUTH

For Lacan, truth is not a quality of propositional statements, the mark of complete or pragmatically sufficient understanding, or the happy outcome of collective verification efforts. On the contrary, truth is associated with discrepancy and ambiguity, with the unremitting inconsistencies or anomalies that motivate renewed attention to phenomena we thought we had successfully grasped. From the side of the subject, truth names our *incompetence* in the face of what exceeds our cognitive powers, disrupts our relational facilities. From the side of the object, truth is associated with the Real, the unintelligible kernel around which meanings circulate.

Truth is not a resting point but a provocation. Resounding with the inchoate dimensions of phenomena and psychic activity, those dimensions that are lost in the horizon of meaning yet propel its incessant recreation, truth is the spur to meaning, its motivation and limit.[154] From the side of the subject as much as from that of the object, truth bespeaks lack, limit, finitude. Truth is testimony to becoming.

Approximation to or accordance with truth, Lacan stresses, is more a matter of opening and sustaining a question than ending a statement with a self-assured period; more a matter of charting a series of (determinate?) negations than arriving at an unshakable conviction; to put it a touch dramatically, more a matter of occlusion than conclusion. Truth is less aligned with discursively reconstructable fantasies underlying behavior, as Klein would stress, than with endlessly enigmatic signifiers. Abrasive with respect to the order of discursive knowledge,[155] truth is the limit to the propriety of propositional attitudes. It is the rub of phenomena or psychic activities as they resist assimilation to our various conceptual schemes and relational horizons. Truth is what cannot be brought back to *us*. In a strikingly Platonic vein, Lacan affirms that truth is always on the horizon. When Klein thinks she has gotten down to the truth of Dick's suffering by uncovering his Oedipal anxieties, from Lacan's perspective, though this conviction is decidedly *useful,* she could not be more off-base with regard to the *truth* of the matter. Klein loses the dimension of truth through her eminently pragmatic compulsion to *know*.

From another angle, truth concerns the ethical stance we assume, or at least try out, as we seek to divest our commitments to demonstrative certainty, to clear and distinct representation, generally, to cognitive and instrumental mastery, of their overwhelming force and attractiveness. In this respect, truth is a matter of fidelitous attention to the indelible becoming- and appearing-otherwise of phenomena, to the unsuspected "other scene" harbored in what we feel we know most well, to that which dimly insists in and through our frameworks of understanding, causing them to tremble, or, at the limit, calling them into crisis. Truth is registered in an ethos, a form of attention—akin to the "suspended listening" of the analyst—that is in(de)finitely attuned to the yet-to-be: the in(de)finite futurities latent in physical and psychic phenomena and the as-yet-unnoticed or as-yet-undeveloped significance of such phenomena.

Truth is always a *difficult truth* insofar as (1) tarrying with the rupturing of phenomenalization or the dimension of the inchoate is eminently unsustainable (such tarrying is vitiated by our engrained habits of understanding, in tension with our need for a sufficiently stable world-orientation, and so on) and (2) attending to the resolutely indeterminate truth of phenomena is, strictly speaking, attending to nothing, to no thing, to a force of nothingness or negativity, to the *freedom of phenomena*. Though phenomena may be largely governed by causal and probabilistic laws, they are *free to appear and become significant* in unsuspected, perhaps in principle unpredictable, ways.[156] Truth is registered in the fracturing of our most coveted certainties, in the faltering of our habitually useful and highly invested forms of attention, in moments of crisis or transition, and in the indelibly *belated* or *retrospective* character of our knowing. Truth shows itself most distinctly in distortions, interruptions, lies, retreats, mistakes and retakes, in the stuttering momentum of meaning-making. Truth is always the truth of excess, a sublime truth.

Lacan's notion of truth is intimately intertwined with his notion of speech: "speech constitutes a new emergence of truth" (*E*: 318/381).[157] Speech is always free speech: free to mean, resonate, and position addressor and addressee in ways that exceed intentional control. Truth, then, is a task of attuning to what is not directly said, perhaps cannot be said, in speech; a task of keeping attention keyed to the unsaid, to that which *may have been* meant or indicated or initiated by various speech acts, e.g., to themes barely broached or vaguely drawn upon; to relational configurations initiated, hesitantly explored, or asked after; to all that tends to be concealed by the overtones of intentional communication. The task of truth is fidelity to the freedom of speech.

Truth is a task of becoming vigilantly attentive to the barely articulate resonances that *may* dwell within speech and to what various utterances *may yet* come to mean. The task of truth is more a matter of ecstatically relinquishing bodily and ego boundaries and the normative ideals with which they are bound up than of establishing masterful interpretive competence. However, the task of truth is not fulfilled simply through concern for the amorphous or virtual. The explication of truth is the explicitation of ambiguity *in and through* determinate meaning. Accepting this task means sustaining awareness of the sensory *significance* that subtends and exceeds the imagistic and discursive elaborations to which it gives rise, not ignoring the latter for the sake of a purportedly pure immersion in the former. To speak the truth is to speak in such a way that determinate meanings bear indeterminate resonances, forces, and fates, to allow ambiguity to seep into the foreground of or carve crevices in determinate meaning, disrupting and disorganizing communication while not wholly confounding it. To hear the truth in speech is to listen bifocally: to both the intentional, determinate content of an utterance and to the meanings, proto-meanings, and nonmeanings that are briefly opened or dimly alluded to in the course of the utterance. Truth emerges *in and through*, not as a result of, lucid speech. True speech is enigmatic and condensed, infused with horizons of meanings and abysses of nonmeaning that only dimly and briefly open in the course of an utterance and are quickly paved over by the forces of communicative competence. True or "authentic" speech is thus speech welled up, perhaps overflowing with ambiguity, filled to the brim with possibilities of meaning-otherwise, studded by elements that resist full integration into the order of meaning. Truth resides in the intimate dialectic of determinacy and indeterminacy.

To become a friend of truth is to lavish attention upon both what is intended and what dimly echoes in the furthest corridors of speech. Thus Lacan insists that "What is at stake [in psychoanalysis] is the realization of the truth of the subject, like a dimension peculiar to it which must be detached in its distinctiveness in relation to the very notion of reality (*Seminar I*: 21/29). The distinctiveness of truth is its abrasiveness with respect to the meanings we find persuasive, avowable, sensible, and thus "real." The true is the contrary of what is yielded by the *sensus communis*; it is difficult, even intolerable. The truth of which Lacan speaks is a truth we can never quite assume as our own, a truth that disrupts the facility of the "I think" that is said to accompany all our representations, that is *as nothing to me*, the truth of madness. For psychoanalytic practice to realize the truth of the subject, it would need to habituate analysands to attend to what seem to be the most impossible, indistinct, and unavowable resonances of their speech, to come to question, and sustain as a question, what they might have meant or might have been doing with their speech, that is, to call themselves into question. The subject is, in truth, a problem to herself.

More specifically, for psychoanalysis to realize the truth of the subject, it must acclimate analysands to entertain their complicity with meanings that, in their most cherished self-image(s), they could never, would never, have really meant. This is to confront, indeed confound, analysands with the unavowed multiplicity of their meanings and with the dimension of nonmeaning that haunts their meanings. This means confronting analysands again and again with the *question* of what they mean or might have meant and with the nonsense that inhabits—disrupts and mobilizes—their various meanings. This is not just a matter of rendering the ordinary extraordinary; it is a concerted effort to mystify what had been taken for obvious. Such a practice will clearly be incredibly frustrating, even prone to provoke outbursts of rage and/or withdrawal. However, for Lacan, there is no other way, or no better way of which he is aware, to expand the analysand's sense of self to the point where no clear self-image can hold, to the point where any self-image *feels* violently reductive and constrictive, or at least to the point where the captivating force of prevailing self-images is significantly diminished, whereupon the desires foreclosed by these self-images can be entertained. The realization of the truth of the subject is the cultivation of a sense of oneself as a question to oneself. This seems to be what Lacan has in mind when he proclaims that "the decisive function of my own response [as analyst] thus appears, and this function is not, as people maintain, simply to be received by the subject as approval or rejection of what he is saying, but truly to recognize or abolish him as subject. Such is the nature of the analyst's *responsibility* every time he intervenes by means of speech" (*E*: 247–48/300).

The truth of the subject, then, names the subject's constitutive mobility and ongoing indeterminacy, her irreducibility to any conceptual scheme, her phenomenal freedom. In Lacan's words, "[t]he most corrupting of comforts is intellectual comfort" (*E*: 336/403). The truth of the subject is a matter of emphasis and exaggeration, specifically, an emphasis of the subject's proneness to become, to want, to fantasize, and to mean in ways she could not anticipate and may not be able to acknowledge from within the interpretive horizon established by her privileged self-image(s). Likewise, the truth of *desire* names, in an emphatic voice, desire's exorbitance, its perpetual breaking free from determinate form—which is, from another angle, a matter of its being always on the way to, perhaps always already involved in, yet another determinate configuration. To attune to the truth of the subject, or what is much the same, of *desire*, is to allow our interest in determinate, stable, secure cognition and relations to subside as we open onto the (in)definite becoming of the subject, of *desire*. Truth names the "horizons" of understanding and relationality in which we learn to expect the unexpectable.

It is now possible to catch Lacan's drift when he writes that "The status of the unconscious, which, as I have suggested, is so fragile on the ontic plane [i.e., the unconscious cannot be fully demonstrated, is incorrigibly speculative and/or somehow evident beyond reasoned demonstration], is ethical: in his thirst for truth, Freud says, 'Whatever may happen, it is imperative to go there'" (*Seminar XI*: 33). Truth is a matter of "going there," of following (in)definite phenomena and the (in)determinate meanings of speech wherever they may lead. Or at least this is what, on Lacan's account, Freud establishes as an analytic imperative in a moment when he is consumed by a thirst for truth. On the one hand, the Freudian dictum is a reasonable directive to get over one's moral delicacy and listen attentively to whatever the analysand has to say (whether directly or in defensively distorted form—in which case, "going there" means going exactly where the analysand has indicated s/he would prefer to avoid). Generally, the council is to avoid passing judgment, all the more so precipitous judgment, and get on with the work of analysis. On the other hand, sourced in a consuming thirst for truth, this imperative gives exaggerated voice to an exaggerated desire. Accordingly, it is to be taken with a grain of salt, something that requires judgment in its application. Lacan, lending his voice to the spirit of Freud, inheriting and amplifying what he construes as the "ethical" exaggeration of the Master in order to work toward a truth tendentially concealed, nonetheless keeps open a critical perspective on the inherited imperative, making sure it does not turn into an absurd, death-driven doxa. The pursuit of truth is not easily undertaken; even initiating it requires effective provocation—say, the provocation provided by the authority of Master Freud delivering a direct imperative, coupled with whatever authority Lacan can muster and the ethical characterization of the pursuit.

Part of the difficulty is that the pursuit of truth requires courage and creativity: the courage to tarry with the forever enigmatic significance of the material (*of ourselves*) as it unfolds before us yet beyond us; the creativity to chart the unfolding of truth in excess of our engrained habits of understanding. Truth requires the courage and creativity to judge, to formulate opinions, thus to risk understanding, even to act on the basis of fragile and incomplete understanding, while yet attending to, or at lest not fully forgetting or otherwise neutralizing, the dimension of phenomena (of ourselves) that complicate and confound such decisively useful understanding.[158] That the unconscious is fragile on the ontic plane means, in part, that the propositions we develop *about* it—the propositions in which we treat the unconscious as an entity, a storehouse of determinate contents, e.g., phantasies and beliefs, undergoing transformations according to specific laws and tendencies (the Freudian-Kleinian exaggeration)—deform the meaning of the unconscious, miss something essential. Such propositions miss precisely the (*non*)*meaning* of unconscious phenomena, i.e., their excessiveness with respect to our cognitive capacities, their radically nontransparent, indelibly distorted character. When discovered, the truth, e.g., the truth of psychic phenomena, is simultaneously created (inflected, perspectivally figured, exaggerated) and thus in a way lost. When he says that the status of the unconscious is ethical, Lacan suggests that attunement to the truth of the unconscious is tantamount to giving up, at least with regard to knowledge of the unconscious, our attachments to apodictic certainties, propositional attitudes, and clear, contentful statements, *and yet not giving up on the prospect of knowing.* To investigate the truth of the unconscious is to become the sort of inquirers who tarry with the (in)definite—both determinate and indeterminate—fate of unconscious phenomena without either reducing them to established schemas or simply throwing away such schemas. It is to become the sort of inquirers who, able to bear and what's more, allow profit to be yielded from ambiguity, will explore what is *psychically real* for the particular analysand along with her by allowing her to create/discover the meaning of her unconscious phenomena *for her*. Truth is in this sense profoundly personal, a matter of what phenomena will have meant or will come to mean for a singular subject.

The ethical ambition of Lacan's notion of truth—an ambition manifest in his teachings and in his clinic—is to induce and sustain a fundamental exposedness. This is not achieved through a willful denial of determinacy but rather by keeping the most highly refined, highly determinate judgments interwoven with the perplexity occasioned by the propensity of the phenomena with which they are concerned to become and/or appear otherwise. In Shoshana Felman's apt words, "This is, in my view, the quintessential service that Lacan has rendered to our culture: to have derived from Freud a way of reading whose unprecedented thrust and achievement is to keep an entire system of signification open, rather than foreclose it, so that the small, unnoticeable messages can grow, by virtue of the fact that the big ones are kept still, open and suspended" (1987: 15–16). Notice that, on Felman's account, Lacan's achievement is to have developed "a way of reading" that, by bracketing the obtrusively obvious meanings saturating the foreground, allows background resonances to "grow." Lacan's achievement is not to have obliterated the foreground, i.e., the dominant regime of intelligibility, nor has it anything to do with an assault on determinacy as such. Rather, the achievement is identified as the development of a manner of reading that causes the foreground to give way to the development, thus the determination, of what had been condemned to near insignificance in the background. The achievement is not identified as the overcoming of determinacy, the collapse of all definite meaning, but rather as the development of a manner of reading open to the multiplication of determinacies, which, in turn, causes foreground and background to waver. Later, Felman brings Lacan's fundamental contribution into finer relief by recalling the difference between Lacan's and Marie Bonaparte's readings of Poe. "For Marie Bonaparte, what is compulsively repeated through the variety of Poe's texts is the same unconscious fantasy: Poe's sadonecrophiliac desire for his dead mother. For Lacan, what is repeated in the text is not the content of a fantasy but the symbolic displacement of a signifier through the insistence of a signifying chain; repetition is not of *sameness* but of *difference*, not of independent terms or of analogous themes but of a structure of differential relationships, in which what *returns* is always *other*" (44).

This ethical ambition is reflected in Lacan's distinctive clinical practices. Lacan's theory of pathology is, to a great extent, an account of how and why we become immured in static forms of life, as if cut off from the eternal wellspring of *desire*, uncreative and unmotivated apart from the energetic work of symptom formation. He worries deeply about monofocal trajectories of desire, stagnant fantasy formations, firm guideposts or protocols for living, generally, about anything akin to enclosure, captivity, or finality. Lacanian psychoanalysis aims at freedom, at our inconclusive liberation from rigidified forms of attachment, desire, and self-relation, so much so that, at times, he comes close to pathologizing stability, e.g., cultural rootedness or embedding in stable forms of life. But this is in the service of unsettling our unavoidable conservatism, our altogether understandable, indeed inestimably valuable, tendency to ritualize and thus stultify our desire.[159] Lacan is not naïve or insensitive enough to unconditionally advocate ongoing detachment from any and all forms of life, as if giving free reign to and identifying with the death drive were an unproblematic good. Given his cultural climate, he would likely see this as the height of ideological complicity with the deterritorializing forces of capitalist globalization, at best a cruel joke to those who suffer enforced uprooting from their traditional communities and forms of life. And it would be, as indicated above, self-defeating: a melancholic, or as a last resort, self-idealizing, trajectory. Lacan is not absurdly denying the contributions that various forms of life make to our survival and wellbeing. However, he is continuously, exaggeratedly, suspicious of rigidification on the ground of its complicity with various forms of suffering and pathology, especially as these involve the sapping of our courage and creativity.

We often suffer, Lacan suggests, from fixations, from deadlocks of irreconcilable desires and gridlocks of competing and seemingly mutually exclusive fantasies—all of which promote symptom formation.[160] For instance, we attempt to adopt the ideals of another (the other's ego ideal or ideal ego) as our own in order to secure the other's love and all we believe it harbors. But (1) in order to sustain our identifications, in order to fortify and thereby preserve our newly acquired treasure, we assume an antagonistic stance toward our *desire*, threatening as it does to exceeds the orbit of, and so in a way destroy, our coveted, recently acquired self-images and ideals. We turn against ourselves, developing an antagonism toward our *desire* that tends to manifest as repression and other forms of (sometimes quite global) defense, condemning ourselves to rigidity and suffering. (2) Since the other is structured by multiple, incompatible ideals and desires objects, relations, etc. that cannot be practically coordinated, assimilating the desires and ideals of the other condemns us to reproduce the other's deadlocks and the suffering they entail. And (3) the fantasy of Absolute Satiation leads to the discounting and disparaging of partial satisfactions attained, thus to wild self-loathing.

Though consistent self-affirmation is impossible, though conflicts at the level of desire are inevitable (desire is always the conflictual desire of the Other), though it is impossible to break free from the hold of the Imaginary in any sustained way, there is still progress to be made in opening ourselves to our truth, the truth of *desire*, and this would forestall at least some measure of suffering.[161] Therefore it is imperative that the analyst speak in a condensed or oracular manner, in a manner that is resonant, suggestive, and mobilizing rather than structured by clear-cut, precise statements that the analysand's ego can simply affirm or reject.[162] In the clinic, in the lecture hall, and in his publications, Lacan aims to stir things up: to induce symbolization (rather than the rote repetition of insights offered by the analyst, lecturer, or writer),[163] to foster creative self-examination (to induce the other to be the one who does the analyzing—the *analysand*), to free the subject to desire otherwise (say, by miming the analyst's attention to and symbolization of the remote echoes of her desire).[164] Lacan's simultaneously ethical and clinical ambition is to facilitate the analysand's confrontation with and accommodation to her in(de)finite truth, her lack (*manque-à-être*), by enhancing the symbolizing capacity through which she perpetually renews her efforts of self-creation/discovery.

In sum, for Lacan, truth is always the truth of lack, of inner discontinuities and ruptures, the truth of our inability to fully grasp what we know, or say, or want—the truth of finitude, of belatedness.

1. We misrecognize what we know by mistaking a perspectival account of the phenomena with which we are concerned for a final pronouncement with which we can rest content: we all-too-quickly turn from the sublime rupture of phenomenalization to the substantivized entities, states of affairs, or causal connections about which true propositions can be stated. Anxiously, we retrench ourselves in the horizon of calculability.
2. We misrecognize what we say by attending predominantly to the meaning that will have become apparent only when an utterance is completed or the intention "behind" the utterance authoritatively clarified. In the course of speaking, many pathways will have been opened, many signifiers will have been employed that could lead us—have already nudged us—in other directions, directions neglected but not transcended. Language speaks us: this is to say, as we speak, we draw upon a number of words and phrases that mean or can be taken up in compositions of meaning that bespeak a fundamentally *other* direction. We misrecognize what we say by attempting to shake off or suppress the branching out of our utterances into innumerable corridors of meaning, proto-meaning, or nonmeaning in order sustain the fantasy of univocal meaning. Our self-understanding is beclouded by a perspective illusion. From where we stand *after* a statement has been articulated, ordinarily, its meaning seems quite clear. But from an "insider's perspective," from the perspective of the units of meaning in the process of composing an utterance, meaning is far from given, far from certain. From the perspective of the units of meaning (the signifiers) that, though they may be heading in an eminently anticipatable direction, also reach out into the unknown, meaning is unstable, unruly, rhizomatic.
3. We misrecognize what we want by allowing ourselves to believe that it is this or that object or quality of object relation for which we are truly pining. But from the perspective of the subject, this is and must be "not it." Neurosis, from this angle, is a defense against truth, against the truth of in(de)finite lack. The neurotic cannot bear that desire is without a specific object, an object that can ultimately satisfy or at least one that promises absolute sat-

isfaction and whose pursuit can give meaning and coherent shape to a life. The neurotic wants the other to specify exactly what s/he wants, wants the comfort and security of determinate wanting and the embrace of a fantasy that promises final satisfaction. The neurotic cannot abide the lack in the Other, the incompleteness in the Other; s/he cannot abide *desire*.[165]

VI. From the Imaginary to the Symbolic

Now that some crucial terms have been elaborated, we can return to the explication of the Imaginary by putting the problematic with which we left off in the terms of the following analogy. The paradox of the superego is that efforts to live by its strictures amplify the guilt they mean to relieve. We would not be so committed to living in accordance with the superego's "moral" code if we did not desire to transgress it—if, at the level of desire, we had not already transgressed it and find ourselves likely to do so again. Obedience to the superego can only enhance its severity: "Whoever attempts to submit to the moral law sees the demands of the superego grow increasingly meticulous and increasingly cruel" (*Seminar VII*: 176). The superego becomes increasingly stern due to the pressing temptation to transgress it manifest in the acceptance of its authority. Additionally, our disappointment with ourselves for failing to live by the superego's standards, at least at the level of desire, as well as our profound aversion to the self-constraint these standards enjoin, generates abundant aggression, which then may be channeled back into the superego, further enhancing its severity. Analogously, the identifications through which we seek to attain Imaginary integrity are self-defeating. Evincing our *want of coherence* and forever failing to provide the coherence they promise, they cannot but magnify the need to identify once again, which disrupts the immediacy of identity and eventually leads to a partial dissolution of the specific forms of coherence previously attained via identification. The identificatory mechanism through which we seek solace in the calm ambience of coherent self-possession incites the most manic agitation, opening onto an implacable dissolution of subjective determinacies.

By means of identifications with the ostensible (ultimately enigmatic) objects of others' desires, we attempt to win their approval. By conforming to their wishes and becoming what we think they want or lack, we keep open the prospect of winning our caregivers' or significant others' all-abundant love, the demand for which, Lacan claims, tends to be harbored in every expressed desire. Because it is through our caregivers', and, later, significant others', love that our worlds become inhabitable, because it is through this love that we come to have a world at all, we madly, insatiably seek to secure it—at least so long as the fantasy of Absolute Satisfaction remains dominant.

However, since the objects of others' desires with which we might identify in order to secure their love are ultimately enigmatic, as much as the Imaginary seems to name a series of closed, dyadic relationships in which we seek the narcissistic splendors of self-cohesion and recognition as *the* object of the other's desire, it also bears the abyssal question of the desire of the other. According to Lacan, it is quite clear to children *that* their primary caregivers want something of them. But *what* they want is altogether obscure. Even when primary caregivers try to be upfront about what they want, e.g., weaning, bowel control, tidiness, obedience to the rules of the household or social order, various developmental or social accomplishments, etc., their desire still strikes the child as enigmatic. The nontransparency of the desire of the other provokes a permanent questioning that keeps us at a certain distance from even our most promising identifications. But this questioning and the mobility it induces are limited because the questioning is only a questioning after what the other wants. Even when the child latches onto a self-image that she believes will make her lovable and therewith, to a great extent, quells her worries about persisting in a state of fragmentation and helplessness, the very desirousness of the other, this desire which, she senses, is an enigma even to the other, makes her wonder, Is this it? Bruce Fink puts the point nicely:

> Even when they do tell us what they want—"You're going to be a lawyer when you grow up, and that's final!"—the message may not be as transparent as it seems. Apart from the fact that we may opt to accede to such wants or revolt against them in protest, we may sense that, while our parents are saying this (perhaps even demanding this), they would actually prefer something else: that we be something they had always wanted to be but were unable to be—or that we *not* be what they had always wanted to be but were unable to be, since they would feel threatened by this, preferring to see us as failures or "ordinary people" like themselves. (1999: 54)

This means that (1) we have reached the deadlock of the Imaginary and will have to look to the Symbolic for a less self-defeating, suffering-inducing form of life, and (2) already within the Imaginary, there are traits of the Symbolic (permanent questioning, attention to enigma, etc.). But before we proceed with the explication of the Symbolic, let us see if our now more nuanced understanding of the Imaginary (and the terms related to it) will help us identify and address the significance of the differences between Klein and Lacan regarding Dick's case.

VII. Back on the Case

From Lacan's perspective, as Klein regulates Dick's anxiety sufficiently for more secure object ties to develop, she introduces him to the seductive comforts of the Imaginary, extruding him from the Real—or more precisely, partially preempting the shattering of all forms of experience named by the Real. Granted, from Lacan's perspective, Dick would be immune to Klein's interventions were he not already in some respects implicated in the Imaginary and the Symbolic. Consider that, first, there are certainly signifiers—"dark," "void"—to which Dick responds and these signifiers are clearly relevant to his suffering. This indicates that Dick is in some way implicated in the Symbolic. Second, would Dick be open to the authority of Klein's interpretations were his enclosure in a horizon of diffuse anxiety not both incomplete and unbearable, i.e., were he not already looking for a way out, concerned with the desire of the Other as he seeks release from the terrors of his unnamable dread? At least in some respects, there is for Dick already an Outside, an Other. Otherwise, why would he latch onto and respond to Klein's interpretations so readily? Already engrossed in the Imaginary, it seems, Dick covets the authority of the One who can grant respite from his suffering. So Klein does not exactly *initiate* Dick's Imaginary captivation. But, Lacan insists, she surely secures its hold as she assumes the role of a god who can relieve Dick of his pain.[166] Does Klein not effectively invite Dick to share in a narcissistic salvation fantasy? Is this not the consummate Imaginary seduction?

Klein's Oedipalizing interpretations offer Dick a discursive blanket to drape over the terrible anxiety in which he is submerged and (what may be the same) with which to cover over the disorienting overfullness and overproximity of the Real. (If Dick does not yet experience the Real, the discursive blanket preemptively impedes access to it.) Offering Dick symbolic equations—Dick is the little train, daddy is the big train, mummy is the station—Klein supports Dick's fledgling ability to recognize unities, to home in on univocal and stable meanings. She initiates him into a propositional attitude. Through the orientative force of her *speech*, that is, through the performative efficacy more than the veracity of her interpretations, Klein promotes Dick's ability to recognize coherent meanings: to recognize himself, others, and objects as wholes in determinate relations with one another, e.g., Oedipal relations. Paving over phenomenal dispersal and ambiguity (which may have been just under the surface of his anxiety or something to which he could become attentive subsequent to being released from his intense anxiety), drawing attention away from the dissonance between the inchoate upsurge of phenomena and their schematic representation, Klein's interpretations metaphorize: convey Dick to a more comfortable and manageable world. But the risk is that securing his place in a world of coherent objects, others, and relations enforces a twofold neglect or suppression. (1) A neglect or suppression of the form of experience—modeled on the *corps morcelé*—wherein phenomena disclose their dimension of excess, their irreducibility to conceptual and relational schemas, thus their in(de)finite amenability to creative reschematization.[167] The risk, in other words, is of the concomitant enervation of subject and object. (2) A neglect or suppression of the truth of *desire*, of his status as an in(de)finite void of *desire*, of his givenness to (in)determinate strivings that will not be placated by any particular form of satisfaction. Granted, Dick may have been alienated from both the Real and his *desire* by his diffuse anxiety. But even if Klein is not exclusively responsible for this alienation, her cure reinforces it.

To elaborate, in the first case the risk is that Klein's authoritative interpretations will quell Dick's impulses (1) to creatively and continuously symbolize, which is the only way to avoid the depersonalization—the nihilism—that follows from assuming a cynical distance toward externally imposed, rigid meanings, specifically, and (2) to explore those possibilities that seem precisely "impossible" from the purview of entrenched regimes of intelligibility and normativity. Klein's interpretations risk suturing the gap between possibility and actuality; from here on, possibility may well be filtered through what Dick's sense of actuality, mimetically incorporated from Klein, deems possible, i.e., plausible, "realistic." Corralled into Klein's *sensus communis* and blinded to the in(de)finite becoming- and appearing-otherwise of phenomena, Dick will be foreclosed from acceding to, affectively and symbolically metabolizing, and thereby developing in response to the unexpected—both underdetermined and overdetermined—unfolding of phenomena. Call it a radical diminishment of his response-ability. For Lacan, it the intrusion of the Real that shatters entrenched expectations and schematic simplification, that introduces the possibility of radically new beginnings and genuinely novel developments, and this intrusion is exactly what Dick becomes insulated from as a result of Klein's authoritative interpretations. His analysis becomes the "primal scene" of social domination.

Klein's interpretations are Oedipalizing in the sense of effecting in Dick, or at least substantially amplifying, a receptiveness to Law, a binding to the Word of the Other. His asylum in Klein's Law is granted on the condition that he sacrifice his experience of—or potential experience of—phenomena as excessive of *any* law, of the world as an unruly manifold not yet or not completely captured by any conceptual, evaluative, or narrative order. Thus of the world as a (potential) secular achievement. Dick must learn to forget or perpetually turn a blind eye to the form of experience named by the Real; he must come to forget or neglect the abrasiveness of experience vis-à-vis the hegemonic terms through which it is filtered. Something in Dick must die or is mutilated in advance of its development—something that, for Lacan, is at the core of the impulse to freedom.

In the second case, the risk is that Dick will come to debase *both* (1) the in(de)finite character of his longing by measuring it against an image of full and final satisfaction (leading to wild self-loathing and interminable frustration, and then perhaps to depression, reactive and brittle narcissism, etc.) and (2) the partial character of his satisfactions insofar as they are felt to be inimical to the suppressed but not wholly enervated surging of his *desire* (again leading to massive frustration). Securing Dick's place in a world of coherent objects, others, and relations, Klein militates against his prospects for working out a relation to the volatile, ephemeral, and ultimately incoherent character of his *desire*.

In sum, promoting the development of object permanence, stable object relations, and secure, univocal meaning entails alienation from the abyssal truth of the subject and the incoherent overfullness of the Real. From Lacan's perspective, Klein's words are possessed of a *beneficent violence* which fosters subjective and relational rigidity and alienation in the midst of a mad pursuit of meaning. Lacan is extremely wary about these interventions, but, to be sure, since their efficacy in implanting Dick within the Imaginary provides him an unquestionably better life, and since, generally, immersion in the Imaginary is both developmentally advantageous and to some extent inevitable, a minimally generous reading will grant that Lacan is also greatly appreciative of these interventions. Klein's Word makes of Dick a believer, a believer in meaning; she grants him the assumption of sense, and he undoubtedly profits from this bestowal, as prone to manipulation and unwitting consequence as it may be. In general, Lacan is less wont to extol the virtues of others' work than he is to highlight its unintended effects and unrecognized dangers. By attending to the *effects* of Klein's speech rather than the veracity of its content, Lacan is able to bring into view what Klein's ego cannot see—generally, what cannot be grasped from the standpoint of the ego. In this case, this involves not just risks unwittingly courted but also the principle of her success.

Let us now briefly recap some of the major differences between Klein and Lacan that manifest in their differential foci.

- Klein focuses on the phantasmatic meanings of objects and the subject's relations to them, while Lacan focuses on the subject and object's destabilizing resistances to and provocation to creative renewal of the order of meaning.
- Klein focuses on the therapeutic consequences of valid (or valid enough) interpretation, while Lacan focuses on the unintended effects of Klein's interpretations.
- Klein attempts to buttress Dick's ego by bringing him into more-settled relations with various objects, while Lacan is wary about ego strength and identification with the standpoint of the ego.
- For Klein, desire is the desire to *have* an object, to secure a relationship to an object or set of objects that will, first and foremost, mitigate anxiety and

thereby facilitate developmental maturation, even the flowering of spontaneity; while Lacan stresses that the desire to *have* an object, insofar as "having" means possessing a fully and finally satisfying object, is a self-defeating and suffering-inducing abdication of the truth of the subject. Such a formation of desire bespeaks a wanton heteronomy (desire as the desire of the other) more than it establishes the conditions for psychological maturity or personal spontaneity—the desire to *have* such an object is precisely infantile. For Lacan, desire is at least as much the desire to *be*—to perpetually become and be recognized as—a subject of *desire* (this is his sense of in[de]finite spontaneity) as it is to *have* this or that relationship with this or that object and on its basis develop in the ways Klein seeks to support. To *have* this or that relationship with an object is, within the Imaginary, to *be* for the object what one imagines it wants one to be or what it would be complimented and completed by. This bespeaks a fantasy of completion that, according to Lacan, condemns us to self-torment.

- Klein stresses that there is an initial relation to an object (the mother) or at least a part-object (the breast), while Lacan emphasizes that the Real must be suppressed for object relations to become established. For Klein, certain object relations are primordial *givens*, while for Lacan they are—perhaps also—forms of defense against the Real, against the ruptures and dissonance registered by the form of attention elaborated on the schema of the premature body in bits and pieces.[168] Though the paranoid-schizoid position implies an emphatic experience of fragmentation and dissolution, it is more structured than the experience of the Real; it is elaborated according to various phantasmatic *narratives* that Klein assumes structure the relation to the primary object and then all subsequent objects.
- For Klein, object relations mollify or enhance anxiety, while for Lacan anxiety must be considered—at least also—as generated by the intrusion of the Real, by the experience of the lack in the object, the object's incoherence and inconsistency.
- For Klein, Dick is an aberration from the norm. Usually, symbol formation begins on its own, via projection and identification, and naturally transforms latent into manifest and thus diminished, and further diminishable, anxiety. Therapy merely lends nature a hand. For Lacan, if Dick is submerged in the Real, the *extent* to which he is may be quite unusual, but that he is beholden to the Real is not. Dick's suffering highlights a universal dimension of experience, a dimension that ordinarily is to no small extent suppressed by the imperatives of development. Klein's therapy is not simply a handmaiden to nature, it is profoundly socializing: it extrudes Dick from the Real (or partially preempts his experience of it) and ensnares him in social authority. If Dick's anxiety is diminished, it is not just because latent anxiety has been transformed

into manageable, manifest anxiety, it is also because his therapy closes him off from the anxiety-provoking encounter with the Real, thus from a valuable source of creative symbolization.

- For Klein, maintaining an object relation may be either an end in itself or a way of diminishing anxiety, while for Lacan, object attraction, at least within the Imaginary, is bound up with attraction to one's desired self-image: love of the object is love of the form of wholeness and what this form promises. Object relations, Lacan stresses, are initially and persistently narcissistic—manners of securing one's desired integrity and of insinuating oneself into the perceived narcissism of the Other. Lacan is concerned with our capacity to break free from Imaginary captivation, while Klein seems to be dead-set on settling us within it.
- Though Klein and Lacan agree that we experience ourselves and objects as initially and persistently disintegrating, Klein, with her great therapeutic-beneficent urge, seeks to mollify this experience as much as possible, while Lacan, with his great commitment to freedom, is attentive to the value of disintegration. The horrors of latent anxiety and the destructiveness of the death drive caution Klein against "tarrying with the negative," while Lacan sees therein promising emancipatory potential.

THE SYMBOLIC

In one respect, the Symbolic names the organization of interpretive and behavioral norms—the expectations and imperatives, written and unwritten codes—that we otherwise refer to as culture or tradition. Perhaps Lacan speaks of the Symbolic rather than of culture or tradition because the latter tend to connote homogenous values, univocal meanings, stable, embedded expectations, and well-ordered relations. This would be culture in its hegemonic articulation, in its ideological self-assertion, not in its inevitably heterogeneous, antagonism-ridden actuality. Culture here would be the voice of the dominant.[169] Such an understanding of culture or tradition only speaks to one dimension of the Symbolic: its provisional yet inevitable stability. Lacan's notion of the Symbolic seeks to underscore both the inertia of dominant norms of interpretation and relation (in this respect, the Symbolic is the Law) and their ongoing susceptibility to reconfiguration and reinflection (in this respect, the Symbolic suggests revolutionary potential).[170] The interpretive and evaluative norms that constitute the Symbolic are never fixed once and for all; in order to achieve whatever stability they may, they must be passed down and established as if anew, reaffirmed at the site of their inheritance, which means that the possibility of differential inflection or redirection is internal to them. "What [the] structure of the signifying chain discloses is the possibility I have . . . to use it in order to signify *something quite other* than what it says" (*E*: 420–21/505; trans. modified). Repetition always involves a chance of alteration, even of radical re-creation. When Lacan asserts that there is no Other to the Other, he means in part that there is no perspective outside the Symbolic from which one could confirm its completeness, that there is no guarantee that its development is finished, no external point of view from which Symbolic developments can be authoritatively gathered (synthesized, schematized) and pronounced complete, their significance thereby fixed.[171] Within the Symbolic, the possibility of the new emerges—cannot but emerge, if only in fledgling and fragile form—in and through the extension of what is being passed down.[172] The Symbolic thus names the belonging together of identity and (potential) difference, the dialectical unity of historical resiliency and (potential for) novel innovation.

The notion of the Symbolic attempts to register (1) the weight and force of culture, its ability to bind us to its terms and work through us, to structure us in ways we can never fully get a handle on, as much as (2) the contingency of culture, its principled openness to reworking. In both respects, the Symbolic is the "Big Other." Specifically with respect to the order of meaning, Lacan's notion of the Symbolic gives equal due to (1) the *process of symbolization* by which we bring into the order of meaning that which was and to some extent remains partially opaque and (2) the *products of symbolization* into which we are born and through which we acquire our cognitive and relational bearings. In other words, Lacan's notion of the Symbolic gives equal due to (1) our relation to that which forever exceeds us (the Real, phenomenality in excess of schematization, the enigmatic quality of signifiers, especially master signifiers[173]) and (2) the determinate forms (structures of meaning, norms, identity categories, etc.) that are always already sedimented as our dominant cultural horizon and into which we are unavoidably, if incompletely, recruited. It gives equal weight to (1) the *form-giving impulse* by which we attempt to symbolize that which is, at the limit, inimical to determinate symbolization and (2) the *formative givens*, the cultural conditioning through which our impulses and sensations are proximally and for the most part mediated.[174] Or with respect to the order of values and relational norms, the Symbolic names the hegemonic universalization by which particular judgments and practices come into social prominence, become entrenched and internalized, passed on from generation to generation, eventually becoming the backdrop of everyday life, the normative texture of the ordinary. But it also speaks to the ways in which these values and norms (and their ritual, institutional, etc. bearers) are forever contestable and revisable. Social norms, however hegemonic, are placeholders for the abiding question of the good and other such existential questions, questions that resist being laid to rest. The Symbolic order is orientative for social life but never sufficiently orientative to quell the existential questions to which it responds or block social developments that seek to respond to these questions in new ways. Though it may become oppressively stagnant, the social cannot be sutured.[175]

For Lacan, because the basic unit of the Symbolic, indeed the basic unit of the psychic, is the signifier[176]—the kernel of nonmeaning that spurs (motivates and inhibits) the meaning-making process—the Symbolic is always potentially unstable, amenable to developing and reconsolidating otherwise. The Symbolic names the coming-into-prominence of meanings, patterns, forms, identities, values, etc. from out of an abyss of indeterminacy that lines them, causing them to quiver. *Form vibrates with the insistent excess of that which it attempts to articulate.* On the side of the subject, this excess is associated with the anxiety of freedom. On the side of the object, it is associated with phenomenal excessiveness or sublimity (*objet a*). The Symbolic thus names (attention to) the presentification of that which will never be fully present, the surging into perspicuous form of that which is ultimately enigmatic and elusive. The Symbolic is the bearer of an insistent question, a provocation that throws us into a state of permanent unrest—whether the unrest of creative cultural work through which the reigning Symbolic is transformed or the unrest of ongoing efforts to reconsolidate the Symbolic status quo. This "question" has many names: the dimension of the Real, the enigmatic signifier, phenomenalization, the sublime, the insistence beyond or below existence, maybe even Being (in excess of its epochal determinations) or the question of the meaning of Being.

As should be clear, the coherence of the Symbolic is an effect of hegemony. Lacan tends to discuss the achievement of hegemony in terms of the working of the master signifier, *trait unaire*, or *point de capiton* (the "quilting point" that binds together a series of heterogeneous elements in a way that seems to produce, and in certain respects does produce, a homogenous fabric). This is to say, Symbolic coherence is itself Imaginary: a product of our penchant to home in on determinate and stable form, the appearance of stability and consistency forged by social power. For instance, from Lacan's standpoint the stability and coherence of an order of meaning is produced by authoritative identifications of certain signifiers with certain signifieds or by the authoritative grouping of certain terms in determinate relations (x, y, and z are instances of v; a:b::b:c). Notice in this light how Klein's authority arises in conjunction with, perhaps from, her success in alleviating Dick's anxiety, in providing him with a partial escape route from the diffuse cloud of anxiety in which he is enveloped (an escape route that is, perhaps, experienced as the path to the promised land), and how this authority, paradoxically condition for and conditioned by her success, allows her to identify certain signifiers with certain signifieds (this is Dick train, this is daddy train), align certain experiences (Dick runs to the space between the doors) with determinate meanings (Dick is attracted to and frightened by dark mummy), and establish certain relations (Dick is to the little train as daddy is to the big train; perhaps Dick's "little" desire to roll to the station/mummy is proportional to daddy's "big" desire to roll to the station/mummy, or at least a relation is established between Dick's desire to roll the train to the window/station and his desire for mummy) in a way that is compelling, binding for Dick. For Lacan, it is social power, or, more broadly, *authority*, that keeps meaning univocal and relations fixed. The gap between authority and absolute sovereignty is what secures the contingent space of the Symbolic, and it is this gap that, Lacan fears, Klein renders inconspicuous, even partially sutures.

As much as the Symbolic is a sedimented product of human practices, it belies our sovereign conceit. The Symbolic is the Other in the sense of that into which we cannot intervene without being controlled by it in ways we will never fully comprehend. We are spoken by language even as we speak (because the domain of the speakable is conditioned, if not fully determined, by prevailing regimes of intelligibility and because our words, as they resonate with intended and, as is always possible, unintended addressees, may signify in ways that exceed our control). Once an action is performed, i.e., taken up within the Symbolic matrix, it may always initiate consequences that exceed its determining intentions. To give one final example, we are alienated in the Symbolic insofar as the terms or roles through which we understand ourselves are not fully our own, insofar as these terms or roles are imbued with resonances and trajectories that we have not put into them. The Symbolic is as much the site of the personalization, the singular redirection or reinflection, of meanings and values as it is.

With this initial elucidation of the Symbolic guiding our way, we can further clarify Lacan's disagreement with Klein over how to understand what transpired and is at stake in Dick's treatment. From Lacan's perspective, Klein's authoritative "symbolic equations" may have released Dick from the brunt of his overburdening anxiety, but the risk of this procedure is that Dick will become blind to the contingent dimension of the Symbolic into which these interpretations induce him, blind to the contestability of the authority that holds the symbolic equations together. To name one implication among many, Dick may be forestalled from the creative development of a singular subjectivity, from symbolizing his affective life, wanting which his Symbolic universe may eventually become stale and collapse. The riveting authority of Klein's Oedipalizing interpretations may result in their reification; it is not just that these interpretations implant the phantasies they seek to describe, they establish these phantasies as the nonnegotiable terms of Dick's experience. His unconscious is articulated by the discourse of the Other. "[T]he child symbolizes the reality surrounding him out of this palpitating cell of symbolism which

Melanie Klein has provided him with" (*Seminar I*: 85/100; trans. modified following Felman 1987: 114).[177]

Or, if Dick associates his diminishing anxiety with the authority of Klein's interpretations, Klein runs the risk of implanting or activating in Dick a craving for strong, even absolute, authority as the only thing that can alleviate his suffering, or at least as a default mechanism of anxiety alleviation. Might he not become a submissive authority addict (whether the authority be political-ideological, amorous, or sensual)? Are there not profound personal and political dangers residing in Kleinian practice?

Dick's induction into the Symbolic throws him deep into the Imaginary. What is performatively figured by Klein's authoritative identifications is perhaps an image of herself as a godlike—omniscient and omnipotent—redeemer who can grant relief from his suffering and bestow upon him a coherent and complete object world so long as he heeds her Word. Or at least these interpretations may cast Klein in an image of authoritative self-possession that may become enormously enticing to Dick. (Aside from the political dangers to which this enticement may lead, is Klein not enticing Dick to measure himself against a model of sovereignty to which he can never live up, an ideal self-image that may then become a source of endless self-debasement?) Is Klein not positioning herself as Mary? The Mary to whom, more easily than to the Son or the Father, prayers are directed or the Mary who gives birth to God (i.e., to a figure of absolute self-sufficiency)? Or perhaps both at once? To what extent is Klein's phantasy life or counter-transference running the show, Lacan wonders.

Klein claims she is clarifying, Lacan insists that she is saying—and doing—much more than she presumes. Klein thinks she is being descriptive, Lacan suggests that she is highly creative, even covertly identifying herself with the creativity of Maternity and/or the Divine (or at least risks coming across this way). The risk, then, is that Klein will preempt Dick's (1) eventual awareness of the contingent operations of social authority, thus of its amenability to revision, and (2) expression of creative impulses, impulses to creatively symbolize the world and his place in it, to breathe affective life into the dead letter of the Law. In both cases, she risks sapping his spontaneity and planting the seeds of suffering.

The problem with Klein's authoritative identifications, then, is twofold:

First, Dick may become resolutely uncritical of hegemonic formations of meaning, value, etc. for fear that any backsliding from univocity and stability will reactivate a state of dire helplessness in which he will be overwhelmed by diffuse, tormenting anxiety. His would be a phobic world indeed. This is to say, the risk is that Dick will become staunchly and unreflectively entrenched in whatever meaning and value horizons impose themselves upon him most forcefully, that he will become a docile subject par excellence. Or he may become emphatically attuned to, always on the lookout for, absolute authority and despair of its absence, oscillating between hysteria and melancholy. The sociopolitical implications are clear: Dick may end up becoming extraordinarily feeble and pliable, a subject of administration rather than a subject of *desire*. Or what is no better, he may become a surface iconoclast desperately seeking out the true Authority who or that can withstand his critical barbs. Under the guise of a critical, antiauthoritarian disposition, a hysterical search for the genuine artifact can proceed. Or he may succumb to the moaning resentment of compliance: complaining bitterly, he will obey all the same. At stake here is nothing less than his prospects for agential self-assertion, or, in a more overtly political register, for resistance to the eclipse of democracy via bureaucratic rationalization and demagoguery. And if his docility becomes a source of dissatisfaction, as it very well may, Dick may become all too amenable to the "obey authority from above, sadistically trample on those below" mentality cultivated by corporate hierarchies and fascist ideologies. Generally, the risk is that Dick will become rigid, indeed mortified, enraptured by a frozen Symbolic order or the prospects thereof, perhaps shifting his commitments from symbolic/normative regime to regime but never questioning the one he is in while he is in it (or questioning it only because he hopes to provoke its authoritative rejoinder, its cruel suppression of his insolence)—that is, so long as it can stave off an overt crisis of authority. Or, if there is an overt crisis of social authority, rather than abandoning the social order for one that impresses him as more consistent, stable, and authoritative, Dick might take the hysterical route of unremitting criticism in the hope that, if sufficiently provoked, the faltering social order will right itself, resume its rightful standing as an authoritative and seamlessly coherent totality. Generally, according to Lacan, the hysteric's attacks on the weakness of the Master (the Master does not live up to her mandate, she has betrayed her/our core values, etc.) are appeals for a stronger, more consistent, more authoritative Master. In this case, despite his incessant criticisms, Dick would be rigidly entrenched in the social order whose injustices he relentlessly decries. His critical posture would be the mode of his complicity with, indeed a manner of firm adherence to, the social order he publicly denounces. By vehemently insisting on the need for social transformation, Dick would not be seeking social justice so much as the return of a believable image of totalizing social authority. In either case, Dick would be alienated from the subversive character of *desire*, from the excessiveness of phenomena vis-à-vis their dominant symbolic representations, and from the futurities latent in but suppressed by dominant discourses. The risk, in sum, is that the rigidity of life overburdened by diffuse anxiety will be not relived but replaced by the rigidity of a wholesale commitment to certainty and security. Dick would become Descartes.

To put one more gloss on this first problem: Dick's induction by Klein into the Symbolic is no tentative rendering of drive, affect, and sensation into sense; the order of meanings into which Dick is initiated by Klein's *speech* is suffused with such resounding *certainty* and *clarity* that Dick may become profoundly averse to indeterminacy as such. This would be a sorry state for any subject of the unconscious, all the more so for a subject of modernity. He may come to fear the very contingency of the Symbolic, the in(de)finiteness of *desire,* the upsurge of phenomenality insofar as they threaten regression to his prior state of diffuse anxiety, which is to say, he may become fundamentally averse to himself and his world. Dick, fixed in a zero-sum, either-or mentality in which there is definite meaning and clear value orientation *or* unspeakable terror, would be deprived of the in-between, of the space for reflection, creativity, possibility. And fetishizing his place in the Symbolic, foregoing the exploration of the fates it might hold for him, he may foreclose on his prospects for happiness.[178] Or even if not, he may forego exploring the more radical possibilities opened by *acts* that refuse the comforting coordinates of the given Symbolic regime, *acts* that attempt what seems precisely impossible from the standpoint of the sociosymbolic status quo. Statically fixated and rigid to the core, Dick would fail to heed his *desire.* The risk is that he will become massively averse to risk. Or from a slightly different angle, as a result of the rigidity induced by Klein's authoritative identifications, Dick may fail to negotiate a relation with the Real—with the elements or dimensions of life that cannot be simply assimilated to established patterns of meaning or value horizons and are thus vital sources of personal and cultural innovation. In any case, as a result of the *force* of Klein's interpretations (irrespective of their veracity), specifically as a result of the authoritative force of their clarity and certainty, Dick may become bound to a deeply conservative life course. From Lacan's perspective, Klein is programming an automaton.[179]

Second, Dick may become blind to the social constitution of meaning, thus to its revisability, and as a result he will be ill-equipped to personalize meaning, to find ways through, places in, or modes of inhabiting the Symbolic that feel authentic (responsive to and reflective of his subjectivity, both in its nonexchangeable, singular determinacy as well as in its indefinite plasticity) or at least promising, i.e., opened to a future that may be more accommodating to his needs and desires. This is similar to the worry that Klein covers over the Real and the claims of *desire* with her Imaginary interpretations, but the twist is that this suppression—generally, Klein's enforcement of the standpoint of the ego—may install Dick in an order of meaning and value that is totally gripping yet felt to be utterly external, obligatory yet bereft of personal significance. Sensuousness and symbolism would at one level come apart and at another level be collapsed into a rigid identity, both to devastating effect. If Dick's relation to his own life practices becomes a matter of simply going through the motions, if he participates in cultural institutions, his routines and relationships, etc. not in virtue of their compelling claim on him or in virtue of their potential to accommodate and express his singular *desire* but because the risk of even limited noncompliance is too much to bear, then cultural in general and everyday life in particular would be totally gripping and yet meaningless, inauthentic. Dick would be at once grasped firmly by the dominant discourses and feel himself to be utterly adrift.

The risk is that Klein will induce a posture of passive nihilism: a firm commitment to an order of meaning and value that is not *really* believed in, an order from which Dick will remain at a cynical distance but cannot break free. This would be an order of meaning and value that he "believes in" only in the sense that he truly believes that the Other (initially, Klein) believes in it and that, therefore, *he must* believe in it. All prospects for genuine social bonds—and, by implication, their affective mediations: compassion, empathy, solidarity, etc.—would be devastated. And of course this passive nihilism may be easily exploited by the stern imperatives of a tyrannical superego: because the order of meaning or value is not *really* believed in, the subject can accommodate any number of absurd falsehoods, fanatical delusions, glaring inconsistencies, etc. What's more, the experiential externality of meaning and value may prompt intense paranoid counter identifications, excessive counter investments in the order Dick feels distant from, even unjustly excluded by, to the point that although he feels radically alienated from this order, he can respond in no other way than by assimilating himself to its codes ever more completely. To lay out one more scenario: it may be that as Dick becomes firmly fixed in a symbolic horizon that yet feels artificial, unreal, he will develop an intense paranoia in order to psychically metabolize his discomfiture with the artificiality of the world to which he is bound. And if paranoia is, as Lacan claims, a mechanism of rationalizing one's sense of discomfort and alienation—one's constitutive dislocation—by attributing it to the invidious operations of some determinate other (often an external enemy figure), then Klein's practice may be quite dangerous not only for Dick but for those held responsible for his suffering, prone as they are to become targets of aggression.

Another risk is that if Dick is induced to assume a cynical distance from the meaning of his experiences, the efficacy of his analysis may be severely jeopardized. Bruce Fink lays out the abreaction problem nicely:

> Psychoanalysis shares a problem with a number of the social sciences and humanities, although this may not be immediately apparent. Psychoanalysts, in their work with patients, often find that, despite myriad interpretations and explanations—which both analyst and analysand may find convincing and even inspired—the analysand's symptoms do not go away. A purely linguistic or interpretive analysis of the events and experiences surrounding the formation of the symptoms does not suffice to eliminate them. . . . It is only when the patient is able to articulate his history and *feel something* at the same time—some emotion or affect—that change occurs. (2004: 141–42)

Of course, the first set of dangers is by no means mutually exclusive with the second. What terrors might their conjunction hold in store for Dick?

In the backdrop of Lacan's worry about Klein's work with Dick is the question of how we learn to accommodate ourselves to the truth of our Symbolic condition, which is another version of the question of how we can come into accord with the truth of our (in)determinate *desire.* Accommodating ourselves to the Symbolic is a matter of assuming our alienation *and* our resistance to it. This involves assuming the limitations and discontents that are part and parcel of viable life in a particular social order (sustaining loss rather than attempting to triumphantly transcend or redeem it) *as well as* our resistance to the particular forms these limitations and discontents take.[180] Though repression, frustration, foreclosure, injury, and loss are inevitable, the particular forms they assume are not. Lacan's worry is that, as a result of Klein's astonishing efficacy, Dick will know nothing of this.

We are interpellated into subject positions through which we become legible to ourselves and one another—e.g., recognizable as agents, claim-bearing beings, or potential objects of attachment and so of mourning—only on the condition of the repudiation of certain forms of life, that is, only on the condition of complicity with social policing efforts in which certain forms of life are set on display as uninhabitable. If our forms of attachment, relation, and desire do not sufficiently conform to social norms, ordinarily, they will not find the support they need to be sustained, let alone flourish. Ordinarily, only by accepting social limitation, which means excising, suppressing, or sublimating certain of our aspects or potentials, do we become socially viable—subjects whose forms of life can be socially recognized and supported, subjects who can live in view of a death that may be experienced as a loss rather than a dissolution of an enigma or the decay of brute stuff, thus subjects who can affirm the significance of their lives. Very early on and continually, we learn that love is conditional: we can secure the coveted love, or, more broadly, the recognition of our primary caregivers, and later our social cohorts, only if our manner of desirous relations and pursuits proceed within certain parameters, only if they do not trespass too far into the outskirts of social abjection. Cultural viability implies "castration": the constitutive exclusion of certain forms of life that serve as placeholders within a particular culture for the abject. But however necessary, "foreclosure" is contingently formulated. The abject there will be, though it need not take this or that particular form. Thus, to assume our Symbolic condition, to assume our *desire,* is to avow our limitedness as well as the contingency of various limits.[181] It is to assume both the necessity of "self"-restrictions (the restrictions through which a socially viable self comes to be) and the revisability of the particular forms these restrictions take. For Lacan, the urgency of freedom and the imperfect achievement of it define the human condition,[182] which is to say, from Lacan's perspective, that Klein's authoritative interventions are precisely dehumanizing.

As Dick becomes more interested in and adept with names, this indicates to Lacan that he is becoming interested in their (and his own) place in the Other, in their (and his) relation to the desires, activities, and concerns of others (first Klein, then his nurse, then his parents), or, more broadly, the Other. Dick's interest in language suggests that he is beginning to negotiate his connection to and separateness from others/the Other. Our interest in language, from Lacan's perspective, reflects our becoming a question to ourselves, which is in part a question of where we stand in the "minds," the affective life and concerns, of others. Consequently, it opens the way to the question of where we stand or may come to stand in the Other qua sociosymbolic order. Dick's captivation by language bespeaks an opening onto a world of others and the Other, onto a world in which others have particular intentions, understandings of how things do and should work, as well as projects, desires, and concerns that are, or at least may be, independent of him. Interest in the Symbolic indicates a waning of one's infantile sense of omnipotence and entry into the initial stages of the assumption of subjectivity. What Lacan wants to draw attention to is that Dick begins to work out acceptable forms of connection to and separation from others and the Other as a result of Klein's authoritative identifications, though they may stall his progress at this very early stage. Klein's "symbolic identifications" initiate but also risk shutting down Dick's investment in the Symbolic as a forever fraught domain, as a space characterized by indeterminacy and unsuspected possibility as much as by determinacy and limitation, by multipilicitous displacements as much as by unifying norms, by hegemonic upsurges as much as by the insistent remainder of the heterogeneous. What may be shut down is Dick's capacity to invest and take pleasure in relatively determinate indeterminacy, in the specific but never fully anticipatable progressive potential of his life context, in faint yet glimmering prospects for living otherwise. Authoritatively propelled into a very particular (Oedipal) order of meaning and value, Dick may be inhibited from assuming his *desire*, his agential (though not exactly self-legislating) capacity to unsettle or rework the norms to which he is beholden, indeed his humanity.

A final worry follows from this, namely, that Kleinian practice is at least complicit with and likely enhances her clients' cravings for coherent world pictures and the frustrations that follow therefrom. For Lacan, assuming our Symbolic condition involves avowing both our ineradicable impulse to lend intelligibility to phenomena (the form-giving impulse) and avowing the insuperable resistances of the phenomena we sometimes harass, or may simply cajole, into determinate orders of representation. The nihilistic forces of modern culture and our form-giving impulse converge to make us insatiable glutens for meaning, addicted to coherent world pictures and the possibilities for active intervention into our fates that they promise yet never quite make good on. Kleinian practice would be, on Lacan's reading, a collaborator with modernity's manic drive for meaning. And making matters worse, if the promise of robust agency is one of the major lures through which we become attached to the status quo in *whatever* form it takes, and the promise of robust agency is an element of the attraction of a totalizing world picture, then Kleinian practice collaborates with the most unreflective currents of social conservatism. The promise of unconstrained agency, of absolute autonomy—in other words, the ideology of individualism—energizes and thereby co-opts and distorts our form-giving impulse. As a result, we tend to project enigma, indeterminacy, and excessiveness as ultimately reducible, if only by extirpation, thereby blinding ourselves to the insuperable resistance of phenomena and so condemning ourselves to ceaseless work, endless frustration, perhaps atrocity. What a subject under the sway of Klein's authoritative identifications is unlikely to see is that form-giving is always a matter of giving form to that which resists or exceeds form's determinacy, of channeling into concepts that which remains other to conceptual articulation; what such a client is unlikely to have eyes for is material singularity. If the incessant impulsion to form-giving bespeaks the insuperable resistance of phenomena corralled into form, then our capacities to order and manage the world are limited, though Dick and other such clients will never know this, suffer as they will from their ignorance. What Dick and other such clients will never see is that significance is an intimate admixture of determinacy and indeterminacy, of intelligibility and enigma. Thus they will never be able to assume their form-giving impulse in a manner that allows them to become stewards of form, provisional caregivers of form that may yet fade or develop otherwise, that is, in a way that acknowledges indeterminacy, the fold of life itself, as other than a motivation for the reassertion of form. Klein, inducing her clients to hyperbolically identify with the standpoint of the ego, causes them to suffer frustration in want of an unattainable ideal of meaning without gap.

To be sure, this is all a matter of the *risks* run by Klein's procedure. Also, since accommodation to the Symbolic is a complex and perhaps inconclusive achievement, even if, later, Dick fails in various ways to affirm his Symbolic condition, these failures cannot be wholly attributed to Klein. Not only should we refrain from a blanket condemnation of Klein, we should pose the question that Lacan's critique paves the way for and in some ways gestures at, but does not explicitly address: How does Klein *also* foster the conditions in which Dick might make his way from Imaginary captivation (a one-sided immersion in the Symbolic qua consistent and coherent order of meaning and value) to the truth of the Symbolic? Actually, there are two questions here. First, more concretely, what does it mean to affirm our Symbolic condition? Second, what does Klein do that might set Dick along the path of affirming his *desire*, his lack or finitude, the fullness of his Symbolic condition? Though quite critical of Klein, on his own terms Lacan should be—perhaps he is?—deeply appreciative of Klein's contributions to Dick's capacity to transition from Imaginary captivation to a more full-fledged assumption of his Symbolic condition, his *desire*.

One way to affirm one's Symbolic condition is to identify with one's current social positioning *when this is done in a certain manner*. To identify with one's particular place in the social order as a given datum, as a necessary fact or fate enjoined by History, Destiny, or Divinity, or by one's analyst or party leader, is to deny the contingency of the Symbolic, the in(de)finite—not unlimited, but open and uncertain—possibilities it harbors. However, one might identify with one's particular place in the social order by assuming one's social (ethnic, national, religious, gendered, sexual, etc.) particularity *as an index of finitude*. This would mean affirming one's limitedness and partiality, affirming that one is "not all," by assuming one's complex social particularity rather than taking a cynical distance from social identifications and thereby preserving a sense of subjective purity beneath "compromised" social appearance. It would mean a fuller accommodation to the Symbolic.

But this alone is insufficient. To affirm one's Symbolic condition is also to assume one's social particularity in a manner that sustains its availability to transformation. Social intelligibility requires that one assume some particular, recognizable identity coordinates, but a more full the affirmation of the Symbolic involves an affirmation of a *minimal distance* between the identifications one assumes and one's abyssal truth, the truth of in(de)finite *desire*.[183] What this affirmation will mean in practical terms is hard to say at this level of generality, but certainly it is no mere cognitive achievement. Neither is it a matter of cool, ironic detachment from the identifications one nonetheless assumes. Rather, it is a matter of performing social identities in a way that displays a commitment to the norms of which they are permutations and yet keeps them available as sites for reconfiguration, available to the insurgence of *desire* and the creative transformations that may follow. It is a matter of exemplary inhabitation, of personalizing one's roles, and thereby keeping them publicly available for inhabitation otherwise. It is a matter of living one's identifications such that they are always already given over to the other. It is a matter of learning how to live in the liminal zone between the abyss of *desire* and the fixation of the Imaginary. The minimal distance between the roles we assume and the truth of our abyssal *desire* is lived when our social identifications are experienced as both comforting, practically indispensable sources of social orientation—more, as valid, thus something that would be betrayed if abandoned—*and* as subtly fractured by the insurgence of *desire*, by the *desire* to live and love (which means also to hate) otherwise, by the desire to see what these identifications might become as *we* live them out. Affirmation of the Symbolic, then, involves critical inhabitation of one's identifications; it is thus to risk performing social roles in ways that may not be immediately legible as permutations of the relevant norm, and so to risk failure, and, at the limit, social death. Affirmation of the Symbolic succeeds and fails as modernist artworks succeed and fail. Such works succeed when their claim to be art, despite the fact that they are unrecognizable as art by prevailing criteria, thus formally ugly, is approved, acknowledged in its evidence beyond logical derivation or empirical demonstration. To succeed is to reinvent the meaning of art (via one's particular medium), and so to warrant succession, which means that success—or one dimension of it, redefining the meaning of (the) art—is necessarily inconclusive. Analogously, reconfiguring the norm it claims to instance but clearly does not fall neatly under is how a critical inhabitation of a social role succeeds. It fails, like modernist art fails, when the look of a promising future turns out to be but semblance, i.e., when inheritance proves unworkable.

Or affirming our place in the Symbolic is a matter of keeping ourselves minimally attentive to, and at times allowing ourselves to be propelled into different courses of life by, the discomfort and uneasiness we face in fitting ourselves (or being violently coerced into) into social categories, wondering Is *that* really all there is to me? Affirming the Symbolic, then, means sustaining awareness of our suffering from categories that tend to highlight our social substantiality, or recognizable social identity, rather than our processes of and prospects for becoming otherwise. Or, affirming our place in the Symbolic may be a matter of acknowledging the *inevitable* inconsistency of our social roles or our manner of performatively recasting them. For the violation of the normative demands of the identity categories to which we are committed gives an oblique indication of our unreconciled and irreconcilable *desire*. In any case, what is at stake in acknowledging the Symbolic is an acknowledgement of contingency, inconsistency, lack—in a word, "castration."

From Lacan's perspective, what is at stake in Dick's case is, in part, the assumption of "castration," that is, traversing the fantasy of omnipotence or otherwise assuming his (and, at another level, our) inconsistency and lack. Insofar as she contributes to this, Klein is due recognition. Though she may position herself as a figure of limitless authority, at least she counteracts Dick's inability to acknowledge his dependency (recall his refusal to call out to others for help) and the significance of others (initially, he treats her as indistinguishable from the room's furniture), both of which may suggest strong undercurrents of omnipotence feelings or radical alienation from the finitude implied by insuperably expositive, relational, and desirous life. By helping him acknowledge his dependency and the independence of others, Klein establishes, or at least initiates, two conditions necessary for Dick to assume the truth of his Symbolic condition: explicit recognition of lack and explicit recognition of otherness. Dick will be able to repudiate, complicate, or nuance Klein's authoritative interpretations, or any authoritative interpretations for that matter, only if he recognizes his lack, specifically his lack of fit with the identity categories through which he becomes intelligible to himself and others. Though the recognition of his nonabsorption by the social categories into which he is nonetheless recruited may be a long time coming, it is to Klein's merit that she may have started him down the path toward it by inducing him to acknowledge the gap between self and other, specifically, the gap between others' desires and his own (manifest in the question, What do the others desire such that they are not immediately here to answer my call?).

If accommodation to the Symbolic requires our infantile sense of or desire for omnipotence and completion to fade sufficiently to be able to acknowledge that we cannot have it all or be it all, that what is boundless is nothing but finitude, then even if Klein's interventions inhibit Dick from experiencing the boundlessness of *desire* and so from experiencing himself and his world as possessed of in(de)finite possibilities worthy of consideration, even if she is responsible for a great deal of Dick's Imaginary rigidity, even if she implants or encourages a desire for a complete and fully satisfying reconciliation of self and other, at least she curbs his belief in his omnipotence and completeness. Or if one is convinced that Dick's overwhelming anxiety is not remotely compatible with a sense of omnipotence and completion or even with the desire for omnipotence and completion, that is, if one is convinced that Dick's anxiety must have been so all-consuming that the very ideas of omnipotence and completion could not even make sense to him, then one could still say that insofar as Klein breaks up the diffuse barrier of anxiety that immunizes Dick from concern with others and orients him in a world that is, quite clearly, not simply of his making (*she* is the one laying out its basic coordinates), she paves the way for his assumption of finitude. Klein's interpretive authority may be too heavy-handed, but at least it attunes Dick to an Other, to an Outside, to his limits. And only once Dick recognizes the Other may he become interested in carving out a place for himself in it.

What's more, through the authoritative interpretations by which she makes it clear that the world is not simply reducible to his perspective on it (existence is not just a blanket of diffuse anxiety; there are determinate objects in determinate relations), perhaps to some extent Klein initiates Dick into an eminently *interpretable* world. That is, the unintended effect of Klein's authoritativeness may be to suggest to Dick that the meanings she establishes, the phantasies she elaborates, may not be the only way of seeing things. As the compelling force of his prior perspective fades, it may come into view *as a perspective*. And this may become the basis for questioning the fit between phenomena as such and their perspectival presentations, a germinal moment of critical consciousness. Or the striking force of Klein's interpretations may suggest that this is how things are *for her*. Her emphatic authority may work against itself, suggesting not that "this is how it *is*" but "this is how *I* see it" or "how you *must* see it." Though Klein's authority may captivate Dick, though it may compel him to see things her way, it may also indicate, now or later, that this is *a way* of seeing things, *her way*.

Following Lacan's lead by attending to the *unintended effects* of Klein's speech, we can say that, though her interpretations may promote Imaginary fixation, they may to some extent counteract it as well, or at least establish the conditions for its eventual questioning and unsettling. Even if Klein's interpretations interpellate Dick into a world structured by univocal, stable meanings and fixed relations, the act of interpretation itself—the level of *speech*—may convey something that the authoritativeness of the interpretation suppresses: that the phenomena identified by the interpretation (e.g., the space between the doors and dark mummy) are not simply identical, that there is a difference between phenomena and their phantasmatic meanings or between phenomena and their meanings for others. Though Klein induces Dick into a propositional attitude ($x = y$), the extreme force with which she does so may partially counteract itself: her interpretations might be heard as insisting on, or just dimly suggesting, an equivalence of *different* terms. Though the authority of her voice foregrounds the equivalence, perhaps the act of identification itself brings into view, however faintly, the *differences* of the terms identified, her assertiveness overflowing and counteracting its intent. In this way, Klein's hyperbolic identifications may both highlight and suppress the in(de)finite interpretability of the world and thereby establish a crucial condition for Dick's accommodation to the Symbolic. Or, more immediately, they may pave the way for Dick to recognize the difference between his phantasmatic interpretative schemas (perhaps implanted by Klein) and the world as subject to construal otherwise. This may be the germinal moment of reality testing (which of course Klein and Lacan understand very differently), which (on either interpretation) may be crucial to Dick's capacity to resist or recast the hegemonic terms of the Symbolic and thereby accommodate himself to its (in)determinate truth.

To summarize this first thread: perhaps, paradoxically, precisely by means of the striking authoritativeness of Klein's interpretations, she may expose Dick to a world in which meaning is neither invented or imposed by him nor intractably given. Or, if this seems too generous, one can still appreciate that as Klein exposes Dick to a world populated by beings who are at least to some degree independent subjects (Klein, nurse, mother) she paves the way for him to assume his finitude, to develop relations with, forms of connection to, and separateness from others.

Now onto the second thread. Inhabitants of this world think, sense, and want from particular perspectives. As we have seen, to affirm that we are *not all*, that our position and perspective, though compelling, is one among in(de)finitely many, a provisional stabilization that may yet give way to something new, is to affirm ourselves as enfolded within the Symbolic. Affirming our place within the Symbolic is a matter of simultaneously acknowledging our social reification and our in(de)finite possibilities for becoming otherwise as we discover/create the unsuspected fates that our Symbolic horizons will have held in store. This involves risk, great risk (e.g., the risk of social death, or sometimes physical death, as in the cases of Woolf, Plath, and Tsvetaeva) and so great courage. Insofar as Klein promotes in Dick a sense of security and self-assurance, insofar as she opens him onto a world that is much more intelligible and hospitable to his development, perhaps she establishes, or at least contributes to the consolidation of, another condition necessary for his accommodation to the Symbolic: the possibility of courage. Perhaps the risk of implanting Dick in an order of stable and univocal meanings and relations is coextensive with the possibility of delivering him to a world sufficiently regulated to feel at ease in and in which to gain his bearings; and perhaps only if he feels relatively at ease and sufficiently well-oriented will he start taking risks.[184] If acknowledgment of the Symbolic involves owning up to both our unity and our splitness, to our cultural moorings as much as our constitutive dislocatedness (dis-possession by the unconscious, by *desire*, by others and the Other), to our deep tendencies and structuring habits as well as to our insatiable and world-opening *desire*, and if a baseline sense of security and agential efficacy is necessary to attend to the complexities and indeterminacies of ourselves and our world, and so to forge a future that might yet be ours in ways the status quo surely is not, then Klein's provisioning Dick with a greater sense of security and self-assurance, her imparting of a sense of being grounded and placed, her ability to make him see that others care for him and can alleviate his anxiety, as well as everything she does that contributes to the development of his ego and so to his sense of self-possession, coherence, and competence, may be important precursors to Dick's capacity to accommodate his Symbolic standing.

Now onto the third and final thread. Lacan maintains that we are conveyed into the Symbolic by the paternal metaphor, that is, by internalizing prohibition, by accepting that you can have this but not that, that you can be many things but not everything to everybody. Insofar as prohibition gives rise to a sense of oneself, and, more broadly, the human horizon (or more), as emphatically, irredeemably lacking, wanting, the establishment of "castration" is a manner of induction into the Symbolic. However, if one accommodates oneself to various prohibitions (weaning, toilet training, restricted forms of intimacy with one's kin, etc.) with the expectation that ultimately they will be lifted,[185] on the basis of a belief that obedience now is somehow necessary for fulfillment later, the assumption of finitude that the paternal metaphor is supposed to effect has not fully taken hold. And this is regularly the case. The father is no sovereign. At first, internalizing the paternal metaphor perhaps cannot but be a matter of acceding to the various demands of others—obedience as a ploy of Imaginary seduction. Hopefully, though, this initial accession plants the seeds from which a more robust sense of incompleteness grows. Even ideally, though, full internalization of the paternal metaphor would mean nothing less than irrevocably shutting down omnipotence and utopia as possible horizons of experience or expectation, a resolute acknowledgement that neither self nor other can be perfectly fulfilled. Only sustaining the discovery of the *ineliminability* of lack (both in oneself and in the other) and the forms of life that proceed on this basis amount to a successful internalization of the paternal metaphor; assuming finitude is a complex accomplishment never fully achieved.[186]

The paternal metaphor, otherwise known as the Law or Name of the Father, stipulates that life is full of indefinitely many *but limited* possibilities that human lack cannot be filled in. One might imagine—captivated by the Imaginary, we tend to imagine—that it is social norms (e.g., courtly etiquette or a repressive political regime) or particular invidious persons or groups that keep us from absolute fulfillment. As a result of the incomplete assumption of "castration," one's life often becomes intermittently given to, or, in certain cases, dominated by, aggression, revolt, or rivalry through which one seeks to overthrow the various gatekeepers barring the way to resplendent bliss (which means given to identifying—to some degree creating—new ones when previous successes fail to yield the desired result). We tend to be lured by the insistence of an infantile sense of omnipotence into believing that lack or want is itself contingent rather than contingently articulated. The crucial distinction is between a sense of one's current limitations as contingent and a sense of limitation itself as contingent. It is the latter that would be shut down by the paternal metaphor. To the degree that the paternal metaphor is effective, one acknowledges the constitutive "castration" of the human condition, whence such impossible rebellion becomes less likely—not that rebellion becomes less likely, but rebellion that imagines the end of the need for rebellion, subversion, ever renewed effort, rebirth, the unending oscillation of destruction-construction becomes less likely. But, as noted, the assumption of the paternal metaphor may be forever in jeopardy due to our Imaginary proclivities.

Now we can see that Lacan's claim that Klein's interpretations are Oedipalizing means not only that she grafts an Oedipal narrative onto his experiences, which only questionably fit its parameters, but that she is the bearer of the paternal metaphor, more specifically, that through the force of her interpretations, through the authority of her speech, she succeeds in generating a rift in the unbearably homogenous anxiety in which Dick is submerged. However ambivalent and incomplete the accomplishment, Klein succeeds in opening a gulf between

Dick and others, between his desires and theirs (or whatever it is that keeps them from immediately and perfectly responding to his). Her interpretations expose Dick to lack, to his need for others and perhaps to the lack in others, that is, to others' desires as both directed at and beyond him—desires into which he can insinuate himself but can never fulfill or even captivate exclusively. In this way, Klein opens the prospect that someday Dick will be able to acknowledge (1) not just this or that particular need or want for others but his *constitutive* dependency and (2) that others are irrevocably unfulfilled, wanting and imperfect, unable to administer a perfect world. Were he to do so, he would be on the way to a more complete accommodation to the Symbolic.

Recall that, initially, Dick treats Klein "as if she did not exist, as if she were a piece of furniture. And nevertheless she speaks to him. She literally *gives name* to what—until then has been, for this subject, nothing but reality pure and simple [i.e., reality as pure, undifferentiated positivity, not reality as fundamentally interpretable, which is how Lacan regularly uses the term[187]]—certainly, he already has a certain apprehension of some syllables, but . . . he does not assume them" (*Seminar I*, 83; trans modified following Felman 1987, emphasis added). What Lacan seeks to underscore is that Klein's speech intrudes into the all-too-stable enclosure of Dick's anxiety. The question, then, is Did Dick so readily respond to Klein's interpretations because they corresponded to his fantasies (Klein's view) or because they verbalized, gave form to, his inchoate suffering (Lacan's view) and perhaps alluringly indicated that he too might learn to do so, i.e., become, like Klein, a subject of language (a Lacanian view, perhaps Lacan's)? On Lacan's reading, Klein's speech intrudes into Dick's solitude, into the fusion of the Imaginary and the Real, and breaks it open. She opens Dick onto the in(de)finite life of *desire* or at least the prospect thereof; her speech implants enigmatic signifiers that may forever mobilize meaning and desire. From this perspective, Klein's speech—naming, equating, interpreting, narrating—does not so much speak the truth (content) of Dick's unconscious as it installs him on the Other scene; the efficacy of her interpretations is not really a matter of either their validity or their ability to localize and diffuse anxiety but of her *symbolic graft*. What Lacan stresses is that Klein initiates Dick into a life of desire-suffused symbolism, allows him to "assume" his place in a symbolic order irreducible to either her intended meanings or the meanings with which he may one day seek to replace hers, a symbolic order necessarily incomplete because belated with respect to the affective life it shapes. What is at issue is not anxiety dissipation as much as the institution of a rupture, a gap between signifier and signified. What is at stake is the assumption of "castration" and the role of Klein's *speech* in initiating it.

As the bearer of the paternal metaphor, Klein allows Dick to see that meaning is given by the Other (initially Klein but perhaps eventually the Other qua Symbolic order; or perhaps Dick already senses that the Other, some anonymous authority, is speaking through Klein), that meaning is in some sense anonymous (might not the anonymity of meaning be conveyed by the immediacy and authority of Klein's interpretations? Might their matter-of-fact character not suggest that they are simply given, true, parts of the metaphysical architecture rather than Klein's personal speculations?), beyond his control (whether meaning comes from Klein or from the Other, it does not come from him) and even his understanding (does he really understand what Klein means when she says that Dick is in dark mummy?), perhaps ultimately beyond anyone's control and understanding.

What's more, even if Klein coerces Dick into the Oedipal narrative she assumes is structuring his experience, at least this narrative allows him to experience others as significant, to experience his desire for others, to experience others as desiring something other than himself (e.g., the standard Oedipal parents' desire for one another) and perhaps to question what others want, what they are lacking (e.g., why their behavior does not simply conform to his desires or why, if what they want is truly one another, they are still unsatisfied). For Lacan, Klein's interpretations overlay Dick's inchoate experience with meaning yet are perhaps at the same time "castrating" in the sense that they impart to and inscribe within him an inescapable and affectively significant *question* about his place within a symbolic and relational horizon that exceeds him and is irreducible to him, yet to which he is bound.

THE SIGNIFIER

The basic unit of the Symbolic, indeed of the psychic, is the signifier.[188] The signifier is a differential element: it may be a phoneme, a word, a sentence, a phrase, a proverb, or any idiomatic unit, so long as it is irreducible.[189] The signifier is a figure for the elemental, a "hard core" that indefinitely resists dissolution into more basic components. More precisely, on the basis of repeated experiences of its indissolubility, the signifier is said—imagined, supposed, acknowledged in its evidence?—to indefinitely resist dissolution. It is a principle of material resistance, an incessant provocation that both calls forth and unsettles meaning. A paradigmatic signifier, then, to give a nonlinguistic example, would be the desire of the other, say, the inchoate yet decidedly impacting experience of our primary caregiver's desire as it calls forth but cannot be reduced to phantasies and other manners of meaning-determination. The signifier is a force of attraction and repulsion: it gathers meaning around itself yet thwarts the consolidation of that which it collects. In this respect, the signifier is akin to the Real: we return to it again and again yet can never quite conclusively discern its meaning; it "never stops not being written."[190] For the signifier does not *have* a meaning, at least not in the sense of possessing a stable, clearly defined signified that the proprietary laws of the psychic economy or Symbolic order would secure as *its*. The signifier does not *have* a meaning so much as it sparks the meaning-making process that tends to but can never fully cover over its enigmatic instigation. However hegemonically a signifier is associated with a determinate signified, a signifier is always an enigmatic signifier, a medium of meaning that may be associated with any number of meanings but can never be fully reconciled with any of them:

> Interpretation . . . has the effect of brining out an irreducible signifier. . . . What is there is rich and complex, when it is a question of the unconscious of the subject, and intended to bring out irreducible, *nonsensical*—composed of nonmeanings—signifying elements. . . . Interpretation is not open to all meanings. It is not just any interpretation. It is significant interpretation, one that must not be missed. This does not mean that it is not this signification that is essential to the advent of the subject. What is essential is that he should see, beyond this signification, to what signifier—to what irreducible, traumatic, non-meaning—he is, as a subject, subjected. (*Seminar XI*: 250–51)

Whence the enigmatic quality of the signifier? Its enigma results from its moorings in the body and in the expositive and relational matrix of human life. The signifier reaches down into the depths of the body, into the undercurrents of affection, and though it names the surfacing of significance, it respects, indeed expresses, the material mystery the body remains. The signifier is bodily life surging into, overflowing, and unsettling the order of signification.[191] Or, one might say, the signifier names the nascent, prediscursive meaningfulness of a bodily event, whether this event arises from "within" (a drive surge, an experience of need) or from "without" (the experience of an other's desire as somehow impacting on and implicating oneself), being brought into the order of meaning. The enigmatic quality of the signifier bears witness to an imperfect alliance between experience and meaning. The signifier is the impact of experience insofar as it impresses us as inchoate yet somehow significant, insofar as it presses into but is not identical with the order of meaning, insofar as it motivates yet outstrips meaning-making. It is the haunting element that, however authoritatively associated with various meanings, keeps them at some level in question: "the signifier . . . materializes the agency of death" (*E*: 16/24; trans. modified).[192]

While Klein and many other analysts are committed to some version of an "anatomy is destiny" thesis, e.g., are concerned with erogenous zones and the phantasies that, purportedly, they naturally inspire, Lacan is concerned with the enigmatic kernels, the signifiers, the metabolization of which gives rise to a partition of the body into erogenous zones (a somatic schematization) and thus to an imaginary morphology, both of which conceal but cannot fully efface the enigma of the signifier, the yet-to-be-decided significance of experience. Though the signifier, like the Real, is elusive, definitionally resistant to objective presentation, for Lacan, it insists time and again, resisting *and* motivating the establishment of meaning, self-images, and even forms of bodily organization.

On a linguistic plane, the signifier is always a floating signifier, a plexus or container that, however historically freighted, carries meaning through an indefinite detour, keeping it open, unstable, punctuated with a question mark. The signifier does not incarnate a prior ideality but is rather enmeshed in a vast web of associated signifiers that it "means" in the sense of drawing them into the horizon of meaning, associating to them or activating them, thereby simultaneously enhancing and in(de)finitely deferring the consolidation of meaning.[193] (More classically but imprecisely put, the differential relation of the totality of signifiers yields meaning. The imprecision of the classical Saussurian statement follows from its eclipse of the diachronic and of the bodily, relational, and expositive matrix expressed by the enigma of the signifier.) For instance, as a particular signifier is pronounced, it calls into the horizon of meaning, with greater or lesser intensity and consequence, other signifiers with which it has become, or is now, as a result of the particular utterance, associated in the singular psychic matrices of speaker and addressee. These associations open new horizons, introduce new dimensions and resonances, that cause the intended meaning to swerve—not to a new terminus at which meaning would be finally given, but into a labyrinthine web of proto-meanings and incalculable resonances. Even the most masterful efforts of direct communication cannot but produce indirect and unanticipatable resonances because the terms (or phonemes, sounds, rhythms, images, etc.) deployed are, as a result of their prior usage and psychic metabolization, invested with an wide range of significances and associated with a number of other signifiers that will have been activated with greater or lesser intensity. What we will have meant, what our speech will have opened us and our interlocutors onto, cannot be stabilized by sovereign intention. The signifier is an anticipation of meaning, an element of the future: what keeps meaning (in)determinate, yet-to-be-resolved by the regulatory violences that inevitably intrude upon the scene of indefinite resonance.

For instance, a period or other such grammatical device may retroactively determine the meaning of the signifiers that compose a sentence (given that my utterance went *there*, I must have meant such and such all along), but the retroactive stabilization of meaning cannot entirely suppress the pathways of significance opened and resonances provoked by signifiers as the sentence is articulated. There is more laden in the (temporalized) whole than can be comprehended by the form of attention that seeks to integrate its various parts into a consistent and coherent unity. This is the basis for Lacan's objection to hermeneutics: returning to the parts out of which a "whole" (sentence, paragraph, text, etc.) is composed in view of our provisional understanding of that whole may surely advance our understanding of each part and of their relations, and this process of return may, in turn, give rise to a renewed understanding of the whole that, then, may motivate a return to the various parts, which again gives rise to a new view of the whole, and so on ad infinitum, but the implicit commitment to the part/whole framework of interpretation detracts attention from the horizons of meaning and resonance that each part, *dissociated from the whole*, opens onto.[194] As we read with an eye to the whole, we gloss over the *holes*, the vortexes of significance, the fractures in the composite structure, which, if attended closely, may, and likely will, lead in directions that cannot be comprehended by the orbit of the whole. Lacan's emphasis is properly *analytic* in the sense of dissolving the bonds of meaning in order to liberate our attention, allow us to focus on and follow the trajectories of the elements out of which intentional meanings are composed, and in order to emancipate experience from the rigid meanings from which we suffer.[195] And of course, though his emphasis does not fall here, dissolving the bonds of meaning is a condition for their creative recomposition.

Lacan is interested in the process of enunciation more than its intentional aim. He is interested in what has not been fully said, what echoes in the darkest and most remote corridors of meaning, in what is most dimly alluded to or unwittingly initiated through intentional communication. Lacan listens to all speech as poetry, or, more precisely, as *poeisis*. He attends most closely to the *effects* of signification, to what speech acts will have meant when one is prompted to tarry with their various components and movements; to what speech acts will have effected in a particular interlocutory situation; to what speech will have effected in the psychic economies of the addressor and addressee. Lacan is interested, for instance, in what Klein's speech will have given rise to more than what Dick's behavior or statements supposedly mean within the context of her favored schemes of intelligibility (e.g., the Oedipus myth). In contrast, Klein is interested in the *content* of signification, in what various objects, processes, or relations are identified with in Dick's psychic economy, and especially his phantasy life.

From Lacan's perspective, again, the risk is that Klein's focus on content will be mimetically incorporated by Dick, propping up the standpoint of the ego and so contributing to his Imaginary ensnarement. Specifically, her desire to understand may motivate Dick to seek clean and coherent understanding as a way of working out what he needs to do in order to be "good," in order to secure the love of the Other that, presumably, is the condition for his fulfillment, or at least for avoiding the worst. Lacan is concerned with the *effects* of Klein's interpretive performance more than with their veracity. As much as Lacan emphasizes and habituates his addressees to tarry with ambiguity, with the complex admixtures of determinacy and indeterminacy that cohabit each instance of speech, Klein emphasizes and habituates Dick (and her readers) to focus on determinate meanings, to locate the meaning of behaviors, dreams, history, feelings, etc. in the narratives she will provide or prompt her addressee(s) to "discover."

While Klein's model signifiers are clear, recognizable components of pre-Oedipal and Oedipal narratives (the space between the doors *is* dark mummy), Lacan's model signifiers are culled from dreams and symptoms precisely because these signifiers are uncoupled from their sedimented semantic histories and conventional ties to particular signifieds. In a dream or a symptom, Lacan suggests, anything can refer to and be associated with anything else.[196] To make the clinical implications of this difference clear: for Lacan, it is because signifiers are uncoupled from their conventional signifieds in dreams and symptoms that the analyst's tasks are to (1) diminish the force of the analysand's structures of defense as much as possible, e.g., to weaken the analysand's proclivity to render certain meanings inadmissible, (2) refrain from interpreting or coming across as "knowing" as much as possible, especially in the early stages of analysis, and (3) encourage the free associations by which the analysand returns to certain signifiers again and again, discovering and creating their significance in the course of repeated encounters, for only thereby may the analysand reach the core signifiers around which turn *both* the latent and manifest content of the dream or meaning of the symptom. Implicitly, Lacan's conception of the signifier situates Kleinian practice (and most other forms of psychoanalysis) as superficial and potentially counterproductive.

For Lacan, though elusive, indeed, like the Real, definitionally resistant to objective presentation, signifiers are most conspicuous in *speech*, specifically in speech understood as the speech of the subject that, bearing the eventfulness of bodily life, overflows with impulses and resonances that cannot be expressed in propositional utterances. Significance is more gesture than accomplishment. Thus Lacan maintains that "half-saying is the internal law of any kind of enunciation of the truth" (*Seminar XVII*: 110/127; trans. modified). This is to say, speech that speaks the truth speaks more than the person speaking or any interlocutor, no matter how ideal, can comprehend. Truth can only be half-said because truth is the processual becoming otherwise—the self-discovery/creation—of the desiring subject. Thus our efforts of clear and concise self-exposition fail, lie, repress, half-say our truth. Unveiling veils, confession conceals. Speech is an ex-pression of the subject, the pressing out of allusions, resonances, and impulses, into the field of the Other, whereupon speech, like the subject, loses control. Speech is "full" when it is both full of meanings *and* full of holes, that is, filled up with signifiers that motivate yet elude our habitual forms of intersubjective understanding.[197]

While Klein focuses on certain privileged signifiers, specifically signifiers privileged by her account of pre-Oedipal and Oedipal development, Lacan seeks to systematically deprivilege the signifiers we tend to find most important in order to focus attention on the ambiguity of meaning, the in(de)finitely multiplicitous resonances and asignifying vortices of speech, the genesis of meaning from and its ongoing mediation by experiences of the exposed and vulnerable bodies we are.

Clinically, this is related to Klein's and Lacan's different orientations toward transference. From Lacan's perspective, Klein works with Imaginary transference, ego-to-ego transference. Her ego is attuned to what, she presumes, her client's ego cannot abide but is manifest in the subtext or structure of his transferentially laden discourse and behavior. This discourse and behavior, she believes, is transferentially organized from the beginning: the client is acting out or otherwise involving the analyst in desires and anxieties that have their roots in his relationship to his primary caregivers. Klein, then, will translate this material into ego-syntonic interpretations (interpretations agreeable to both her and her client's ego) in order to allow her client to acknowledge what had been heretofore inadmissible or to support the development of the client's ego with a view to anxiety alleviation. On this reading, Klein's attention is structured by the signifiers privileged by her client's ego/defenses, the signifiers (themes, desires, ideas, etc.) to which the client returns time and again in his associations or makes manifest in his symptoms, behaviors, dream recounting, play, etc. The ego is controlling the scene in three senses: (1) the client's ego selects the signifiers to which Klein will attend: what is negatively privileged by ego, i.e., what the ego defends against, captures Klein's attention; (2) Klein's ego and its imperative for understanding compel her to focus on what can be readily understood within the terms of her privileged interpretive framework; and (3) Klein renders interpretations in a manner that, she believes, will be palatable to her client's ego given its current state of development, context of excitation or distress, etc.[198]

Just because this orientation to transference centers on and consolidates the Imaginary does not mean it is to be avoided, if only because positioning of the analyst as a subject who Knows provokes analysand to speak.[199] Besides, such an orientation allows for important disclosures of affect, desire, and anxiety; and it allows the analyst to home in on the client's projections, introjections, and identifications. But what this orientation will not reveal are the enigmatic dimensions of the client's unconscious signifiers, attunement to which, for Lacan, is crucial both for therapeutic success and for the attainment of the measure of freedom available to us.

There is one further clinical implication of Lacan's effort to systematically deflate the signifiers we tend to find most important and inflate the ambiguous, unfinished character of meaning to which attention must now be drawn. It is related to Lacan's various efforts to undermine the fantasy that the analyst possesses expert knowledge that would allow her to effectively alleviate the analysand's suffering. Through such efforts, he encourages the analysand to take responsibility for her fate, to assume her complicity in her suffering. For only if the analysand acknowledges that the meanings of the experiences, relations, conflicts, etc. from which she suffers are not simply given, intrinsic and immutable, but are at least to some extent her own construction, an effect of her giving shape and weight to relatively inchoate experiences (however strong the natural or social prompting to do so may be), or at least an effect of her ratifying and complying with meanings that may be to some extent naturally or socially inescapable,[200] may she be motivated to work out new ways of negotiating with, new ways of symbolizing, the relevant experiences, relations, etc. (e.g., What am I to the Other? What does the Other desire?).[201] Or at least only on this condition may she be enlivened by the prospect that other interpretations, and so other futures, are possible. Of course, this would be extremely insensitive, indeed downright cruel, if the point were equivalent to the paternalistic injunction "just get over it." Lacan is not saying anything like, "You think you know what happened, but you don't. And it's all just a matter of interpretation anyway, so why go on seeing things in a way that causes you to suffer? Why not just give up your pathological interpretation for something that would suit you better? Why are you doing this to yourself? What's wrong with you?"[202] Rather, his aim is to unsettle the analysand's pathogenic interpretations *as much as possible and in full recognition that they cannot be simply willed away.* Even if new meanings of and possibilities for responding to the questions, conflicts, experiences, etc. from which the analysand suffers are developed, they will coexist alongside the (now subdued) pathogenic interpretations that once prevailed. Hegemony can be broken, perspectives and relational orientations can shift, fixations can diminish, but what was once dominant invariably persists. Though progress may be possible, temptation is ineliminable, thus mourning remains an ever-urgent task. It is precisely due to Lacan's recognition of this point that his clinic aims not at something as ambitious as a cure but at the capacity to achieve and sustain whatever degree of freedom is possible for a particular analysand.[203]

Simply put, from Lacan's perspective, Klein is too content-heavy. But from Klein's perspective, Lacan's refusal to acknowledge the Oedipal significance of children's behavior demonstrates his complicity with a pre- or anti-Freudian desexualization of the child. Generally, his attention to the dissociated, in(de)finitely interpretable element bespeaks a symptomatic evasion of underlying structure. The Lacanian rejoinder, of course, would be that (1) he is downplaying, not denying, the Oedipal dimension and (2) Klein is working with a limited, adultomorphic conception of sexuality (she is genital-centric, etc.). On this latter point, would not Lacan's question be Why not acknowledge the inchoate but impacting, i.e., exciting, experience of enigmatic signifiers and the form-giving impulse they spark as themselves "sexual"? Is not the "pre-Freudian" gesture to conflate sexuality with genitality or a psychosexual developmental trajectory that concludes with normative heterosexual genitality? Maybe, Klein could reply, but are there not, as Dick's case amply demonstrates, good clinical reasons to "overemphasize" Oedipal dynamics? With regard to the general concern about attention to the fragmentary, isolated, and dissolute as symptomatizing an evasion of totality, Lacan would likely have to bite the bullet. However, to mitigate this concern he could of course draw attention to the elements of his practice that conduce to the consolidation of meaning, albeit provisionally: he does not let analysands indefinitely digress from significant motifs, dream recountings, and so on; his punctuation techniques (the short session, scansion, etc.) aim to call a provisional halt to the sliding of signifiers; even isolating a signifier (a loaded term, slip, etc.) from its intended context and emphasizing its enigmatic character makes it available to the retroactivation of different meanings.

The differences between Klein's and Lacan's respective orientations toward signifiers, and, more broadly, symbolism and the Symbolic, may be best illustrated by their different understandings of the phallus.

A criticism commonly leveled at Lacan is that he naturalizes the culturally contingent association between the penis and the phallus and further naturalizes the penis/phallus as *the* definitionally desirable object, the prime mover with respect to which all other longings are derivative. Might this criticism be more appropriately directed at Klein? Though for Klein the phallus is imaginary, that is, imagined to be inside the mother's body, and though it is not the sole object of desire, she insists that the phallus is definitionally desirable within the Oedipal phantasmatics of early infancy, and from there onward. Of course, the twist is that, according to Klein, the phallus is *displaceable* cannot be simply identified with the penis: the phallus names the good stuff inside the mother's body, and though this good stuff is universally phantasized as the father's penis, this is only one of its phantasy forms.[204] But still, in Klein's account the penis/phallus, the phallus *as* penis, even if one element of a larger relay, is posited as desirable by definition. To be sure, Klein's conviction on this matter is predicated on a great deal of analytic experience. But, problematically, this conviction is raised to the level of an axiom and thereby insulated from potentially disconfirming evidence. Come what may, Klein steadfastly maintains that there is intrinsic unconscious knowledge of and desire for the penis/phallus (as well as the breast, etc.).

The point is not to assess the appropriateness of the charge of phallocentrism, whether leveled at Klein or Lacan.[205] Rather, the point is to highlight that, for Klein, the phallus/penis as much as the breast names an object that at the level of phantasy is a *natural correlate* of desire, while for Lacan, as we will see, the phallus indicates, quite to the contrary, the noncorrelation between *desire* and its objects.

Given her duplex model of the mind, Klein will read various clinical presentations as *signs* of phantasmatic contents. Lacan, on the other hand, tends to frame the same clinical material as *symbols* of the in-sistence of *desire*. What is at issue here is not deciding who is correct but rather unpacking the disparate theories of truth implied in these divergent clinical emphases. There is surely interpretive violence on both sides; Klein's emphasis on the phantasmatic meaning of clinical material is no less violent and monofocal than Lacan's emphasis on the material as instantiating, yet again, the exorbitance of *desire*. Klein's understanding of symbolism is bound up with a theory of truth as adequation. On this model, our representations of, say, the phallus can be adequate (or not) to its *given actuality* in the mind of the infant or client. Lacan, on the other hand, is unconvinced that there are universal objects of desire, thus that desire is amenable to systematic theorization, let alone that clinical phenomena straightforwardly refer to such objects or their phantasmatic elaborations. Lacan is far less interested than Klein in *understanding*: he works with a notion of truth as intrinsically excessive of representation and focuses on the (in)determinate *effects of speech* rather than the ostensible *meaning* of speech or behavior. The truth, Lacan stresses, is the truth of the Real: the truth of phenomenalization in excess of schematic presentation; the truth of *desire* as an in(de)finite longing that, though object-oriented, is not quite object-directed—desire loops around various objects and swerves from object to object, never resting content with any of them; it is always on the way to something else, the principle of perpetual natality. To assume that desire is naturally inclined toward various objects, e.g., the breast or the father's penis in the mother's body, is to misunderstand desire completely.

What Lacan's emphasis on the exorbitance of desire brings into view is that Klein's theory of mind turns on an image of mechanical subsumption and translation. It is as if, for Klein, there are preset phantasmatic templates into which various objects or experiences are inexorably slotted.[206] This is an image of mental life as primed from the get-go to narratively configure, or at least formally coordinate, experience—rather peculiar for the great theorist of the death drive, psychotic anxieties, and the like. This is an image of mental architecture as prior to and always to some degree immune from social mediation—rather peculiar for the consummate theorist of primary (erotic and aggressive) sociability. Lacan's theory of the mind, on the other hand, turns on the belief that though schematization is for the most part unavoidable, something as rigid as psychic slotting is (1) at most a culturally and historically particular form of schematization rather than a basic operation of our mental architecture and, (2) even if operative, limited by the enigmatic quality of the signifier and the excess of phenomenality vis-à-vis representation. For Lacan, phenomenality/experience is incompletely assimilable by available "slots" (e.g., phantasy frames), attempted subsumption and containment by which may initiate a reorganization of the presumptively immutable categorical grids and schematic templates.

So, while for Klein the phallus has determinate phantasmatic referents, for Lacan the phallus, at least the Symbolic phallus, is a signifier of the signification process itself[207]: a signifier of the (non)relation, or, more precisely, the contingent and multiform relations, between signifier and signified,[208] *desire* and its articulation, phenomena and their representation, or expectation and satisfaction. In *Seminar XX*, for instance, the phallus is identified with the "bar" between the signifier and the signified (40/39). This suggests that it is the signifier of incompleteness, of lability, e.g., of the unsettled relations between a phoneme and its denotative range and connotative resonances or between desire and its aims and objects. The phallus is essentially plastic. As a signifier of multiplicity, of motility, indeed of signification itself, the phallus is more akin to a symbol than to a sign in that it points to something that cannot itself be made present. It is also important to underscore that, in the Symbolic register, the phallus names insurmountable lack and nonreconciliation; it is the signifier of "castration." "The phallus itself is nothing but the site of lack it indicates in the subject" (*E*: 745/877).

The Imaginary phallus, on the other hand, is the placeholder for *the* object or relation that promises unmitigated and inviolable satisfaction. It is the scaffolding of the Imaginary. The Imaginary phallus is a fantasy image of limitless satisfaction marked—or, more precisely, retroactively posited—as such precisely when it comes into view as off-limits. Prohibition risks exorbitantly amplifying the desire for the prohibited, and not just because the efficacy of prohibition may require ongoing attention to the object *as* illicit; keeping the object at a distance means making it available to unconstrained fantasy. For instance, weaning may mark the breast (and all that is later associated with it via the metonymic and metaphoric operations of desire) as *the thing* that, were we allowed to return to it, would satisfy us completely. Or, to give another example: prohibitions against genital masturbation, genital incest (as opposed to strongly affectionate familial relations), or genital relations before a certain age or outside the sacraments of marriage may mark the genitals as bearing the promise of full and final satisfaction, a promise that would be immediately fulfilled if only the relevant prohibitions were lifted and fully expunged from our psyches. If only we could abolish the law, and thus our inhibitions, guilt, and anxiety, we would enter a domain of absolute sexual bliss. Or so we are duped into believing. For here we can see how the law's elaboration of transgression is a crucial means by which it binds us to its terms: "Transgression in the sense of jouissance is accomplished only by supporting itself on a contrary principle, on the forms of the Law."[209] We may seek to directly or indirectly overthrow the law (e.g., we may chose to ignore the incest prohibition or find a partner who very much reminds us of the prohibited object or, even more indirectly, become vehemently anti-establishment, anti-authority, etc.), but precisely in so doing we allow the coordinates of our desire to be determined by it. Further, since the Imaginary phallus comes into view as a figure of the prohibited, our questing after it will be tinged with anxiety about what the law might do to prevent us from obtaining it or to punish us would our quest prove successful—thus tarnishing its pursuit in advance.[210] And, in part, it is our tendency to convert this anxiety into or defend against it by hyper investing our longing for *that thing* that would bring both our anxiety and our longing to an end that keeps us tethered to the Imaginary, and so to the Law. The intense desirability of transgression may be an effect of the law, a way the law ensnares us in its terms.

The Imaginary phallus is that which one wants to incarnate (to be) or to possess (to have), either directly or vicariously (e.g., by securing a partner who "has" it or "is" it). It thus seems to be a figure for what one desires in one's heart of hearts. But the Imaginary phallus alienates us from our *desire*, from our truth. The Imaginary phallus is an answer to the crucial question upon which Imaginary captivation turns: what does the Other want (of me)? We desire to be or to have whatever would fill the lack in the Other and thereby secure his or her unconditional love and the perfect world we believe this love can provide—this is the Imaginary phallus. What we seem to want most dearly, *our thing*, is what we want to give the Other: in love, Lacan claims, we give the other what we do not have.[211] The Imaginary phallus is the signifier of what I am (not quite, not yet) for the desire of the Other; it is the signifier of the desire of the other. In this way, the phallus is the signifier of both lack (the Imaginary perspective on the present) and possession (the Imaginary anticipation of the future).

It follows that if for a particular individual the penis is the phallus this is because s/he believes—likely in no small part due to widespread cultural subtexts—that this is what s/he must secure (be or have) in order to lock in the all-providing care of the Other. The penis becomes the phallus *when one comes to believe that the penis is what the Other is lacking*. The most pressing question for Lacan, then, is not What is the phallus? (is it the penis, the breast, etc.?) but, rather, How can we avow our *desire* such that the claims of the Imaginary phallus lose their hold on us to the greatest extent possible? For Lacan, the question is How can we open ourselves to the in(de)finite striving of *desire*, how can we cultivate a love for incessant mobility, (in)determinacy, tension, insecurity, etc.?[212]

That the identification of the penis with the phallus is common, indeed extraordinarily so, is in no way denied by Lacan. What he is concerned with is not demonstrating *that* this is the case but rather exploring *how* and *at what cost* this identification takes place. To be sure, at times, Lacan certainly uses the term "phallus" to refer to the penis—especially prior to 1958. But then the question follows: is Lacan assuming a natural correspondence between the penis and the phallus, or is he *deploying* a culturally hegemonic identification? And, if the latter, to what end? We can begin to work out a response to these questions by noting that, for Lacan, though at a particular time in a particular culture the phallus may come to be identified with the penis, this would amount to a hegemonic filling out of an essentially empty placeholder for *that thing* that would fulfill us completely. It would bespeak the cultural prevalence of the Imaginary more than a natural feature of human longing. It is also important to note that, for Lacan, the phallus inevitably participates in both general and idiosyncratic networks of meaning. Within a particular cultural horizon, the phallus names the objects, states, or relations promoted by that culture as manifestly desirable, the greatest goods on offer. But since "culture" cannot sovereignly dictate the desirable, since its power is limited by a crucial medium of its expression, namely, individual instances of desiring that may, and often do, fail to reproduce its decrees perfectly, the phallus also names that which will have become desirable for singular individuals, what we pine for that is illicit from the point of view of, or simply unanticipated by, cultural norms. The phallus, then, is both (1) whatever attributes, abilities, objects, and so on are intensely socially prized and (2) the signifier of nonidentity, specifically of the individual's desire in excess of its cultural conditioning. Using the term this way, as both general and particular, Lacan habituates his addressees to the duel register of the signifier: a signifier, e.g., "phallus," can never be fully dissociated from its sedimented Symbolic determinations, but it may also assume an idiosyncratic valence unanticipated by cultural norms.

Now, I believe, we are in a better position to speculate about why Lacan sometimes so cavalierly refers to the penis as the phallus. When he does so, perhaps he is referring to the socially determined meaning of the phallus, and in so doing, calling upon his readers to own up to the inexorable influence of culture on their desire, to the social mediation, the impersonality, of what is presumptively most their own. Perhaps, for Lacan, vehement insistence that the phallus is *not* the penis symptomatizes a fantasy of personal purity. For the one who says such a thing ("The phallus is *not* the penis!"), perhaps, refusing to cede on what he consciously experiences as *his* desire is *his thing*. Perhaps *his thing* is a fantasy of unmediated authenticity that, paradoxically, contributes to his alienation by securing him to the Imaginary. By "simply" referring to the penis as the phallus, perhaps Lacan is calling on his addressees to acknowledge, following his lead, that the penis, as a placeholder for whatever culture marks as desirable, *does* in fact promise full and final satisfaction. And perhaps he does this because only upon acknowledging their being in thrall to this promise may his addressees take a step toward traversing the fantasy of fulfillment.[213] Just as Freud suggests that mourning requires recollecting the depth and breadth of the lost object's significance,[214] perhaps traversing the fantasy of fulfillment requires recollective return to all the objects around which it has been constituted, traversal being a matter of going through the fantasy *as* fantasy.[215]

Drawing these two threads together, we can now say that in the Symbolic register the phallus names Imaginary fullness *as* Imaginary. The Symbolic phallus is the sublation-cum-explication of the Imaginary phallus: by being it or having it we become keenly aware of our lack, aware that we do not and will not have it, cannot be it. To be or to have the Symbolic phallus is to be "castrated," perhaps to pursue the current incarnation of our *thing* but knowing full well that *this is not it*, that its attainment will not yield paroxysms of bliss or the steady stillness of contentment, and thus, perhaps, to be available to the incessant displacement of desire. This is why Lacan describes phallic jouissance as inevitably disappointing yet almost unavoidably enticing: invariably partial—both incomplete and favoring an object that/who is not-all—it promises more than can be redeemed but promises nonetheless.[216] The phallus is a figure for what we desire or will come to desire that but also a maker of the nonsatisfaction which having or being it—or having a relationship with one who has or is it—inevitably entails, thus a gesture toward the unknown.

The phallus names both (1) the incessant insurgence of *desire* and (2) the captivation of *desire* by *the thing*, by the Imaginary, indicating the inexorable intertwinement of the Symbolic and the Imaginary. The phallus indicates both what we strive after as well as the stance we take toward our desire: fulfillable or not. Its multiple meanings suggest that "it" is not some phantasmatic object to which representations can correspond and of which various clinical phenomena are the sure-fire signals.

The differences between Klein's and Lacan's respective orientations toward signifiers, and, more broadly, symbolism and the Symbolic, are stark. As much as Klein focuses on the *determinate contents* of desire (and anxiety), tending to overemphasize their legibility, Lacan focuses on the (in)determinacy—the pliancy and ambiguity—of *desire*, tending to overemphasize its illegibility. As much as Klein is in thrall of the expectable, even inevitable, objects and vicissitudes of desire (and anxiety), Lacan is enamored of *desire's* singular and surprising articulations. To be sure, this is all a bit exaggerated; Lacan's exaggerations bring Klein's into view and vice-versa. It is not as if Klein is only listening for the narratives of anxiety and desire with which she is familiar. Nor is Lacan so enraptured by the flight of desire that he cannot discern or is unwilling to in any way heed its mundane, ordinary and expectable, articulations. In many ways Klein and Lacan are much closer than they would likely care to admit.

A brief coda: It has been said a number of times that the basic unit of the Symbolic and the psychic is the signifier. How can this be? Appeal to the Lacanian dictum that the unconscious is structured like a language will only takes us so far in addressing this question. When Lacan claims that the unconscious is structured like a language, he means, primarily, that the primary principles of unconscious organization are displacement and condensation, analogous to metonymy and metaphor in the linguistic register, and that it is by means of these principles that signifiers are webbed together in a particular psychic economy. Other quasi linguistic principles of the psychic association of signifiers include alliteration, assonance and consonance, homophony, synonymy and antinomy, being part of a larger word or phrase, synecdoche, connections between letters, etc. In this context it is less important to detail the myriad ways signifiers are metabolized than to underscore that, for Lacan, wishes, phantasies, drives, etc.—what are ordinarily considered the basic elements of the psychic, and what Klein in particular considers to be such—are *secondary*. They are the products of the psychic metabolism of signifiers, responses to the persistent enigma, the spur to meaning, of the signifier.

Signifiers come into prominence, they become important to us, only because they are contingently associated with, e.g., happen to be in the backdrop of, impacting experiences. Signifiers register these experiences *in their import*[217] *but not quite in their meaning*, for this is yet to be worked out. Certain experiences impress us as somehow freighted with significance, though we know not what this might be. Associated with these impacting but inchoate experiences are signifiers, formally configured impressions of various sorts, that may be only incidentally related to the experience (e.g., an experience of maternal affection is associated with the aromas of the kitchen—the signifiers—in which this affection is expressed) but will be the crucial terms around which their meaning is later worked out. One source of the arbitrariness of the signifier is its roots in prediscursive, sensuous excitation. To put it in developmental terms, signifiers (structured sense impressions) abound prior to the development and consolidation of the concepts and schemas (structures of intelligibility) through which the meaning of various experiences will be elaborated, that is, before routine connections between signifiers and signifieds are established via socialization. Once these connections are established, experience will proceed for the most part in their terms. But even when social schemas are in place, their efficacy is imperfect; they can never altogether assimilate the (inchoate but sensuously structured) impact of affectively charged experiences into given orders of meaning. Experience is, on Lacan's account, irreducibly excessive, emphatic, gesturing toward yet always eluding the symbolic forms through which it—*this* sensory configuration—will be shaped, clarified. The signifier is Lacan's name for the excess of somatic force over social meaning, for the residue of sensuous excitability in stabilizing schemas. The signifier is the basic unit of the psychic, then, insofar as it names the register of experience (logically and chronologically) prior to the work of symbolization. The signifier *becomes* the basic unit of the Symbolic as it spurs symbolization, as it indefinitely activates the form-giving impulse.[218]

If a Symbolic order is a culturally particular organization of signifiers in which various signifiers are regularly related to various other signifiers and aligned with various signifieds by way of authoritative identifications (elaborated both by the routinization of experience and direct decree), then the psychic is an idiosyncratic particularization of this general cultural order. The difference is analogous to that between *la langue* and *la parole*. If the Symbolic names a general patterning of signifiers and of the relation between signifiers and signifieds into which each individual is born, the psychic names the idiosyncratic patterning that develops as a result of the singular sequence and composition of individual experiences and the singular structures of attention—the perspectives—through which these experiences are filtered. For instance, imagine an infant rent by the experience of some inchoate upsurge of need or desire not currently being met. Certain signifiers are in the backdrop: the color of the walls, the mood prevailing prior to the surging forth of desire, the words said by mother on the phone, street traffic, or whatever. These signifiers will be forever laden with the intense and unintelligible affects, (proto) questions, etc. with which they are associated (though obviously this valence is not always in the fore).[219] Further, these signifiers may come to be connected with the fantasies, feelings, further experiences, etc. (and the signifiers that are and come to be associated with *them*) associated with this and other such experiences of vulnerability and with various manners of working out this vulnerability. In this way, an associational nexus of signifiers and a web of relations between signifiers and signified will be established. The singular sequence and composition of events an individual undergoes in the course of her life gives rise to the singular sense of the signifiers forged therein.[220] The "content" of a signifier (the experiences, affects, ideas, other signifiers, etc. with which it is associated) and the connections between signifiers as well as those between signifiers and signifieds will be, on the one hand, regulated by the prevailing Symbolic order but, on the other, as contingent and idiosyncratic as an individual's life course. Within the psychic, signifiers have a personal history irreducible to their cultural history, which is why the psychic significance (the "psychic reality") of signifiers can be quite disparate from their sedimented cultural significance, and thus extremely obscure to an external observer. Whence Lacan's insistence that clinicians bracket understanding, e.g., bracket what they think they know about what various experiences mean for their clients, and his dedication to developing analytic practices conducive to the exploration of the often unexpected significance of clinical material, practices in which, paradoxically, both parties learn to expect the unexpectable?

To give one final example, think of the visual signifier "red" in Hitchcock's *Marnie*. In the film's "primal scene," Marnie is roused in the midst of sleep, removed from the bedroom she shares with her mother in their cramped apartment, and put onto a couch in the foyer so that her mother, a sex worker, can use the bedroom with a client. The sailor visiting that night hears Marnie whimpering from a nightmare and comes out into the foyer, presumably to console her. But rather than console her, the sailor begins to fondle her, which throws Marnie's mother into a rage. A fight breaks out, ending only after Marnie's mother has suffered a crippling injury to her right leg and Marnie has killed the sailor. Red is the color of the blood Marnie sees as the sailor and her mother are slumped over together—he dying, she injured and distraught.

Condensed in this signifier "red" are, perhaps: (1) Marnie's experience of helplessness and abandonment (her mother sees to her clients rather than caring for her child; she removes Marnie from the comfort of slumber in their shared bed and fails to go to her when she has a nightmare; for most of the scene, Marnie feels she cannot save herself or her mother from the sailor, and even though she kills the sailor she will not have been able to save her mother from severe injury or herself from the traumatic impact of the assault; her mother has "allowed" the fondling by not preventing it, which may give rise to worries about her mother's nonomnipotence and the horrors of a world in which one is left to one's own devices; perhaps her mother's failure to prevent the assault is also associated with her particular line of work, and so with sex, desire, etc., and with the particular site of this work, and so with the domestic); (2) whatever anxieties or inadmissible excitements were present in the nightmare; (3) Marnie's Oedipal desire and rivalry (she is displaced from the bed she shares with her mother to make room for various men) and consequent deadlock of guilt and aggression; (4) her guilt over somehow motivating the terrible seduction, and thus a fear of her sexuality or even of her body or perhaps of rest and comfort (Marnie is depicted throughout the film as highly mobile, traveling from town to town and assuming multiple false identities—as if in manic flight from stability); (5) her guilt over the injury to her mother and the death of the client, which are likely fantasies of a child forced to sleep outside her sex-worker mother's bedroom and thus perhaps related to Marnie's fears over her own omnipotence—what she fantasized *actually came true*; (6) the excitement of witnessing, even being perversely recruited into a scene of, her mother's sexuality; (7) her identifications with, and perhaps a certain envy of, either her mother, the sailor(s), or both, and thus her relation to sexuality and sexual difference in general or heterosexuality and its normative gender articulation in particular; (8) the terror over her mother's seemingly fathomless sexuality; (9) the insecurity and jealousy arising from the her mother's attention being directed elsewhere, beyond their intimate dyad (and so perhaps the question of what if anything could ever satisfy her mother, the freighted question of the desire of the other); (10) the terrors of sexual assault, loss of innocence, violation of personal integrity; (11) the likely plaguing question of her origin (Marnie's mother was silent on the issue of her father, who was mostly likely a customer—was the sailor she killed that night her father?

Notice the simple anagram: marnie = marine.); (12) the questions and fears that correspond to the identification between herself and her mother implied by the sailor's sexual advances ("Is this terrible fate what it means to be identified with my mother? Is this what my fantasies of and desires for symbiotic merger with my mother really mean? Does being [a] mother mean that I am a whore? That I am, like she is, hypersexual, unsatisfiable, insensitive, injurable or injured, guilty? What does it mean that the sailor can treat me as he treats mother? Do I exist as a distinctive individual?"); (13) an desire for recognition through which Marnie could disprove the sailor's identification of herself and her mother (Marnie always returns home and acts the dutiful daughter between her "jobs," perhaps thereby attempting to secure a needed sense of identity conferred by maternal recognition; furthermore, when Marnie's mother "adopts" the little girl next door, Marnie is overcome with jealousy, rage, and disappointment); (14) a feeling that identity or identification, as in the identity between herself and her mother implied by the sailor's unwanted advances, is coercive (and so, perhaps, a feeling that categorization or interpretation is coercive—even though, later, Marnie rightfully exposes the chauvinist aggression and self-inflated presumptiveness behind Mark's [her captor/husband] efforts to "interpret" her, the magnitude of her rage and malicious character of her response may suggest that something else is at play); (15) a confusion about the difference between child and mother/adult; (16) the phrase "red with rage" (recall that her mother was manifestly enraged by the sexual assault) with which a little girl might be familiar; and so on.

And this is only to speak to what may be condensed in the signifier at this particular moment. As Marnie goes about her neurotic, criminal life trying to make sense of and obliquely responding to what transpired that terrible night, further experiences and the signifiers associated with them will come to be associated with this core signifier "red." For instance, when it becomes clear that Mr. Rutland has *read* a number of books about the sexual life of the criminally insane in order to "fix" Marnie, she lashes out against him. Marnie's response is altogether appropriate, but here we would do well to focus on what this lashing out (perhaps) *means to Marnie* irrespective of the fact that it is *also* a justified and quite clever response to Mark Rutland's efforts to secure her sexual enslavement. The point here is that the visual signifier "red," though it may be more amenable to certain significances than others, has its meaning built up by (1) that with which it comes to be associated in a particular cultural milieu (through ordinary American socialization, red will come to be associated with love, rage, etc; furthermore, this signifier may become connected by sound resonances with "dead," "bed," "said," "fed," "wed," etc. or larger words of which it is a part or words made up of other words or syllables that it bears an auditory resemblance to, e.g., *med*ication, and thereby with all that these latter terms come to signify under conditions of ordinary and expectable acculturation) and (2) the particular experiences of the individual that occur, we might say, in the midst of "red," that is, when "red" is prominent in the backdrop of affectively weighty experiences. "Red" will become an anchoring point for a number of experiences and signifiers that develop internal associations by way of being connected with or by "red."

What this discussion of the signifier should make clear is that Lacan's emphasis tends to fall on the heterogeneity of culture, on the idiosyncratic particularization of cultural meanings, while Klein's emphasis tend to fall on the relative homogeneity of culture, on the dominant, even universal, terms, narratives, etc. through which life with others is psychically processed. We are, for Klein, first and foremost enamored with the mother/breast of and, from then on, indeed *as a result*, condemned to oscillate between paranoid-schizoid and depressive anxieties and defenses. This is not so certain for Lacan. He remains skeptical about both this deduction and the use of such generalizations as the paranoid-schizoid and depressive positions when attempting to account for and respond to individuals' sufferings and desires. This differential emphasis—on the heterogeneous as opposed to the homogenous, the ineffable or enigmatic rather than the intelligible, the resistant particular rather than the narratively cohesive—colors everything. For instance, with regard to repression, Lacan is interested in the repression of various signifiers and the fundamental fantasies composed by and around them, while Klein is concerned with the repression of determinate desires, wishes, fantasies, fears, anxieties, etc. Or, more starkly: Lacan is concerned with the foreclosure of the Real as a result of which the Symbolic tends toward the stultifying consistency of Imaginary reification, while Klein is concerned with the repression of various desires and anxieties as a result of which life feels radically inconsistent, besieged, etc.

While Lacan is focused on the Other that precedes and exceeds us, Klein is focused on the other, the particular other—both real and phantasmatic—with respect to whom our object relations are in better or worse shape. Specifically, she is concerned with our relations with that particular other known as (or, Lacan would insist, schematized as) the breast. As one prominent Lacanian puts it, "Object relations theory, in spite of all its variations of emphasis, postulates the irreducible relation to a primary object—namely the breast—which determines to a greater or lesser extent the internal world of the infant and thus, eventually, the adult."[221] For Klein, the breast is *the* other, the one or "the Thing" that conditions the entirety of psychic life—that to which one must appeal "in the last instance." The breast is as if an axiom from which all else follows, the term without which psychoanalytic theory and practice are bound to founder. Lacan, on the other hand, seeks to turn our attention away from *the* object or other (the breast) and redirect it toward the Other, or, more precisely, Otherness. He seeks to turn our attention to Otherness in ourselves, Otherness in the other, Otherness in the socio-symbolic order. He seeks to turn our attention toward the insuperability of Otherness in the sense of lack, perpetual reformation or reconsolidation (re-symbolization), nonsymmetry and inconsistency, etc. Against Klein, who focuses on *objects* (internal or external, good or bad, part or whole), Lacan focuses on the pulsating *signifiers* (de)composing object representations and relations, with respect to which object representations and relations are secondary, even defensive. When he does concern himself with object representations and relations, it tends to be insofar as they are structured by fundamental fantasies that arise, at least in part, from the need to process signifiers. A duality—a duel?—of exaggerations: Klein exaggerates the breast, Lacan the signifier. Each has their articles of faith, even some vision of the elemental. To be committed to psychoanalysis, is this not always a matter of conversion?

THE REAL

While the Symbolic and Imaginary are forms of attention, the Real names the collapse or impossibility of the selectivity of attention. There is little that can be directly said about the Real other than that it is the dimension of the ineffable that lines the Symbolic and the Imaginary, causing them to tremble yet serving as the impetus for their perpetual reconsolidation or transfiguration. More precisely, it is not the Real per se that motivates the reconsolidation or transfiguration of the Symbolic or the Imaginary. The Real is not an agency: it is an overwhelming excess, a force that both throws us off balance and motivates us to reestablish our bearings.[222] The encounter with the Real is the *spur* of the form-giving impulse: its motivation and limit, irritant and impasse, that which gives rise to the activation energy for symbolization but also the jagged rocks upon which symbolization is thrashed. The Real is the "hard kernel" that cannot be metabolized by schematization or any other manner of psychic processing yet that in response to which it is propelled yet again—either into a repetitive, futile attempt to capture the Real or into new and imaginative transformations that are equally futile as attempts at its capture. The Real is the condition and limit of repetition; it is what turns analytic discourse into mythology.[223]

The Real names a principle of material resistance or excess, but speaking at this level of generality misses something crucial: the notional structure of the Real is, formally, quite unusual, indeed utterly idiosyncratic—what the Real "is" is a question for each individual. This is to say, the Real is registered in each individual's tendency to *repeatedly return* to certain scenes (behaviors, fantasies, semantic choices, oratorical rhythms, relationships, etc.) without knowing why and often without realizing it. The Real is registered in the compulsive, unreflective quality of those things we do almost despite ourselves, e.g., in words and deeds that seem motivated (driven) by principles that will forever elude us and are often contrary to self-interest. The Real is the inexplicable.[224] In experiential terms, the Real names a sense of *being here, yet again, and yet not knowing exactly what one has gotten oneself into.* We partake of the Real when we "just do it."[225] The Real cannot be decoded; it is not subject to analytic deciphering as repressed desires, fundamental fantasies, and even core signifiers may be; it has no determinate content. It is both under- and over- determined, as under- and over-determined as the core signifiers around which turn and out of which are organized the associational networks structuring each individual psyche.[226] The Real is endogenous yet inimical to the order of meaning; it is the extimate kernel of representation and self-representation, that which must be excluded for one's images of self and world to maintain their consistency.[227]

In one sense, then, the Real names our irremediable diremption, our inhabitation by an endlessly opaque "other scene." But the Real is not the unconscious. It is a name for our emphatic passivity, a passivity beyond passivity, a passivity that cannot be converted into any form of self-directed activity. Such conversion precisely marks one's distance from the Real, the subsiding of its sublime force. Though we may learn to avow various unconscious impulses, fantasies, and perhaps to some extent our *desire* itself, the Real cannot be so avowed. There is no way to accommodate ourselves to the Real or cultivate forms of acknowledgment appropriate to it. "It" is beyond the floodgates that must remain closed if our cognitive maps, projects, self-representations, and world-orientations are to remain stable enough for us to get on in the world. Opening onto "it" would throw us into a limbo from which there would be no foreseeable return. The admission of the Real—allowing the full force of the Real to be felt—would be devastating, cause our worlds to crumble.

The Real is the limit. It is the indigestible kernel that cannot be incorporated into the metabolic processes of the psyche without unraveling it entirely. The Real is *the* figure of inadmissibility in Lacan's thinking. Its admission would catastrophically unravel the structures of admission and exclusion by which experience is structured, would overwhelm the principles of selectivity through which the world comes into focus. The constitutive finitude of experience presupposes the foreclosure of the Real. While various figures of abject life (psychosis, criminality, *homo sacer*, etc.) may serve as cultural placeholders for the Real, their very figurability bespeaks their distance from the Real. Hence the ironic idiocy of the term. The Real is the name of the paradoxical principle (*archē*) of anarchy that is held at bay in order for the ordering operations—the patterning and structuring—of human experience to take hold.[228] Admitting what were once abject forms of life into the fold may modify the structures of inclusion/exclusion around which a particular community is organized in incredibly important ways (this is often a matter of life and death), but insofar as the community can reorganize itself, and especially insofar as it can recognize this orientation as a continuation of a longstanding—however mutated—legacy, it has not admitted the Real.

The Real, as noted, can be figured as the upsurge of phenomenalization prior to and forever in excess of schematization; it is the constitutive outside, the exception or excess that must be excluded if reality is to remain in any way consistent. Again, the configuration of a cultural order may change significantly once it alters its practices of constitutive exclusion, but to diminish hostility toward or even extend hospitality to those against whom one's identity has been negatively defined is not to utterly shut down the very possibility of experience, which is what the admission of the Real would entail. The Real is a "principle" of massive, insurmountable inconsistency, of catastrophic disorientation, of ravishing chaos. If one insists on framing it as a form of experience, it could be said to be distantly akin to that of *le corps morcelé*, i.e., to the experience of bodily organs or zones, barely defined in themselves, striving for their own satisfaction, resisting consolidation into any totality.

To put one final gloss on it, one's sense of reality may admit of a great degree of latency, but the admission of the Real would amount to the utter breakdown of the capacity for selective perception through which latencies come into view as the possible horizons of *my* life course. In the face of the Real, one can no longer say "I" or "we." The Real names the radically impossible—that which cannot be extrapolated as a potential fate of the world we have come to know. The Real is both "too much" and "not enough": it is the elemental upsurge of life irreducible to its anthropocentric registration, that which cannot be contained within the bounds of possible experience.[229]

REALITY

It is important for our consideration of the differences between Lacan and Klein to specify (1) the difference between the Real and reality and (2) how each understands the nature involvement in and commitment to reality. Recalling what was said earlier about the rhetoric of experience and its analogues in Klein's work, we can say that up to a certain point Lacan and Klein agree that *reality is fundamentally interpretable*: there are no immediate, self-evident truths to be told about oneself or the world; rather, experience is both uncircumventable and elaborated through structures of attention and symbolization that are eminently contestable because necessarily selective and constructive. Of course, where Klein would stress that the chaotic confusions of silent suffering, or its converse, hysterically inept loquaciousness in speech and deeds, may be relieved by the therapeutic beneficence of the clarifying word, Lacan would stress the therapeutic and theoretical consequences of remaining attuned to the persistence of enigma. And of course, at a certain moments, both Lacan and Klein backtrack from this shared vision of the in(de)finite interpretability of experience, privileging particular interpretations so emphatically that it seems as though they are absolutely convinced that they know what's *really* going on. But still, at least at certain junctures, both consider reality a field of the inexorable becoming and appearing otherwise, the aspectival unfolding, of phenomena.

More precisely, of phenomena that concern us. For both Klein and Lacan, *reality is invested with significance; it matters to us.* Reality is not organic and inorganic matter governed by universal and probabilistic laws but phenomena that are alive to us, that implicate and animate us, that matter. Lacan, as we have seen, insists that acquiring a sense of reality is a normative, indeed normalizing, accomplishment, a consequence of submission to the structures of concern and symbolic orientations embodied by our primary caregiver(s), and, later, our social cohorts. Klein would agree that reality is not the brute indifference of what is evacuated of subjective, thus distorting, coloration but something given only in and through our investments. For her, though, a sense of reality is less a normalizing than a developmental accomplishment, one that marks the consolidation of cognitive and relational schemas that provide a flexible yet firm world-orientation, schemas that delimit a domain in which we have a place along with objects and others in which to work out our anxieties and attachments.[230] Lacan emphasizes the constriction that a sense of reality entails, while Klein emphasizes the flip side, the opening of possibilities. These emphases are by no means incommensurable; as Kant demonstrated, a limit is at once a condition of possibility.

Klein and Lacan tend to frame the question of reality less in terms of ontology than in terms of ontologization: the promotion of certain objects and processes that captivate and constitute our interest to the—honorific—status of "real." We have already shown this to be the case for Lacan. On Klein's side, so much is reality other than the self-evident that she says of Dick, even after much therapy, "he is *beginning* to establish a relation to reality" (1975: 228; emphasis added). For Klein, perception alone is not an indication, let alone a guarantee, of a relation to reality; perception may merely serve as the pretext for the activation of intrapsychic processes that phantasmatically overlay phenomena, totally overcoding and obscuring reality. As Dick expresses a desire for the presence and attention of his mother and nurse, as he both idealizes and develops an anxious rivalry with his father (this, I presume, is what Klein means when she speaks of "indications of the normal Oedipal attitude"), as he establishes more firm relations to objects, tries to makes himself intelligible, and works to better his vocabulary, he develops a relation to reality in the sense of investing in, indeed becoming a part of, a broader world that is independent of yet connected to him. Reality, for Klein, names not the domain of truths subject to external corroboration or immediately self-evident but rather a vital connection to a world irreducible to one's wants, needs, and fancies. Reality is not a matter of objective presence but of affective presence: the mutual implication of self and other/object. More precisely, Dick begins to attain a relation to reality when *concrete others and objects*—particular beings who/that may or may not respond in desired ways: others who are seats of subjectivity, agents in their own right, or objects that are relatively independent, materially resistant—become the anchor points of his libidinal and fantasmatic investments. Attaining a relation to reality, for Klein, amounts to a process of *worlding*: becoming a part of an experiential manifold that is irreducible to, persistently in excess of, oneself yet vitally responsive to one's needs, wants, and so forth. Reality names the experience of self, objects, and others as significant beyond the parameters of fantasized omnipotence. Even if the ego is there from the beginning, a relation to reality is not thereby implied.

This, however, is only one side of the story. Though Klein intimates that a relation to reality is developed rather than simply given, she also holds that a relation to reality obtains from the beginning. Considering that, for Klein, a relation to reality results from (1) the earliest activities of the ego (latent anxiety is unbearable, creating/discovering specific objects as determinate sources of anxiety transforms latent into manifest—thus diminished and negotiable—anxiety and thereby provides for a more felicitous existence) and (2) the epistemophilic impulse, which seeks connection in the form of "knowing" the contents of the mother's body, her intimations that a relation to reality *develops* must concern only the quality of this relation, not its existence. For Klein, the ego (or something like it) is there from the beginning; it is an agency that, unless overburdened, will attune the infant to reality in order to facilitate the minimization of anxiety. Hence Klein says that as the ego develops a "true relation to reality is gradually established out of . . . unreal [phantasmatically dominated] reality" (1975: 221). This is to say, though a relation to reality changes qualitatively over time—specifically, as the infant learns to differentiate between appearances and affects that arise from the world as opposed to those that arise from within—it obtains, at least in rudimentary form, *ab initio*. Even phantasmatically overcoded reality, "unreal reality," is reality. Because the development of the ego and the relation to reality depend on the ego's capacity to tolerate the pressures of anxiety situations, the technical lesson deduced from this bit of metapsychology is that the analyst must support the faltering ego, remove impediments to its natural development, and thereby allow the anxiety-alleviating relation to reality to establish itself (1975: 221).[231] "The only possible thing to do in analysing this child who could not make himself intelligible and whose ego was not open to influence was to try to gain access to his unconscious and, by diminishing the unconscious difficulties, to open up a way for the development of the ego. Of course, in Dick's case, as in every other, access to the unconscious had to be by way of the ego. Events proved that even this very imperfectly developed ego was adequate for establishing connection with the unconscious" (1975: 229).

The presuppositions guiding Klein's statement are that (1) the infant's (in this case, Dick's) *ego* is governed by the pleasure/unpleasure principle and (2) both the ego and the unconscious exist from the beginning. Lacan does not share the first presupposition, at least not in this form, and he explicitly rejects the second. Though Lacan supposes infantile life to be regulated by the pleasure/unpleasure principle, for him this does not entail the existence of the ego or the unconscious. The unconscious, for Lacan, will develop as the associational webbing of signifiers (implanted by the desire/discourse of the Other) congeals *subsequent to* the primary repression of certain core signifiers, which effectively binds the Real. And the ego will develop as the infant's efforts to secure the love of its primary caregiver(s) motivates the mimetic incorporation of their structures of attention and concern. Klein's account of development presumes a natural course that, Lacan stresses against Klein (though perhaps in her spirit), is socially mediated. Though Klein assumes the intrinsic sociality of the infant—the infant is always already psychocorporeally related to the mother—she also assumes robust limits to the work of social mediation: the infant will develop more or less programmatically given adequate care. While Klein is attuned to the natural opening out of the infant's ego onto the world and to the diminishment of anxiety that follows from this, Lacan is emphatically attentive to the infant's openness to the Other and to the incorporation of the Other's sense of reality that results from this. Where Klein seeks to chart the course of natural linear development, Lacan is riveted to dialectical involutions: primordial permeability shows itself to be the condition for confining captivation.[232] And while Klein's assumption of the originary existence of the ego and the unconscious bars her from a thought of the Real, Lacan's attention to our exposure to social norms prior to and continuous with the development of the ego allows him to implicate the development of the ego and of a sense of reality in the foreclosure of the Real.

Klein is concerned with the development of the ego's powers, not with the development of the ego as such. Though she says that Dick is at a certain point beginning to develop a relation to reality, she also says that "[t]he sadistic phantasies directed against the inside of the mother's body constitute the first and basic relation to the outside world and to realty" (1975: 221). Bracketing the question of how to reconcile this claim with those postulating or implying an originary amorous engrossment in the maternal presence, peculiarly, this "first and basic relation to . . . reality" obtains prior to "the beginning," that is, prior to the beginning of Dick's relation to reality. There is for Klein always already a fledgling relation to reality, specifically to the mother's body, "hardwired" into human development. Though the infant's earliest reality is predominantly phantasmatic, the infant is already attuned to reality insofar as its phantasy life takes its cue from, is the initial psychic metabolization of, the real world (the experience of the mother). From Klein's perspective, there is no need to broach the question or assess the impacts of the psychogenesis of a relation to reality. She need only attend to the relative success or failure of this relation and support it when it is found feeble or wavering.

Furthermore, Klein assumes a "hardwired" symbolic network, an originary unconscious structuration of phantasy. It may be later modified, but it is there from the beginning and will serve as the scaffolding for all further developments. The objects of anxiety with which the infant is surrounded—excrement, organs, various part-objects, things animate and inanimate—are *to begin with* equivalent to one another, symbolically equated with one another *from the beginning* (1975: 221). This symbolic organization of experience is not, as Lacan would hold, acquired by subjection to the forms of attention exemplified by primary caregivers or otherwise *learned*; rather, such symbolism is posited as *originary*.

For Lacan, our commitments to our acquired sense of reality and to the Symbolic serve two vital functions: (1) keeping the Real at bay (overproximity to the Real translates into unbearable anxiety and risks massive destructuration) and (2) keeping us connected to others whose care is of inestimable importance for our psychophysical wellbeing. For Klein, primordial connection to others and immersion in a symbolically mediated reality is simply supposed as what keeps (natural) latent anxiety at bay and under wraps.

For Klein, there is no Real that, outlining the Symbolic, the Imaginary, and reality, causes them to quiver, sometimes to quake. There is only an in(de)finitely interpretable reality that one can relate to more or less felicitously. For Lacan, part of the import of the distinction between the Real and reality is to highlight that the Real, unlike reality, *is not interpretable*. The clinical stakes of this distinction are enormous. From Lacan's perspective, by not attending to the Real—which is the prerogative of the ego—Klein locates her practice within a field of unlimited interpretation. She will interpret and interpret again, forever failing to confront the analysand with her radical alterity, with her desirous excess, with her implacable nonsense and abyssal truth—with the dimension of the Real, which, if dosed appropriately, will gradually unravel the dominant structures of the analysand's psyche and thereby open her onto a future that can be had in no other way. Only tactfully provisioned encounters with our nonsensical dimension can motivate *separation* from the fantasies in which we are ensnared.[233]

Klein supports the adeptness and capaciousness of the ego rather than introducing a distance between the subject and the ego. She works in service of the assumption that meaning can be had, and thus, Lacan insists, risks colluding with (1) the addiction to control and/or docile submissiveness that often follows from this assumption and (2) the fantasy of meaning's inviolable and all-enchanting attainment from which follows endless frustration, aggressive retribution, and so on. Retrenching her analysands in their fantasies of coherent and cohesive, altogether satisfying meaning, she promotes the disavowal—which often amounts to a socially pernicious displacement—of their insistent unintelligibility, intolerance for their and others' insuperable obscurity, for the enigma that they *are*. Reinscribing her analysands in the order of meaning, e.g., by tending to modify rather than fundamentally challenge her analsyands' identifications and favored forms of object relations, Klein is bound to amplify those forms of suffering that arises from taxing commitments to intelligibility. Because she understands suffering to result from natural/automatic and socially mediated upsurges of anxiety, Klein responds to suffering by supporting the ego's capacity to tolerate tension, confusion, the ambiguity of intertwined love and hate, and so on—that is, by enhancing and stabilizing the analysand's identification with his or her ego. But if the ego is the seat of social normalization as much as the agency of individuation, if identification with the ego tends to project an ideal against which we will forever find ourselves wanting yet from which we cannot break free, then this strategy risks running severely awry.

Lacan's clinical practice, on the other hand, regularly refuses support for the ego's development for fear of (1) turning psychoanalysis into an unwitting support for faltering social normalization, which may mean preserving the decaying corpse of irrational social forms, and (2) underwriting the Imaginary investments that give rise to the problems discussed above. Lacan tends to confront his analysands with the unexpected, inconclusive, and otherwise unsettling meanings of their words and deeds and with their nonsense, their alterity to the order of intelligibility, in order to promote disidentification with their Imaginary and Symbolic positions—with the Imaginary and Symbolic identifications by which they have been captivated and that have generated the suffering that brought them to analysis in the first place. His aim is to loosen the grip of constraining social norms in order to open his analysands onto the in(de)finite itinerary of *desire*, that is, to help them cultivate a sense of themselves as at least minimally different from their current desires, projects, and social roles, thus as able to take some responsibility for their fate, or, ideally, to help them cultivate a sense of themselves as an ongoing problem and process. The aim, simply stated, is freedom.

For Lacan, Kleinian—or any other version of—object-relations theory is yet another ego psychology. Of course there are differences between Klein, on the one hand, and Hartmann, Kris, Lowenstein, Anna Freud, etc., on the other. First of all, though Klein does not assume, as Lacan does, that the ego arises from partially abandoned object cathexes and primary mimeticism, neither does she assume, as do the ego psychologists, that there must be an ego from the beginning *because* there is action, perception, and thought (ego functions) at the outset of life. If there were no ego, ego psychologists tend to claim, action, perception, and thought would be a function of the id, which makes no sense. Though Klein does not share their reasoning, she does share their conclusion: the ego is given from the outset.

Second, Klein does not share the moralistic axiom (and genetic fallacy) that informs ego psychology: the ego must be there from the beginning if it is to have the autonomy from the id that it *must have* if we are to be the conflict-free, autonomous, and rational beings we *must be*.[234] Again, though Klein does not share their reasoning, she shares ego psychologists' presupposition of the originary existence of the ego and the id (or in her case the unconscious).

Third, though Klein does not share Anna Freud's belief that transference cannot be established prior to a solidified relation to one's primary caregivers (which is based on the assumption that if the place of these primary caregivers is not fixed in the unconscious it cannot be transferred onto others), and though she does not share Anna Freud's belief that a child's ego can only be educated, not analyzed at the level of unconscious conflict, she shares with Anna Freud the focus on the ego as the site of intervention.

Via these assumptions about the ego, generally, via the priority she affords the ego, from Lacan's perspective, Klein blinds herself to the ego's constitutive envelopment in the work of keeping the Real at bay and under wraps. Thus she will fail to develop analytic practices in which the signifiers that bind the Real are discovered and reorganized—a reorganization that Lacan associates with a radical re-creation of the subject. While signifiers must bind the Real in some way, they need not do so in the ways that have been developed heretofore—ways that have produced the fantasies, identifications, etc. from which the analysand suffers. Klein will support Dick's subjectification and worlding, not the desubjectification and unworlding through which *desire* is allowed a line of flight beyond its current organization. Klein will promote adaptation to and more meaningful immersion in the world rather than the freedom to risk large-scale desubjectivation or destructuration, which is the first step toward a radical renegotiation of one's place in and relation to the Symbolic.[235]

In sum, if, as Lacan insists, the Real insists or persists in ways that are not recuperable in the order of meaning, then Klein's refusal to lend consideration to the Real is at one with her conviction that the unconscious is a law-governed container of meanings (phantasies) whose conflicts can and should be worked through in order to achieve a maximally felicitous relation to the social world. Unconcerned with anything akin to the Real, Klein conceives the unconscious not as organized around enigmatic signifiers that spur meaning but around the contents of phantasies that can be, in principle, successfully decoded and, once decoded, either avowed, repudiated, or otherwise worked through *by the ego*. Klein works in the ambit of meaning while Lacan seeks to expose meaning's constitutive outside. Where Lacan would detect the possibility of intervening at the site of the subject's relation to the Symbolic, Klein will see the need to integrate the client more fully into the dominant Symbolic order, to induce her to assume it as her own. Finally, her neglect of the Real insulates her belief that the unconscious is not an *effect* of "introjecting" without being able to symbolize the discourse/desire of the Other but rather is simply there from the beginning; and as a result of this belief she will be blind to the effects of her discourse as it impacts Dick, specifically as it contributes to the formation of his unconscious.

VIII. Summation

On the basis of the foregoing, Lacan's initially obscure claims that Klein's interpretations are Oedipalizing and that the unconscious is the discourse of the Other should be much more comprehensible, as should be the stakes of these claims. Further, on the basis of this exposition the significance and stakes of a great number of Lacan's differences in emphasis from and disagreements with Klein, as well as the contours of his unique perspective that emerge in the course of these differential accentuations and disagreements, should come more clearly into view.

Klein tends to emphasize the terrors of latent anxiety and the anxiety-alleviating potential of ego development; the meaning of phantasies and their linguistic and behavioral signs; the fortuitously concomitant development of the ego, symbolization, and worldliness; the need for a world in which one is sufficiently connected to and separated from objects and others, and the forces that disrupt this equilibrium; the intrinsic sociality of the infant and, specifically, the originary import of the mother; the goodness of the world when object relations provide the conditions for the diminishment of anxiety and fulfillment of desire; the natural development of—or when this fails the need for therapeutic assistance for—an anxiety-reducing relation to "real reality"; all that Lacan describes as Imaginary. Klein is keyed to anxiety, to its terrible consequences as much as to the propitious developments that follow from successful responses to it—responses that usually proceed by nature but sometimes need a bit of analytic assistance.

Lacan tends to emphasize the exorbitance of *desire*; the normalizing constrictions implied by ego development and reality testing; our indelibly partial integration into and nonreconciliation with cultural regimes of intelligibility and value; the potential for freedom that follows from exposure to the lack in and nonsense or enigmaticity of self, other, and world; the effects, especially the unpredictable effects, of speech and deeds; the hazards of measuring oneself against impossible ideals; the Otherness that inhabits and mediates (over- and under-determines) desire, discourse, and object relations—the Otherness that keeps them both stable and available to transformation, the alienation and subjective rigidification effected by Imaginary structures and fundamental fantasies, and the possibility of traversing these fantasies or otherwise gaining distance from the affectively weighty questions that motivate Imaginary ensnarement; the prospects for desubjectivization and resymbolization as a result of which one's sense of self and world may alter radically; the in(de)finitely (in)determinate—irreducibly polyvalent and polysemic, excessive, enigmatic, and inconclusive—dimensions of desire and discourse. Lacan is keyed to the possibility of possibility, to freedom and whatever forces of rigidification impede it.

While Klein conceives therapeutic success in terms of diminished anxiety, ego development, and more secure and hospitable object relations, Lacan conceives therapeutic success in terms of the analysand's ability to become and sustain herself as a problem to herself.

For Klein, Dick's case suggests that even the most closed-off, psychotic children can be humanized, i.e., develop "normally" (Oedipally), with the right sort of therapeutic assistance, specifically through the efficacy of valid interpretation—which in turn suggests the universal and mutually supporting validity of her theoretical and practical commitments. For Lacan, Dick's case suggests that the unconscious is the discourse of the Other, thus that each analysis is unique and that the effects of speech are at least as important as its veracity.

Given these enormous differences in emphasis, in what respect can it be said that Lacan and Klein are concerned with "the same" case? For us, Lacan and Klein are names of unique perspectives, of differential foci, that elaborate and respond to "the same" phenomena in very different ways. With Lacan, the accent is on difference and desire; with Klein, the accent is on integration and anxiety. When these perspectives are paired, shown to be responsive to "the same" material, it becomes clear that in each case theory is radically underdetermined by evidence and that clinical procedure is in no way directly dictated by the material at hand. The Lacanian perspective will never be able to demonstrate its necessity or value in a way that simply renders the Kleinian perspective irrelevant or shows it to be demonstrably false, and vice versa. Psychoanalytic knowledge and practice—both in these two forms and, I would suggest, generally—is exaggerated, implacably one-sided, informed by structures of concomitant blindness and insight, the elaboration of a perspective, thus subject to acknowledgement or avoidance or neglect, but never to irrefutable demonstration.

And not only are reasons for commitment to one school rather than another wanting in demonstrative force, so too are the reasons for commitment to one interpretation rather than another. Even when we are attuned to "the same" clinical phenomena, choosing between (not to mention among) Kleinian and Lacanian assessments and responses becomes no easier. Nothing is resolved by appealing to the particular. Yet lurking around psychoanalytic circles is a certain positivist temptation to believe that were we to get our clinical descriptions *just right*, we would be able to see what the appropriate theoretico-practical framework to drawn on would be. This will never work. Detailed descriptions of clinical phenomena are unavoidably theory-laden, and even if they weren't we would be no closer to resolving the question of how to best describe and respond to the phenomena at hand. Clinical description in particular and psychoanalytic thinking in general are inescapably questionable, speculative constructions no matter how empirically sensitive, but not for that reason rationally dismissible. Performatively elaborating the skeptical moment of cognition of matters psychic is how psychoanalysis acknowledges its material conditions—its rootedness in singular analyses and the various emotional, unconscious, defensive, etc. involvements incumbent thereto—and so how it shapes its claim to rationality. Its rationality would not be that of deduction from first principles or that of systematic empirical induction but that of attestation. Attesting there where classical canons of cognition see only another occasion for skeptical dismissal or its twin, system-building recruitment, psychoanalytic knowing returns the authority of cognition to its objects and constitutive practices by explicating its dependence on them. Here, performative expressions of cognitive insecurity are rational avoidances of over inflating subjectivity or system as all-encompassing, which leads inexorably to skeptical or dogmatic collapse. Like art criticism for Adorno, psychoanalytic knowing is an effort to master subjectivity in order to make room for the claim of the object, its rationality at one with its modernist commitment to the unprecedented but not unmediated singularity of its object. Yes, it is a value-laden rationality, but can it be any other way?

At least within psychoanalytic circles, where it tends to be doggedly buried or defensively sidestepped but where it has a chance of being productive, the skeptical moment of psychoanalytic knowing is in need of much more robust and refined consideration. Perhaps, if the insistent questionability of psychoanalytic knowing were given more sustained consideration, it would provoke questions of why one is committed to one particular camp or interpretation rather than another (at least intermittently) and thereby (1) take the analyst's self-analysis in potentially new and fecund directions and (2) sustain the tenuousness of psychoanalytic knowing sufficiently for doctrinal rigidity to slacken. What is at stake in acknowledging the insuperable questionability of psychoanalysis is nothing less than the possibility for psychoanalytic *thinking*, for the development of psychoanalysis beyond stalemated partisan polemics, as engagements between Kleinians and Lacanians tend to be. And this leads us to our final topic: the ways in which Lacan's perspective is organized by an imperative to keep thinking in motion. We will broach this topic through a consideration of how to read Lacan.

IX. How to Read Lacan

It is hard to deny the impression that Lacan is staunchly dogmatic ("In the beginning was the Word, which is to say, the signifier"[236]; desire does not seek satisfaction, it seeks rearticulation; "to love is to want to be loved"[237]), prone to wild exaggerations ("there is no other resistance to analysis than that of the analyst himself"[238]; "the essential function of the ego is very nearly that systematic refusal of reality which French analysts refer to in talking about the psychoses"[239]), and frequently given to moralizing ("do not cede on your desire"; "the only thing one can be guilty of is giving ground relative to one's desire"[240]; "the subject should come to recognize and name his desire"[241]; "there is never a subject without an ego . . . but this is what we must always try to obtain from a subject in analysis"[242]). It is equally difficult to deny the impression that he is inordinately preoccupied by a select few topics (desire, jouissance, the Other) and that as a result his teachings are one-sided and exaggerated and his readings of Freud and of the clinical material he draws upon are forced. Has any reader of Lacan not been vexed by the impression that his criticisms of others' work presuppose the absolute value of his own theoretical and therapeutic orientation (Klein and the ego psychologists are remiss for propping up the standpoint of the ego; they promote adaptation rather than freedom and so must be corrected) or by the sense that to read him is to masochistically submit to an overwhelming barrage of language—to subject oneself to mystification so extreme, to an onslaught of association so intense and unremitting, that the very act of reading, let alone reading critically, is thwarted? Can one avoid feeling manipulated, even sadistically accosted, by linguistic intricacies that seem to call for reflection and unpacking but in the end may well confound the expectation of meaning, let alone meaning worth the effort? Is not reading Lacan to struggle anxiously with the feeling of being manipulated by stage-stealing wordplay, of being recruited into a self-indulgent narcissism or hysteria, of having wasted one's time? Has any reader not worried about Lacan's tendency to abandon once-complex and -nuanced claims and stride into rigid oppositions, especially when these seem both facile and overblown, as they often do, e.g., desire as lack versus jouissance as substance, the Symbolic versus the Imaginary, the subject versus the self, meaning versus nonsense, empty speech versus full speech? And his predilection for the obscure cannot but seem excessive, even at times contrived. Often he refuses to even acknowledge the overt meanings of the phenomena with which he is concerned as he rushes headlong to ferret out their unsuspected resonances, unexamined significance, and abyssal underside.

When reading Lacan, one cannot but become frustrated, even incensed, by his evasion of argument via the distractions of indirection, seduction and flirtation, humor, and wordplay, and all the more so by his haughty penchant for "arguing" by parody, slander and insult, irony, elliptical commentary, and especially by assertion and definition: castration *is* loss and incompleteness; being-split *is* desire *is* the subject; to accommodate oneself to desire *is* to come into one's truth, etc. Likewise, one cannot but become troubled, at the very least, by Lacan's indulgence in raising various of his claims to the level of axioms, as if via self-authorized election and elevation they would become immune from critical contestation. Is there any way of arguing with Lacan's assumption that due to our prematurity and the absolute dependence it entails we are radically open to the discourse and desire of the Other (i.e., [via] a primary caregiver), and in response to the frustrations and sufferings associated with infantile prematurity and the ultimately enigmatic, exciting discourse and desire of the other we become gluttons for meaning, coherence, stability, and finality, locking ourselves into fantasy formations from which we will suffer and from which only the therapy of desire will provide emancipation, however qualified? Does one not sense that Lacan would dismiss outright any empirical evidence to the contrary?

When reading Lacan, one cannot but become vexed by the way he hyperbolically privileges, even to the point of primordializing, i.e., rendering as ontological basics, certain themes or tropes that seem part of a larger picture that is resolutely suppressed, e.g., the anxiety of freedom. In Oedipal rivalry, Lacan asserts, we defend against the infinity of *desire*, the void of subjectivity.[243] *Really*, our Oedipal rivalry has nothing to do with, say, wanting to be (like) mother because she has captivated father's attention. *Really*, it is about our defense against *desire* as such. Really?

When reading Lacan, one cannot put aside the impression that his emphases are all too decided and one-sided. Often one eventually succumbs to complacency, if somewhat anxiously; well, it's Lacan, so of course he is going to emphasize certain topics: the unsuspected depth and breadth of our subjection to and alienation by various schemas and strategies through which we seek to secure social recognition and world orientation; the unwitting coerciveness of the desire of the other and the limits it imposes on acceding to our truth; the interruption of the Real that unravels comforting consistencies and structures of significance, unsettling and displacing us but perhaps thereby paving the way for subjective and social-symbolic renewal; the rigidity and constriction of the fundamental fantasy and the need to traverse it; what is always already behind our backs and forever in excess of cognitive or instrumental mastery; the hazards of consistency, strength, and cohesion, both in terms of subjectivity and theoretical production; the need to put one's whole life into question, to move from stable and stabilizing demands to the lability of *desire*. Is Lacan not rather predicable? Does he not come off—formally—as something of a fairly reliable if eccentric character from a piece of nineteenth-century fiction? Time and again, will he not focus, searchingly, on the effects of speech rather than respond to the manifest content of what is said? It is Lacan, yes? So of course he will insistently emphasize the level of idiosyncratic psychic reality rather than the level of intersubjectively established meaning. Of course he will be suspicious of meaning, especially if it concretizes our sense of what ails us, allows us to hold others or specific aspects of ourselves at fault, and thus opens the way for punishment or other forms of expiation whereby guilt is temporarily assuaged and our probing into the causes of our distress demobilized. At least at times is Lacan not rather formulaic, proceeding as if on autopilot? Or, one might say, driven, given to compulsive repetition, mad?

Lacan's ethico-clinical ambition seems to be equally decided and one-sided: to undo or at least shake up subjection, to enhance freedom and liberate desire (come what may?), to promote a nonidealized relation to others and the Other, to sap the force of Imaginary ensnarement, to promote the affirmation of finitude, lack, desirous singularity. Is this always the best way to go? What makes him so confident? Does he offer any plausible arguments to this end, or, again, does he just assume the absolute value of his ambitions and expect us, in the long term, to come to see things his way?

In these ways and more, Lacan often seems dogmatically rigid and heavy-handed. The question that preoccupies him always seems to be What is the individual's relation to the Other's desire? The hysteric provokes the Other's desire but refuses to be the object of his or her jouissance, i.e., to satisfy. She tries to deny her lack (the Other's desire qua enigma in her) by evoking in the other a state of manifest lack, i.e., desire. At the other end of the spectrum, the pervert tries to do away with the Other's desire by becoming the object of his or her jouissance or by presuming that the question is irrelevant (and thus in every way responding to it) because he or she has found the object that truly satisfies: *it*. Somewhere in the middle, the obsessive tries to avoid the question by allowing him- or herself to believe that both s/he and the Other are satisfied and complete. The complex rituals of obsessive neurosis, along with its typical thought and speech patterns, are ways of avoiding both one's desire and the desire of the other. Even if the terms "hysterical," "perverse," or "obsessional" are not diagnostic categories into which various clinical phenomena will be slotted, still, is the question of how one relates to the desire of the other the only or even the most-pertinent question? And to the extent that clinical phenomena are subsumed by this categorical apparatus—how can this be altogether avoided?—will this not be a backsliding from Lacan's repeated insistence on the need for the utmost attention to the singularity of the clinical material?[244] A performative contradiction? For that matter, what are we to make of the many contradictions, both at the level of content and performance, that riddle Lacan's thought?

Can we read Lacan's work without becoming distressed by its wildly oppositional, even reactionary, character? Is not Lacan's thought often, even usually, set against prevailing social forces? Specifically set against those that promote normalization, rationalization, and reification, but not just these? Likewise, is Lacan's thought not set against both the prevailing and newly dominant ambitions, concerns, and theories of other analysts? Lacan is evidently against the hermeneutic focus on part/whole relations as much as he is against the subordination of psychoanalysis to the natural sciences, against adaptation to social norms as much as he is against "hysterical" opposition to them, against the focus on and cultivation of stable and meaningful object relations (object relations theory) as much as he is against the focus on and cultivation of socially productive defenses (ego psychology). He sets himself against narrative coherence, against idealization, against all forms of Imaginary captivation, against Freud's lucidity,[245] against understanding:

> What counts, when one attempts to elaborate an experience is less what one does understand than what one does not understand. . . . Commenting on a text is like doing an analysis. . . . [O]ne of the things we should be watching out for most, is not to understand too much, not to understand more than what there is in the discourse of the subject. Interpreting is an altogether different thing than having the fancy of understanding. One is *the opposite* of the other. I will even say that it is on the basis of a certain *refusal of understanding* that we open the door onto psychoanalytic understanding. (*Seminar I*: 73/87–88; trans. modified and emphases added)

Against, against, against. Does Lacan not seem dead set on refusing—refusing, not refuting—everyone else's ideas and ambitions to the point of neurotic nay-saying? Does one not suspect that no matter what social or psychoanalytic trends became dominant Lacan would set himself against them? So strongly does Lacan set himself against prevailing and newly arising trends and ambitions that his negativity verges on self-parody, putting one in mind of Groucho Marx's "Whatever It Is, I'm Against It."[246]

On a more serious note, can one avoid suspecting this manner of guaranteeing oneself a place in the limelight as the consummate critic colludes with a deadlocked narcissism—empty yet ravenous? And does his oppositional stance not collude with his perhaps defensive vagueness in elaborating and reticence to warrant his own ambitions, values, and ideas? For is it not that his ambitions, values, and ideas come into view for the most part as the negations of what others uphold? Even the truth of *desire* is for the most part elaborated through a continual negation of what others describe as fulfillment and developmental success. Is this not a negative theology of *desire*? And, if so, can we argue with it? How are we to receive it? Is it is merely incidental that Lacan's work tends to be received by either devoted disciples or exasperated critics?

Another cause for distress when reading Lacan is the moralizing tenor that regularly crops up. Does Lacan not claim to have discovered *the truth* of subjectivity? And on the basis of this revelation does he not propose strategies by which we are to accede to our truth? Are the various injunctions not to cede on desire precisely moralizing insofar as (1) their ground is not and perhaps cannot be made available for reflective scrutiny and, (2) on his own terms, we can never fulfill this injunction sufficiently? As antinormative as he poses himself in relation to prevailing social, theoretical, and psychoanalytic norms, Lacan is by no means averse to positing regulatory ideals. Lacan says repeatedly in *Seminar VII* that "The only thing of which one can [finally] be guilty is of having given ground relative to one's desire" (319, 321, 322). In formulating this injunction, Lacan appears to raise a certain human potential—accommodation to one's desire to the greatest degree—to the level of Truth. This injunction must be read as a regulatory ideal[247] since it explicitly forbids identifications (identifications with the desire of the other would be precisely ceding one's ownmost desire), but for Lacan identifications are inevitable. "[T]here is never a subject without an ego—a fully realized subject—but this is what we must always try to obtain from a subject in analysis" (*Seminar II*: 246). But is it certain that an individual is possessed of a stratum of desire that is properly his or her own, a stratum of desire that can be wholly isolated from, or, if not, is yet somehow independent of, the history of mimetically incorporated desires? And is it not Lacan who suggests that identification may be an avenue through which desire sustains its mobility? In any case, the call to live "authentically" by not ceding on one's desire[248] is moralizing precisely to the extent that it evangelically asserts—as if testifying to a transcendent value—an ideal against which we should measure ourselves but with respect to which we will forever come up wanting. To be sure, teaching us how to live in the space of inevitable failure is part of the Lacanian ambition. But does positing this ideal not court many of the risks Lacan outlines in relation to Kleinian practice? Even if this ideal demands incessantly mobilized desire, ongoing desubjectification, etc., doesn't its formal role as the highest good make it a potential source of pathological suffering? And what are we to make of the impression that Lacan's ambitions *regularly* run many of the risks that he identifies in others' work?

On the one hand, these impressions, worries, questions, and vexations are not off base. Lacan is dogmatic, moralistic, excessively contrarian, given to ridicule where argument seems appropriate, and so on. When reading Lacan there is always reason to be wary. But on the other hand the foregoing is a highly one-sided, indeed quite-exaggerated, presentation of Lacan's teachings. Though not wrong, it is not quite right either. These sorts of concerns need to be confronted if we are to learn how to read Lacan, but to unqualifiedly assert or deny them would be to miss something crucial. As we will see, Lacan is a creature of contra-diction.

Immediately encumbering any proposals for how to read Lacan is the difficulty of identifying exactly what is to be read, for so much of Lacanian thought is composed by Lacan's inheritors. This is true of many pathbreaking thinkers but of Lacan especially. There is so much ambiguity, tension, and inconsistency in his writings and teachings, and such a paucity of explicit argument for so many of his most significant claims, that a coherent and transmissible "Lacan" could not but be a product of subsequent interpretations. And this is exactly how Lacan wanted it. When, in a letter to René Diatkine, Althusser proclaimed that "Lacan's claim and his unique originality in the world of psychoanalysis lie in his being a *theoretician.* Being a theoretician . . . means producing a *general system* of theoretical concepts, rigorously articulated with each other and capable of accounting for the *total set* of facts and the field of analytic practice," Althusser missed the boat entirely.[249] As Lacan directly claims in *Seminar XVI*, "[w]hat I enunciate about the subject as himself an effect of discourse absolutely rules out the possibility that my discourse could constitute a system" (Nov. 27, 1968). Lacan's overriding impulse is not to systematize and totalize. His distinctiveness emerges most evidently in the moments when the urge to systematization and totalization, or, more precisely, to universalization, meets with and is offset by a deflationary countercurrent, by an impulse to expose the provisional, exaggerated, and so eminently contestable character of his claims. In order to situate itself as a perspective, as emphatically partial, but a perspective that must be taken seriously, Lacan's thinking both is suffused with exceptionally bold claims and implacably exposes itself to alterative perspectives. To be sure, Lacan is no fan of easy pluralism. He calls upon the force of *compelling* alternatives—both those of prominent psychoanalytic figures and those he induces his addressees to develop—to situate his own claims as something other than definitive pronouncements, to allow his claims to emerge as compelling insights with which we can work rather than as revealed truths with which we can rest content.[250]

A dialectic of inflation and deflation is at work in Lacan's teachings and writings. This is quite clear, for instance, in the tension between the universalizing thrust of his mathemes, which are supposed to be completely transparent and transmissible,[251] and the opacity of his texts and seminars. The mathemes seek to describe structural truths that can be precisely formulated and affirmed with the utmost certitude, while the opacity of the texts and seminars keeps us wondering whether anything has been understood (either by Lacan or by us, his addressees). Another instance of this dialectic manifests in the tension between, on the one hand, Lacan's promotion of *desire* to the truth of subjectivity and his establishment of its liberation as the highest analytic goal and, on the other, his claims that "desire is a defense, a defense against going beyond a certain limit in jouissance" (*E*: 699/825) and that psychosis is characterized by the disintegration of the ego, ego ideal, and other such Imaginary forces of unification and stabilization that presumably impede the liberation of desire (*Seminar III*). Traces of this dialectic are also evident in Lacan's framing of his insights, bold as they are, as *readings* of Freud. Lacan's scrupulous interrogations of Freud's texts, and especially his attention to their tensions, ambiguities, and amenability to being read quite otherwise than they have been—e.g., their availability to Lacan's efforts to retrieve their spirit, which effectively makes their message unrecognizable to the Freudian orthodoxy—keeps the problematic character of these texts alive and in view. Thus when Lacan presents some of his most significant claims as readings of the very texts he calls into question, the problematic character of the Freudian texts subtly seeps into the bold claims he makes on their basis.

Generally, Lacan proposes radical innovations in psychoanalytic theory and practice while at once, though often only implicitly, calling for critical hesitation regarding just these proposals. By soliciting alternative perspectives to illuminate his own *as a perspective* rather than a clear-cut claim to truth, Lacan seeks to keep psychoanalytic thinking vital, enmeshed in a scene of antagonism whose loss would be, as we will see, the loss of the specific character of psychoanalytic truth. The effort is to sustain psychoanalysis as a problematic field, to keep genuine conflict alive, and thereby to keep psychoanalysis responsive to the peculiar status of its objects.[252]

For Lacan, psychic objects (perhaps phenomena as such) are ontologically indeterminate. They are relatively inchoate, neither immediately given nor positive contents to be decoded and brought to consciousness. Psychic objects are complex blends of sense and nonsense, determinacy and indeterminacy, content and enigma, structure and void. By no means does Lacan want to suggest that psychic life is simply meaningless or that our efforts to uncover unconscious phantasies, beliefs, attitudes, and so on are condemned to utter failure—one can, indeed one must, guess at them: "the analyst . . . strives to get the analysand to guess [*lui faire devenir*—to divine, to become subject to the befalling or revelation of]" unconscious meaning (*E*: 492/589). But one can do no more than guess. This is to say, the rational confidence that one's discernment of unconscious meaning is conclusive, valid as deductions from first principles or systematic empirical inductions are valid, is not forthcoming, though to repudiate what has been discerned or to abandon the ongoing guesswork of analysis on this basis would be to ask for more precision than the subject admits of, to succumb to unreasonability in the name of reason, perhaps to anxiously evade that which recalls exposure to skeptical unrest, which is to say, all matters of significance. One can do no more than guess: this is also to say that even what strikes as a revelation is not to be extracted from the orbit of skeptical secularity;

circumspectly revolving around what has been revealed, one may encounter areas of opacity, hazy topographical features, even uncharted continents, and other motives to guess on. Lacan does not want to obscure the persistent mystery and ultimate ineffability of psychic phenomena nor shroud the evident significance of what has been determined. The aura of revelation or divination is that of mystery. Accordingly, psychoanalytic thinking at its most rigorous will mirror its object's admixture of determinacy and indeterminacy. Psychoanalytic knowing requires a mimetic moment, a performative registration of the complex admixture of determinacy and indeterminacy of its object. In this precise sense, Lacan is to be read as a materialist.[253]

On the one hand, Lacan is committed to psychoanalysis as a problematic field within which conflict and creativity can and should be sustained. On the other hand, he proposes extravagantly bold and evidently conclusive insights to which he is equally committed. This tension between deflation and inflation is plainly visible in Lacan's style. His style is declarative, apophantic rather than demonstrative. This is most emphatically the case in the written texts and the seminars of the 1970s, but by no means consigned to them. By *not* providing demonstrations or often even examples[254] of his most important and novel claims, Lacan at once (1) calls upon his addressees to accept what has been asserted and (2) urges us to think, to provide arguments and examples that would substantiate—support and concretize—his/our convictions. This is most explicit when Lacan famously says, with regard to his *Écrits*, "one either takes [i.e., appropriates] what they formulate or one leaves them."[255] By speaking and writing in a manner that is conspicuously opaque and condensed, that is difficult,[256] indeed barely intelligible, sometimes contradictory, and in need of unpacking at every turn, Lacan urges his addressees to ruminate over what he says, or, more precisely, to create/discover what this discourse might mean: "You don't understand dis writing [*stécriture*]. So much the better—it'll give you a reason to explain it."[257] "I strive to ensure that access to the meaning [of what I say] not be too easy, such that you must contribute some elbow grease of your own (or work hard at it) [*mettre du vôtre*]" (*Seminar XIX*, Jan. 6, 1972; trans. modified following Fink 2004: 178). His discourse means to motivate its resymbolization, its personalization. His language seeks to bind and unbind, to associate and individuate. Communicating specific insights while at once inducing his addressees to associate to his claims in ways that may make of them something the author never could have intended, he invites his addresses to become coauthors. In this way, Lacan both assumes the position of master and professes his commitment to a radical egalitarianism. Contra-dictory to the core.

Drawing attention to their style, Lacan's teaching and writings make it perfectly clear that psychoanalysis, at least in its Lacanian incarnation, does not presume to apodictic certainty. It may be dogmatic, but what the exquisitely self-aware dogmatism of this discourse gives us to see is that it is never sufficiently warranted.[258] Paradoxically, dogmatism is a display of exposure, unrest, and incompletion, a way of making room for others. By not speaking clearly, providing demonstrations, or offering all that many examples, and by speaking in a manner that, at least initially, seems rushed and overfull, in a manner that requires us, again at least initially, to just go along with it, Lacan induces us to associate to his claims both consciously and unconsciously, to think them through and to be unconsciously moved by them (as an analyst would). Obviating the logical order of step-wise, predictable progression is no extravagance; it is a constitutive condition of his discursive practice. Perhaps tactless, Lacan is a consummate tactician—able to circumvent without debilitating the ego. He puts us in a position where we can acknowledge both the compelling force of his claims and the insuperable partiality of his/our knowledge, the limits to his/our (cognitive, but not just cognitive) mastery.[259] He puts us in a position where we can see ourselves as both subjects of understanding and subjects of the unconscious. Is this not the position of the analyst?

Lacan's structure of address is quite complex. He positions himself as both analyst and analysand. As analyst, he is both the one who Knows (the classical conception of the analyst) and *objet a*, the "cause" of the addressee's desire (the Lacanian conception of the analyst[260]), both sage and provocateur. But especially in his seminars, Lacan explicitly positions his addressees as his analysts.[261] A megalomaniacal move? But this in order to provoke individuating resistance? Positioning his addressees as his analysts, he suggests that his discourse is to some degree transferentially inflected, subtended by "insane and irreducible" signifying chains (thus casting doubt on his ability to assume the role of the one who Knows), that he is to some extent obeying the rule of free association, that he is distortive and defensive, working out his own emotional-historical issues, passionate, "mad"[262]—i.e., a subject of the unconscious, subject to forces over which he will never be able to gain full control that influence his articulation of the material with which he is concerned—and that he is offering material for interpretation, not a doctrine. But, then again, positioning himself as an analysand he may mean to recall the "invention" of psychoanalysis by a patient and thereby recuperate some measure of authority.

Perhaps Lacan's infamous difficulty and obscurity, and his abstention from providing much in the way of demonstration and exemplification in particular, are signals of self-inflated presumptuousness—or, more generously, signals of fidelity to convictions beyond rational redemption—*and* ways of urging us to phrase his claims in our own ways, to find our own examples for them, thus to make these claims our own. Ever the provocateur, Lacan seeks to have an *effect* as much as, and sometimes more than, he seeks to communicate a content of knowledge. Is this a mechanism of self-aggrandizement? Maybe. Does it focus too much attention on his own performance and detract attention from the material under consideration? Perhaps.[263] But perhaps by being forced to make his claims meaningful through our own elaboration and exemplification we will be induced to go further in our own thinking and perhaps in our own analyses: Lacan does say that he is ever training.[264] And if psychic objects are ontologically indeterminate, always amenable to rearticulation, perhaps this will become clear to us as we recurrently resymbolize the phenomena to which Lacan draws our attention.

At stake here is a dialectical dimension of psychoanalytic discourse and so, as we will see, the specific truth value of psychic objects. Proposing bold theses, Lacan lends them an air of universality: we are to take seriously the possibility that these claims speak the Truth. But since we must support these claims by rendering them in our own ways, by finding our own examples for and applications of them, and by developing our own arguments for their veracity, these claims become particularized.[265] They become meaningful within the space of our commitments, sensibilities, and concerns—they take hold of us. And yet they immediately disseminate. Making these claims our own by finding our own ways to substantiate, illustrate, articulate, or apply them, we invariably morph them, particularize them, but only on the basis of their capacity to resonate and perhaps to flourish in ever new contexts. Making these claims our own we are immediately disappropriated, exposed to the in(de)finite interpretability of that to which we have laid claim, and so to the feeble violence of that claim. The claim, like the psychic object for which it seeks to account, is inconclusive, subject to an ongoing dialectic of creation and discovery. It is not given, there to be simply transmitted, decoded, or taken over. Rather, its reception requires the work of thinking (both conscious and unconscious). We are always cocreators of the Lacanian innovation and thus coresponsible for its fate. Lacan's difficulty is at one with his efforts to promote responsible resymbolization.

To allow psychic objects to manifest in their truth is to keep alive the dialectics of universalization and particularization and of creation and discovery. To elaborate only the dimension of universality *or* the dimension of the particularity, only the aspect of discovery *or* the aspect of creation, would be—even if possible—to lose the object in its fullness, in its truth—which is inevitable, but not in such an egregious manner. The truth of a psychic object is won, to the extent that it can be, as *its* complex admixture of determinacy and indeterminacy, *its* meaning and irreducibility to this meaning, is kept alive and in focus. The object comes into its truth through its abrasiveness to and incitement to reworking of the universalizing claims that attempt to systematically integrate it into a standing body of theory or otherwise clarify it completely and its inassimilability to and partial reconfiguration of the somewhat more restrained discourses that explicitly, self-consciously, elaborate it according to a particular perspective. This is to say, the object comes into its truth incompletely, as necessarily but not wholly distorted by universal claims and more attenuated discourses, in its manner of resistance to or standing apart from its conceptual and schematic determinations, in the mode of gesturing toward its futurity. In Lacan's words, "the unconscious is what closes up again as soon as it has opened" (*Seminar XI*: 143/131).[266]

It would seem that, tragically, the object's specific admixture of determinacy and indeterminacy is partially obscured and its specific proneness to become and appear otherwise is partially obstructed by the terms through which it can do so, our terms. The dimension of its truth can manifest in and through its continual rearticulation, though the object never entirely comes into its truth. But it is not as if our terms are merely impediments that, upon dissolving, would allow the object to come fully into its truth: such would be a falsifying and endlessly frustrating fantasy of escape from finitude. To the contrary, the object can come into its truth in no other way than through these terms. Indeed, the language of "distortion," "obscuring," and "obstruction" is somewhat misleading, just as it is somewhat misleading to speak of "the object's specific admixture of determinacy and indeterminacy" or "its specific proneness to become and appear otherwise." For it is not as if somewhere "deep in the mind" there is a pure, undistorted psychic object to which, in principle, our terms could correspond. Neither is it as if truth is a property of the object that is diminished by our handling of it.[267] Rather, the object's coming into truth is a matter of coresponsiveness between subject and object, a matter of mutual becoming. Truth is between subject and object, the mattering of their mutual implication. The object comes into its truth as claims about it are received, taken up and reinflected, redirected, or otherwise particularized—which is to say, the truth of the object is registered in our impulsion to formulate, attend to it, or, most broadly, respond to it ever anew. As we should suspect, from a Lacanian perspective, truth is less a matter of correspondence between propositional statement and object or of fulfilling intersubjectively established validation procedures than it is an *effect*.

The truth of a psychic object is manifest in the tension between the universalizing claims that pronounce its determinate meaning(s) and the particularizing claims that register its resistance to these universal generalizations and through which they are challenged and qualified. The truth of the object is manifest in the tension between the claim to decisive discovery and efforts of (re-)creation or resymbolization, in the tension between knowing and not knowing, between retaining, discerning, and anticipating, in the tension of thought.[268] The object hangs in the balance between what has been given to be seen and what may yet unfold. Insofar as we are committed to speaking the truth of the psychic object, we can forgo neither universalization nor challenging and reworking it, neither claiming to have discovered the meaning and structure of the object nor striving to complicate or at times undermine what has been asserted. To the extent that we are committed to the truth of the psychic object, we will seek to do justice to the object's amenability to universalizing articulation *and* its implacable resistance to it, to our capacities for being moved to associate, respond, and discern otherwise—that is, to our capacities for cobecoming with the object—*and* to the limits the object sets to this mutual development.

Lacan's teachings do not constitute a doctrine.[269] They are more like a provocatively intense suggestion. To be sure, there are claims to Truth throughout Lacan's corpus, *many* such claims, but these are to be read in this "suggestive" context.[270] Lacan's discourse is evocative and challenging; it interrupts easy assimilation by the novice as much as the initiate's pretension to understand.[271] At both surface and depth, one can never be exactly sure about what Lacan is saying or enjoining. In order to preemptively fight off his inheritors' temptations to repose in whatever mastery of his work they have achieved, Lacan comes up with ever-new formulations of his basic insights and even, to a certain extent, radically changes tack in his theory and practice. By doing so, he seems to be suggesting that (1) a true insight will survive its first formulation[272] (inflation, universalization) and (2) the insight is never as clear as its confident presentation suggests, especially when it is an initial presentation, as much more may be than is now evident (deflation, particularization). Again, there is a dialectic of assertion and retraction, of inflation and deflation at play. Lacan's discourse is *expansive*: it is composed of commentaries and conceptual developments bearing on the most diverse psychoanalytic themes, given to regular alternations of rhetorical atmosphere and especially of guiding metaphors and prominent tropes, strewn with literary, philosophical, political, and religious-historical references and allusions, and coursing with thematic and normative currents and countercurrents. Is this discursive multiplicity, the seemingly endless itinerary of Lacan's transdisciplinary assemblages, not a means of gesturing toward what cannot be expressed in any one sector and thus a way of keeping psychoanalytic thinking keyed to the persistent (in)determinacy of its objects, to their amenability to being said and specified otherwise? Might the Lacan's theoretical discomposure mean to avow the unsettling force of the experiences theorized?

Lacan's style is evasive, multilayered, and surprising. It keeps us off-balance, on edge: between trying to anticipate what may yet come and trying to catch up with what we have been through. His discourse is emphatically condensed, over- and underdetermined, subject to multiple displacements, contra-dictory,[273] and polylingual: it speaks the languages of mathemes, set theory, structuralism, anthropology, modern and classical literature, European philosophy, etc. And rather often a seemingly trivial gesture or remark—a brief note, a particular turn of phrase, an undertone, a connection only alluded to—represents something of great significance. Call this Lacan's penchant for the short circuit. With this discourse, Lacan seeks to habituate his addresses to tarry with the evasive, multilayered, surprising, often obscure, contra-dictory, and ultimately ineffable nature of the unconscious in particular and of psychic phenomena in general (maybe phenomena as such). His discourse mirrors its objects; thus even if Lacan's claims are found wanting at the level of content—e.g., even if one shows that his readings of Freud fail to take something crucial into account or that his concepts fail to register something of the utmost importance or even that his claims are disproved in some fashion—something true is conveyed through his manner of *speech*.

Yes, Lacan is difficult to read. Both performatively and thematically, he emphasizes opacity, incompleteness, and the need for continual re-elaboration—the need for a thinking that will never quite correspond to its object but may be co-responsive with it, a thinking that will respond to the object and allow the object to respond to the thinking by both manifesting itself in its terms and resisting total assimilation to them, thereby, perhaps, provoking their reconfiguration. The interminable resistance of phenomena is, for Lacan, the spur of thought. But Lacan is not all that incomprehensible. Even if particular statements or formulas arise in a context that they do not fit neatly within and this gives one to worry that, given their dissonance with what has lead up to them, what follows them, and all that is associated with them either in the immediate context or more tangentially, nothing has been understood, still it is not as if we are so vertiginously displaced that all hopes for understanding are dashed. Lacan's texts put forward clear-enough ideas and take reasonably intelligible positions. He is not trying to confuse us for the sake of confusion. Rather, he is trying, for instance, to habituate his addressees to attend to the least-likely meanings or the more-expansive-than-imagined range of meanings of the phenomena with which he is/they are concerned. Expressed in Lacan's writerly practice—which is not confined to his written texts—is a striking commitment to the marginalized and vehement resistance to all forms of totalization. The point is not to be confusing for its own sake but rather to allow psychic objects' singularity to shine forth from the clarifying conceptual schemas in which they are enshrouded. The point is to both *capture* psychic phenomena within the privileged terms of his perspective and *release* them from these terms, with the hope that with this exemplary performance he can induce us to do likewise. Thereby, Lacan aims to (1) forestall as much as possible the death of psychoanalytic speculation and (2) attune us to the dimension of the objects (and so of ourselves) that demands yet eludes symbolization.

In these ways, Lacan insists upon or strongly suggests—for he cannot definitively demonstrate—the ongoing incompletion of psychoanalytic knowledge. This knowledge, like its object, is transient: it may come to rest in a provisional stability, but what has consolidated will soon give way. The Lacanian conception of psychoanalysis is resolutely modernist: radically self-critical, self-transgressing, incessantly self-revolutionizing—never having said the last word.

To read Lacan is to read a self-consciously exaggerated discourse, a discourse that refuses to hide the exaggerated quality of its claims and thereby seeks to (1) draw out the suppressed exaggerations of others' claims (are Freud, Klein, Hartmann, etc. any less prone to exaggeration? Does Freud not exaggerate the persistence of our libidinal history in the organization of our present forms of life and in our availability to the future? Does Ferenczi not exaggerate the import of empirical experience, e.g., pathogenic experiences of the breakdown of trust and sympathy and the reorientational experiences provided by Ferenczian therapy? Does Winnicott not exaggerate the drive to (re)development and the import of the caregiving environment in pathology and healing? Do ego psychologists not exaggerate the value of the ego, reality testing, self-determination/social integration, and, broadly speaking, adult capacities? Does Kohut not exaggerate the significance of the selfobject matrix and narcissism and our prospects for personal and social integrity?) and (2) undermine stultifying conviction in both his own and others' claims (are they not all a bit exaggerated? Can we rest content with any of them?). But to read Lacan is also to read a fairly straightforward discourse on psychosexuality and other standard psychoanalytic topics, a discourse that calls attention to certain phenomena with which we are not yet sufficiently familiar and calls upon us to take its claims about these matters seriously. To read Lacan is to immerse oneself in a discourse that has *internalized* the dialectics of inflation and deflation and of universalization and particulatization that, often without remark, structure the history of psychoanalytic thinking.[274]

Part of the difficulty of reading Lacan stems from the fact that his discourse is imbued with the tension of conflictual extremes: yes and no, absolutely and not so fast, here it is and not yet. Exaggerations (e.g., the unconscious is structured like a language; the Real cannot be symbolized; there is no sexual *rapport*; the superego commands us to enjoy; there are no unconscious affects, let alone repressed affects, etc.) meet with and offset deficiencies (failures to think through that to which Lacan draws attention). And deficiencies (our inability to fully make out what he is saying; the scantiness of warrants and examples) meet with and offset exaggerations (the boldness of his claims). With Lacan, there is no outside to exaggeration. For instance, an excessive emphasis on epistemic and ontological insecurity meets with and is tempered by audacious claims about "the way it is." Or an excessive emphasis on radical heterogeneity is met with and tempered by excessively bold claims about psychic structure (the mathemes) or motivation (*the* inescapable question of the Imaginary is "What does the Other desire?"). Or an excessive deflation of the dominant readings of Freud (Klein, the ego psychologists, the orthodox Freudians, etc. get it totally wrong) or of the taken-for-granted convictions of prevailing psychoanalytic theory and practice (transference provokes countertransference, the tradition upholds; no, Lacan proclaims in his reading of the Dora case, countertransference provokes transference) meets with and is tempered by the strategies through which Lacan excessively deflates his own claims. Excess is set into tension with counter excess; thinking cannot come to a rest.

Even when Lacan's discourse is quite clear, it is perhaps for that reason all the more mad. As Lacan maintains, the psychotic's refusal of doubt is just as mad as the neurotic's perpetual doubt. If, as Lacan claims, psychotics never doubt the meaning of their discourse and to whom their messages are addressed, and if, conversely, neurotics compulsively doubt the meaning of their discourse and to whom their messages are addressed, then does Lacan not display both neurotic and psychotic structures as a way of both making a claim about what they are and undermining his authority to do so? This is what Lacan gives us to think.

Lacan is interested in what can be known of the meanings of dreams, parapraxes, symptoms, etc., but his emphasis falls on that which cannot be raised to the level of thematization or conscious knowledge or otherwise reflectively recuperated. He is interested in the aims and objects of satisfaction, but he exaggerates the in(de)finite, insatiable, and enigmatic character of *desire* and by doing so wrests it from the obscurity to which the tradition had condemned it. Lacan is interested in understanding and drawing from the psychoanalytic tradition but more so in unsettling received opinions. Generally, he is interested in redressing the blind spots in psychoanalytic theory and practice and opening psychoanalysis onto new horizons, onto new avenues of inquiry whose paths are yet to be plotted. And his discourse reflects this interest at every turn.

X. Once More unto the Breach, Dear Friends (How to Read Lacan, Part II)

Having clarified the basic elements of Lacan's style and strategy, we can better appreciate his criticisms of Klein, especially those that concern the violence of her interventions. Throughout his commentary on Klein in *Seminar I*, Lacan repeatedly foregrounds the violence of her speech. This is how the discussion starts: "She sticks symbolism into him, little Dick, with the utmost brutality, that Melanie Klein!" (*Seminar I*: 68/81; trans. modified following Felman 1987: 118). Is Lacan's rhetorical blast not meant to carve a trench between himself and Klein? Countering by inverting Klein's injurious intrusiveness, does it not aim to establish as much distance between himself and Klein as possible, to articulate a clear polarity between Klein the brute and Lacan, by implication, the complex and patient reader? Is this not a rhetorical imposition of a forced choice: either side with Lacan, who, aligned with poor little Dick, is outraged by the savagery of a violently normalizing strain of psychoanalysis, or admit to identifying with the aggressor and side with Klein?[275] Generally, do not Lacan's polemics call upon us to take sides and ultimately, of course, to side with him?

In this first sentence and throughout, Lacan appears to be drawing the lines of partisanship. In order to caution against following the Kleinian path, he eventually goes so far as to intimate that Klein's frame of interpretation is motivated by, perhaps nought but an expression of, her fixation on sadistic sexuality. Lacan pathologizes her—and, vicariously, her current and would-be pundits—in order to position himself on the side of clear thinking (analysis) and draw us to his side, as if a general amassing his forces. He, Lacan, is the analyst; she, Klein, is the brute—one of those miscreants responsible for the bad name of psychoanalysis from whom we should establish as much distance as possible, the more spectacular the ostracism the better. From the first sentence, Klein's work is openly repudiated for being overly schematic and violent, at which point, again, it seems that we are to side with Lacan and thus with patient and careful analysis, indeed with *analysis* as a sophisticated and ethically self-aware, even nonviolent, activity. Lacan encourages us to identify with the victim of this brute, with poor little Dick, with poor little Dick who, Lacan suggests, we know to be wonderfully empathetic—unlike his analyst—by the fact that he says "poor Melanie Klein" in response to the sight of pencil shavings on her shirt. We are subtly implored to identify with this basic human empathy and thus to take a stand against the brute who has unleashed such extreme interpretive violence against this fragile and fundamentally good little creature, little Dick.

It is as if by identifying Klein's "illness" (her fixation on sadistic sexuality) and inducing us to identify with the victim (and through the victim with Lacan, who is manifestly on his side), Lacan is calling us to his side, enticing us to side with him both in his reading of the case and generally. It is as if he is seducing us to the side of the loving father or older brother who wants to protect us/Dick from the sadistically invasive mother. The moment we attend to the rhetorical dimension of Lacan's text, to the text as speech, as addressing—positioning and interpellating—its audience, we see quite clearly that there is a subtle, even quite sly, effort of persuasion at work. The question, then, is this: are Lacan's polemics simply designed to carve out a gulf between himself and Klein (or whomever his current adversary may be) and compel us to take his side, or do they subtly raise the question of how psychoanalytic disagreement can proceed if analytic perspectives are underdetermined by their supporting evidence, that is, if the strength of psychoanalytic readings are never sufficient to compel the conclusion that this perspective rather than that one is right—which is at root a question of the shape and stakes of psychoanalytic judgment?

Continually pointing to the insufficiencies of Klein's theory and practice, as if compelled to introduce ever more evidence for a case won but not quite closed, Lacan cannot demonstrate that Klein is altogether wrong about Dick or that her violence and the risks of her approach decisively warrant dismissing her orientation in favor of his own. He can only fight it out. This is not to say that vituperative polemic is the only way to proceed in contests that cannot be decided in the tribunal of Reason (deductive or inductive logic), just that with regard to such matters polemic—conflict, struggle, etc.—no matter how delicately refined, is unavoidable. Might it be that, for Lacan, heated, even outright vicious, polemic is a dramatic device, the medium of choice to convey both the depth of his conviction and the undecidability of the question under consideration in virtue of its exaggerated shunning of conciliatory, civic reason? *One* may develop forms of polemical engagement that abjure Lacan's aggression, but given his commitments to foregrounding the unavoidability of conflict (inconsistency, nonclosure, etc.) there where harmony is sought or supposed, *he* can only fight it out. Might it be that by being so blatantly malicious and unfair to Klein and so manifestly coercive with respect to his readers Lacan is at once giving voice, strongly, to his sincere conviction, expressing fidelity to an interpretive orientation, the material sources and practical significance of which compel his resolute commitment—a commitment that would be as nothing, betrayed, were he not to facilitate its claim on others—and attempting to draw to the fore the undecidability of interanalytic conflict? And thus the need for decision, for individual judgment? Even for violence? Might Lacan's rhetoric be a way of keeping the antagonisms structuring the analytic field manifest *as* antagonisms in order to provide a more clear picture of what it is to inhabit and work in this field, specifically to reveal the ideological kinship of the scientific credo that progress in formal logic and/or the empirical sciences will provide the tools to resolve analytic conflict and the amicably intended dismissal of such conflict to the domain of the "technical detail"? Or maybe he's just mean and self-aggrandizing.

Perhaps Lacan's polemics are designed to compel us to take sides and ultimately to side with him. But it may well be that Lacan's criticisms, here as elsewhere, are not nearly as condemnatory as they initially appear. Could it be that Lacan seeks to systematically subvert the position of external judge—the position of the *sujet supposé savoir*—from which he seems to denounce his various psychoanalytic interlocutors? And could this destabilization of the position of the external critic—of the expert, moralist, or inflated executive—not aim precisely at opening the space of responsive and responsible reading? A superbly democratic gesture? Is Lacan, even in this violent assault on Klein, covertly insisting on the necessity of judging for oneself the matters he will so forcefully weigh in on?

Approaching these questions, let us begin by noting that as much as the violence of Klein's interpretations certainly trouble Lacan this violence may not be a sufficient reason to reject her orientation and embrace his. Not even for Lacan. Though it certainly seems this way, it may not be a question of Lacan *or* Klein, the Symbolic *or* the Imaginary, desubjectivization *or* ego development.[276] It may not be an either/or sort of question. It may well be that Lacan systematically solicits and subverts our desire to fall in with neatly demarcated psychoanalytic camps, generally, to succumb to the authority of a master. The pathos of the statement in which Lacan charges Klein with brutality ("She sticks symbolism into him, little Dick, with the utmost brutality, that Melanie Klein!") is quite complex and warrants close consideration, as does the complex tenor of his engagement with Klein throughout *Seminar I* and elsewhere. Let the following considerations stand as a call for a return to Lacan, a return to his text, to the letter of his text and to the distinctive voice(s) manifest therein, a call to discern the subtle operations at play in Lacan's teachings that are so often obscured by pundits and critics alike.

Lacan forthrightly calls Klein's interpretations brutal. He even implies that she is aggressively "masculine" in her penetrative insertion of symbolism into Dick: she "*sticks symbolism into him*, little Dick," or in Forrester's translation, "She *slams the symbolism on him* with complete brutality, does Melanie Klein, on little Dick!" Is not Lacan openly repudiating Klein's work and casting aspersions on her character? If so, might this righteous rage indicate a defensive posturing on Lacan's part? Might it be that Lacan focuses on and rhetorically magnifies Klein's violence in order to detract attention from the masculine violence of his vituperative assault? Is Lacan's positioning of Klein as an ignorant brute a way of demeaning the speaker and thereby prejudicing us against what she has to say? Is it an instance of a more pervasive sexism? Is it a way of concealing the difficultly of decision about which perspective to affirm (on the case or in general), Klein's or Lacan's? Does Lacan not subtly project an ideal image of himself through his expulsion of this sin-saddled brute—as if engaged in some self-purifying rite? In other words, is Lacan just being slick and rather mean-spirited here?[277]

Or might it be just the reverse? Might it be that a knowing intimacy with and great appreciation for Klein's work reverberate in the subtext of Lacan's charge of vulgar brutality? Could this charge somehow be an expression of appreciation of her efficacy and admiration for the consistent care she provided for her patient? Perhaps Lacan's opening statement is not the blanket repudiation it appears to be. Perhaps it is not so much a covering over of the difficult decision of which perspective to affirm as it is an oblique way of raising this question and anticipatorily sustaining it as a question.

Though Lacan is obviously troubled by Klein's violence, the way he presents her work also suggests that because she cared enough to be brutal and stupid she worked wonders for the boy. *Her violence and her efficacy may be inseparable.* It works, Lacan soon proclaims; Klein's interventions work. There is no question about it. "It is clear that as a result of this interpretation something happens. That is what it's all about" (*Seminar I*: 68/81; trans. modified following Felman 1987: 108). This "something," Lacan goes on to suggest, is nothing less than Dick's accession to humanity. Klein's brutal interventions effect an ontological transmutation: what was once not yet or not quite human becomes recognizably human. Prior to his analysis with Klein, Dick did not feel in the least concernfully connected with others, and on Lacan's account, as exaggerated as this claim may be, he did not yet have an unconscious. Klein's interventions institute in Dick an unconscious and a sense of negotiable connectedness to and separateness from others: in both senses he becomes a *subject*. As a result of Klein's interventions, Dick comes to feel addressed by others and is able to address himself to them in turn. He is initiated into the human fold. Klein binds Dick to the Symbolic—and what we should not fail to notice is that *perhaps this is not despite but because of the violence of her speech.* If, on Lacanian grounds, the violence of initiation into and continued life within the Symbolic is a necessary violence, and if this violence is best conceived as an enabling *and* constraining violence, then, again on Lacanian grounds, the violence of Klein's interventions may not be a reason to prefer Lacan's orientation (to the case or in general) to hers.

To be sure, Lacan paints a dreadful picture of Klein. After the opening salvo, he quickly proceeds to state that "This text . . . comes from a therapist, a woman of experience. She feels things, she expresses them badly." But, he continues, "one cannot blame her for that" (*Seminar I*: 68). Perhaps blaming—specifically, assuming the position of external judge from which one denounces the other and implicitly valorizes or at least invokes the innocence of the self—is precisely the temptation to be avoided. By following Lacan's text closely and patiently, which does not mean without a certain willfulness and even violence, we may find it insisting on the insuperability and the value of avowing complicity. Even complicity in violence. Is this not one of the primary goals of Lacanian analysis, to have the analysand avow her role in and commitment to the suffering that seems to besiege her from without?[278] Perhaps Lacan's oblique suggestion is that blaming, judging from a site of presumptive exteriority, succumbing to the comforts of an either/or—you're in the wrong, I'm in the right—framework is a simultaneously ethical and theoretical failure. The text written by this "woman of experience," Lacan proclaims in the space marked by the ellipsis, "is a precious one." And, really, can Lacan blame Klein because she "feels things"? Or because she "expresses them badly"? As voiced by Lacan, can we hear either charge, and especially the latter, without at least a tinge of irony? She feels things—as if Lacan's writings and seminars are in no way directed by intuition or given to fits of feeling. She expresses herself badly—if there ever were a case of the pot calling the kettle black! *She* is a woman of experience . . . but does *he* not attempt "to elaborate . . . experiences" (*Seminar I*: 73/87)? Did he not later mention in the preface to *Seminar XI* that, "as always, I was entangled in urgent cases as I wrote this" (ix)? However latent, is there not a knowing intimacy in this critique? What would its consequences be?

If we are to appreciate the value (the preciousness) of Klein's text and the efforts it records, it is perhaps best to avoid a facile and misleading contrast between Klein, the violent and unthinking woman of experience, and Lacan, the sensitive, reflective, and theoretically adept man who would redeem the good name of psychoanalysis. Even though this seems to be exactly how Lacan sets things up. Ultimately, it may not be, or may not simply be, a matter of choice between their respective orientations. Even though this is how Lacan appears to frame his commentary, or at least a framing his discourse readily allows. The choice between Klein's and Lacan's readings—say, between focusing on content and the Imaginary as against speech and the Symbolic—may be much more complex and difficult than it seems. And it may be this difficulty with which Lacan's text, however surreptitiously, confronts us. If Klein's and Lacan's orientations are not as mutually exclusive as Lacan directly declares—Is there not a profound confluence between Klein's description of Dick's phobic world-construction and the Lacanian claim that phobia may be in the service of shoring up the precarious status of the *Nom-du-père*?[279] Does Lacan not seem to be in agreement with Klein about the primordiality of object relations when he suggests that an infant's cry is addressed to an other, specifically to the mother?[280] Are there not interesting parallels between Lacan's mirror stage and Klein's depressive position, both of which are said to set in around the age of six months? Isn't Klein's account of the tyrannical nature of the superego, specifically her emphasis on its imperatives to do good or make good, i.e., imperatives to reparation and idealization, in accord with Lacan's emphasis on the obscene, terrorizing injunctions of the superego?

Don't Klein and Lacan similarly emphasize the death drive as a unity-dissolving force rather than as aiming at homeostasis, tension-reduction, or inorganic inertness? Is there that much difference between Klein's account of envy of the breast and Lacan's account of envy of another's relation to jouissance?—then *if* we are to decide between them, we are plunged into an abyss, forced to decide on necessarily insufficient grounds . . . which would be the unavoidable condition of decision. But is such decisiveness, if indeed this is what is called for, or if this is something we cannot altogether avoid, not an act of violence? Would we, in siding with Lacan against Klein's brutality, be immune from violence, innocent from entanglement in that which we denounce?

Though the particular form of violence enacted by Klein's interpretations may not have been necessary, though Klein might have found ways to proceed other than the mechanical imposition of Oedipal interpretations ("slamming symbolism into him"), it is consistent with Lacan's thinking to say that some form of violence will have been necessary to liberate Dick from his Imaginary solitude. If reality and the Imaginary are fused, as Lacan suggests they are at the outset of Dick's treatment, then some violence in wresting the two apart will be unavoidable if the treatment is to proceed. To say that reality and the Imaginary are fused is to say that, for Dick, there was neither reality nor the Imaginary properly speaking. Their confusion means their collapse. Notice, then, that *Dick's case, and specifically Lacan's reading of it, calls into question the scope of the categories that Lacan is constructing in the course of his early seminars and related writings.*[281] If reality is unendingly interpretable, necessarily represented through mechanisms of selection or filtration, then Dick had no sense of reality. Equally, if reality names the hegemonic discourses and practices through which phenomena are conceptually and evaluatively predigested, Dick had no sense of reality. And if the Imaginary involves efforts to integrate phenomena into hard-cast cognitive and relational frames, to constitute a world by rendering experience narratively or otherwise symbolically cohesive and establishing felicitous and sustainable patterns of practical involvement with objects and others, then Dick was not yet, not really, a creature of the Imaginary. Equally, if the Imaginary turns on the question of what one is/can be/must be for the desire of the Other, Dick's manifest lack of concern with others suggests that he was not yet caught in the Imaginary. Though it may not be exactly "Imaginary solitude" from which Dick needed to be wrested (this phrasing overestimates both his integration in the Imaginary and his investment in life with others, which is a precondition for solitude if by this we understand, as Lacan seems to, deprivation of desired forms of life in common), Lacan and Klein agree that Dick was in need of emancipation from the flatness of his overanxious existence, i.e., initiation into a less rigid, static, and suffering-suffused form of life.

To be sure, the question of the exact trajectory of this emancipation—should the analyst support the development of his ego and object relations as

Klein contends or promote accommodation to the truth of his self-differentiating *desire* as Lacan claims—is a significant point of contention. Though the disagreement between Lacan and Klein concerning the goal of Dick's liberation is, on the one hand, a matter of emphasis (accommodation to the truth of *desire* requires a significant measure of ego development and relatively secure object relations if the individual is to avoid collapse,[282] just as developments of the ego and object relations would become oppressively stale or extremely frail were the propulsion and space for subjectivization opened by desirous differentiation wanting), it is, on the other, a matter of irreducibly antagonistic emphases that reflect the distinctiveness of their respective orientations. These differences in emphasis reflect the distinctive foci, the theoretical and practical commitments, constitutive of each perspective.

But if we bracket this debate for a moment, if we simply stay on Lacanian terrain and say that Dick needed to be initiated into the Symbolic, then we may notice something most peculiar given the vitriol animating Lacan's characterization of Klein's violence. Regularly in Lacan's work entry into the Symbolic is associated with violence, with the cut of symbolic prohibition, castration, and the paternal metaphor, as well as with the violence of alienation and separation. The "charge" of violence, then, may be tautological, thus trivial. There is, on Lacanian grounds, no other way to break the shackles of absorption in an Imaginary attitude and assume one's Symbolic status than through the imposition of a certain violence.[283] And there may be no way to sustain one's Symbolic position without undergoing ongoing violence.

In the Lacanian lexicon, the force that breaks us out of the Imaginary attitude is associated with the law and the father, both of which, in turn, are clearly associated with violence. More precisely, becoming a *subject who* can attempt to accommodate herself to the truth of her desire, that is, becoming a subject of the Symbolic, involves becoming *subject to* certain foreclosures and constraints, e.g., to those limitations of desirous subjectivity/relationality effected by primordial repression and continuous social interpellation. Violence and exclusion are, for Lacan, indissociable from the incessant process of subjectivization, of self-(de)limitation. Prospects for affirming the truth of one's desire, of one's Symbolic condition, require that one's desire manifests in socially intelligible—thus circumscribed—ways. Subjectivity presupposes intersubjectivity as the condition for its singular assertion—which is to say, without the stabilizing support of social recognition, which means liability to misrecognition, without the social facilitation of the forms of desirous subjectivity/relationality one most wants to cultivate and claim as one's own, which means ongoing exposure to failure, efforts of singular self-assertion are but a fantasy of sovereign hubris.

Or to put another gloss on it, if accession to familial and then broader cultural belonging involves acquiring a sense of dependency and then mutual dependency, of the insuperability of exposure and then mutual exposure, of the need of others for the satisfaction of one's basic needs and for the pursuit of one's desires and then of their need of you for the satisfaction of their basic needs and the pursuit of their desires, that is, if accession to the Symbolic involves something like the reflective comprehension and affirmation of basic trust, the dawning without disdain of one's irrevocable vulnerability to the affectively significant presence (or absence) of others, to their care and desire (and the faltering thereof), then accession to the Symbolic involves the violence of wresting the infant, or what is persistently infantile in the adult, from the ambit of her fantasized omnipotence, from the partially or entirely retrospective and fantasmatic comforts of symbiotic fusion.

If a certain violence is intrinsic to Symbolic life, and if what Dick needs is to be bound to the Symbolic, then what is the point of accusing Klein of violence? Is it just to rhetorically enhance the risks run by Klein's procedure that Lacan will go on to intimate? But it is not as if Lacan presents evidence that the violence of Klein's brutal and mechanical Oedipal interpretations is simply superfluous or did some long-lasting damage to Dick that could have been avoided. So what is at stake in this accusation?

Lacan's opening gesture of accusing Klein of violent brutality cannot be taken at face value. It is too exaggerated, too theatrical; its very excessiveness suggests that there is irony at play. One indication of this is that, ultimately, the accusation of interpretive violence is more appropriately directed at Lacan's near-calumnistic engagement with Klein's work than at Klein's interpretations of Dick. For though on Lacanian grounds Klein's violence is necessary—in some form, though not necessarily in the particular form it takes—Lacan's aggressive berating of Klein's violence surely is not. There are much more subtle and nonaggressive ways of making his point. The temptation to be avoided, though, is to turn the tables on Lacan and reject him on the grounds he lays out for rejecting Klein. Such a critique would be too immanent, bespeaking a disavowed, quasi-hysterical obedience to the master: "Lacan says reject brutality, and so I will!" The point of calling attention to Lacan's violence, or, more precisely, of attending to the surplus violence that Lacan displays, that, perhaps, he stages and allows to be seen at the opening of his engagement with Klein, is to suggest that Lacan's viciousness may be superbly ironic.

Could it be that this opening line is not the blanket condemnation it appears to be and is instead, by virtue of its theatricality, an indication that Lacan is playing the part of the "beautiful soul," the sensitive and attentive critic who sees evil everywhere but in his own accusatory gaze? This enactment, this staging of the beautiful soul, if this is what Lacan is up to, would be an ironic and parodic warning against assuming precisely this position. It would be a way of warning us against *our* propensity to assume this position of knowingness, of presumptive clarity, against our penchant for facile judgment and easy morality, simplified position taking and sterile polemics. It would be a warning against the facility of blame and the faltering of self-interrogation—ultimately, the enfeeblement of thinking—that runs along with it. It would be a warning against our tendency to take sides, either for or against Lacan (or Klein, or whomever), if this means failing to attend to the complex textures and not always immediately evident value of the work of those we admire or repudiate or to the complexities of the phenomena with which such work is concerned. It would thus be a way of urging ever-renewed *reading* against the consolation of partisan commitment. It would be about as serious and as modern as melodrama can be.

If this is his game, then Lacan is urging critical scrutiny and hesitation in the face of the concepts and interpretive orientations he will be developing and advancing in his seminars, and perhaps by implication all his future work. Perhaps part of Lacan's ambition when reading the Dick case is to begin to cultivate in his audience the critical habits requisite for the proper reception of his teachings. Might it be that Lacan is attempting to intervene in the scene of his reception, trying to establish the conditions in which he would be able to address himself to a scene of tense critical ambivalence rather than an all-too-receptive audience awaiting the master's bestowal of the newly forged interpretive key that will unlock all social, cultural, and psychological matters[284] or just seeking yet another critical-theoretical novelty or intellectual curio? Could it be that at stake in his address is not just the communication of content but an attempt to cultivate the subjectivities without whose discerning engagement his discourse and the practical orientation it means to promote would be massively distorted, surely fail to achieve its radicalizing potential? Recall that we are dealing with *Seminar I* here, with the first seminar held at Sainte-Anne Hospital after the creation of the Société Française de Psychanalyse (S.F.P.) and the first seminar open to the public, with a seminar now granted a significant institutional backing and authority, with a seminar that is planned to continue for years to come, and so, perhaps, with questions that are provoked by these new conditions: questions of authority, of legacy, of the relationship between subjectivity and insight.

Lacan's ironic strategy of assertion-retraction, his insistence upon the need for critical caution concerning the concepts and orientations he is advancing to the point of self-parody, I take it, aims to sustain a twofold dialectical tension. It aims to sustain the dialectical tension between psychoanalytic perspectives and between psychoanalytic schemas and the phenomena they render. In both cases, sustaining dialectical tension involves keeping attention keyed to the coming-into-perspicuity of phenomena *through*—(1) as mediated by and (2) in excess of, but never altogether outside—their conceptual[285] articulation and thus to the need for ongoing rearticulation. That is, sustaining dialectical tension involves keeping attention keyed to:

- The emphasis embedded in each act of conceptual determination, i.e., to the perspectival—value- and sensitivity-expressive—character and so genetic conditions of conceptualization, specifically to conceptuality's mutually implicated dimensions of blindness and insight, and thereby to the necessity of a mutually challenging and mutually supplementing dialectic of psychoanalytic perspectives that, ideally, will progressively clarify the phenomena conceptualized while drawing attention to the suspicious idealism of the asymptotic approach that posits the full truth of phenomena as external, out there, given but unavailable to us.
- The excessiveness or resistance of phenomena vis-à-vis conceptual articulation, the conceptual inexhaustibility of the phenomena themselves, their hospitability to in(de)finitely many manners of conceptual construal no single instance of which nor any systematic arrangement of which can absorb the full significance of the phenomena, i.e., abolish temporality, thus again to the necessity of a mutually challenging and mutually supplementing dialectic of perspectives.

The former—the emphasis embedded in the conceptual casting of phenomena and thus the need for a plurality of perspectives to draw out the valences and significance of the phenomena that a particular perspective must elide and/or the range of potentially pertinent phenomena it must neglect in order to constitute itself as an incisive and illuminating perspective—is highlighted by Lacan's theatricality. This theatricality calls attention to the pathos-suffused scene of conceptualization and position taking (the performative or rhetorical register, the register of *speech*) and to the perspectival character of his discourse, thus to the need of other perspectives to challenge and correct the contingent and constitutive blind spots of his perspective. Lacan comes across as quite a character, quite a card, really, and thereby forestalls the dissociation of the concepts he forges and positions he propounds from their roots in his singular perspective, keeps them manifestly moored in his particular sensibilities, larger ambitions, theoretical and normative inheritances and commitments, and so on, thus signaling a need for competing perspectives if particularity is not to be falsely universalized. Because Lacan is so flagrantly embroiled in an impassioned polemic with Klein, because his critique is so wildly scathing, we are kept aware of the pathos-suffused context of his conceptual and therapeutic innovations and perhaps thus encouraged to become suspicious of, even wary about, the validity of Lacan's perspective or of any other perspective, immured in a pathos-suffused context of conception as it likely is. Lacan's strategy, it seems, is to prevent the subject of enunciation from fading behind the content of the utterance and, by calling attention to the indelible moment of subjectivity, resist the reification his statements nonetheless impose and release the phenomena under concern into the in(de)finite expanse of articulation otherwise—which can be sustained and, in being sustained, can mount a much-effective resistance to reification, only if constituted by vibrant and viable alternative perspectives.

The latter—the excessiveness or resistance of phenomena vis-à-vis conceptuality—is manifest *not* by direct appeal to "the phenomena themselves," as the always disappointed ideal measure of their concepts as if there were a privileged point of access to phenomena in their aconceptual purity and immediacy (this would be the impossible identity of positivity and emptiness, something like Hegel's "being pure being"); rather, this is manifest, or, more precisely, gestured at, by keeping explicit the work of conceptualization as simultaneously and coextensively revealing and concealing. By displaying his conceptual innovations as able to disclose dimensions of the case that Klein's conceptual apparatus was bound to miss, mischaracterize, or downplay, and, by implication, reflexively suggesting that there are dimensions of the case that his conceptual apparatus is bound to elide, obscure, misconstrue, etc., Lacan intimates—wittingly or not—that phenomena endlessly resist conceptual exhaustion.

What Lacan strongly suggests, or perhaps allows to be seen, is that phenomena, because they are shot through with latency (a characterization *particularly* true of psychic phenomena, e.g., unconscious ideas recurrently undergoing condensation, displacement, articulation into symptoms, all manners of new associative connection, etc.), because their manifestations, thus their significances, are socio-historically and otherwise contextually mediated, cannot give themselves fully, once and for all, to discursive articulation. By avowing, indeed openly parading its impulse toward reification, Lacan's teachings and writings release phenomena from the conceptual casts they nonetheless impose—respecting their mystery. The self-explicitation of the work of conceptualization renders conspicuous the excess of phenomenality over the particular instance of conceptualization and thereby gestures toward, for it can never demonstrate, the irreducible excess of phenomenality over conceptualization. The self-explicitation of the work of conceptualization—Lacan's letting it be seen that he is conceptualizing phenomena that others, e.g., Klein, have conceptualized otherwise and that, by implication, may yet be conceptualized in heretofore unimaginable ways—gestures toward the irreducible priority of the object. Manifestly wrangling phenomena away from the conceptual apparatus of his interlocutors and into his own conceptual casts, Lacan grants the (in)determinacy of phenomena its evidence, allowing it to pierce the confidence of the concepts into which it is marshaled.

Theatrically calling attention to his performance *as* a performance and thus to his perspective *as* a perspective—as perhaps one among in(de)finitely many possible perspectives—Lacan keeps as explicit as possible, i.e., gestures at, the *withdrawal* of phenomena from even the concepts that seem best able to account for them. By highlighting the mutual implication of blindness and insight in the work of conceptualization (Klein sees certain things that Lacan cannot and focuses on aspects that he will not, and vice versa) Lacan allows to be seen the receding of the phenomena with which he is concerned from his conceptual grasp—in general, the receding of phenomenality from total intelligibility. Or, put positively, he grants the evidence of the temporalization of phenomenality. Paradoxically, he allows to be seen that to which he must blind himself, immersed as he is in the perspective he is in the process of elaborating.

Part of Lacan's brilliance, I would suggest, is that his text is smarter than he is. It allows to be seen what he cannot quite see. By means of the strength of subjectivity—through the strength of his judgments about what is important in the case, how to theorize the material, and what clinical conclusions to draw, that is, in and through his best efforts of conceptualization and judgment, specifically, in and through acts of conceptualization and judgment that explicate themselves as such—Lacan attests to his weakness, his constitutive permeability and secondariness. Through the strength of such judgments he sustains the primacy of the object, its status as conditioning and exceeding, determining without programming, its discursive presentation and the conclusions drawn from it. The turning in of conceptuality onto itself, the self-explicitation of conceptualization as a work of bracketing and selecting, focusing and inflecting, a work of simultaneous disclosing and concealing, allows the phenomena conceptualized to manifest as organizing yet exceeding their conceptual presentations.

To keep dialectical tension alive, then, means keeping attention keyed to phenomena as both compellingly disclosed through particular conceptual determinations (only the rigorous and compelling character of conceptual determination will prevent the deflationary moment from devolving into a paralyzing or trivial and dismissive skepticism) *and* as liable to manifest otherwise, as prone to display features that cannot be seen from the point of view currently inhabited. It is to keep an eye on the impossible, to allow what is constitutively excluded to insist as such, however indeterminately, to allow the constitutively excluded dimensions of the phenomena with which one is concerned to remain as the opaque lining of their compelling conceptual clarification. In this way, concealedness comes to condition, to haunt and interrupt, conceptual clarity. Here too psychoanalysis shows its allegiance with mythology.[286]

This mutual implication of clarity and opacity in conceptuality is what Lacan's concepts allow to be seen only because they are framed by a polemic with Klein. Klein's reading, though it seems to stand for the mere appearance of insight that Lacan will see through as he reveals the truth of the matter, is, let us recall, "precious." Because it is clearly valued by Lacan, reading Lacan fidelitously means taking Klein's reading seriously, seriously enough for it to become, at a first moment, the perspective from which Lacan's insights are situated at the level of mere appearance, seen through in order to access the truth of the case.

Because it enjoins us to take Klein's reading seriously, Lacan's commentary offers itself to be read from a Kleinian point of view, a point of view from which it is bound to be found faulty, or at least limited and exaggerated, distorting however disclosive. At a second moment, because both Lacan's and Klein's readings must be taken seriously—this is what Lacan's commentary demands—the framework of mere appearance versus truth or surface versus depth cannot be sustained: it is doubled, inverted, and thereby suspended.

Because on Lacanian grounds Klein's reading must be taken seriously, it will be able to situate Lacan's perspective as a perspective, i.e., interrupt the totalizing impulse of Lacan's conceptual apparatus, and thereby bring Lacan's concepts into their truth. It brings them into their truth as limited and provisional, even if universally applicable, articulations of the phenomena with which they are concerned, and, as such, more fully responsive to such phenomena than they would be otherwise. Truth is, in part, a matter of form. Sustaining truth in this context—perhaps generally—means acknowledging the continuing need for other perspectives, for continuing dialogue, for through such acknowledgment the excess of phenomena over their conceptual presentation is given voice.

Truth—as a complex admixture of determinacy and opacity, of conceptual clarity and phenomenal excessiveness—is emergent not in the thinking of this or that psychoanalytic theorist alone, but in the dialectical tension of the field. Or perhaps in the thinking of this or that thinker insofar as it manages to incorporate the tension of the field. Klein's reading of the case, as inscribed in Lacan's presentation, serves as a placeholder for the in(de)finitely many other readings of the case, for the in(de)finitely many features of the phenomena written up as the case study that, under a different set of pressures and sensitivities, may claim someone's attention as significant, motivating a thoroughgoing reconception of the significance and stakes of the case, thus as a placeholder for the consequences for psychoanalytic theory and practice that might yet be drawn from such alternative readings, and therewith as a placeholder for the self-transgressing and self-reinventing character of the psychoanalytic field. Klein's reading is positioned as the inherence, the "internal" overflowing, of the future of psychoanalysis from out of the Lacanian field.

This is not to say that "the true is the whole" but rather that truth emerges in psychoanalytic thinking *in and through* the taught dialectical tension of mutually challenging, mutually qualifying, and mutually supplementing perspectives. This is not a plea for eclecticism: each perspective must justify itself rigorously. At least concerning matters psychic, truth requires, truth demands—at stake here is a chiasmus of theoretical and practical reason—both rigorous conceptual clarity and attentiveness to, some way of acknowledging, what is elided in each instance of conceptualization. *Truth demands another orientation, another mode of discursivity.* Truth requires both attention to phenomena as compellingly conceptually articulated *and* to that which conceptual clarification will have glossed over. Truth demands the exaggerations of conceptualization—demands a willingness to be false in a certain way—as well as critical caution concerning the total transparency that perhaps cannot but be promised by conceptual insight, enthusiastic as it is to testify to the striking experience of having seen and to amplify the luminosity of and therewith generalize the encounterability and preserve from relapse into neglect that which it has retrieved from concealedness. It is only in this double bind that truth emerges in its withdrawal, as a shading into oblivion.

In psychoanalysis and, perhaps more broadly, to be committed to truth is a matter of honoring others and thereby the potentiality of the object: its amenability to yielding itself otherwise, according to the concerns, sensibilities, and urgencies composing another scene of inquiry. Dialectical thought—psychoanalytic thought at its best—responds to and sustains the overfullness of phenomena, the potentiality of phenomena to manifest otherwise. Yes, to potentiality, to phenomena's abiding beyond actuality, beyond what is currently manifest, beyond agreed- or insisted-upon reality. Is all of this not implied in Lacan's conception of reality as a *sensus communis*? What self-conscious, self-explicitating conceptualization may allow to be seen, if faintly, is potentiality itself, i.e., temporality, as an element of phenomena with which claims to truth must reckon.

On a first approach, we might say that the simultaneously ethical and theoretical virtue at stake in keeping dialectical tension alive would be an honoring of the potentiality of phenomena to withhold or withdraw from particular conceptual articulations as they become manifest in them, an honoring of the temporality of phenomena, of the proclivity of phenomena to yield in and through an evolving plurality of perspectives, and of our endless need for others, for other viewpoints and sensibilities through which phenomena may yet yield something of themselves to which we have been blind and so through which we may attain some awareness of our blind spots. In a classical idiom, this would be the virtue of self-aware self-limitation. In a modern idiom, the virtue at stake would be the avowal of finitude: the mourning work of acknowledging the inherence of dependency in our most self-assertive endeavors, the infinite finitude of cognition, no matter how well systematically integrated. Avowing finitude (e.g., "castration" and separation): is this not at the core of the Lacanian project?

But sustaining dialectical tension is a way of reigning in hubris *and* of acknowledging its all-too-human, perhaps insuperable, character. Startled, even awestruck, by insight delivered from the depths of obscurity and perhaps marveling at its practical consequences, subjectivity is engrossed and expanded by its discovery: a lover at first sight, as if possessed. Wanting to proclaim "this is it" to all with ears to hear, to insist on the evidence and/or significance of the insight so emphatically that its compelling character will never fade—even if this means hyperbole—subjectivity reels from the shock of discovery, enamored and inflated perhaps to the point of hubris. And this is hardly lamentable. Sustaining the availability of the insight may require nothing less than the language of love.

Thus for dialectical tension to be sustained, attention would need to be doubled, split between absorption and reflection, keyed to both phenomena manifesting as conceptually-framed (intentional consciousness) and to the frame itself (self-consciousness that shades into "ob-ject" consciousness).[287] Attention would need to be devoted to both the object manifesting in the frame (without manifest reference to the frame, as if immediately giving itself in its evidence) and to the frame (e.g., concepts, forms of attention, guiding concerns, etc.) through which phenomena are disclosed *and thereby* framed-off, cut-off, concealed in order to be revealed. On the one hand, the either/or framework of object consciousness *or* self-consciousness may be misleading: self-consciousness (of the framework) and intentional-absorptive consciousness (of the object) may be mutually supportive, mutually enhancing rather than mutually exclusive or mutually paralyzing.[288] But not necessarily. The risk that attention will swerve strongly to one pole or the other—the possibility of adopting the attitude of the specialist or the historian of ideas—cannot be relieved. Difficult as it is, by simultaneously advancing compelling new concepts, readings, and therapeutic suggestions and inscribing a hesitation about them Lacan not infrequently manages to sustain the tension between phenomenalization and conceptualization and between alternative perspectives and thus to honor the potentiality of the object and the need of others' perspectives and thereby keep psychoanalytic thinking in motion, which is the proper setting of its truth. This is the immanent standard of his work.

If the cagy irony of assertion and withdrawal is Lacan's game, *if* he is staging the perspective that troubles him deeply (the beautiful soul) in order to draw attention to and undermine it, then we would do well to attend to the ways in which, continually, Lacan is willing to go down with the ship. This courage of complicity is one of the most distinguishing, and often disturbing, traits of the Lacanian perspective.

And *if* this is what Lacan is up to, the stakes of his venture are high, extending far beyond his relation to Klein, even beyond the field of psychoanalysis. According to Lacan, "[t]he ego of modern man has taken on its form in the dialectical impasse of the beautiful soul who does not recognize his very raison d'être in the disorder that he denounces in the world" (*E*: 233/281; trans. modified). What is at stake in his encounter with Klein, then, may be nothing less than beginning to work through *the* dialectical impasse of modern subjectivity, nothing less than disrupting and resisting *the* paradigmatic form of the modern ego.

Just how intimate are Klein's and Lacan's perspectives then? And what more may be at stake in this clandestine intimacy, if intimacy it is? Although Lacan condemns Klein's harshness harshly, as we have seen, this does not necessarily mean that he believes there to be some nonviolent way the analysis could have proceeded. Lacan's opening line may not be a blanket condemnation of Klein's work: either of her work with Dick or, by extension, of her work in general. Might not the aggressive pathos of this opening line conceal and enact (symptomatize?) a profound intimacy? Strikingly, Lacan's harshness seems to *mirror* Klein's. Might his harshness, mirroring hers, bespeak an Imaginary identification with Klein and thus perhaps a dimension of rivalry? Throughout his commentary, Lacan appears to be engaged an eminently anti-analytic ad hominem attack on Klein. Apparently inconsistent in his accusations, Lacan comes off as madly vituperative: Klein is too theoretical (she mechanically imposes Oedipal interpretations) and yet is unconcerned with theory (she expresses herself badly, is a "woman of experience"), and in both cases she is in the wrong; she feels too much and thinks too much, and again in both cases she is in the wrong. Does the hyperbolic quality of Lacan's attacks not suggest a dimension of rivalry animating his engagement with Klein? And if rivalry there is, if Lacan finds himself locked into some sort of Imaginary dyad with Klein, or at least if this is how he is staging things, then given his claims about how Imaginary dyads tend to generate paranoid feelings and fantasies of persecution and generally distort perception and thinking, perhaps the point of the wild and willful aggression is, here too, to allow us to see that he is not in a position to simply pronounce judgment on Klein's work. Does he speak from a position of critical clarity immune from the aggression and other invidious Imaginary tendencies he detects at work in Klein's text, and, more broadly, in her psychoanalytic orientation? Is Lacan not manifestly "invested?"

Lacan's mirroring of Klein's violence invites the following sets of questions:

1. Is it just Klein who is feeling while Lacan is thinking? Or are the thought processes of both guided by experience, affect, and structures of sensibility? Is thinking ever divested of affective and historical-experiential determinants and dimensions? If not, how should an inheritor of the Freudian discovery approach theoretical production and reception? Could it be that the hardly concealed mirroring of Klein's aggression in Lacan's text means to signal that thinking is never fully divested of affective currents, specifically unconscious affective currents, and so is inevitably wanting for self-transparency? That articulating thought always involves saying and doing more (and less) than intended? Thus demands to be *read*? How then are we to read? If authorial intention cannot be the gold standard for adjudicating between better and worse readings, how are we to distinguish between the better and the worse? Is an appeal to consequences enough, e.g., is it enough to say that following Lacan opens theoretical pathways and yields clinical insights that following Klein

does not? But of course Kleinians can say the same. And one need not consult Plato's *Republic* to know that asking after what constitutes the advantageous is a terribly vexing enterprise. To what extent can appealing to consequences suffice when the question is what makes for a better or worse reading?

2. Is it just that Klein is violent while Lacan is the epigone of critical sensitivity? Or is violence manifest on both sides? Generally, is violence extricable from the scene of interpretation? And if we cannot simply side with nonviolence, how are we to adjudicate the debate between Lacan and Klein about the meaning and stakes of Dick's case, which means, more broadly, about how to inherit Freudian psychoanalysis? If we cannot take the easy way out (she is violent, he is on the side of the oppressed), how are we decide which psychoanalytic orientation to favor? What criteria might be relevant? Are there protocols that can be drawn upon, or are our commitments to particular psychoanalytic persuasions inevitably underwarranted? If the latter, is the insecurity of commitment—its exposure to criticisms that cannot be answered in a knock-down sort of way—something to be lamented, valorized, or neither?
3. Is the mechanicity of Klein's Oedipal interpretations, this ostensibly compulsive repetition, an indication that her thinking, but not Lacan's, is rigid and constricted, too focused on a selective set of issues, indeed *unthinking*? Or could it be that a certain hyperbolic reductionism is coextensive with psychoanalytic thinking, especially in the case of the pathbreaking thinking of figures such as Lacan and Klein, even with thinking as such?
4. Does Lacan's mimesis or enactment of the Imaginary terms and tendencies he explicitly identifies as the structuring principles of Klein's text (both in her study of Dick and generally) indicate a contingent faltering of consistency or suggest that the Imaginary cannot be so easily evaded, if at all? If Lacan is enacting or staging an Imaginary rivalry with Klein, if understanding his commentary requires attentiveness to its Imaginary features, then is Lacan really proposing, as he seems to be, that we should choose between the Imaginary and the Symbolic, between Klein and himself? What structure of supplementarity is Lacan's commentary urging and assuming?

Once we become aware of the mimesis of violence at play in Lacan's commentary, the floodgates open fast and we can see how much mirroring there is throughout. And so perhaps how much rivalry—or maybe intimacy—there is. Where Klein's voice ends and Lacan's begins is often difficult, sometimes downright impossible, to discern. At many points, it is unclear whether Lacan is simply reconstructing Klein's point of view or giving his own assessment of the case. For instance, the third paragraph begins as follows: "You will have noticed the lack of contact that Dick experiences. That's where the defect of his *ego* is. His *ego* isn't formed" (*Seminar I*: 68; original emphases). Is this Klein's claim, her emphasis on the ego, or Lacan's? Since one of the primary charges Lacan will bring to bear against Klein is that she is too focused on the ego, these sentences would seem to be a way of distancing himself from this focus, in the service of setting up a major point of contention. But it is not altogether clear that Lacan—even though he continually resists the privileging of the ego—disagrees with the diagnosis that Dick's ego is defective. Even though it is certainly clear that Lacan thinks Klein places far too much emphasis on the ego and other Imaginary elements, it is not clear that he specifically disagrees with this portrayal of Dick. It is not even clear that she, rather than he, is the author of this diagnosis.

Or take another example. When Lacan specifies that Dick's awakening to affective immersion in the discourse/desire of others occurs not when he responds to Klein's nomination of the trains as, respectively, Dick train and daddy train but subsequent to "an initial ceremony" in which the child seeks "refuge in the dark space in order to renew contact with the container," this eminently Kleinian description of the dark space as a (maternal) container and of Dick's desire to renew contact with it are taken over by Lacan, his voice blending with hers (*Seminar I*: 85/98; trans. modified). We would expect Lacan to object to this characterization of Dick's behavior, but he does not. We would expect him to make it clear that he is citing Klein's case report in order to establish the targets of his criticisms and establish a specific point of contrast to bring into relief his claims about what is at stake. We would expect him to make it altogether clear that he is not ratifying this account. But he doesn't. Their voices are in unison.

Throughout the commentary, there are many such points of indistinction between Klein's voice and Lacan's. Are these moments of staged identification? Are they symptoms of identification? What fragile narcissism and fantasy framework is propelling (or putting on display as propelling) this identification? And what are we to make of it? It is well known that Lacan was once a great reader and admirer of Klein, that he agreed to translate her first book, *The Psychoanalysis of Children* (1932), when they met in 1949 . . . even though that same year Lacan claimed to have first formulated the fantasy experience of the fragmented body to which that very book speaks (and Karl Abraham's work before that), not giving Klein (or Abraham) credit until the 1966 publication of "De nos antécédents" in *Écrits*. How much rivalry is there in Lacan's text, what sort of rivalry is it (conscious or unconscious), and what are its effects?

Once we begin to notice the Imaginary register in Lacan's commentary—which may be what it strategically provokes us to do—a number of striking features rush to the fore. Lacan's account of Kleinian theory and practice is manifestly oppositional, dualistic, aggressive, and reductively schematizing, i.e., Imaginary. Lacan's commentary frames Klein's work in an aggressively totalizing manner, treating Klein's text as if it were a fully legible signifier that points to a univocal, stable, and determinate signifier: *the* picture of what she was up to with Dick and, by extension, *the* picture of her theory and practice in general. It makes it seem easy to understand and evaluate Klein's text and her orientation in general and easy to reject both in favor of the Lacanian alternative. Is this a hysterical response to disappointed love? An adolescent storming out of mother's house? Or is this how Lacan attempts to win our love, to situate himself in the desire of the Other? Lacan frames Klein's text in a way that seems to forget his insistence on reading and listening for the complex—polyphonous, polysemic, ambiguous, discontinuous, overdetermined, and partially nonsensical—play of signification. *And it frames the text as if in willful ignorance of the fact that Klein's case report was presented to the seminar not a (diagetic) moment ago, through the mediation of a seminar participant, Mlle. Gélinier.* Lacan charges Mlle. Gélinier with giving an account of "Melanie Klein's point of view" through a reading of Klein's "Importance of Symbol-Formation in the Development of the Ego" (*Seminar I*: 67). Then he proceeds to treat Klein as if the Kleinian point of view is perfectly manifest in this article, as if this article were wholly transparent, completely at one with itself, and unproblematically illustrative of Kleinian theory and practice in general. He treats it as an ideal matrix, making no effort, for instance, to read Klein's emphases on the inner world and the anxieties by which it is wracked as a self-consciously exaggerated counter to Anna Freud's focus on adaptation to the external environment or Klein's inflated concern with the death drive as responsive to the rampant romanticization of Eros. And he acts as if Gélinier was not charged with the specific task of rendering perspicuous the differences between Klein and Anna Freud, as if this would have no impact on the image of Klein presented. Despite these layers of mediation, Lacan's commentary frames Klein's text (and, reflexively, itself?) as a sign rather than a symbol, making it seem as if Klein's text (and, by implication, his commentary?) is transparently intelligible, fully and finally decodable. Lacan demands a caricature and then condemns Klein as overly schematic. He refuses to understand.

Also notice that Lacan's reading is explicitly violent and subsumptive. He makes no effort to understand Klein—as if assuming that since she has plenty of acolytes he can leave the work of understanding to them.[289] He even seems to willfully misunderstand her from time to time. For instance, when Lacan claims that Klein speaks "out of habit," i.e., mechanically applies the Oedipal scenarios upon which *she* is fixated, he completely ignores Klein's cautionary statement that Dick's case is unusual, calling for an anomalous strategy.[290] Never does he try doing justice to her work—say, by reconstructing her metapsychology and technique as accurately as possible and then indicating their tensions, inconsistencies, and insufficiencies in light of their guiding premises and problematics. And notice the violent dismissal of Klein, and by implication any pundit of the Kleinian perspective, as a potential interlocutor, an equal. Never does Lacan support his disagreements with detailed theoretical arguments and clinical illustrations with which, at least in principle, Klein (or her pundits) could argue. Instead, he brackets Klein's concerns and her reasons for being so concerned in order to attend to the *effects* of her intervention: effects that will shore up his claim that attention to the Symbolic is requisite for understanding what transpires in analysis and for effective interventions therein. Thus Lacan asks, "So what did Melanie Klein actually do?" (*Seminar I*: 85/99), "What is the specific function of the Kleinian interpretation?" (*Seminar I*: 74/88). Lacan emphasizes the illocutionary and perlocutionary dimensions of Klein's speech, bracketing the constative claims (urine is poison, etc.) on which she places such great weight. Since, for Lacan, entrance into the Symbolic, which he suggests should be the focus of the case, assumes/produces a nonsymbolizable remnant, a kernel of the Real, that serves as the fulcrum for the development of the unconscious, a full account of Dick's initiation into the Symbolic will require attention to a dimension of psychic life beyond meaning and so very much beyond Klein. Subsuming her text to his own concerns and theoretical assumptions, Lacan's violence to Klein is extreme.

Importantly, the palpable disrespect of this disdainful refraining from argument indicates that Lacan's ultimate rejoinder to Klein is not a series of propositions or theses that, if effectively demonstrated, would shatter Klein's convictions. Rather, it is a shift in attention that situates her speech as an event, *as not simply subject to understanding and thus agreement or disagreement*—even though disagreement seems to be exactly what Lacan urges at every turn. Lacan attends to Klein's speech, to the performative dimension of her enunciations and their various unintended effects, and thereby shows that there is more to what is said than what Klein (specifically, Klein's ego) intends. This is not exactly, or at least not obviously, a counterargument, let alone a refutation. Rather, it is a backgrounding of Klein's point of view in the service of opening another point of view from which other significant elements—which Lacan insists are *the* significant elements—of the case become perspicuous. (However, notice that some manner of respect seeps back in—Klein's perspective is acknowledged as compelling by the exertion with which it is suppressed. Even if Lacan is—or postures as—unimpressed by what has taken so many in, the effort that goes into relegating it to the background attests to its compelling claim, at least for many. Again, Lacan is impressed by her efficacy.[291]) While inveighing against "understanding" and mechanical subsumption, Lacan subsumes Klein's text within his habits of understanding, mechanically imposes his reading protocol. And thus doing violence to Klein's text, he discloses what a "just" reading—a reading that takes up Klein on her own terms—never could. The commentary mirrors the violence and mechanical schematization it attributes to Klein, and like Klein's interpretations it works: "it is clear that as a result of this interpretation something happens. That is what it's all about." Lacan puts the point in these terms:

> What counts, when one attempts to elaborate an experience is less what ones does understand than what one does not understand. . . . Commenting on a text is like doing an analysis. . . . [O]ne of the things we should be watching out for most, is not to understand too much, not to understand more than what there is in the discourse of the subject. Interpreting is an altogether different thing than having the fancy of understanding. One is the opposite of the other. I will even say that it is on the basis of a certain refusal of understanding that we open the door onto psychoanalytic understanding. (*Seminar I*: 73/87–88)

Lacan provides illumination by refusing to understand, by refusing to comply with Klein's insistence on what is significant. Is this not a bit reactionary? Is there not an element of fascination and aggressive rejection at play? Is there not a question of Imaginary object relations looming?

Also of note is that after the first sentence ("She slams the symbolism on him with complete brutality, does Melanie Klein, on little Dick!") Lacan proceeds as follows: "Straight away she starts off hitting him [with] large-scale interpretations. She hits him with a brutal verbalization of the Oedipal myth, almost as revolting for us as for any reader—*You are the little train, you want to fuck your mother*" (*Seminar I*: 68). While clearly admonishing Klein, Lacan's commentary mirrors the objects of its critiques at every turn. To begin with, notice that however stark the opposition established by the severity of Lacan's critique its grand finale—"*You are the little train, you want to fuck your mother*"—fuses Lacan's voice with Klein's. However much this literalizing and vulgarizing parody of Klein's interpretation succeeds in displaying Lacan's revulsion in the last instance, his voice and hers coincide.

Is this just an unhappy coincidence, or does Lacan's recitation of (what he presents as) Klein's interpretation, Klein's voice, indicate that he is identified with it? Does identificatory fusion not bespeak Imaginary rivalry? Is it not a response to the question of what the Other desires? Does the commentary not show (enact or stage?) Lacan to be unconsciously identified with Klein—fused, complete, all-knowing? Might it be that it is only on the basis of the abundant confidence that such fusion provides that Lacan can so recklessly claim to know Klein to be in the wrong and himself to be in the right?

Next, note that Lacan replicates every malpractice of which he accuses Klein in this passage, specifically, through a performative enactment of exactly what he condemns at the level of content. Aggressively, Lacan accuses Klein of aggression. He accuses her of starting with "major interpretations," and he himself starts off by providing a "major interpretation" of Klein's efforts. This major interpretation, like those that he attributes to Klein, is both remarkably bold (Lacan is supremely confident that what Klein is saying about the trains has a clear-cut Oedipal meaning) and pretty much off the mark (he summarizes the thrust of Klein's early interpretations as "*You are the little train, you want to fuck your mother*"; surely there is a moment of truth in this caricature, but as far as Klein is concerned what is primarily at stake is the fragility of Dick's ego, his capacity for investment in symbolism and intersubjective life, not aggressive and incestuous Oedipal desire. A primary attachment to the breast, envy, and so forth may play a role, and Klein does think that part of the problem is a too-early onset of genitalization, but she is *not* simply saying to Dick "You are the little train, you want to fuck your mother." The one who says this is Lacan; this is *his* "major interpretation."). And accusing Klein of mechanically and violently imposing Oedipal interpretations, Lacan mechanically and violently reconstructs her interpretations to fit this image.

Again and again when attending to Lacan's rhetorical performance, one is struck by the redoubling of the object of critique in the form of critique—by Imaginary mirroring. Lacan accuses Klein of being too literal, too simple minded, too dead set on giving the Oedipal interpretation. But it is *he* who literalizes Klein's interpretations; even if she intended a routine Oedipal interpretation, as voiced, her interpretations are somewhat ambiguous, at least compared with Lacan's vulgar literalization. In a certain way, is it not *he* who is dead set on giving the Oedipal interpretation? Is it not Lacan who seems dead set on understanding Klein as fixated on and mechanically reproducing Oedipal interpretations as he ignores her remarks about Dick's anomalous case calling for an unusual strategy? Do these comments not suggest that Klein, much more than Lacan, is prone to respect the singularity of each interpretive situation? And, of course, the "brutal verbalization" of which Lacan accuses Klein is mirrored in *his* brutal verbalization of what he construes as the content of her interpretations: "You are the little train, you want to fuck your mother." Is there a more brutal verbalization than this? Finally, by literalizing and vulgarizing Klein's interpretations, Lacan foregoes attention to the enigmatic dimensions or multiple meanings of her *speech*, which is exactly what he accuses Klein of doing by dint of her mechanical Oedipal interpretations. Is "commenting on a text" really "like doing an analysis" (*Seminar I*: 73/87–88)?

In general, does Lacan's text not seek to supplant Klein's interpretive framework with his own? Does it not push for a decision between the two perspectives? Ultimately, does it not solicit affirmation of Lacan's point of view and therewith our love and admiration for Lacan? Is the *demand* of the text not to unconditionally love Lacan, at least in want of any better objects of affection? What Imaginary extravagance! Is there not a current of narcissistic self-inflation discernable in Lacan's portrayal of Klein's text and practice as so base that it cannot but reflect his own as sensitive, careful, thoughtful?

Opposition and rivalry, schematization and totalization, the demand, mirroring, fusion, narcissism, aggression, intense concern with and symptomatic expression of the question of the desire of the Other, etc.—all these are associated with the Imaginary. Are they regrettable oversights, contingent failures of consistency? Or does the flagrant self-display of its Imaginary features allow the commentary to speak to the perils of ignoring the Imaginary even though, *or precisely because*, this would contra-dict—speak against and inscribe a hesitation concerning—Lacan's overt claim that attention should be shifted from the Imaginary to the Symbolic? If the Imaginary names the predilection of the ego to seek clear and coherent images of oneself and others, then do not the all-too-vivid pictures of Klein the brute, and, by implication, Lacan the sensitive soul, suggest the necessity of attending to the Imaginary dimensions of Lacan's commentary and what is covered over therein? Does not the simple, static, oppositional relationship between Klein the brute and Lacan the thinker, between the Imaginary and the Symbolic, suggest the invidious hold of the Imaginary and thus, on Lacanian grounds, warrant attention to what is concealed thereby?[292] Does not the demand for unconditional affirmation of Lacan's perspective suggest the risk of Klein's claims having been distorted, the value of her text and practice summarily judged? Lacan's commentary exhibits striking Imaginary features, but it seems ironically, at a distance that holds them out for critical scrutiny. Perhaps complicity with the object of critique and critical scrutiny are here at one.[293]

The basic paradox is this: if the Imaginary names a penchant for reductive totalization and all that is associated therewith, then the simplifying opposition between Lacan's emphasis on the Symbolic and Klein's emphasis on the Imaginary is itself Imaginary and thus, on Lacanian grounds, misleading. Lavishing attention on neither the Imaginary nor the Symbolic will suffice: to do so would be to distort both Lacan's commentary and Klein's case study, both the Symbolic and the Imaginary.

If the Imaginary names the perspective of the ego, and if, following Lacan, the perspective of the ego is systematically defensive and distorting, once we are keyed to the Imaginary dimensions of Lacan's commentary are we not precisely on Lacanian grounds called to inquire further, to read more closely—specifically, to read in a way that challenges this reductive framework of Lacan or Klein, the Symbolic or the Imaginary? Lacan's commentary, we might say, is *sous erature.* It releases the excess of the phenomena with which it is concerned by subverting its claims to theoretical totalization. It releases phenomena from the grasp of the concept into the space of reading. It calls for coauthors, retakes, rebeginnings. These are the marks of Lacan's profound commitment to pluralism and reason to be wary of those who would dismiss Lacan as a mere dogmatist as much as those who would acclaim and amplify a Lacanian dogmatics. Once we are attuned to the Imaginary dimensions of the commentary, are we not challenged to return to both Klein's and Lacan's work afresh, to attend to the phenomena reduced, distorted, or concealed by schematic presentation in both Klein's account and

Lacan's account of Klein? Are we not called back to "things themselves," to phenomena as they manifest or may come to manifest in excess of Lacan or Klein's presentations, thus propelled forward into an evolving scene of psychoanalytic pluralism? Or, if we have no pressing reason to return to the phenomena with which Lacan and Klein are concerned in order to unlock dimensions and draw consequences they cannot, are we not urged to remain aware of the provisional and limited character of these efforts of conceptualization and conclusion drawing? Are we not urged to strive to keep sight of the mutually implicated dimensions of revealing and concealing in each act of reading, and thus of course in our own? Are we not called to read, to judge, to avoid becoming mere acolytes of either Lacan *or* Klein, to take caution with respect to the facility and distortions of the judgments to which we are urged?[294]

Now let us concentrate more intensely on the consequences of the intimacy with Klein's perspective to which Lacan's commentary attests. What this intimacy reveals is that (1) the distinction between the Symbolic and the Imaginary is hardly categorical, (2) Lacan's perspective requires the internalization of Klein's in order to fully articulate itself, i.e., to speak itself truthfully, and (3) avowing complicity in violence is a crucial dimension of accommodation to the Symbolic.

As for the first point, the intimacy with Klein's voice and with her violence as well as the other moments of mimesis suggest, at the level of Lacan's performance, the insuperability of the Imaginary, its intertwinement with even that which would displace it, and thus a perhaps-ongoing need for attention to the Imaginary in the name of accommodation to the Symbolic. *Even Lacan* manifests a tendency to become embroiled in Imaginary rivalry and in the course of a Seminar that ostensibly attempts to turn our attention away from the Imaginary, from questions of identification, rivalry, aggression, etc. (the whole Kleinian ambit), as overdone and, insufficient, and furthermore, as if unwittingly via his performance—that is, precisely in the register of *speech*. Is this effort to turn our attention away from the Imaginary an unconscious tactic of distraction, i.e., an effort of preemptive autoimmunization? Is this effort in some way an expression of Lacan's desire to insulate himself from a critique that, he fears, would proceed on the basis of close attention to the Imaginary dynamics at work in his text? Or is it a form of autocritique? Is it totally unreasonable to suggest that Lacan is putting this mimesis on display, that he wants it to serve as a gateway to the question of the Imaginary structuration of his commentary, perhaps of his work as a whole, even of *speech* as such? Or if one suspects that Lacan is not so clever, that he is rather more of an arrogant show-off, perhaps one would accept that, ironically, his text is smarter than he is.

As we have seen, in the course of criticizing Klein, while seeming to distance himself from her as much as possible, Lacan mimes (performatively repeats and caricatures) her—her voice, her violence, and the Imaginary structures he marks out as her area of concern, even her perverse fixations—undercutting the clarity of the distinction between himself and Klein, between the Symbolic and the Imaginary, while at once insisting that distinction there is. What is crucial to underscore now is that it is not that differences are effaced but that, rather, they proliferate, becoming more complex and subtle. *How* Lacan criticizes Klein's text suggests the continued urgency of attending to the Imaginary, thus qualifying his overarching claim that we must eschew questions of the Imaginary—of the ego, aggression, self-images and object relations, etc.—and tempering its moralizing verve. The manner of Lacan's criticism substantially mitigates his implicit claim that Klein is "wrong" for being too concerned with what is merely Imaginary; it communicates qualified content. Lacan's mimesis is a medium of differentiation: through it, Lacan returns us to the Imaginary at the level of *speech*, thereby suggesting that the Symbolic and the Imaginary are much more interpermeated, thus that the distinctions between them are much more subtle, than the overt content (i.e., Imaginary dimension) of his commentary and related work stipulates.[295]

So pronounced are the Imaginary features of Lacan's speech that it seems that the gambit of the commentary is, first, to direct attention to speech and the Symbolic, away from content and the Imaginary, and then to facilitate a more sophisticated return to content and the Imaginary *at the level of speech*. Lacan's performative-mimetic point, the point we can discern *after* having affirmed with Lacan that the register of *speech* is vitally important, that is, after exposure to the absorbing efficacy of Lacan's hyperbolic exaggeration of the import of the Symbolic, is something like the following: If I, Lacan, cannot escape the Imaginary, what makes you believe it can be escaped? Are we—i.e., we Lacanians—so committed to a developmental or stage-ist framework (so it is not only Klein who succumbs to this vice?) that we are primed to believe that once we achieve some measure of accommodation to the Symbolic, the Imaginary is simply left behind? Have we jubilantly suppressed the difficulty of working through the arduous and perhaps ever incomplete work of mourning? Yes, we must not focus so much on the Imaginary. Yes, attention to rivalry and aggression is more than a bit overdone, especially by the Kleinians. But how can we *not* attend to the Imaginary if it is a fundamental register, an inescapable mode of psychic organization? How can we *not* attend to the Imaginary given that it is bolstered by dominant discourses and manipulated by hegemonic social formations? Given to the Imaginary as we are, can we afford to ignore it, either clinically, theoretically, or ethico-politically? If we put the analysis of the Imaginary on the backburner, are we not setting ourselves up to misjudge the extent of our success in affirming our Symbolic character, our in(de)finite *desire*? And if we are tempted to conclude that, regarding our accommodation to the Symbolic, much more has been accomplished than really has been, do we not risk complacency there where complex strategy and yet another effort are needed? *Is not a condition for accommodating to the Symbolic, to our desire, a perpetual working through of the Imaginary? And is not a condition of (im)possibility for accurately assessing our accommodation to the Symbolic an acute awareness of our captivation by the Imaginary?*[296]

As for the second point, continually, there is a profound intimacy with Klein asserted just beneath the surface of Lacan's text—or so very much on the surface that it's easy to gloss over. By asserting this intimacy, Lacan time and again undermines the position of external judge from which he appears to attack Klein and thereby allows the Lacanian and Kleinian perspectives to confront and challenge one another, perchance to render each other more complex and sophisticated, or at least to explicate the admixture of opacity and clarity, of blindness and insight, constitutive of each approach. Paradoxically, as we become more aware of the conflictual intimacy of the two perspectives, the specificity of each perspective as a perspective—as striving for totalization in its own way, yet equally in its own way internally inscribed with a hesitation (coming from the other) concerning precisely this—comes more clearly into view.

Yes there is a rhetorical assault underway from the first sentence that distances Lacan from Klein profoundly. But notice that from the beginning this distance is evidently unstable. At the final moment of this first sentence ("that Melanie Klein!") a bit of irony, humor, and thus intimacy is introduced. "That Melanie Klein!" Lacan exclaims, as only intimates can. "Oh, you!" he seems to say, in a coy and friendly—if also outraged and exasperated—tone. Are we really to take a criticism that ends with "that Melanie Klein!" as completely serious? To be sure, the phrase "*that* Melanie Klein" objectifies her, sets her at a distance, figures her name as a sign of a mechanical procedure, generally defames and caricatures her. Yet this finale is over the top; at least for a moment, it topples over the acerbic tone of the sentence and undermines the distance it establishes—which is equally crucial for bringing Lacan's concern with the singularity of each analysis, generally, his perspective, into relief. This first sentence, initially suffused with aggression and outrage, ends on something of a light note: even if one reads "that Melanie Klein!" as "that poor, stupid fool!" or "that brute!", even if one reads "that Melanie Klein!" as "damn her, that Melanie Klein!", it is difficult to deny, in light of Lacan's clear esteem for her "precious" text, that lurking in the complex, perhaps enormously overdetermined, pathos of the phrase is an amicable "Oh, that Melanie! There she goes again!" By implicating himself in a scene of bemused—if also genuinely troubled—friendship, Lacan makes it difficult to sustain the position of external judgment that is developed earlier in the sentence and will crop up throughout his engagement with Klein, allowing Klein's perspective to return as a necessary challenge to his.[297] With this final moment of ironic intimacy (Oh, you! There goes Melanie, at it again!), Lacan deflates some of the overheated pathos of the sentence's admonishment, allowing Klein to reemerge as a genuine interlocutor. The gesture humanizes Klein, figures her as an old pal as much as it objectifies her as *that over there, that thing*, sustaining the ambivalent ambiance and qualified form of claiming appropriate to a perspectival thinking. Specifically, it mitigates in advance the distance we might be tempted to take from Klein once she is depicted as aggressing against poor little empathetic Dick. (A self-aware hermeneutic gesture? If so, this would gesture toward the possibility of the self-interruption of the Imaginary.) Thus the loss of perspective on the concepts and interpretive orientation Lacan will be advancing that require her critical vantage point. Klein will be demonized, but she is also, in advance, situated in the space of friendship, intimacy, and humanity. (It is as if she is split in order to be preserved from mounting aggression.)

The phrase "that Melanie Klein!" must be read along with the "Oh, that Lacan!" that Lacan just about addresses to himself when he says, later on, "You are going to say to yourselves, Of course, being Doctor Lacan, he uses this to go on about language again." (*Seminar I*: 83). Is the jovial though honestly concerned tone of this preemptive pseudo-self-criticism not also at play in "that Melanie Klein"? Just as one might believe, reductively, that Klein can't stop herself from making the Oedipal interpretation, from going on about the breast, phantasies, object relations, the ego, and the like, one might believe that Lacan cannot stop himself from going on about language. Both appear beset by mechanistic, even compulsive, repetitiveness. But would the ludicrousness of reducing Lacan to his concern with "language" not be the same as that of reducing Klein to her concern with "phantasy"? Would it not be as facile of the critic who says at this point, "Of course, being Doctor Lacan, he uses this to go on about language again" to assume s/he knows what Lacan means by "language" as it would be to assume we know what Klein means by "phantasy" without having extensively studied her large body of work? On the other hand, there seems to be a kernel of truth to "Of course, being Doctor Lacan . . ." as much as there is to "that Melanie Klein!" Does Lacan not emphasize language as much as Klein emphasizes (pre-)Oedipal phantasy? Preoccupation, even obsession, with a number of themes and structures of psychic life, Lacan performatively suggests, is not something from which he is immune. It is something, the commentary suggests, from which no one can be immune. Emphases and exaggerations, thus distortions, exclusions, and marginalizations, condition insight. This suggests that Lacan must—and that we must—read Klein *from out of* (on the basis of, but allowing liberation from) his—and our—most entrenched habits of attention and understanding. *To an extent, Lacan will read Klein as Lacan would. This is why disrupting his own reading or at least urging such a disruption—e.g., via hospitability to, a certain manner of "internalization" of, Klein's perspective—is a necessary moment of it.*

As for the third point, by undercutting the point of exteriority from which a criticism of Klein's violence could be leveled, Lacan raises the prospect of an all-implicating violence, consideration of which may be crucial for advancing our understanding of and accommodation to the Symbolic. If violence is not just on the side of Klein's mechanically Oedipal or otherwise brutal interpretations but is coextensive with acceding to and inhabiting the Symbolic, then accommodating to the Symbolic may require avowing and engaging violence.[298] Rather than repudiate Klein the aggressor, there may be reason to identify with and work through the violence she emblematizes, for to automatically condemn violence and dismiss its representatives may mean turning a blind eye to certain crucial if unnerving features of the Symbolic. Following through on the Lacanian ambition—theoretically clarifying and practically accommodating to the Symbolic and *desire*—may require retracting or at least substantially qualifying the criticism of Klein through which this ambition is initially formulated.

By performatively collapsing the facile distinction between violence and nonviolence and allowing violence to appear all-pervasive, if gradated—e.g., differentiated into enabling versus constraining forms, though of course these regularly overlap—and especially by rendering perspicuous the link between the Symbolic and violence, does Lacan not incite us to ask ourselves how we feel about and what we have made of the violence that, on his account, is coextensive with our initiation into and continual interpellation by the Symbolic? Are we not induced to ask, What are the psycho-affective consequences of this structural violence? Does this violence feel like a violation?

And if it does not, what social and/or psychological pressures might be obstructing its affective registration as violation? For instance, if one cannot bear even the suggestion that structural limitation can feel like loss or might provoke the expression of grievances even while known to be unavoidable in some form or another, if one is given to vigorous disavowals of the grievability of broadly shard limitations or structural violences as unrealistic, impractical, and so on, is this because one resents those who would dare declare injury as vicarious embodiments of those repudiated aspects of oneself that would like to abandon the stoic stronghold that subjectivity, seeking to secure itself against its ongoing exposure or specific consequences thereof, has become, and because one resents oneself for being moved by them, for having failed against one's stoic ideal? Or is this because one so intensely desires change deemed impossible or is so profoundly frustrated with and disappointed, say, by an intense desire to belong when one feels that one's prospects for acceptance are extremely imperiled (generally because one is so captivated by Imaginary fantasies of completion) that one is prone to reactively assert full, affectively uncomplicated accommodation to the status quo?

Or if this violence does feel like a violation, what social and/or psychological pressures might be amplifying its registration as such—for instance, fantasies of perfect self-expression through which an infantile presumption of the transparency of one's thoughts to one's primary caregivers, thus the prospect of perfect fulfillment by them, is sustained, or forces of social manipulation that seek to mobilize discontent against an unsolvable "problem" in order to secure the lasting relevance of their efforts to redress it?[299] And, most importantly, if this violence does feel like a violation, how do we psychically elaborate or manage it, to the extent that we do? (Or even if the violence does not register as violation at the level of unconscious affect, how do we unconsciously metabolize it?) With what proximal causes of suffering—or presumptive causes of suffering—has this primordial violence, the violence of the Symbolic or of acculturation, been associated? Are there certain beings who or forms of life that, associated with the violence of the Symbolic, bear the brunt of our reactions to it? Are there certain beings who or forms of life that we *project* (an eminently Kleinian theme) as the sources of our sense of violation and constriction, perhaps in order to figure this violation as contingent (a consummate Imaginary gesture)? Has there been a vengefulness or reactive violence on our part, a scapegoating of various others as stand-ins for the felt violation of the Symbolic that we have yet to adequately avow and work through? Would such working through not be an important component of our accommodation to the Symbolic? Which others? Foreigners, political enemies, parents, or other ready-made sources of non-satisfaction? Teachers, government representatives, or other socially tried and true figures of invasive constriction? Women, the impoverished, or other socially and politically disenfranchised figures who can easily stand in for our deplored dependency and finitude? With what purificatory rites and exclusionary practices has our failure to work through the violence of the Symbolic been connected (this is, again, a very Kleinian question)? Generally, might being ill at ease with the violence of the Symbolic give rise to a great number of *Imaginary* effects? And when these involve object relations, fantasies, aggressive outbursts, and social or political demands, as they often do, are they not precisely the sort of scenarios that Kleinian-type readings are so very adept at illuminating? Might disavowals of the structural violence of the Symbolic—of endless finitude—be connected with an Imaginary projection of "a metaphysical mirage of universal harmony" and with the violence that may follow from the frustration of its non-attainment?[300] Might not attention to the Imaginary—say, to violent object relations—be involved in accommodating to the Symbolic?[301]

Finally, might there be organizations of the Symbolic that allow us to more directly confront its violence, perhaps therewith mitigating or impeding the tendency to lash out against its representatives? In other words, are there socio-political conditions for fuller accommodation to the Symbolic? If so, what exactly are they?[302]

The final paradox is this: although Lacan's displays of intimacy with Klein can be discerned only by incorporating, reproducing in our own readings, Lacan's exaggerated emphasis on the Symbolic, they aim to systematically subvert his authority, to release us from captivation by his perspective. This auto-destabilization aims to open the space of responsive and responsible reading, a space within which we can problematize and ultimately gain some critical distance from the absorbing authority of the Lacanian inheritance that opened this space in the first place. Do these displays of intimacy, then, not give rise to the question of how to judge, indeed *whether or in what respect to judge* Klein's efforts? Let us return once more to Lacan's commentary in order to see how it poses these questions.

The force of repudiation that Lacan's performative expressions of intimacy are working against is severe. When Lacan says that "She begins right away by hitting him with the major interpretations," he seems to be saying more or less what is conveyed by the standard joke about Klein now told in Lacanian circles: *A patient of Klein's is ten minutes late for his appointment. When he arrives, Klein looks at him and says, "You missed the first interpretation!"* In this joke, as in Lacan's statement, concern is expressed about the plausibility and value of early and deep interpretations. Do these interpretations not reflect Klein's anxiety, which is perhaps related to the difficulty she faces in containing her client's anxieties, terrors, etc. or to her Imaginary anxiety in the face of in(de)finitely interpretable or infinitely labile *desire*? Might these interpretations not collude with intellectualization to keep deeper dreads unacknowledged and unimpacted, causing Klein to systematically miss chances to "make contact with the patient's experience of living in an incomprehensible world"?[303] To be sure, Lacan is reticent about working through the layers of the ego in order to eventually access the deep unconscious. When this reticence dominates, he tends to insist that the analyst's task is to circumvent the ego, to trick it with enigmatic and equivocal speech and other techniques that allow the analyst's speech to resonate with, to vitalize or even volatilize the analysand's unconscious. But remember that as far as Lacan is concerned, Dick does not yet have an unconscious. And if there is no unconscious, there can be no transference—which makes the point of such early "major interpretations" altogether obscure. Even if Lacan's claim that Dick does not yet have an unconscious is overblown, the point about transference still holds. Klein seems misguided at best, brutal at worst. Claiming that Klein is "hitting" Dick with major interpretations from the get-go reinforces Lacan's claims about the violence, brutality, and stupidity of the Kleinian approach. Lacan goes on, "She throws him into a brutal verbalization of the Oedipus myth, almost as revolting to us as to any reader whatever."

Could it be that, again, what seems a wholesale condemnation of Klein is anything but? Perhaps Lacan's strident accusations of violence, brutality, and so on mean to explicate and acknowledge what, in his estimation, the average seminar attendee, or perhaps any reader of Klein, is bound to feel but may be unable to confront. Remember that this is the first seminar open to the public; contending with public perception may be very much on Lacan's mind. Could it be that, paradoxically, by raining down slander upon Klein, by judging her so severely, *Lacan makes it possible to read her*—specifically to read her in a way that would not be as inhibited by unacknowledged rage or identification with the victim (Dick) as would those readings that proceed without the benefit of having experienced his exaggerated enactment (his explicit "airing") of these impulses? Perhaps judging Klein, condemning her, means to release her from the scene of easy judgment into the space of responsible reading.

"I am revolted, we are revolted," Lacan publicly protests (in paraphrase), and in saying it perhaps he means to encourage his addressees to acknowledge and take responsibility for their revulsion. There are four discrete aspects of this strategy, if strategy it is. First, by staging repugnance Lacan brings it into the open, making it more difficult to immediately assume. Second, through the public airing of righteous rage, Lacan may mean to vicariously discharge his addressees' felt sense of duty to condemn and shun, their (our) moralized impediments to reading—i.e., he may mean to placate the superego: Okay, she has been admonished. Now perhaps we can read her. Third, the extreme violence of his condemnation may mean to make it feel ugly, untoward; it is repulsive, thus not so easy to assume oneself. Might his caustic slander motivate some concern for its target? A newfound empathy even? Fourth, by so violently condemning Klein's violence, Lacan confounds our endeavors to simply side with nonviolence, to take sides with him and against Klein, to judge her from afar or from the safety of the Lacanian encampment.

If staging in order to vent and render unseemly our initial abhorrence of Klein's violence is what Lacan is up to, is this not an intervention at the level of the Imaginary, specifically at the level of our object relations vis-à-vis Klein (and what she may stand for at the level of phantasy)? If so, does Lacan's commentary not performatively complicate its claims about where our attention should be focused? But, again, Lacan does not just abandon his criticisms. This intimacy gives to be seen the violent valences of interpretation in both Klein's practice and Lacan's assessment of it. As per usual with Lacan, caricature gives exaggerated form to the target of his criticism—it does not wholly invent it.

Lacan is *complicit*—he com-plies with, folds his thinking into, the faults of his adversaries in order to expose a mutual failing, but also to recover the value of what is found faulty. Generally, by allowing his discourse to become contaminated by the various objects of its critiques, Lacan calls into question his qualification to judge . . . and our desire to see him do so, with all of its Imaginary implications. Specifically, Lacan undermines the position of external judgment, i.e., collapses the dichotomy between Klein who feels things and Lacan the theoretically adept, by means of this revolting enactment of revulsion. His theatrical scorn acknowledges his subjective position of enunciation: he is revolted, overwhelmed, or at least seriously beset by emotion. It is not just she who feels. It is not just she who is a "woman of experience." Who then is to judge if, as Lacan seems to imply, we are all in a state of emotional turmoil, subjects of the unconscious? And what does judgment mean for such subjects? Must judgment mean deciding once and for all in favor of or against? Would such judgments not amount to an Imaginary resistance to *desire*? Judgment may be necessary, but it will never be easy. Through his enactment of condemnatory judgment, might Lacan be urging us to acknowledge that decisions concerning a great number of issues—say, for or against Klein, for or against Lacan—however well warranted, are never sufficiently warranted to fully forget or repudiate what was decided against?

What is at issue in these expressions of intimacy is nothing less than truth, truth in its alliance with *the perturbation of the question*, as something not altogether assimilable to definitive, systematically organized answers that put our questions to rest.[304] Rather, the provocation of truth emerges here as an incitement to both attain the most well-defined and -substantiated insights *and* sustain the shroudedness that will cause our insights to shudder and stumble, to become awkward, perhaps interminably adolescent. The truth of Klein's writings to which Lacan's intimate attention directs us concerns both their specific insights *and* their spur to renewed reading (of their interpretive modality and of the phenomena with which they are concerned). By destabilizing without abandoning his interpretive and evaluative claims regarding Klein's work, Lacan insists that both aspects of their truth are to be pursued rigorously.

It is also important to note that by displaying intimacy with his unthinking, violent, emotionally embroiled antagonist, Lacan subtly implicates his thinking in Klein's framework, gives his commentary over to her perspective. Lacan is evidently beset by revulsion, he finds something unbearable, and, as any Kleinian would note, he may thus be prone to externalize and condemn that which he finds unbearable. Perhaps only to later make reparation. From Klein's perspective—the perspective that Lacan's text solicits vis-à-vis its own operations even as it condemns it—Lacan may be *projecting* and thus may be wracked by paranoid-schizoid anxieties. Is this not a reason to be suspicious of such damning judgment? Or at least Lacan may be encumbered by aggressive object relations vis-à-vis Klein that call for a Kleinian frame of analysis. Could Lacan be in implicit agreement with Klein about how we tend to handle unbearable anxieties? Or at least conceding that her take on the matter is a viable interpretive opinion even if he means to challenge its content and consequences? Does Lacan's staged intimacy then not allow each perspective to manifest as a perspective, to put itself to the test? And is this not in the service of forestalling the devolution of perspective into dogma—in Lacanese, facilitating separation?

Once we are lead to consider that Lacan may agree with Klein about how we tend to handle unbearable anxieties, we are provoked to ask, Is Lacan projecting, revolting, throwing out something with which he identifies? What are the effects of this identification or even this rivalry, if this is what is operative here? Specifically, whence the appeal to "any reader whatever"? Is Lacan identifying with an imagined audience? Is this his figure for a "good object"? Is he taking solace in cohesive solidarity? If so, would this not be an Imaginary gesture par excellence? What is troubling him so much that he needs to take shelter in an imagined crowd, lose himself in an angry mob, or fantastically call on a band of brothers to slaughter the corrupt matriarch? Is Lacan herein admitting the inevitability—or at least the deep temptation—of a desire for cohesive self-images? Might he be giving expression to an anxiety of solitude and neglect? In light of these questions, one may begin to suspect that, once again, precisely when Lacan is speaking against the Imaginary he shows himself to be ensnared by it. Might this be a way of allowing the Imaginary to appear in its inescapability and thus an incitement to investigate this dimension of psychic life with all due caution and rigor?[305]

Finally, through this intimate entanglement in the Imaginary, Lacan may mean to further our understanding of the Symbolic. Having noticed the incessance of Imaginary trends, one might ask after their conditions. Might it be *desire* that is intrinsically unbearable and so prone to be dealt with in Imaginary ways? Might the motor of the Imaginary be not a positive longing for Completion (or not only that) but (also) *desire* itself—or, to put it in a classical idiom, the anxiety of freedom? If so, the investigation of and accommodation to *desire* and the Symbolic cannot proceed apart from concern for the Imaginary. In the end, the Kleinian perspective is demonstrated to be at the very least a necessary supplement to the Lacanian perspective, or, more strongly, internally inscribed in its full articulation. However incompatible their orientations may be, perhaps Lacan and Klein require one another.[306] At the level of Lacan's "textual unconscious," are not Lacan and Klein secretly—or now not so secretly—betrothed? Might Klein be Lacan's Thing?

Though Lacan's explicit claims are that Klein works too much within the space of the Imaginary and fails to attend to the performative dimension of her speech and its effects, as we have seen time and again, his implicit claim is that when we follow his lead and attend to the register of *speech* we find reason not to throw off our concern with the Imaginary but to track down its effects there too. Following Lacan's lead, we end up back on Kleinian territory. Klein may be encumbered by the intensity of her focus on identification, aggression, and other features of the Imaginary, but this is no warrant to dismiss the Imaginary altogether in favor of attention to the Symbolic—even though this is exactly what Lacan does, at least at the level of *content*; but recall that throughout his critique of Klein, this is a level about which Lacan councils us to remain suspicious. Lacan will largely abandon and council against explicit concern with the Imaginary, but perhaps we can now see that in doing so he accepts the risk of a one-sided violence that, like Klein's violence, may be indissociable from his project's efficacy. Perhaps this risk of a one-sided emphasis on the Symbolic is a necessary mode of *reparation* for its historical marginalization.[307]

With Lacan, there is always a double injunction, a yes and no, a state of emphatic undecidability, complicity and contamination all around: a call to judge. Yes, we must downplay object-relations, Oedipal positioning, the phantasmatic meaning of Dick's behavior, and all other kinds of Imaginary concerns in order to ask after the effects of Klein's speech and the conditions for the liberation of *desire*, both in Dick's case and generally. If we fail to do so, we will completely misunderstand what transpired in the course of the treatment and fail to draw the appropriate therapeutic and theoretical consequences. Yet no, we cannot simply ignore the Imaginary, the ego, and so on. If Klein were to do so, Dick would surely be worse off. And if we were to do so, (1) much of the depth and significance of Lacan's commentary, along with its distinctiveness, its voice(s), would be obscured, and (2) our efforts to accommodate to the Symbolic, to affirm *desire*, may be substantially impeded. So yes, Lacan will turn away from the Imaginary and toward the Symbolic, and with good reason. But his dramatic exit is a means of preparation for a more effective return. He turns away from the Imaginary and toward the Symbolic in part because this hyperbolic rejoinder to Klein is, in his estimation, the best way to set things in motion: the best way to begin making a case for attention to matters tendentially obscured and neglected and at once the best way to mobilize the work of critical reflection that will hopefully forestall the devolution of his strategically exaggerated claims into a dogma. Lacan's methodological claim seems to be that, at least initially and to some degree persistently, excess can only be deflated by counter excess. In order to keep thinking in a state of taught dialectical tension and thus maximally responsive to its objects and maximally respectful of others, which means establishing the conditions in which his claims will be qualified and challenged, Lacan risks one-sided, highly exaggerated claims, even quite violent claims—he gives us something to resist.

Drawing toward a conclusion, let us ask the following: *If* Lacan's ambition is to call his interpretive and evaluative claims into question by displaying intimacy with and even embodying the objects of his criticisms (the ego, the Imaginary, violence, mechanical routine, etc.), *if* Lacan is imploring us to resist facile discipleship, to keep psychoanalytic thinking critical and on edge, if his goal is to call into question the entirety of the psychoanalytic tradition from within, his own contributions included, all the while making advances in this tradition, should he not just come right out and say it? Would his ambition not be clearer and thus more effectively realized were he to explicitly say, "Though I am convinced that I am right here, or at least largely so, do take care to take this with a grain of salt" or "Though what I say certainly seems correct and/or the most productive way of viewing things, this is only a provisional and partial perspective on the matter"? Perhaps the major movements of his thinking could have been clarified much earlier had he said something like this. Perhaps had he offered some such explicit proviso the astonishing dogmatism of a great many Lacanians would have been avoided, along with the malicious barbs of some of his more aggressive critics. But at what cost? Is it not much more effective to allow us to come to these conclusions about the status of Lacan's claims and the dynamics of his writerly strategy on the basis of close readings of his texts? These texts, because they are so obviously problematic, because they are so manifestly complicit with what they denounce, induce suspicion. By promoting a questioning attitude, do they not have a decent chance of producing the proper conditions for their reception? Are critical impulses not best cultivated by provocation rather than dictation, i.e., pedantic assertions of the necessity of scrupulous reading? Would it not be counterproductive for Lacan to attempt to destabilize his authority via an authoritative pronouncement? Is it not much more effective to allow the texts to show themselves as problematic at every turn if one means to implant the urgency of critical scrupulousness as opposed to stating from afar, from a position of presumptive expertise or authority or ethical righteousness—from a position that assumes one's discourse to be, precisely, not *problematic,* not a field of problems, conflicts, questions, etc.—that "one must be scrupulous, read closely and critically, etc."?

Were Lacan to be straightforward about what his texts demand of his addressees, would he not risk his audience simply accepting or rejecting the demands of the master? Perhaps Lacan's reticence to make clear the demands of his texts is related to his cultural diagnosis that even the revolutionaries are seeking new masters. Perhaps too it is related to his claim that, often, our attachments to a master are predicated on our awareness that s/he can be duped by superficial compliance—that is, on awareness that we can maintain a minimal distance from the master, keep open a certain private space, by remaining cynically distant from the decrees we nonetheless obey. And perhaps it is related to his contention that we are prone to overly idealize and quickly lose confidence in our masters. If we are, his question would then be, Why risk the dissipation or even dissolution of the critical impulse by tying it so tightly to confidence in the master? Lacan, whose position within the French psychoanalytic scene and, all the more so, the international psychoanalytic scene was forever precarious and especially so around the time of *Seminar I*, perhaps knew better than to bind the demand for continual scrupulousness of and within psychoanalysis to his personal charisma or institutional authority. Generally, Lacan might well wonder, Why submit the urgency of critical reading to the context of master-disciple relations and all the difficulties incumbent thereto?

Finally, do we not learn what it means that Lacan's claims are partial and provisional—that they rise up from and take a stand within a space of interpretive plurality, that though they are forged and insisted upon with the utmost strength, they are irreparably submitted to a stumbling or wavering as they are caught in the interpretive winds blowing from all directions—*in much more concrete ways* by submitting his texts to the critical scrutiny they inspire? Would some relatively abstract yet explicit pronouncement that the claims to follow are "perspectival" be nearly as effective on this front? Is systematic self-complication not a much more effective way of advancing the imperative of continual critical scrupulousness?[308]

Singularly, at a certain point Lacan's work regularly manages to complicate itself, even to rigorously undermine or bring itself into crisis. And it does so self-consciously, with the aim of inducing us to follow suit. Lacan's perspective is different from other psychoanalytic perspectives *as perspectives*—it tends to be more truthful (even when, at the level of content, it is clearly in the wrong), more self-conscious, more fully responsive to its material conditions. Certainly self-questioning is evident in the work of other psychoanalytic theorists, but not with the regularity and rigor we find in Lacan. Lacan's ethico-theoretical ambition is to keep thinking alive by sustaining the exposure of his claims to complication and challenge by the phenomena they render and by others' perspectives. Even his most cherished insights, even his most characteristic interpretations, even his most fundamental premises are brought into question. He exposes his exaggerations as exaggerations by, somewhere, somehow, taking up the opposite claim or at least providing space for its articulation. Though he may act as judge and jury, at least for a moment claims contrary to his are given a hearing. In this way, the inassimilable outside of the Lacanian perspective—the abject—is brought into the interior, causing the Lacanian perspective to tremble, and precisely thereby to come into the medium of its truth.

The truth of the Lacanian perspective, as a perspective, is won by keeping it manifest as a perspective. Dialogue is its internal requirement. With Lacan, there is always a claim and counter-claim, a moment of inflation and of deflation. With Lacan, we are always in the space of the undecidable. Even though, with Lacan, there is always an urging of decision, a demand to side with him rather than the competition. To be sure, Lacan solicits our assent, and yet at some moment or other he calls into question that with which we would agree. Unlike any other, Lacan's perspective systematically resists reification into a doctrine that could be finally validated or invalidated, affirmed or rejected. Though his concepts, insights, and interpretive orientations attain to a certain stabilization and even obstinacy in the face of criticism, they are always, at a certain point, troubled, allowed to display themselves as ways of proceeding among others, as perhaps advantageous but never the best without qualification. Lacan's claims are advanced as insightful but "not all"; this, we might say, is an expression of his feminine wile.

What Lacan gives to be seen is that the singularity of a perspective is not only manifest in what it reveals, what it conceals, and where it leads—it is not reducible to its content and consequences. Rather, the singularity of a perspective manifests in its manner, its way of proceeding, its style or voice(s): its *ethos*. The singularity of a perspective is expressed in how it frames itself as a perspective, in the stance it takes on what it is to take a stance, to shape and stake a claim. Expressing a distinctive structure of sensibility and urgency, and a number of theoretical and practical commitments, a perspective manifests a life and is to be honored as life is honored: in its plurality.

Notes

1. Cf. Dieter Henrich, *The Unity of Reason: Essays on Kant's Philosophy* (London: Harvard University Press, 1994).

2. Melanie Klein, *Love, Guilt, and Reparation: And Other Works 1921–1945* (New York: The Free Press, 1975), 230. Hereafter 1975.

3. Julia Kristeva, *Powers of Horror: An Essay on Abjection*, trans. Leon Roudiez (New York: Columbia University Press, 1982).

4. It is unclear whether this means to be a summary of a clinical hypothesis confirmed in the course of the therapy or the record of an established interpretive schema that proved to be effective in this case and may be useful in others. The status of Klein's interpretations and specifically of the rhetoric of "reality" ("it *really* had to do with . . .") and "standing for" ("doors and locks stood for . . .") will be addressed below.

5. Jacques Lacan, ed. Jacques-Alain Miller, trans. John Forrester, *The Seminar of Jacque Lacan: Book I, Freud's Papers on Technique 1953–1954* (New York: W. W. Norton, 1988).

6. Compare Freud: "After all, conflicts will only be successfully solved and his resistances overcome if the anticipatory ideas he is given tally with what is real in him" (*SE* 16: 452).

7. The treatment is admittedly unusual. Klein cannot rely on her ordinary play-technique, which "follows the child's symbolic representations and gives access to his anxiety and sense of guilt" due to Dick's inhibited investment in symbolization (1975: 224). Thus, initially, she turns to the symbolism that was "revealed in the details of his general behavior" (1975: 224).

8. Klein's assignment of the two trains as "Dick train" and "daddy train," respectively, can be understood in at least two ways. (1) The interpretation induces Dick to enact a phantasy of fearful flight wherein the anxiety-provoking proximity to the daddy train—or, perhaps, simply the proximity to an *other* [train], to a non-Dick, which may just as well be his mother, various part-objects associated with her, or a figure of *otherly terror* that has nothing to do with either mother or father in their empirical concreteness or even their imagoes—provokes him to flee to the soothing space of the mother/station. Dick flees to a site that—despite the relative lack of love on the mother's behalf noted by Klein—evokes a memory of consolation or satisfaction because it is associated with his mother. Here we would understand Dick as developing the rudiments of signal anxiety and enacting Oedipal desires. (2) Since Dick's world was largely undifferentiated, the two trains ("Dick train" and "daddy train") were quickly identified despite their difference in size. Once mentally merged, Dick's rolling his train to the "Station" expresses the desire of (what he perceives as, imagines as, or desires to be) the "daddy train." The thread-bare differentiations organizing Dick's world allow for a remarkable openness to and assumption of the desire of the other: Dick/daddy, as an undifferentiated monad, roll to the mother. Of course, these two interpretations are by no means mutually exclusive. The point is simply to underscore from the beginning the undecidability of Dick's behavior even within a standard Kleinian framework.

9. Or in a Kristevan vein, one might say that Dick runs to a space of thirdness (associated with the "individual father of prehistory"?), a space that establishes his distance and difference from the incestuous scene of the "Dick train" rolling into the station (mother and/or father), its phantasized consequences, or, who knows, something else altogether that is, within Dick's idiosyncratic psychic economy, connected with the daddy train. Thereby, perhaps, Dick triangulates himself, whether with respect to Klein and the station (the desire of the mother), the daddy train and the Dick train (homosexual desire), Dick train and station (heterosexual desire), or other such configurations. What is at stake may be an enactment of individuation, and, if so, Klein's diagnosis of Dick as just about wholly overcome by undifferentiated anxiety may be off the mark. Or quite to the contrary—though a contrary interpretation need not be an incompatible one—recognizing something of himself in the train named after him, Dick may be using the train to play out a desire for connection, perhaps fusion, with the mother. Both when the train rolls into the station *and* when Dick runs to the space between the doors, perhaps he is attempting to touch mother. "Dark" may signal the comfort of nighttime ministrations. The point here is simply that neither the Kleinian nor the Lacanian interpretation will exhaust the interpretability of this or other such scenes.

10. The claim about projection is peculiar, though. Is not assuming as established the symbolic import that transforms throwing toys into projection a bit precipitous in this context?

11. For instance, in 1946 she distinguishes her approach from Fairbairn's by underscoring that while his "approach was largely from the angle of ego development in relation to objects," hers is "predominantly from the angle of anxiety and its vicissitudes" (*Envy and Gratitude & Other Works, 1946–1963,* [London: Virago, 1988], 3). Are these two perspectives identical but for their angle of approach? Are they fully interchangeable, theoretically and practically? Surely not. If, as the claim implies, differences in manner

of approach, i.e., perspective, are not merely superficial but rather are significant enough to define the theoretical and practical differences between Fairbairn and Klein, or at least are that to which Klein turns our attention in order to shed light on these deep differences, then much more needs to be said about the nature of perspective. Yet about these matters Klein is silent.

12. Or so Klein's texts regularly suggest. One cannot but wonder, though: Does Klein tend to frame her interpretations in the language of body parts and processes because she found this language to be experientially near to and thus most helpful for the highly disturbed children with whom she was working? Is the reproduction of this language in her metapsychological works but an oversight or a device designed to return the reader to the clinical ground of, and perhaps thereby to the ultimately clinical significance of, her metapsychological formulations?

13. For more on Klein's claim that certain phantasy contents and associations are innate, cf. Danny Nobus, "Theorising the Comedy of the Sexes: Lacan on Sexuality," in *The Klein-Lacan Dialogues*, eds. Bernard Burgoyne and Mary Sullivan (New York: Other Press, 1999), 100.

14. Compare, for instance, the following excerpt from "The Early Development of Conscience in the Child": "In attacking its mother's inside . . . the child is attacking a great number of objects, and is embarking on a course which is fraught with consequences. The womb first *stands for* the world; and the child originally approaches this world with desires to attack or destroy it, and is therefore prepared from the outset to view the real, external world as more or less hostile to itself, and peopled with objects ready to make attacks upon it. Its belief that in thus attacking its mother's body it has also attacked its father and its brothers and sisters, and, in a wider sense the whole world, is, *in my experience*, one of the underlying causes of its sense of guilt and of the development of its social and moral feelings in general" (1975: 254; emphases added).

15. However, the possibly defensive function of Klein's repeated appeal to the language of experience should not go unremarked. Klein's employment of the language of experience makes it difficult to keep in mind that often her claims are grounded in retrospective reconstructions rather than direct observation of infants and very young children. Other than her own children, Klein's youngest patient was thirty-one months, and most a good bit older—somewhere in the Oedipal years.

16. This tension is by no means consigned to this one essay; it is everywhere in Klein's work. To cite just one more instance: "*We know* that the destructive instinct is directed against the organism itself and *must therefore* be regarded by the ego as a danger. *I believe* that it is this danger which is felt by the ego as anxiety" ("Early Stages of the Oedipus Conflict and of Super-Ego Formation," in *The Psychoanalysis of Children* [New York: Free Press, 1984], 126; emphasis added).

17. Or it may be that by drawing on associative links with potent earlier (often infantile or early childhood) material, a current event and/or the material it becomes associated with becomes traumatic. In this case, the attempt to symbolize and integrate a current experience backfires by reviving material (prior experiences, fantasies, etc.) that had been lying dormant but now, upon revival, cannot be borne. Such material was not traumatic within the framework of prior self-conceptions, values, and so on but only becomes so upon being revived in a new context of commitments.

18. Cf. Julia Kristeva's *Powers of Horror*, especially pgs. 133ff.

19. My reading of Lacan may initially strike many readers as "generous." But consider the following. Lacan's teachings and texts are so massively inconsistent, so dictated by rabid polysemy, so extraordinarily suggestive at every turn—that is, ever opening onto new horizons while continuing to plumb the depths of older themes and advance previously established positions—that one cannot but be selective when reconstructing the major movements of his thought. Lacan was emphatically averse to systematization; often he was even wont to provide arguments for or clarifying examples of his most significant concepts and theses. Filling in the blanks by providing the warrants, connections, arguments, and examples, i.e., substantiating his claims, inevitably entails reinflecting, even redirecting them. In short, if we are to speak of Lacan coherently at all, construction is unavoidable. So why not allow a spirit of generosity to be our guide? Whether my "generous" reconstruction involves reduction or misconstrual I leave for the reader to decide.

20. "[T]he stake of analysis is nothing other than this—to recognize what function the subject assumes in the order of symbolic relations which cover the whole field of human relations" (*Seminar I*: 80); "In order to know how to respond to the subject in analysis, the procedure is to determine first of all the place where his *ego* is . . . in other words, to know through whom and for whom the subject poses *his question*. As long as this is not known, there will be risk of misunderstanding concerning the desire that is there to be recognized and concerning the object to whom this desire is addressed" (*Écrits: The First Complete English Edition*, trans. Bruce Fink, [New York: W. W. Norton & Company, 2006], 250/303; trans. modified. Hereafter cited as *E*). Dany Nobus provides a nice example of what it means to ask after the structure of address: "if an analysand says, 'I am doomed to ruin every relationship I am engaged in,' the analyst . . . ought to concentrate on the fact that something is being said from a particular place, the exact source and intention of which remain unclear and require further exploration. When the analysand is saying, 'I am doomed, etc.,' the subject of enunciation is not necessarily herself. The statement may very well represent the discourse of her mother and she may easily produce these words for the analyst to believe that they are hers and for him to try to convince her that she is not doomed at all." "Lacan's Science of the Subject: Between Linguistics and Topology," in *The Cambridge Companion to Lacan*, ed. Jean-Michel Rabaté (Cambridge: Cambridge University Press, 2003), 62.

21. Here and throughout discourse is not limited to verbal productions. For Lacan, discourse is an expressive medium (expressive of desire) that may be verbal, behavioral, and so on.

22. Indeed, for Klein, every drive, need, impulse, and impression is phantasmatically elaborated, i.e., in some way *meaningful*.

23. Compare Klein's claim that "the psycho-analytic procedure . . . to put it in a nutshell, consists in understanding the patient's mind and in conveying to him what goes on in it" ("The Psycho-analytic Play Technique" in Klein 1988, 129) with Lacan's claim that "[i]nterpretation is a signification that is not just any signification. . . . It has the effect of bringing out an irreducible signifier. . . . What is there is rich and complex, when it is a question of the unconscious of the subject, and intended to bring out irreducible, *non-sensical*—composed of non-meanings—signifying elements" (*Seminar XI*, trans. Alan Sheridan, ed. by Jacques-Alain Miller [New York: W. W. Norton, 1998], 250) and

his claim in *Seminar X* that that the symptom does not call for interpretation—it is not an impasse to be deciphered by analytic expertise—but pure jouissance addressed to no one (unpublished manuscript).

24. Cf. *Seminar XIX*, June 21, 1972; and "L'Etourdit," *Scilicet* 4 (1973), 5–52.

25. "We always understand too much, especially in analysis" (Jacques Lacan, *The Seminar of Jacques Lacan: Book II; The Ego in Freud's Theory and in the Technique of Psychoanalysis*, ed. Jacques-Alain Miller, trans. Sylvana Tomaselli [New York: W. W. Norton, 1988], 103).

> What counts, when one attempts to elaborate an experience, is less what one does understand than what one does not understand. . . . Commenting on a text is like doing an analysis. . . . [O]ne of the things we should be watching out for most is not to understand too much, not to understand more than what there is in the discourse of the subject. Interpreting is an altogether different thing than having the fancy of understanding. One is the opposite of the other. I will even say that it is on the basis of a certain refusal of understanding that we open the door onto psychoanalytic understanding." (*Seminar I*: 73/87–88; trans. modified)

On the first page of *Seminar XX*, we find Lacan saying "I don't want to know anything about it" (*The Limits of Love and Knowledge, 1972–3: Encore. The Seminar of Jacques Lacan; Book XX*, ed. Jacques-Alain Miller, trans. Bruce Fink [New York: W. W. Norton, 1999]). The caution against understanding obviously means to highlight a clinical risk: when the analyst presumes to understand and conveys this understanding, explicitly or implicitly, through her interpretations, she may have failed to appreciate the intensity of the analysand's desire to assimilate himself to the image projected by the interpretation and what is behind it. What looks like an "ideal" response to analytic interpretation, on Lacan's account, may amount to resistance to the interpretation and to analysis generally.

26. The brunt of Lacan's attraction to Structuralism had little to do with the particular research programs developing under its banner. Rather, what captivated Lacan's attention was to a great extent Structuralism's anti-intentionalist/anti-phenomenological methodological commitment, i.e., its commitment that meaning was irreducible to what could be described from an insider's view.

27. Though, as we have seen, these may not be distinct for Klein.

28. *Seminar XX*: 54–55/52.

29. So it seems in Lacan's work too there is a moment of naturalization/mechanicism. Can ambition avoid such a moment? We will return to this below.

30. This is indicated by Lacan's repeated contention that training ("didactic") analysis is pure analysis. In training analysis, the work of desubjectification can be more intensely and consistently pursued because, likely, the analysand is not beset by the sorts of debilitating conflicts and anguishing difficulties that bring others to analysis; hence fewer concessions need to be made to the ego. Cf. Jacques Alain-Miller, *Excommunication* (Paris: Seuil, 1984), 149–53. However, Lacan does say that he is always training: for instance, he says that his "seminar was, from the beginning, *implicated*, so to speak. . . . [I]t was aimed at what is an essential of that praxis, namely, the training of psychoanalysts (*Seminar XI*: 2). Even in the context of "impure" analyses—if there are any—alleviating suffering is not Lacan's primary goal, and here he follows Freud: "Cruel though it may

sound, we must see to it that the patient's suffering, to a degree that is in some way or other effective, does not come to an end prematurely. If, owing to the symptoms having been taken apart and having lost their value, his suffering becomes mitigated, we must reinstate it elsewhere in the form of some appreciable privation; otherwise we run the danger of never achieving any improvements except quite insignificant and transitory ones" (*SE* 17: 163).

31. For Freud, "the dimension proper to analysis is the reintegration by the subject of his history right up to the furthermost perceptible limits," Lacan says approvingly (*Seminar I*: 12).

32. This seems to be the gist of what Lacan is getting at when he later gleans Klein's failure "to grasp the importance of the signifier" from her reduction of "fantasy to imagination." Klein's presumption of an autochthonous imagination is at one with her blindness to fantasy as the mediation of the enigmatic signifiers "which [come] from the Other." As he soon goes on to insist, fantasy is "an image *set to work* in the signifying structure" (*E*: 532/637–38; emphasis added).

33. On the meaninglessness of the signifier, cf. Jacques Lacan, "The Position of the Unconscious," trans. Bruce Fink, in Richard Feldstein, Bruce Fink, and Marie Jaanus, eds., *Reading Seminar XI: Lacan's Four Fundamental Concepts of Psychoanalysis* (New York: W. W. Norton, 1995).

34. Cf. Peter Brooks's reading of Rousseau's *Confessions* in *Reading for the Plot: Design and Intention in Narrative* (New York: Vintage Books, 1985), 30–63.

35. Here it should be quite clear, if it was not already, that the Lacanian questions and concerns pursued herein are constructed on the basis of his work to come and then read back into his engagement with Klein in *Seminar I*. This is an attempt to stage a confrontation that could have—but did not—later take place in order to better explicate the differences in perspective between the mature Lacan and the mature Klein.

36. Though she is usually a superbly deft reader of Lacan, Shoshana Felman's gloss on this scene is wholly off the mark. Felman writes, "And how does Klein's speech act produce the call in Dick? By calling him ('Dick—little train'), by naming him within the constellation of a symbolic structure, by performatively constituting him, through her own discourse, as a subject" (*Jacques Lacan and the Adventure of Insight: Psychoanalysis in Contemporary Culture* [Cambridge: Harvard University Press, 1987], 118). Is Felman not suggesting that Klein engages in a sovereign act of interpellation? That the interpellation functions smoothly and efficiently? Lacan is (as Felman *usually* is—see her *Scandal of the Speaking Body*) much more cautious about the possibility of unilaterally effective interpellation. Consider the following statement: "But if I call the person to whom I am speaking by whatever name I choose to give to him, I intimate to him the subjective function that he will take on in order to reply to me, even if it is to repudiate this function" (*E*: 247/300; trans. modified). On Lacan's account, the act of nomination intimates to its addressee her subjective positioning vis-à-vis the speaker; it does not effectively guarantee the assumption of this positioning. Speech can do no more than forcefully suggest a subject position. This is quite clear when Lacan specifies that the act of interpellation is just as likely to be refused as it is to be assumed. As he says earlier in the essay from which the previous citation is drawn, "What constitutes me as subject is my question. In order to be recognized by the other, I proffer what was only in view of what will be. In order to

find him, I call him by a name that he must *assume or refuse* in order to answer me" (*E*: 247/299; emphasis added). Of course, to refuse an act of interpellation is to be in some way bound up in its terms. But even so, the captivating power of interpellation is, on Lacan's account, limited. Though Dick is deeply impacted by Klein's speech, he "symbolizes the reality surrounding him *out of* this *palpitating cell of symbolism* which Melanie Klein has provided him with," i.e., out of this germinal symbolism substance that will grow and develop in ways that Klein will not have been able to predict or control (*Seminar I*: 85/100; trans. modified following Felman 1987: 114 and emphases added). Moreover, on Lacan's account, Klein's speech could not constitute Dick "as a subject" because, by definition, the subject is what remains beyond interpellation. The subject is precisely the void, inconsistency, or lability that eludes assimilation by the sociosymbolic order. The subject is precisely what persists beyond and guarantees the partial failure of interpellation. On this last point, cf. Mladen Dolar, "Beyond Interpellation," *Qui Parle*, Berkeley: University of California Press, vol. 6, number 2, Spring/Summer 1993: 75–96.

37. Here it is most clear that the Imaginary and Symbolic are dimensions or registers of experience and are by no means mutually exclusive. All too often Lacanians reify and falsely isolate the Imaginary and the Symbolic, most often in the service of an ethico-therapeutic suggestion to find an exit from the intrinsically conservative Imaginary and enter the radicality of the Symbolic. As an example of this lamentable trend, cf. Todd McGowan, *The End of Dissatisfaction? Jacques Lacan and the Emerging Society of Enjoyment* (New York: SUNY Press, 2004).

38. On processual differentiation, cf. Alan Bass, *Difference and Disavowal: The Trauma of Eros* (Stanford: Stanford University Press, 2000), and his *Interpretation and Difference: The Strangeness of Care* (Stanford: Stanford University Press, 2006).

39. *Seminar IV*: 63; though admittedly some comments in this seminar seem to point the other way.

40. Actually, it is unclear in Lacan's work whether (1) it is a *theoretical axiom* that early experiences of fragmentation are so undesirable that they provoke flight into the Imaginary; (2) the unbearability of the body-world in bits and pieces is a retrospective construction based on anxious dreams of such like states and other clinical evidence; (3) there is not so much a flight from the fragmented body as there is an intrinsic impulse to subjective unification; (4) such an "intrinsic impulse" toward integration is implanted by the desire of caregivers and later sustained by cultural inheritors of the caregiver status; (5) the move into Imaginary coherence is promoted by a (suspect) privileging of the penis as a solid, firm entity whose formal features are definitionally desirable, or at least captivating, and that induces the infant (or at least the male infant) to mimetically incorporate its qualities in his desired self-image; (6) it is the unbearable dependency and inevitable dissatisfactions of infancy (preemptory neediness, the surging of sensations that are traumatically intense or intrinsically traumatic because unmetabolizable, etc.) that, because they are *associated* with experiences of fragmentation, provoke the infant to create and/or discover (perhaps in the desire of its caregivers) a more coherent form of self- and world-experience, a form of experience less *associated* with such devastating early experiences; (7) such a flight, if there is one, is conditioned by the extreme permeability between self and other in which the child feels overwhelmed and crowded out, unrecognized and forlorn; (8) on the contrary, such flight—again, if there is one—is a way to overcome a

sense of isolation and abandonment; or (9) all or some combination of the above is what accounts for Imaginary captivation. Although there is much ambiguity about *why* we are impelled into the Imaginary, *that* we are, for Lacan, is evident.

41. "The Mirror Stage as Formative of the *I* Function as Revealed in Psychoanalytic Experience," in *E*: 75–81.

42. It is precisely the Imaginary reduction of subjectivity to character that shows the Imaginary to be fundamentally at odds with narrative intelligibility. The narrated self is forever a problematic subject; successful narratives are those that compel us to acknowledge and help us accept our perpetually problematic character.

43. Cf. Judith Butler, *The Psychic Life of Power: Theories in Subjection* (Palo Alto, Calif: Stanford University Press, 1997).

44. As we will see, both the desire for connection and the demand for tension reduction play a part in Lacanian theory, but Lacan understands their significance very differently than do object relationists and classical Freudians, and he places much less emphasis on them than they.

45. "In psycho-analytic thought, we have heard more of 'imago' than of image. The distinctions between an 'imago' and 'image' might be summarized as: (a) 'imago' refers to an unconscious image; (b) 'imago' usually refers to a person or part of a person, the earliest objects, whilst 'image' may be of any object or situation, human or otherwise; and (c) 'imago' includes all the somatic and emotional elements in the subject's relation to the imaged person, the bodily links in unconscious phantasy with the id, the phantasy of incorporation which underlies the process of introjection; whereas in the 'image' the somatic and much of the emotional elements are largely repressed." Susan Isaacs, "The Nature and Function of Phantasy," *International Journal of Psycho-Analysis* 29 (1948): 93.

46. Some textual support for the claim that the Real at least sometimes names a primordial form of experience can be found in *Seminar XI*. There Lacan comments on Freud's "Wo Es war, soll Ich warden" as follows: "The subject is there to discover *where it was*—I anticipate—the real. *Where it was*, the *Ich*, . . . the subject must come into existence" (45).

47. To be clear, for Lacan ego functioning is not *only* defensive, but it is likely *always* (also) defensive. Here, to speak of defensive ego functioning is not to qualify ego functioning; rather, it is to use the adjective "defensive" to redouble the emphasis on defense encoded in the term "ego."

48. Our sense of non-belonging may be aggravated by various social pressures, but it cannot be fully relieved by any social development, no matter how progressive universalist. For Lacan, the attempt to secure a social order into which we would fit perfectly smacks of defensive denial and should put on alarm those soon to be held responsible for its failure.

49. More precisely, such integration occurs only if the infant is possessed of a sufficient quantity of libido and/or develops its reality-testing capabilities to a sufficient degree.

50. At times Klein describes the whole object as exclusively good, e.g., when she characterizes the ego in the depressive position as coming "to a realization of its love for a good object, a whole object and in addition a real object, together with an overwhelming feeling of guilt towards it" (1975: 270). But for the most part the link between wholeness

and reality is consistent throughout her work. Though there are moments when Klein might have questioned the link between wholeness and reality, indeed when she seemed almost on the verge of doing so (as when she describes the good, whole object as idealized), she never takes this step.

51. To clarify, though the relationships as experienced may be far from static, the *form* of the relationships is in each case quite stable.

52. "The first internal good object acts as a focal point of the ego. It counteracts splitting and dispersal, makes for cohesiveness and integration, and is instrumental in building up the ego" ("Notes on Some Schizoid Mechanisms," in *The Selected Melanie Klein*, ed. Juliet Mitchell [New York: Free Press, 1986], 181).

53. "There is no whole. Nothing is whole" (Jacques Lacan, "Radiophonie," *Scilicet* 2–3 [1970], 93).

> The *dialectic of fantasy objects* promoted in practice by Melanie Klein tends to be translated in the theory in terms of identification. For these objects, whether part-objects or not, but certainly signifying objects—the breast, excrement, and the phallus—are no doubt won or lost by the subject; he is destroyed by them or preserves them, but above all he *is* these objects, according to the place where they function in his fundamental fantasy. (*E*: 513/614; earlier emphasis added)

54. Registration and repudiation of the primary and persistent experience of oneself/the world as fundamentally non-whole would be, in Lacanian parlance, the work of fundamental fantasy, which is identified in the passage above as the secretly controlling framework of Kleinian theory.

55. Cf. Bruce Arrigo, "The Inside Out of the Dangerous Mentally Ill: Topological Application to Law and Social Justice," in *Lacan: Topologically Speaking*, ed. Ellie Ragland and Dragan Milovanovic (New York: Other Press, 2004), 158–61.

56. Compare J. M. Bernstein, "Sexuate Being: Foundations for a Feminist Legal Philosophy?" in *Imagining Law: On Drucilla Cornell*, eds. Renee Heberle and Benjamin Pryor (Albany: SUNY Press, 2008), 81–102.

57. Briefly, let us note another major difference between Lacan and Klein: even if Klein were correct that the epistemophilic instinct is innate, it is far less relevant than she imagines, Lacan suggests. In "Introduction à l'édition allemande d'un premier volume des *Écrits*," Lacan intimates that the passion for ignorance is far stronger than any passion for knowledge, explicitly claiming that the passion for ignorance is a greater passion than even love and hate (*Scilicet* 5 [1975]: 11–17).

58. To be sure, this would be a risky venture. Some of the most obvious rejoinders would be that such a culture would be anarchic, devastating for the least well-off, divested of the security and satisfactions that administered culture provides, open to external attack and internally arising hegemonic forces, and solicitous of the worst in us. This may well be true, but Lacan's continual emphasis on the radicality of *desire* and his efforts to promote *desire* to the truth of subjectivity, however theoretically illicit, ideologically suspect, or even downright dangerous, seems less of a political *proposal* (he is not addressing the government) than a provocation. Perhaps it is a provocation designed to be resisted and thereby reflect back to us our unacknowledged conservatism. Or perhaps it aims to provoke reflection on the questions of exactly what forms of social life are worth pursuing

and why. In either case, it seems designed to enhance self-consciousness, not to open the floodgates to libertine anarchism. Lacan, as we will later see, establishes accommodation to desirous subjectivity as a normative ideal but not an exclusive ideal or unqualified good. Desire is of course always shadowed by anguish. And—albeit in a roundabout way—Lacan avoids manipulating this ideal as a moralizing platform from which to condemn actions that do not conform to it. Rather, his teachings are self-consciously complicit in the dialectical oppositions that he seeks to keep in motion.

59. Here, as elsewhere, there is a veering toward Nietzsche, then, at a crucial moment, a departure, which is followed by a qualified return. Compare the following passage from Nietzsche's *Genealogy of Morals.*

> If we place ourselves at the end of this tremendous process, where the tree at last brings forth fruit, where society and the morality of custom at last reveal *what* they have simply been the means to, then we discover that the ripest fruit is the *sovereign individual,* like only to himself, liberated again from morality of custom, autonomous and supramoral (for "autonomous" and "moral" are mutually exclusive), in short, the man who has his own independent, protracted will and the *right to make promises* [here Lacan diverges sharply from Nietzsche, only to return in a qualified way when the power of self-creation signaled by the "independent, protracted will" and "right to make promises" rather than self-consistency, self-mastery, etc., comes into focus]—and in him a proud consciousness, quivering in every muscle, of *what* has at length been achieved and become flesh in him, a consciousness of his own power and freedom, a sensation of mankind come to completion. (*Genealogy of Morals,* trans. Walter Kaufmann and R. J. Hollingdale [New York: Vintage, 1989], 59).

60. Though, as we will later see, Lacan depathologizes categories of neurosis, he sometimes retains the pathological connotation of neurosis in order to emphasize that the ideals of fulfillment with which neurotics are enamored are sources of *suffering.* For instance, when Lacan claims that "[t]he neurotic's desire is what is born when there is no God," the suggestion seems to be, in part, that the neurotic's unsatisfiable, suffering-inducing desire for completion is born when there is no identifiable agency to which one can appeal for salvation, e.g., for a decisive decree about what one must do in order to be "good" and thus "redeemed" (*Seminar VI,* June 24, 1959; unpublished manuscript). As Nietzsche underscored, theology persists well after "the death of god"—which, in a Lacanian lexicon, translates into the following: various self-images or desirable objects are elevated to the empty place of divinity and the neurotic suffers in everlasting want of them.

61. Though Klein occasionally worries about the tendency of reality testing to arrogate fantasies of omnipotence, thereby becoming self-undermining, even in so doing she maintains that, in principle, reality testing can be completely successful. In contrast, for Lacan, the success and self-subversion of reality testing run together.

62. To be sure, this is no iron-cage theory. The claim that our sense of reality is mimetically acquired by no means presumes to be exhaustive. Lacan would have no interest in denying that via systematic inquiry we can correct our beliefs to some extent. And notice that even at the level of its performative enunciation this claim suggests that we can at least gain some distance from the value-laden, perspectival sense of reality we mimetically acquire from others: becoming self-conscious of mimetically acquiring a sense of reality, our perspective alters; even if, in a quasi-Spinozistic vein, this does not

imply that we gain any new cognitive content but rather a reorientation with regard to what we already know.

63. Actually, it is unclear in Lacan's writings whether we notice self-concern in others or project it onto them.

64. This brings Lacan and Sartre quite close with regard to the solution to the problem of other minds. Consideration of this convergence would reward study.

65. I take it that the great many commentators fundamentally miss this point who interpret Lacan's injunction to "not cede upon your desire" as enjoining the pursuit of authentically individuated desire.

66. A Lacanian reading of penis envy would thus situate it as a matter of being ensnared in the ingratiating stratagem of another—for instance, but not only, of a child—to which all are susceptible. "Penis envy" as traditionally construed would be reframed as the fantasmatic consequence of a largely successful projection of, for instance, a child's desire rather than a natural development of female desire consequent on her "perception" of her lack.

67. It cannot be recalled often enough that Lacan does not simply wave away the need for love, recognition, and a sense of personal integrity. Rather, he seems to think that (1) these topics have been addressed by just about everyone else and, (2) even so, there has yet to be due consideration of what they risk and suppress. In other words, they have not been fully thought through; they have rather been privileged and idealized as a result of their disintrication from their dialectical underside. Again and again, Lacan will exaggerate the suppressed underside in order to keep the dialectic—to keep thinking—in motion.

68. "Nothing forces anyone to enjoy except the superego" (*Seminar XX*: 3/10).

69. For instance, in *Seminar VII* Lacan suggests that the ego is a mirage concealing the subject's (and implicitly the object's) *manque-à-être* (*The Ethics of Psychoanalysis, 1959–60: The Seminar of Jacques Lacan; Book VII*, ed. Jacques-Alain Miller, trans. Dennis Porter [New York: W. W. Norton, 1992], 298). In order to stress his point that the ego should not be ascribed the power of reality testing, Lacan goes so far as to say that "the essential function of the ego is very nearly that systematic refusal of reality which French analysts refer to in talking about the psychoses" ("Some Reflections on the Ego," *International Journal of Psychoanalysis* 34 [1953]: 12).

70. *Seminar VII*: 298

71. *In Seminar III*, Lacan stresses the dialectical-historical interimbrication of recognition and misrecognition named by the ego:

> I tried last time to show you that the ego, whatever we make of its function, and I shall go no further than to give it the function of a discourse of reality, always implies as a correlate a discourse that has nothing to do with reality. With the impertinence that, as everyone knows, is characteristic of me I designated this the discourse of freedom, essential to modern man insofar as he is structured by a certain conception of his own autonomy. I pointed out its fundamentally biased and incomplete, inexpressible, fragmentary, differentiated, and profoundly delusional nature. I set out from this general parallel to point out to you what, in relation to the ego, is apt, in the subject fallen prey to psychosis, to proliferate into a delusion. I'm not saying it's the same thing. I'm saying it's in the same place. (Trans. Russell Grigg [New York: Norton, 1993], 144–45/165)

72. Ibid., 15.

73. Compare Lacan's characterization of *objet a* as the dimension of self, other, and object that is "never there, that is always situated elsewhere, that is always something else" (*Seminar V*: 19; unpublished manuscript).

74. Some readers of Lacan claim, and at certain moments Lacan seems to suggest, that the ego is, from the beginning, modeled on the perceived wholeness of various objects, e.g., say, the penis. Cf. Mikkel Borch-Jacobsen, *Lacan: The Absolute Master*, trans. Douglas Brick (Stanford: Stanford University Press, 1991).

75. "The enigmas that desire—with its frenzy mimicking the gulf of the infinite and the secret collusion whereby it envelops the pleasure of knowing and of dominating in jouissance—poses for any sort of 'natural philosophy' are based on no other derangement of instinct than the fact that it is caught in the rails of metonymy, eternally extending toward the *desire of something else*" (*E*: 431/518).

76. Compare: "I always tell the truth; not the whole truth, because we are not capable of telling it all. Telling it all is materially impossible" (*Television: A Challenge to the Psychoanalytic Establishment*, ed. Joan Copjec, trans. Denis Hollier, Rosalind Krauss, and Annette Michelson [New York: Norton, 1990], 9).

77. Translation modified following Felman 1987: 113.

78. This is one meaning of "*the unconscious is the discourse of the other*. . . . It is Melanie Klein's discourse which brutally grafts the primary symbolizations of the Oedipal situation onto the initial ego-related inertia of the child" (*Seminar I*: 85/101).

79. Cf. *Seminar XI*: 11ff.

80. On the subtopic of (re)symbolization through the creation and re-creation of fantasy throughout the course of Lacanian analysis (as opposed to progressively exhuming ever deeper strata of phantasy, as some Kleinians urge), cf. Bruce Fink, *A Clinical Introduction to Lacanian Psychoanalysis: Theory and Technique* (Cambridge: Harvard University Press, 1999), 70.

81. Though Lacan does at times recommend evacuating all individualizing features of the analyst from the scene as much as possible in order to facilitate projection, as in "Intervention on Transference," in *Feminine Sexuality: Jacques Lacan and the École Freudienne*, ed. Juliet Mitchell and Jacqueline Rose, trans. Jacqueline Rose (New York, W. W. Norton, 1985), 61–73.

82. Cf. Vincente Palomera, "On Counter-Transference" in *The Klein-Lacan Dialogues*: 143.

83. Unless the client is an obsessive neurotic: on this point, cf. Fink 1999: 134.

84. *The Lacanian Subject: Between Language and Jouissance* (Princeton: Princeton University Press, 1996). On the other hand, when Diana Rabinovich claims in "What Is a Lacanian Clinic?" that "[c]alculated vacillation of neutrality . . . is employed because the psychoanalyst should preserve for the analysand the imaginary dimension of non-mastery, imperfection, ignorance . . . facing each new case," does she not provide Lacanian grounds for attending to and even disclosing countertransference? (*Cambridge Companion to Lacan*, op. cit., 221).

85. Lacan goes as far as to suggest that "perhaps it is part of the analyst's role, if the analyst is performing it properly, to be besieged—I mean *really*—by those in whom he has invoked this world of shades, without always being able to bring them up to the light

of day" (*Seminar XI*: 23). Intense emotional embroilment is likely to manifest somehow, and this may assist the analyst in undercutting the analysand's presumption of the salvific power of her expertise.

86. For confirmation of the suspicion that, for Klein, all of the patient's "free" associations can be referred to the transference, cf. Robert Hinshelwood, *A Dictionary of Kleinian Thought* (London: Free Association Books, 1991). For a more elaborate Lacanian articulation of this claim, cf. Eric Laurent, *Lacan y los discursos* (Buenos Aires: Manantial, 1992).

87. For a reading of Lacan that attempts to demonstrate that content-focus does not trade off with sapping the force of the Imaginary, cf. Fink 1999, chapter 3, especially pgs. 36 and 41.

88. Since working with Symbolic transference requires that the analyst put her ego out of play as much as possible, this work can only be intermittent; it is something of a regulatory ideal in Lacanian analysis. Also, at least on the interpretation of one prominent commentator, the early stages of the Lacanian clinic require Imaginary transference since it is "the strange sort of satisfaction that comes from the transference relationship and from deciphering the unconscious" that the analyst must initially provide as a substitute for the satisfaction of complying with the analysand's demands to set his or her world aright (Fink 1999: 9).

89. E.g., *E*: 96/ 118, where Lacan claims that "in analytic experience, the ego represents the center of all resistances to the treatment of symptoms."

90. Cf. Joseph H. Smith, *Arguing with Lacan* (New Haven: Yale University Press, 1991).

91. As Lacan famously suggests in his reading of the Dora case, it is countertransference that prompts transference. This claim underlines his distance from Klein, for whom transference is thought to be at its peak when the patient enters analysis. However, depending on how one reads Lacan's claim that as soon as there is a subject supposed to know there is transference, he and Klein may be in fundamental agreement.

92. "When all is said and done, it is less a matter of remembering than of rewriting history" (*Seminar I*: 14).

93. *Lacan and the New Wave in American Psychoanalysis: The Subject and the Self* (New York: Other Press, 1998).

94. Lacan makes this clear through his reference to the infant in such a state as an "hommelette." The hommlette, broken as eggs are to make an omelette, or scrambled, is not just the infant but the *homme*, man in general, in the diminutive. On the heuristic status of developmental narrative in Lacan, cf. *Seminar III*: 147, 151; *Seminar IV*: 199; *Seminar V*: 55.

95. Cf. Borch-Jacobsen 1991, chapter 3.

96. Perhaps to underscore that he is not providing a chronological narrative of human development, occasionally Lacan alters the chronology. For instance, though usually Lacan claims that the Imaginary precedes the Symbolic, as early as *Seminar II* he claims the opposite: "The symbolic relation is constituted as early as possible, even prior to the fixation of the self-image of the subject, prior to the structuring image of the ego, introducing the dimension of the subject to the world, a dimension capable of creating a reality other than that experienced as brute reality, as the encounter of two masses, the

collision of two balls. The imaginary experience is inscribed in the register of the symbolic as early on as you can think it" (257).

97. Elizabeth Grosz, *Jacques Lacan: A Feminist Introduction* (London: Routledge, 1990).

98. Cf. Borch-Jacobsen 1991: 63–69.

99. Lacan coins the term *hainamour* to capture the interimbrication of hate and love.

100. On the jealous rivalry, hostile aggression, and alienation brought on by Imaginary captivation, specifically that induced by ego-psychological technique, cf. Richard Boothby, *Death and Desire: Psychoanalytic Theory in Lacan's Return to Freud* (New York: Routledge, 1991), 21–45.

101. "[D]esire is borne by death" (*E*: 536/642).

102. These allusions to Heidegger are by no means accidental, though hardly precise.

103. Cf. Deleuze's discussion of the death drive in "Coldness and Cruelty" for a similar line of argument about the relation between particular negations and the Negative (Gilles Deleuze, *Masochism: Coldness and Cruelty & Venus in Furs*, trans. Jean McNeil [New York: Zone Books, 1991]).

104. For a contrary view, cf. Borch-Jacobsen 1991.

105. Jacques Lacan, "Desire and the Interpretation of Desire in *Hamlet*," ed. Jacques-Alain Miller, trans. James Hulbert, *Yale French Studies* 55, no. 6 (1977): 49.

106. "Bare life," as Agamben has shown, is either (1) what a sovereign posits a certain individual or group to be (a mode of inclusion in the law) when they are banned from normative treatment, e.g., expelled from the umbrella of legal protection (a paradoxical exclusion), or (2) that to which individuals are reduced when subjected to such terrible conditions that the quality of their lives no longer seems to matter to them, when the very prospect of humane treatment cannot be tolerated because measuring one's current predicament against it would take one beyond the breaking point—the very standard of humane treatment would interfere with the extreme defenses necessary for mere survival under the conditions of the worst, defenses so extreme that Agamben doubts whether they can even be called defenses. Bare life *might* also mean, Agamben suggests, something akin to what Lacan describes as the subject insofar as it is characterized by joyful spontaneity. But if this redeemed figure of bare life is a form of life (*bios*) that is fully exhausted by—that is, nothing but—its bare, spontaneous life (*zoē*), then Lacan's conception of the subject might be the basis for our suspicions about the covert conservatism of this figure. Cf. Giorgio Agamben, *Homo Sacer: Sovereign Power and Bare Life*, trans. Daniel Heller-Roazen (Stanford: Stanford University Press, 1998).

107. In order to make this point clear, Lacan distinguishes between the death "that life brings" and the death "that brings life" (*E*: 686/810).

108. This line continues: "In order to be recognized by the other, I utter what was only in function of what will be. In order to find him, I call him by a name that he must assume or refuse in order to reply to me." This suggests that the subject is not just a force of self-differentiation but a principle of differentiation generally, a (de)constructive principle. The subject is (known through) its effects. The subject, in order to be (recognized as) a subject, provokes the object of her address to become a question to herself (Am I what I have been called? And what will I do in response to

this nomination?), which is to say, subjectivizes her. By temporalizing the object of her address the subject recursively temporalizes herself (gives herself the problem of responding to the other's unpredictable response), i.e., sustains her standing as a subject. "Full speech is speech which aims at, which forms, the truth such as it becomes established in the recognition of one person by another. Full speech is speech which performs [*qui fait acte*]" (*Seminar I*: 107).

109. Cf. Adam Rosen-Carole, "The Possibility of the New: Adornoian Lessons for Psychoanalysis," *Pli: The Warwick Journal of Philosophy* 21: 62–87.

110. "[T]here is never a subject without an ego—a fully realized subject—but this is what we must always try to obtain from a subject in analysis" (*Seminar II*: 246). When Lacan later says that "the subject is never more than supposed," I take it that he means something like a pure subject, the dimension of the subject bereft of all entanglements with the ego, the question of the desire of the other, etc. (*Seminar XXIII*, cited in Fink 1995: 35).

111. Is Lacan genuinely advocating that we unconditionally affirm desire as it unfolds *in whatever form*? Surely not. Lacan is not naïve enough to suggest that we should or could do so. Lacan's vision, as noted, is utopian: it *has no place* on Earth; it cannot be consistently realized. The point of the utopian advocation, I take it, is to counterbalance—unsettle or at least bring into reflective consideration—the proclivity to conform to culturally prevalent norms and interpretive schemas, to disrupt and call into question our quasi-spontaneous consent to and deep investment in imposed limits. Lacan, ever the proponent of dialectical tension, will speak enthusiastically in favor of the unlimited affirmation of in(de)finitely unfolding *desire* precisely to the extent that culture demands limitation and conformity. His utopianism seeks to keep us unreconciled, to keep our attachments to the specific forms of life we inhabit available to reflection, revision, and renewal. The ambition, as always with Lacan, even when he seems utterly dogmatic, is to promote reflection and judgment.

112. Cf. Jean Améry, *At the Mind's Limit: Contemplations by a Survivor on Auschwitz and Its Realities*, trans. Sidney Rosenfeld and Stella P. Rosenfeld (Bloomington: Indiana University Press, 1980).

113. For an illustration, see the early scene culminating in Boris's (Larry Davis) suicide attempt in Woody Allen's *Whatever Works* (Sony Pictures Classics, 2009).

114. Freedom is perhaps *always* our "little freedom," conditioned by the weight of what it resists. As Lacan would later underscore, the subject has "one foot in, one foot out articulation in the field of the Other" (*Seminar XVI*, May 7, 1969).

115. This is one meaning of Lacan's highly equivocal claim that "desire is nothing other than that which supports an unconscious theme, the very articulation of that which roots us in a particular destiny, and that destiny demands insistently that the debt be paid, and desire keeps coming back, returning, and situates us once again in a given track, the track of something that is specifically our business" (*Seminar VII*: 319).

116. Jacques Lacan, *Le Séminaire: Livre XX; Encore, 1972–73*, ed. Jacques-Alain Miller (Paris: Seuil, 1975), 17. And *Le Séminaire: Livre XVII; L'envers de la psychanalyse, 1969–70*, ed. Jacques-Alain Miller (Paris: Seuil, 1991), 134.

117. For the three basic meanings of Lacan's claim that there is no sexual relation, cf. Dany Nobus, "Thorising the Comedy of the Sexes," op. cit., 108–109.

118. Cf. J. A. Miller, "An Introduction to Seminars I and II: Lacan's Orientation prior to 1953 (II)" in *Reading Seminars I and II: Lacan's Return to Freud*, ed. Feldstein, Fink, and Janus (Albany: SUNY Press, 1996), 23.

119. Lacan also discusses Klein's biologistic, literalistic interpretation of the drives in "The Phallic Phase and the Subjective Import of the Castration Complex" (*Feminine Sexuality*, eds. Mitchell and Rose, op. cit.).

120. An early indication that *desire* may never be pure is provided when Lacan describes "full speech" and "empty speech" as "extremes" between which "a whole gamut of modes of realization of speech is deployed" (*Seminar I*: 50). Full and empty speech, and so desire, may be as extreme as myth.

121. "[T]he dimension proper to analysis is the reintegration by the subject of his history right up to the furthermost perceptible limits" (*Seminar I*: 12).

122. As should be clear by now, I distinguish pure desirousness from specific desires by italicizing "desire" when it refers to the former. However, in what follows, this distinction is difficult to sustain; I caution the reader against assuming that all instances of italicized "desire" are indicative of pure desirousness or that unitalicized desire is thoroughly object oriented and fantasmatically metabolized.

123. Perhaps this is less than a fantasy, maybe only an obscure sense. Or, if it is a fantasy, it is likely retrospectively (re)constructed in order to make sense of later suffering or material arising in the course of a singular analysis with distinctive needs for (re)construction. *If* this is an originary fantasy, and *if* this detailing of the fates of desire means to be a straightforward developmental narrative, which is doubtful given Lacan's concerns about developmental theory articulated above, then, though differences persist, Lacan is in greater agreement with Klein about originary fantasies than he is prone to admit.

124. I take it that Lacan is not and need not be committed to the metaphysical or empirical claim that *there is desire* from the beginning nor, by extension, to the empirical validity (or metaphysical validity, whatever that might mean in this context) of the fates of desire detailed. Here, as elsewhere, Lacan is not primarily interested in establishing an empirically or metaphysically valid developmental narrative. In this case, he uses the frame of a developmental narrative—indeed one so akin to a myth of the fall that it calls out to be received ironically or *as mythology*—as a heuristic devise to highlight what tends to fall under eclipse: the hegemony of Imaginary, its susceptibility to partial dissolution, and the in(de)finite striving of *desire*. Thus the following formulations would be, in this context, equivalent: the excessive, rupturing force of *desire* is quickly, almost immediately, harnessed into fantasies of completeness; the excessive, rupturing force of *desire* is quickly, almost immediately, eclipsed by fantasies of completeness; fantasies of completeness take hold early and impede accommodation to *desire*. What is essential is (1) establishing the antagonism between *desire* and satisfaction, (2) suggesting that the investigation of *desire* can proceed only through an investigation of its compromised fate, and (3) suggesting that accommodation to *desire* cannot be a matter of release from its determinate shapes. The retrospective/(re)constructed character of these claims about the fates of desire should become all the more conspicuous via the use of the notion of "symbiosis" below. Ultimately, Lacan's discussion of the fates of desire is meant to be assessed in terms of its therapeutic efficacy, not its theoretical or metaphysical validity.

125. Let us note in passing that if and to the extent that living on the crisp edge of *desire* is akin to the terrifying vulnerability of infantile experience, accommodating *desire* cannot be plausibly construed as an unqualified good to be monofocally pursued. We will return to this.

126. From a Lacanian perspective, the classical orientation of Oedipal desire toward exclusive possession of its object may be a residual manifestation of the desire for absolute fusion under conditions in which the subject doubts the possibility and/or desirability of dedifferentiation.

127. To the extent that the desirability of *desire* is conceived as an affective registration of freedom or a provocation to encounter and engage with the unexpected, the historical, specifically modern contours of Lacan's thought become more prominent and the presumption that he is engaged in a form of transcultural and transhistorical, i.e., metaphysical, claiming becomes more difficult to sustain, which is not to say that this presumption is altogether incorrect.

128. Cf. *Seminar VIII*: 425; unpublished manuscript.

129. Lacan elsewhere suggests that obsessive neurosis may be in the service of neutralizing desire for a lost object and thereby *desire* generally. Concerning himself intensely with objects that are completely under his control (typically, things rather than persons), the obsessive repudiates a prior loss, and generally the inherent liability of desirous life to loss, via his attachment to a neutralized compensatory object. Disavowing any lack in the other and so securing an illusion of self-completion (like the pervert), the obsessive—e.g., the collector, the hoarder, the miser, etc.—has it all. But even here there may be a covert effort to sustain or reactivate *desire*: the hysteric, unconsciously insisting that he has lost *nothing*, may be giving symptomatic expression to the loss of *desire*, leveling a grievance about his affectively neutralized even if outwardly frenetic existence.

130. To clarify, neither the hysteric nor the obsessional strategy exactly aims at keeping *desire* alive; rather, it would be more accurate to say that each aims to keep libido active and labile or that each seeks to keep alive certain *desire*-like qualities of sexuality or experience.

131. Qua Imaginary, desire is the desire of the other in the sense that it recognizes itself (its imagined fulfillment) in an image of the other as self-sufficient. Desire, seeking its ideal mirror reflection, and thus self-annihilation, becomes trapped in an Imaginary dyad that, as we have seen and will see in greater detail below, may issue in paranoid aggression and self-loathing. Escaping this dyadic ensnarement, desire qua Symbolic is desire for the other as other than herself and thus, ultimately, for oneself as perpetually becoming other. Here, desire is for the other as pure desirousness and from the other of pure desirousness seeks recognition as pure desire. Symbolic desire seeks not its ideal mirror image but the hole or anamorphic stain in the mirror. Qua Symbolic, it seems that what *desire* aims at is not an object but a relation: *desire* is the desire to be recognized as a void of *desire* by another such *desire*. But Symbolic desire does in fact aim at an object of sorts, at a very peculiar "object," a nonobjectifiable object: the *desire* of the other. "Desire . . . is not desire of an object but desire of that lack which designates, in the other, another desire" ("Formations of the Unconscious," summary by Pontalis, approved by Lacan, *Bulletin de Psychologie XII* 4 [1957–1958]: 251; cited in Borch-Jacobsen 1991: 203). More precisely, Symbolic desire seeks the other *as* desire for mutual recognition as pure subjects of desire. Only another subject can recognize me as a subject by in(de)

finitely desiring me as an in(de)finite desirousness. But for Lacan, the satisfaction of Symbolic *desire* may be impossible because the desire to be recognized as a void of *desire* by another such *desire* requires a determination of one's *desire* and seeks from the other a determinate object/configuration of desire (even if it can take indefinitely many forms): a desire for mutual recognition as subjects of *desire*. Call this the aporetic formalism of desire. If *desire* is specified, channeled into a desire for me or the other as a subject of *desire*, then both subject and object of desire are no longer pure desirousness and so unable to recognize each other as such; but in no other way can they express themselves as anonymous instances of pure desirousness. Due to the double determination of *desire* through which *desire* seeks to obtain its end (mutual recognition as voids of desire), *desire* becomes its own impediment. Just as Imaginary desire aims at an impossible end (total satisfaction) and is self-negating (the other who could administer total satisfaction must be annihilated in order to attain it), Symbolic *desire* in its purity is impossible and self-canceling. Many commentators are mislead by the obvious Hegelian provenance of Lacan's claim that *desire* is the desire to be recognized as a void of *desire* by another such *desire* (the dialectic of lordship and bondage is broken with mutual love), failing to see that Lacan's conception of *desire* is structured by an impossibility, a deadlock that resists sublation. As we will see later in greater detail, *desire*, for Lacan, can never be pure. And it may be precisely this to which the aporetic dialectic of Symbolic desire means to point.

132. "[T]he function of desire must remain in a fundamental relationship with death" (*Seminar VII*: 303).

133. Cf. *E*: 336/403.

134. Generally, as should be evident, I take it that what seems like a seismic shift in the later Lacan—emphasis on the jouissance of the drive and the resistance of the Real, insistence on identification with one's sinthome, the developments concerning the Borromean knot and topology, etc.—is anything but, more a matter of emphasis. Thus I take it that the standard characterization of early Lacan as predominantly concerned with decoding and resolving deadlocks of desire and prohibition, supporting Oedipalization, transforming distorted, symptomatic speech into clear and consistent self-expression, and otherwise facilitating the intersubjective dialectic of recognition, etc., is misconceived, though not incorrect, not exactly a Lacanian reading of Lacan. Do the dyadic and symmetrical terms of the standard account of Lacan's development not reflect the Imaginary fixations against which Lacan cautioned from the beginning? Though Lacan's later developments are not logical explications of what was implicit in the beginning, there is a much greater confluence between early, middle, and late Lacan than is often acknowledged.

135. This helps explain the peculiar status of the developmental narrative through which Lacan gives an account of *desire*—this narrative means to be *edifying*, more akin to fable than to empirical research.

136. This is where the normative thrust of Lacan's notion of desire becomes paradoxical: pursuing the maximal development of possibilities (as opposed to, say, maximally developing one's potential in a manner that is compatible with equal opportunities for others) seems tantamount to repudiating normative constraints altogether, save one.

137. Let us note, albeit in passing, that what at least since Hegel has been situated as the great if unfinished achievement of modernity, namely, recognition of the infinite rights of subjectivity, seems to be, for Lacan, part of the fundamental order of things, as

elementary as the Real: "[d]esire . . . is . . . beneath existence, and, for that very reason, insists" (*Seminar II*: 266). Though he agrees with Hegel that its full realization is hardly a fait accompli—indeed, in a Hegelian idiom we might say that, for Lacan, a crucial or perhaps *the* crucial goal of psychoanalysis is the self-consciousness, i.e., full actualization, of the subject *as* desire—unlike Hegel, Lacan seems committed to reading *any* historical scene as, in however subdued a fashion, infused with the desire for *desire*. Whether this implies an irreducible metaphysical moment in Lacan's work I leave as an open question. Might courting the charge of metaphysical assertion be a risk Lacan is willing to run in order to emphasize the insistence of *desire*, to retrieve it from an tendency toward oblivion exacerbated by the fundamental features of rationalized modernity: domination of internal and external nature (or the presumption thereof), rationalization of the economy and law, standardization of culture, generally, ever-expanding interest in minimizing, and, when that fails, repressing arbitrary chance?

138. This may to some extent explain the repetitiveness and peculiar tenor of the injunction not to cede on desire, perhaps too the strangely aggressive tenor of Lacan's normative suggestions and intimations generally: his dogged insistence on sustaining the desire of *desire* may reflect the inevitability of setback, of the reassertion of the Imaginary. Perhaps Lacan is continually confounded by this inevitability—each instance of setback issuing unwittingly in a tenacious reassertion or amplification of the demand. Or perhaps Lacan means to keep the inevitability of setback in view as an implicit caution against the presumption of having accomplished one's task. Or perhaps he means to keep this inevitability in view in order to reflexively draw attention the flailing, flustered, somewhat pathetic character of the voice vehemently demanding that we must not cede on desire and in this way work against its self-arrogation of authority, its auto-moralization. Is there not something contradictory about the *demand* to pursue one's *desire*? Or perhaps the strikingly assertive tenor of Lacan's injunction not to cede on *desire* is better thought to be an element of an ego-placating strategy meant to be eventually abandoned or at least recede into intermittent use. That is, perhaps Lacan means to mimic the harsh voice of the superego and thereby placate the ego's need of firm directives in order to circumvent some portion of the resistances that he suspects may arise from the content of the claim.

139. Of course, this point is not merely "clinical" in the restrictive sense. It speaks to the diminished capacity to enjoy, the fundamental self-loathing, and the cynical self-distancing that wreaks havoc on us all. Lacan's interest in interrupting the Imaginary debasement and disavowal of partial satisfactions becomes more pronounced in his later work when the fundamental aim of analysis is cast as inducing the capacity to enjoy enjoyment (and the concomitant stress of the drive as always attaining satisfaction, i.e., "hitting its mark") rather than setting desire into motion.

140. The neediness interpreted as a first demand is what Lacan understands to be the object of primary repression. The unconscious forms around a kernel of ineffable neediness. Thus, the unconscious, or, more broadly, psychic life, is self-interpreting: always interpreting an ineffable neediness that can never be directly known or satisfied. This entails that analytic interpretation of unconscious material participate in a dialectic of creation and discovery, that suggestion and speculation be inexcisable from analytic knowing.

141. Channeling *desire* into concrete forms, i.e., demands, is not the same as absorbing it into demands. To channel *desire* into demands is configure demands from elements

that will overflow them, thus to sustain the lability of *desire*. Lacan's specification of the goal of psychoanalysis as teaching "the subject to name, to articulate, to pass into existence, this desire . . . which insists" should be read in this light (*Seminar II*: 266).

142. Compare: "The Borromean knot can only be made up of three. The imaginary and symbolic do not suffice. There has to be a third element, which I call the real. This determining solidarity . . . is necessary. The loss of any one of these three dimensions . . . must lead to madness (*Seminar XXI*, Dec. 11, 1973).

143. This is not to say that Lacan completely backed off from emphasizing the "narcissistic" dimension of desire; the overheated romanticism of the day would not allow this. Thus a few years later Lacan strikingly describes copulation as a "masturbatory concession" (*Seminar XIV*; April 12, 1967). Elsewhere he speaks of "love's deception and baseness," declaring that "to love is to want to be loved" (*E*: 723/853). Cf. Borch-Jacobsen 1991, chapter 2.

144. I take it that the notion of the split subject means to resonate with Heidegger's conception of being-in. As recurrent as they are, though, the Heideggerian resonances in Lacan's seminars and writings are too vague to be treated in the context of this work.

145. Let us note in passing that throughout Lacan's teachings it is unclear whether *objet a* is projected or discovered "in" the object/other. This ambiguity is essential. Through it Lacan suggests that distinguishing between discovery and creation (in this case, projection) will never be easy, more precisely, that the line between the intrapsychic and the external is exceedingly difficult to draw, which seems to be an oblique rejoinder to Klein's literalism of part-objects and drives here. Further, through this ambiguity Lacan suggests that, generally, psychoanalytic knowing ought to remain speculative, questionable, provocative.

146. Also cf. *Seminar XI*: 23.

147. To be sure, he certainly sounds as if he is suggesting this from time to time, e.g., *Seminar XI*: 33.

148. Earlier, Lacan had already underlined the connection between freedom and exposure, even exposure to chance, in order to distinguish his use of the term from its historically prevalent determination as autonomy: "the game is already played, the die already cast. It is already cast, with the following proviso, that we can pick it up again and throw it anew" (*Seminar II*: 219).

149. Cf. Lacan's discussion of the suicide of the homosexual woman analyzed by Freud in *Seminar X* (January 16, 1963).

150. Or perhaps is a fantasmatic negotiation with this presence—a rudimentary effort to interpret it in a way that satisfies the wish to be the exclusive target of one caregiver's concern, thus something of a projection.

151. Also, when isolated, some of Lacan's very late comments about anxiety as an indicator of jouissance distorted by fundamental fantasies and self-images contribute to the suspicion that he is a purist of *desire* declaiming the Imaginary for getting in the way of or corrupting the otherwise available pure jouissance of desire or the drive. As will be made clear, I read the return of earlier conceptions of anxiety in the context of Lacan's later work where the conception of anxiety has altered substantially as part of an effort to destabilize, or, better, problematize, the conceptions of the good borne by the various notions of anxiety. In brief, I read the return of the earlier conception not

as a correction of a correction, a return to an original position, but as an effort to keep us unsettled, to keep the irreducible plurality of goods, thus the endless difficulty of self-affirmation, in the fore.

152. Notice that even in the context of his elaboration of anxiety as a suffering from lack of lack, i.e., from a want of freedom, Lacan intimates that desire alone, desire in want of an object, indeed desire in want of a very particular object, may occasion anxiety as well. When Lacan states that "[w]hat is *most* anxiety producing for the child is when the relationship through which he comes to be—on the basis of lack which makes him desire—is most perturbed: when there is no possibility of lack, when his mother is constantly on his back," he clearly means to emphasize anxiety as sourced in the other's overwhelming presence (Dec. 5, 1962; emphasis added). However, with what is "most" meant to contrast? Is there not a subtle intimation that the absence of the object, even the absence of the very object that occasions the anxiety of annihilation, is anxiety-provoking too?

153. It is perhaps to underscore the limited forms of satisfaction available to us that in the late *Seminar XXII* Lacan states that anxiety is to be found in the interior of the body overcome by jouissance (*R.S.I., 1974–75*, ed. Jacques-Alain Miller; *Ornicar?* [1975]: 2, 104).

154. *E*: 213/256–215/259.

155. Hence two dimensions of the highly overdetermined irony of Lacan's *Scilicet* are (1) *scire licet*, "it goes without saying," "you are permitted to know," i.e., you are permitted to know that *it* (truth, *desire*, the subject) goes, moves, elaborates itself, without *saying*, without discursive elaboration, without appeal to criteria for intersubjective validity or even intersubjective intelligibility, is irreducible to discourse, to knowledge; (2) *scire licet*, "it goes without saying," "you are permitted to know," i.e., of course, it is self-evident that it (truth, *desire*, the subject) goes without saying, is abrasive to the order of discursive knowledge, for though evident, this is nothing that can be grounded or simply expressed within the order of discursive knowledge—that it goes without saying, that truth elaborates itself in excess of discursive knowledge, is something that gives itself, permits its evidence to impose itself, cannot be brought back to the self-comprehension of reason. But also, of course, a third dimension would be (3) *scire licet*, you are permitted to know, i.e., I allow it, so do not fear, there is someone who knows, and is even benevolent, will let you know, even if what he knows and will let you know is a terrible truth. Which is counterbalanced by a fourth dimension (4) *scire licet*, you can *know*, i.e., what is to be said or inquired into, as well as the principle of articulation, need not remain a mystery—you need not find your world, indeed yourself, as unintelligible as you had; which implies that *I*, Lacan, am possessed of no special powers or ancient formulas that grant me greater access to these matters than can be had by you, indeed *you* can know (providing of course that you recognize the unbridgeable chasm between *can know* and simply *know*).

156. For a consideration of the extent to which phenomena are governed by causal laws, see the final chapter of *Plurality and Perspective* (Author, forthcoming).

157. Cf. *E*: 435/523ff.

158. Perhaps a faint echo of Nietzsche can be discerned here: "Preparatory human beings—I welcome all signs that a[n] . . . age is about to begin, which will restore honor to courage above all" (*The Gay Science*, sec. 283, ed. Bernard Williams, trans. Josefine Nauckhoff [Cambridge: Cambridge University Press, 2001]).

159. On the unavoidability of the Imaginary, cf. *Seminar XI*: 6.

160. This is of course not his only account of suffering. For instance, in his earlier work Lacan suggests that we often suffer from narratives in the grip of which we feel helpless and condemned to suffer.

161. Given Lacan's focus on eliminating surplus suffering, one might say that he is like Marcuse without the manic enthusiasm. Cf. Herbert Marcuse, *An Essay on Liberation* (Boston: Beacon Press, 1971); *Eros and Civilization* (London: Routledge, 1987); and *One Dimensional Man* (London: Paul Kegan and Routledge, 2002).

162. Cf. *Seminar XVIII*, Jan. 13, 1971; *E*: 86/106ff; "L'Etourdit"; and "Introduction à l'édition allemande d'un premier volume des *Écrits*," 16.

163. The distressingly prevalent trend among Lacanians to apply standard Lacanian formulas to various cultural artifacts (literature, films, etc.), often in a way that leads us to learn nothing of the work to which the formula is applied except that it can be manipulated to illustrate the truth of the formula (as if insecurity about the truth of the formula propels its incessant application), is one of the more clear indications that Lacan has yet to be *read.*

164. When Lacan says that "[t]he intervention takes on a structuring function . . . by dint of its symbolic form," he means that the analytic intervention both attunes the analysand to what in him is profoundly ambiguous and inchoate (in need of symbolic form but never reducible to its symbolic determination) *and* that it promotes the symbolization of this material by way of evoking, in and through the transference, the desire to creatively explore oneself, to discover/create oneself (this is its structuring function) (*E*: 248/301; trans. modified). The meaningfulness of certain material in the analysis will not be simply assumed—as if certain forms of behavior, slips of speech, or whatnot decisively point to their phantasmatic referents, their meaning. That is Klein's presumption, not Lacan's. Rather, with Lacan, the assumption of meaningfulness is extended as a technical measure designed to elicit the analysand's desire to generate his or her own meanings, to produce in the analysand a habit of viewing what heretofore fell in the range of the meaningless (pauses, repeated but unintelligible patterns, peculiar word choices, etc.) as filled with (in)determinate significance, with significance to be created/discovered. So, at another level, the structuring function is an effort of responsibilization. More on this later.

165. This, of course, is not Lacan's only account of neurotic desire. Elsewhere he suggests, to the contrary, that the neurotic suffers from the feared evaporation of her desire. Constructing concepts—e.g., neurosis—with contradictory contents, Lacan seeks to hinder the automaticity of their application, i.e., to forestall understanding.

166. Thus Lacan's claim that, initially, Dick's experience is entirely undifferentiated is wildly exaggerated, even on his own terms. Dick's "profound indifference, his apathy, his absence," noted by Klein, is read by Lacan as incontrovertible evidence that Dick's world is no world at all, that it is, rather, but a completely undifferentiated field of anxiety. "It is clear, in fact, that in Dick what is not symbolized is reality. This young subject is entirely in crude reality, reality unconstituted. He is entirely in the undifferentiated . . . [in] reality pure and simple" (*Seminar I*: 81–82). But Dick is not simply immersed in "undifferentiated . . . reality pure and simple" and cannot be on Lacanian grounds. Lacan's claim is a wild exaggeration, perhaps a dramatic device

designed to highlight the contrast between (1) Dick's initial state of overwhelming and insulating anxiety and (2) his care for his place in a world of objects and others that results from the impact of Klein's speech. We will return to the question of how to read Lacan's exaggerations later.

167. Ironically, since for Lacan the *corps morcelé* is linked to the out-of-jointness that results from the drive, specifically from the death drive, the charge is that *Klein is denying the death drive*! Or at least that she fails to understand it.

168. Cf. Borch-Jakobsen 1991, chapter 2, for a further elaboration of the link between premature experience and truth in Lacan's thinking.

169. For certain inhabitants of the Northwest corridor of the world, "culture" may well mean something like fluidity, an ever-shifting terrain, an experience of perpetual transitoriness, instability, confusion, malleable identity, etc. But this too is an understanding of culture voiced from a hegemonic perspective, namely, from the vantage point of either (1) the transnational capitalist elite who thrive—have been forced to thrive—under such conditions in order to insure continuing profits or simply to survive or (2) consumers who have been taught to relish novelty, the new product or trend that comes into seductive prominence just as quickly as it fades and is replaced by something else. For more detailed accounts of the perspectives from which culture is conflated with liquidity (perpetual and unbinding change), cf. Zygmunt Bauman's recent work, especially *Liquid Love: On the Frailty of Human Bonds* (Cambridge: Polity Press, 2003); and *Liquid Life* (Cambridge: Polity Press, 2005).

170. In Lacanese, this distinction roughly corresponds to that between *la langue* and *la parole*. Note that, to the extent that the analogy is apposite, *la langue* suggests but *is not* a closed system of regulated differences independent of the reality designated.

171. Cf. *Seminar XX*: 43.

172. Or to put the point in a less metaphysical, thus less misleading, manner, the Symbolic is a form of attention awaiting and attracted to unsuspected possibilities emerging from the processual accretion of a normative horizon.

173. A master signifier is a consequential signifier that appears insistently throughout the treatment—in dreams, slips, associations, etc.—yet is at the limit nonsensical ("stupid" as Lacan at one point says [*Seminar XX*: 13]) or only makes "half-sense" (*Seminar XX*: 80).

174. The connection between the form-giving impulse and Nietzsche's will to power, and between acceptance of our formative givens and Nietzsche's *amor fati*, may reward study.

175. The symbolic order is simultaneously non-being and insisting to be. . . . A symbolic order [is always] in travail, in the process of coming, insisting on being realized" (*Seminar II*: 326).

176. "In the beginning was the Word, which is to say, the signifier" (*Seminar VII*: 213).

177. Palpating cell of symbolism: chiasmatic figure of spontaneous life and scripted, schematized mechanicity.

178. Or, as a result of his aversion to ambiguity and indeterminacy, Dick might become concretistic and thus unamenable to future analysis (or to later stages of his analysis with Klein) because (1) analysis implies the possibility of interpretation, of seeing things

in different ways that are not authoritatively guaranteed to be right, and (2) the desire to enter into or proceed with analysis implies that one is not certain and secure about what things mean and how to best live one's life. Though this analysis is confluent with Lacan's, especially with his discussions of perversion, the risk elaborated here is not one Lacan articulates or even implies in his discussion of Klein. On the topic of concreteness, cf. Alan Bass's *Difference and Disavowal: The Trauma of Eros*.

179. Even if, and not only in this context, induced mechanicity is a condition for the emergence of spontaneity, natality, etc.

180. By contrast, the hysteric assumes that utopia is his due and on this basis compulsively denounces the imperfections and inconsistencies of the social order, as if its imperfections and inconsistencies were altogether contingent and revocable, as if they were the fault of some Authoritative Other who has failed to administer the harmonious and absolutely satisfying world He perfectly well could. "[T]he subject seems to speak in vain about someone who . . . can never become one with the assumption of his desire" (*E*: 211/254; trans. modified).

181. More precisely, to assume our Symbolic condition within or under the pressure of the Imaginary is to avow our limitedness *as a source of discontent* as well as the contingency of various limits and the discontents coextensive with them. To assume our Symbolic condition with this pressure relieved, even momentarily, is to have broken the automaticity of the association of limitation and discontent.

182. Lacan would likely agree that, brutally pushed to the limit, human beings may transubstantiate into something that lacks this urge to freedom, i.e., the *Musselman*. For his point is that humanity is not a metaphysical given but a culturally facilitated achievement, something precious and precarious. On the figure of the *Musselman*, cf. Giorgio Agamben, *Remnants of Auschwitz: The Witness and the Archive* (New York: Zone Books, 2002).

183. Cf. Denise Riley's elegant analysis of "linguistic discomfiture" in *The Words of Selves: Identification, Solidarity, Irony* (Stanford: Stanford University Press, 2000).

184. Consider in this context the claim frequently made by Kristeva in her early work (especially *Revolution in Poetic Language*, trans. Leon S. Roudiez [New York: Columbia University Press, 1984]): male artists can more easily take on the risk of unsettling the symbolic because they feel sufficiently part of the relatively well-structured symbolic order they contest, even invested by that order with the authority to contest it.

185. This is often the phantasmatic subtext to "successful" resolutions of Oedipal conflicts.

186. As should be clear from the foregoing, the paternal metaphor need not be associated with an empirical father. In Lacan's words, "the father is there even when he isn't there" (*Seminar V*: 168). Or more explicitly:

> Can an Oedipus complex be normally constituted when there is no father? We've noticed that it wasn't all that simple, that an Oedipus complex might very well be constituted even when the father wasn't there. . . . Oedipus complexes that are completely normal—normal in both senses: normalizing, on the one hand, and also normal in terms of how they denormalize, I mean by their neuroticizing effects, for example—are established in exactly the same way as in other cases, even in cases where the father isn't there. (*Seminar VI*, Jan. 15, 1958; unpublished manuscript)

The initial sense of oneself as lacking may be instituted by (1) repeated experiences of frustration, usually corresponding to the non-presence or partial presence (e.g., distraction or imperfect responsiveness) of caretakers or (2) recognition of our caregivers' desire(s) as always directed elsewhere. Also, less important than how this sense of lack takes hold is *that* we acknowledge it, that we symbolize the m/Other's lack and come to see that the lack of/in the m/Other implies our own lack. Of course, this acknowledgement is difficult to sustain—consumerist culture seems to thrive on its denial.

187. For instance, when Lacan says that "Everything is equally real for him [Dick], equally indifferent," he suggests that, by contrast, reality is an arena of exaggeration, selective focus, passionate perspective.

188. Later, Lacan claims that the most basic unit of psychic *structure* is the matheme. This is not the place to parse the difference.

189. Sometimes Lacan distinguishes between the signifier and the letter, deeming the letter the irreducible element of the Symbolic and the psychic. At other times, though, he clearly states that signifiers are irreducible: "Interpretation . . . has the effect of bringing out an irreducible signifier . . . intended to bring out irreducible, *non-sensical*—composed of non-meanings—signifying elements" (*Seminar XI*: 250); "the signifier—which has no meaning, and is irreducible and traumatic" (*Seminar XI*, 251). Of course, Lacan being Lacan, he says this after discussing the "irreducible and insane character" of "a *chain* of signifiers" (ibid., 212; emphasis added). How exactly can a chain be irreducible, a figure of the elemental? And at times he suggests that the letter is composite, as in *Seminar XX*: "the letter designates an assemblage . . . [or rather] letters *make up* assemblages; not simply *designating* them, they *are* assemblages, they are to be taken as functioning as assemblages themselves. . . . The unconscious is structured like the assemblages . . . in set theory, which are like letters" (46–47).

190. "L'étourdit," op. cit., 17. A similar formulation appears in *Seminar XX*.

191. "Full speech is a speech full of meaning [*sens*]. Empty speech is a speech which has only signification" (*Le Séminaire. Livre XXIV. L'insu que sait de l'une bévue s'aile à mourre, 1976–77,* in *Ornicar?* 12–18 [1977–1979], 11).

192. Lacan's notion of the signifier, as I understand it, is a critical recasting of Freud's theory of signal anxiety. If signifiers name, initially, the inchoate impressions of experience, and if the metabolism of signifiers is a matter of *binding* them to the order of meaning, then the initial experience, in its abrasiveness to the prevailing order of intelligibility, can be characterized as a traumatic excitation and the metabolism/symbolization of signifiers seems to perform much the same function as signal anxiety does in Freud's account: preventing traumatic excitation from impairing the psychic apparatus. However, the difference is that while Freud describes signal anxiety as in the service of the ego and the pleasure/unpleasure principle, and so in the service of tension reduction, homeostasis, and equilibration, Lacan describes the metabolism of signifiers as both facilitating and unsettling the order of intelligibility to which the ego is committed, as both conducive to and impeding homeostasis and equilibrium. The persistent enigma of the signifier both calls forth and subverts meaning, and so the ego.

193. Given the inherence of polysemy in the notion of the signifier, we should not be surprised that Lacan uses it variably, e.g., to designate the entire signifying system of a language.

194. The clinical corollary to this is Lacan's punctual technique. Through scansion and the short session, the Lacanian analyst puts a stop to the sliding of meaning; s/he takes a signifier—a loaded term, a slip, a conspicuous word choice, etc.—out of its intended context and draws the analysand's attention to it, submitting the material to new association and interpretation, that is, to different contexts in which its meaning(s) will be developed otherwise than it would in its original, commanding context.

195. Cf. *Seminar XI*: 7–8.

196. To draw out the implicit swipe at structural linguistics: insisting on the arbitrariness of the signifier and the merely conventional alignment of signifier and signified makes the science of language a science of madness. Either (1) language is much less rational than linguistic science admits, and so much less amenable to scientific inquiry, (2) confronting the madness of linguistic life, the meaning and practice of science are forced to undergo massive mutations that have been hardly begun, (3) madness, and so the arbitrariness of the signifier, is only apparent, concealing a deep logical structure, or (4) it's not just that its signifiers are modeled on those of symptoms and dreams but that linguistic science is itself a symptomatic dream of shelter from (a) a commonness that cannot be borne, i.e., from our essential exposure and so binding to one another in ordinary, public historical life—at once a fantasy of a private language, a global defense against the anxiety of influence, and, on the contrary, an anxious reflection of social bonds in crisis and subject to manipulation by the power hungry or pathological, and (b) the cynical manipulation of our indelible sociality. The first two are supported by Lacan's claim in "Beyond the Reality Principle" that "[t]ruth in its specific value remains a stranger to the scientific order: science can honor itself by an alliance with truth . . . but it cannot by any means identify it as its own end" (cited in Benvenuto and Kennedy, *The Works of Jacques Lacan: An Introduction* [New York: St. Martin's Press, 1986], 68).

197. Cf. Barbara Johnson, "The Frame of Reference: Poe, Lacan, Derrida" in *Literature and Psychoanalysis: The Question of Reading Otherwise*, ed. Shoshana Felman (Baltimore: The Johns Hopkins University Press, 1982): 457–505.

198. "[I]n Dick's case, as in every other, access to the unconscious had to be by way of the ego" (1975: 229).

199. Even though this seems to be a concession to Klein, Klein may not agree that positioning the analyst as the one who Knows is necessary to induce the client to speak. For her, the early onset of transference is likely sufficient to induce the client to speak (or play, act out, etc.).

200. The social inescapability of certain meanings is suggested by Lacan's description of the Other as a "signifying battery" in "The Subversion of the Subject."

201. Even in the context of insisting that "[i]nterpretation . . . has the effect of brining out an irreducible signifier . . . . [of bringing out the] irreducible, *non-sensical*—composed of non-meanings—signifying elements," Lacan indicates that "what is there is rich and complex," i.e., determinately structured and in some way given. Even if the richness and complexity of "what is there" is available to reshaping, it *is there* prior to the work of re-creation, in some way discovered rather than wholly constructed, let alone arbitrarily so. Lacan underscores the limits to interpretive self-constitution as he goes on to state, "Interpretation is not open to all meanings. It is not just any interpretation" (*Seminar XI*: 250–51).

202. Lacan risks being ascribed such callous sentiment when he says, for instance, "When all is said and done, it is less a matter of remembering than of rewriting history" (*Seminar I*: 14).

203. The hope for the miracle of *l'acte* so prevalent among contemporary commentators on Lacan with interests in social criticism—especially when this hope for *l'acte* substitutes for the work of articulating plausible programs to address the social ailments diagnosed through the matrix of Lacanian theory or for the work of specifying the long-term, structural transformations of subjectivity and objectivity requisite for the development of such programs, thus for clarifying the precise shape of the current impediments to their development—seems a gesture of cynical desperation cloaked in enthusiasm, if it is not a barely concealed appeal to idealized authority, the very epitome of the Imaginary demand, and is, to say the very least, often inappropriate in the clinical setting. Another basic Lacanian reason to be wary of valorizations of *l'acte* concerns the proximity of this notion to the traditional conception of enactment. The "revolutionary recklessness" of doing what is deemed impossible (*l'acte*) may be fundamentally akin to enactment classically conceived—a fully Imaginary gesture. What seems an inspired refusal of illusory social constraint may be but an attempt to make the impossible/ideal object present, i.e., an attempt to secure distance from *objet a*. In the context of *l'acte*, satisfaction—the direct realization of what is said to require complex and long-term preparations, if it can be realized at all—may operate as a defense: the shock of the spectacular realization of the impossible may highlight the social unintelligibility of the gesture, thereby calling out for interpretation, for symbolic coding, for this unprecedented actuality to redefine our sense of possibility. This would make *l'acte* transference without analysis, a spectacle.

204. Cf. Judith Butler, "The Lesbian Phallus and the Morphological Imaginary," in *Bodies that Matter: On the Discursive Limits of Sex* (New York: Routledge, 1993). There Butler levels the charge of phallocentrism against Lacan with reference to the non-displaceability of the phallus from its biological male mooring.

205. In order to assess this charge, minimally, the following questions would need to be addressed: Is attraction to the other *as* sexually differentiated a retrospective reconstruction of infantile desire—and if so, in the service of what?—or is attunement to and desire for the other *as* sexually differentiated a natural feature of human experience from the beginning? Can we say that the infant is both aware of and attracted by its caregiver's sexuation? If so, on what grounds can these claims be made? Even if it can be established that the infant is primordially attentive to sexual difference, does this entail that its longing homes in on it? Does all attention imply attraction? Further, is sexual difference, insofar as an infant is aware of it, primarily defined by genital difference? With what tenacity is the infant's longing keyed to sexual difference as opposed to other sorts of particularizing characteristics? In other words, what primacy is to be placed on the longing for an object as a sexually differentiated—specifically, as genitally determined—object? And, again, why would one, and why would an analyst in particular, make this claim, either in the course of therapy or elsewhere? What are the various theoretical and practical stakes of this claim, both with respect to the two authors considered and generally?

206. Klein's commitment to the unconscious as culturally particular, discussed above, is now seen to have its limits.

207. Cf. *Seminar XIX*, Jan. 19, 1972; and *E*: 579/690.

208. Cf. *Seminar XX*: 32/29.

209. *Le séminaire, Livre VII: L'éthique de la psychanalyse*, ed. Jacques-Alain Miller (Paris: Seuil, 1986), 208.

210. Notice that from Lacan's perspective, however much Kleinian technique diminishes anxiety, by retrenching her clients in the Imaginary she may generate anxieties that she is ill-equipped to treat, and, worse, is likely to take as indications of insufficient rather than hypertrophic ego development, leading to a course of therapy likely to enhance her client's anxieties and therewith her self-assurance.

211. *Seminar VIII*: 147.

212. Compare Nietzsche: "The true man wants two things: danger and play" (*Thus Spoke Zarathustra*, "Of Old and Young Women," trans. R. J. Hollingdale [New York: Penguin Classics, 1961]); "The secret of reaping the greatest fruitfulness and the greatest enjoyment from life is to live dangerously" (*The Gay Science*, sec. 283); "thanks to your drunkenness you never break a limb. . . . For us life is more dangerous: we are made of glass" (*The Gay Science*, sec. 154); "another ideal runs ahead of us, a strange, tempting, dangerous ideal . . . a spirit who plays naïvely—that is, not deliberately but from overflowing power and abundance—with all that was hitherto called holy, good, untouchable, divine" (*The Gay Science*, sec. 382).

213. To figure the penis/phallus as a generic scaffolding for the Imaginary is to render it eminently displaceable/replaceable; *this* would be Lacan's moment of iconoclasm.

214. "Remembering, Repeating and Working-Through," *SE* 12: 147–56; "Mourning and Melancholia," *SE* 14: 243–58.

215. Or perhaps, for Lacan, not being offended demonstrates one's (likely partial) disintrication from the promise of absolute fulfillment: offense may express outrage over the sacrilegious demeaning of the phallus via its identification with the mere penis. Another aspect of Lacan's strategy may be this: the frequent and multiform use of the freighted terms "phallus" and "penis," their being webbed into a number of highly variable—and, because this is Lacan's discourse, highly volatile—discursive-affective environments, may mean to desacalize them, to hyperbolically mobilize them and overload them with discursive and affective associations, thereby emptying them out, returning them to their status a mere signifiers: to their inherent openness to signify otherwise and to their brute, nonsensical literality (the gesture would be akin to Stein's "Rose is a rose is a rose is a rose"). If this is what Lacan is up to, the use of the term "penis" to signify "phallus" would ultimately aim to break the connection and, more broadly, to demystify these terms or at least to call attention to their residual mystification and thus to the need for further (and perhaps different forms of) demystification. In another context, Lacan claims that "we must use things like that, old words, as stupid as anything, but really use them, work them to the bone" (*Seminar XX*: 60).

216. Phallic jouissance is set against an Other jouissance, "feminine jouissance," which is a placeholder for surprise just this side of trauma, a jouissance that insists rather than ex-ists, i.e., that cannot be articulated in our symbolic status quo.

217. Kristeva would say their *signifiance*. Cf. Julia Kristeva, "L'engendrement de la formule," in *Semeiotike: Recherches pour une sémanalyse* (Paris: Seuil, 1969), 216–310; *Desire in Language: A Semiotic Approach to Literature and Art*, trans. Leon S. Roudiez

(New York: Columbia University Press, 1980); *Revolution in Poetic Langauge*, trans. Margaret Waller (New York: Columbia University Press, 1984); "The Speaking Subject," in *On Signs*, ed. M. Blonsky (Oxford: Blackwell, 1985); also Roland Barthes, *Image—Music—Text*, trans. Stephen Heath (London: Fontana, 1977).

218. It is in this vicinity that a number of convergences between Lacan and Adorno can be discerned.

219. Of course this does not mean that the association between the intensity of infantile helplessness and the signifiers experientially coeval with it will always be as strong as it once was. There is a certain truth to behaviorism. If the infant repeatedly experiences its helplessness but not the signifiers with which it was at first associated, the association may fade. As experiences compile, the force of certain associations will likely become much more dominant than others. But the difference between Lacan and many versions of behaviorism turns on the Lacanian supposition that, once forged, associations may be overlaid and diminished but do not dissipate entirely. The association may transform into the faintest resonance, but the connection will have been inexorably established. Freud might call this connection a *Bahnung* (*A Project for a Scientific Psychology*, *SE I*: 283–387).

220. Attending the compositional and sensuously indeterminate character of the signifier should relieve some of Derrida's worry about Lacan's appeal to the elemental, though Derrida's broader worry that Lacan is engaged in a quasi-transcendental project would require at least three questions to be addressed: (1) Is significance *afforded* or *attested to* by the signifier? (2) Is the *significance* purportedly guaranteed by the signifier identical to the *meaning* for which the transcendental ambition intends to derive an ideal guarantee? (3) If not, even if the notion of the signifier means to afford or attest to the inescapability of its particular form of significance, what is the specific objection to this? Cf. Jacques Lacan, "Seminar on the Purloined Letter," in *The Purloined Poe*, trans. Mehlman, ed. John Muller and William Richardson (Baltimore: The Johns Hopkins University Press, 1988); Jacques Derrida, "The Purveyor of Truth," in *The Post Card: From Socrates to Freud and Beyond* (Chicago: University of Chicago Press, 1987); and Jacques Derrida, "For the Love of Lacan," *Cardozo Law Review* 16, nos. 3–4 (1996): 699–728.

221. Bice Benvenuto, "Once upon a Time: The Infant in Lacanian Theory," in Burgoyne and Sullivan 1999, 19.

222. "It sets everything on fire, the Real. But it's a cold fire. The fire that burns is a mask, if I might put it this way, of the Real. The Real of it is to be looked for on the other side, the side of absolute zero" (Seminar *XXIII*; translation following Lee Edelman, *No Future: Queer Theory and the Death Drive* [Durham: Duke University Press, 2004] 44).

223. For an elaboration of the relevant notion of mythology, cf. Claudia Baracchi, *Of Myth, Life and War in Plato's Republic* (Bloomington: Indiana University Press, 2002).

224. *Le séminaire, Livre IV: La relation d'objet et les structures freudiennes, 1956–1957*, ed. Jacques-Alain Miller (Paris: Seuil, 1994), 67. Notice the link Lacan makes between the Real and mythology in this passage; also cf. *E*: 722/851–725/854.

225. Of course *after the fact, and most often almost immediately*, we are bound to integrate these acts and the experiences onto which they open into networks of significance—self- and world-interpretive schemas—but the *passage à l'acte* names those situ-

ations in which something cannot be processed (or sufficiently processed) symbolically, situations in which we suffer something—even if what we suffer is precisely our own doing—that cannot be assimilated by our frameworks of intelligibility and thus cannot become an object for reflection and thereby a basis for self-directed activity. The *passage à l'acte* is the enactment of an inchoate "something" in the dimension of the Real. As much as the Real describes a compulsion to repeat patterns of action, relation, and desire as a result of which we find ourselves *here yet again without knowing exactly what we have gotten ourselves into,* it is "essentially the missed encounter" (*Seminar XI*: 55). The Real outstrips experience, eludes cognitive recuperation, throws us off-kilter. At the level of the Real, we cannot but return "here" once again precisely because we miss what we were ostensibly aiming at (e.g., a coherent self-image, a symmetrical and perfectly harmonious relationship, tight-knit social cohesion, or even just a decent, ordinary social encounter).

226. Because of this, in Lacan's lexicon "the Real" sometimes names certain relatively well-structured impasses—say, those turning around the affects or jouissance of parents or previous generations that are unconsciously transmitted—more than a principle of excess that overwhelms our capacity for determinate experience. In this sense, the Real names a relatively determinate unconscious content or pattern but only insofar as this content or pattern articulates an impasse and remains ineffable, that is, insofar as it exceeds our capacities to assimilate it, to make sense of it and move on.

227. If this commentary on the Real is anything like accurate, it should serve as a corrective to those commentators who insist on characterizing Lacanian analysis as involving a progressive draining away of the Real into the Symbolic.

228. In a Kantian idiom, it would be the sensory manifold *prior to* the work of the transcendental imagination (if this even makes sense). One wonders whether the concept of the Real is a theoretical hypostatization of the shock-experiences of modernity.

229. The appositeness of Derrida's critique of Lacan's transcendentalism should be considered in light of the preceding. Cf. Derrida 1987.

230. Let us note in passing that Klein occasionally claims, and more than occasionally assumes in her clinical work, that from the very beginning and throughout life there is always a channel through which we can register objective reality. Transference anxieties, projections, etc., no matter how strong, cannot impinge upon this basic capacity. More precisely, the claim is that children maintain an open channel through which they can realistically perceive their parents, which is why they (and we as adults) can always use interpretations. While, plausibly, contemporary Kleinians tend to claim that the capacity to use an interpretation is an accomplishment, Klein assumed, and occasionally claimed explicitly, that we can always receive interpretations unclouded by transference projections and phantasy, i.e., as neutral content with beneficent therapeutic intent. This is not easily reconciled with the view explicated above.

231. Or as Klein claimed earlier the task of the analyst is to reduce the influence of phantasy (unreal reality) and the force of authority so that "the reality principle will rule in the sphere of thought and established fact" (1975: 24).

232. Lacan will elsewhere intimate that confining captivation in turn becomes a condition for avowing primordial permeability and even amplifying its impact, though this is not where his stress falls.

233. Compare Denise Riley's *Words of Selves: Identification, Solidarity, Irony*, especially chapter 5, with her *Impersonal Passion: Language as Affect* (Durham: Duke University Press, 2005), especially chapter 1.

234. Cf. Hartmann and Kris, "The Genetic Approach in Psychoanalysis," *Psychoanalytic Studies of the Child* 1 (1945): 11–30.

235. "[W]hat is really at issue, at the end of analysis, [is] a twilight, an imaginary decline of the world [or decline of the world as imaginary], and even an experience at the limit of depersonalization" (*Seminar I*: 232). Soon hereafter, Lacan stressed that this "decline" must not wait for the final stages of the analysis.

236. *Seminar VII*: 213.

237. *E*: 723/853.

238. *E*: 497/595.

239. 1953: 12.

240. *Seminar VII*: 321.

241. *Seminar II*: 228–29/267.

242. *Seminar II*: 246; translation modified following Bruce Fink, *Lacan to the Letter: Reading* Écrits *Closely* (Minneapolis: University of Minnesota Press, 2004), 11.

243. *Seminar VI*, Jan. 7, 1959; also cf. Jacques Lacan, "The Neurotic's Individual Myth," *Psychoanalytic Quarterly* 48 (1979): 405–25.

244. E.g., "analysis as a science is always a science of the particular. The realization of an analysis is always a singular case, even though those singular cases lend themselves to some generality" (*Seminar I*: 29); "[a]nalysis is not a matter of discovering in a particular case the differential feature of the theory, and in so doing believe that one is explaining why your daughter is silent—for the point at issue is to *get her to speak*, and this effect proceeds from a type of intervention that has nothing to do with a differential feature" (*Seminar XI*: 11).

245. Cf. Grosz 1990: 13–14.

246. From *Horse Feathers*, 1932, music by Harry Rubin, lyrics by Bert Kalmar.

247. I appeal to the admittedly awkward language of "regulatory ideal" rather than "regulative ideal" in order to avoid the intimation that this ideal can be in principle fulfilled, as regulative ideals can for Kant. Lacan's directive is closer to tragic-impossible.

248. *Seminar VII*: 321: *Je propose que la seule chose dont on puisse être coupable, au moins dans la perspective analytique, c'est d'avoir cédé sur son désir. Cette proposition, recevable ou non dans telle ou telle éthique, exprime assez bien ce que nous constatons dans notre expérience. Au dernier terme, ce dont le sujet se sent effectivement coupable quand il fait de la culpabilité, de façon recevable ou non pour le directeur de conscience, c'est toujours, à la racine, pour autant qu'il a cédé sur son désir.*

249. Cited in Jean-Michel Rabaté, "Lacan's Turn to Freud," in Rabaté 2003: 12.

250. "[A] mistake exists in every form of knowledge, insofar as knowledge is nothing other than the crystallization of symbolic activity that it forgets, once constituted. In every knowledge already constituted there is thus a dimension of error, which consists in the forgetting of the creative function of truth in its nascent form" (*Seminar II*: 29).

251. At least this is the way Jacques-Allain Miller tends to read them. For some support for this position, cf. Jacques Lacan, "Yale University, Kanzer Seminar," *Scilicet* 6–7 (1976): especially p. 26. For a contrary reading of the mathemes as metaphors, cf. Joël

Dor, "The Epistemological Status of Lacan's Mathematical Paradigms," in *Disseminating Lacan*, ed. Pettigrew and Raffoul (Albany: SUNY Press, 1996); and Joel Dor, *L'a-scientificité de la psychanalyse, tome I: L'aliénation de la psychanalyse* and *tome II: La paradoxalité instauratrice* (Paris: Editions Universitaires, 1988/1989). Various interpretative approaches to the matheme can be found in Sherry Turkle, *Psychoanalytic Politics: Freud's French Revolution* (London: Free Association Books, 1978), 182ff; Nathalie Charraud, *Lacan et les mathématiques* (Paris: Anthropos, 1997); Nathalie Charraud, "Matheme," in *A Compendium of Lacanian Terms*, ed. Huguette Glowinski, Zita M. Marks, and Sara Murphy (London: Free Association Books, 2001); and Nathalie Charraud, "A Calculus of Convergence," in *Drawing the Soul: Schemas and Models in Psychoanalysis*, ed. Bernard Burgoyne (London: Karnac, 2003).

252. Though the inconsistencies, contradictions, about-faces, etc. can make reading Lacan extremely frustrating, we should not fail to appreciate the comedy of it all. Like Brecht, Lacan uses humor as a signal of dialectical reversal; dialectical reversals are figured as comic twists, unexpected shifts of perspective. Also of note with regard to Lacanian comedy is his use of "what is at stake" and "what ultimately matters"-type claims. By so frequently making "ultimate import"–type claims, and manifestly inconsistent claims at that, Lacan uses this form of claiming to incite something like free-floating attention: when everything can be a bearer of ultimate import, old hierarchies crumble and what had seemed itinerant indulgences now seem well worth while. This is the jester's gesture, a desacralizing effort.

253. Cf. *E*: 413/495.

254. Cf. *Seminar XIX*, Jan. 6, 1972; and *Le séminaire, Livre XI: Les quatre concepts fondamentaux de la psychanalyse*, ed. Jacques-Alain Miller (Paris: Seuil, 1973), 253.

255. Cited in Marcelle Marini, *Jacques Lacan: The French Context*, trans. Anne Tomiche (New Brunswick: Rutgers University Press, 1992), 65.

256. Cf. *E*: 412/493.

257. *Seminar XI*: 253; trans. modified following Fink 2004: 176–77.

258. Lacan makes this clear not only through his style but also through explicit statements such as "If it is true that our knowledge comes to the rescue of the ignorance of the analysand, it is no less true that we too are plunged in ignorance, insofar as we are ignorant of the symbolic constellation underlying the unconscious of the subject" (*Seminar I*: 78–79).

259. A few years later, Lacan became explicit about this, declaring that he was trying to confound his audience, offering them "the opportunity to not quite understand" (*Seminar III*: 164).

260. Cf. *Seminar XV* and *The Seminar of Jacques Lacan: The Other Side of Psychoanalysis, Book XVII*, trans. Russell Grigg (New York: W. W. Norton, 2007), 38, 106, 176.

261. Cf. *Seminar XVIII*, Dec. 2, 1971; *Seminar XIX*, March 8, 1972; and *Seminar XX*, 1.

262. Lacan was a prolific producer of neologisms, and it is none other than he who writes that neologisms are one of the signatures of psychosis (*Seminar III*: 43–44). Likewise, Lacan insists on interrogating all general terms and concepts for their lacunas, gaps, and inconsistencies, challenges the violent exaggeration of every universal, particularizes all generic assertions, and it is he who describes precisely these activities as hallmarks of hysteria.

263. Here Lévi-Strauss's recollection of Lacan's seminar seems apposite: "What was striking was the kind of radiant influence emanating from his person and from his diction, his gestures. I have seen quite a few shamans functioning in exotic societies, and I rediscovered there a kind of equivalent of the shaman's power. I confess that, as far as what I heard went, I didn't understand. And I found myself in the middle of an audience that seemed to understand" (cited in Elisabeth Roudinesco, *Jacques Lacan & Co.: A History of Psychoanalysis in France, 1925–1985*, trans. Jeffrey Mehlman [Chicago: University of Chicago Press], 362).

264. There is an obvious risk to this procedure, though. Since no reconstruction or exemplification ever seems quite right, there is an ongoing liability to unproductive prolixity. E.g., after a number of well-rehearsed formulas are applied to an expansive range of cultural artifacts without this disclosing much about either the formulas or the objects to which they are applied, the commentator feels pressed to repeat the procedure, recycling failure into the motivation to press on in a perverse rendition of Beckett's "All of old. Nothing else ever. Ever tried. Ever failed. No matter. Try again. Fail again. Fail better" (Samuel Beckett, *Worstword Ho*, collected in *Nowhow On* [New York: Grove, 2010]). Another dimension of the risk is this: due to Lacan's rigorous refusal to demonstrate, it is easy for, say, Zizek to fill in the blanks with Hegel. But it is precisely when Zizek's provisioning of a Hegelian infrastructure is convincing that he distorts Lacan's writings.

265. Of course not all manners of particularization will be valid, let alone equally valid. Of the unsuccessful, some will smack of indulgent self-absorption, others will involve such strained extensions that the coherence of the claim collapses. Of the successful, some will draw out dimensions of the claim that have been there, unnoticed, all along, others will proceed as permutations of the claim that, however strained, can be recognized as confluent with its historical spirit, as novel developments or genuine additions rather than changes of topic. Generally, a genuine discovery in this field will be of a viable theoretical intermediary, an elaboration of the claim that will have been able to be taken over and usefully employed by others, that in expressing its singular site of utterance resonates productively with other such sites, as in psychoanalysis when a higher-order concept becomes a theoretical intermediary as it is associated to—filled out and reworked by—a particular analysand in such a way that a new constellation of the concept emerges that can be usefully employed elsewhere.

266. Or, as he puts it more obscurely, "only in the dimension of truth can something be hidden" (*Seminar II*: 201).

267. Of course, there are ways of responding to the object that prohibit it from appearing or becoming as it otherwise would, as it regularly would, and, in this sense, as it would by nature. The vast preponderance of empirical evidence suggests, for instance, that a child's phantasies will develop differently depending on whether or not the child has been severely abused. Thus there is still reason to speak of *the object's* specific admixture of determinacy and indeterminacy and of the ways in which *its* becoming and appearing are distorted or impaired by our handling of it: the child's passionate attachments and phantasies will develop within given parameters unless something egregious occurs. What blocks this account from devolving into a vulgar subjective idealism is the acknowledgement of the object's tendential unfolding according to certain patterns that can be facilitated or thwarted by our responses to it. These patterns are norms of the ob-

ject's development against which certain responses to it can be characterized as violations and certain elaborations characterized as distortions.

268. "I always speak the truth. Not the whole truth, because there's no way to say it all. Saying it all is literally impossible: words fail. Yet it's through this very impossibility that truth holds onto the real" ("Television," *October* 40 [Spring, 1987]: 7.

269. Though his teaching cannot be consolidated into a consistent, systematically integrated theoretical doctrine, are not Lacan's repeated demands to mutually rearticulate subject and object somewhat doctrinaire? Though these seem to be doctrinaire demands to keep thinking, subjectivity, etc. in motion, even in frenetic motion, Lacan can risk this excess without devolving into doctrinalism because, he presumes, the Imaginary is irreducible and this means that his injunctions to mobilization will be inevitably counteracted by an impulse toward stasis, a sense of sufficiency, etc. The force of Lacan's injunctions to destabilization, destructuration, etc. responds to the unavoidable—and culturally reinforced—penchant to rest content that he identifies as Imaginary.

270. Confluent with this interpretive suggestion is Lacan's description of the human sciences, presumably including psychoanalysis, as "conjectural sciences" as opposed to "exact sciences" (*Seminar III*: 295–97).

271. "There is a danger in public discourse, precisely in so far as it is addressed to those nearest—Nietzsche knew this, a certain type of discourse can be addressed only to those furthest away" (*Seminar XI*: 23). Or, as Nietzsche put it, "The knight of knowledge must be able not only to love his enemies, but also to hate his friends" (*Ecce Homo*, trans. Anthony Ludovici [New York: Dover, 1994], 5). Lacan's address to "those furthest away" should be read in light of the utopian dimension of his discourse discussed above.

272. For instance, cf. Lacan's reformulation of the mirror stage in *Seminar VIII* and Marini 1992: 64.

273. Lacan's discourse is riddled with contradictions, both seeming and real. For instance, though Lacan repeatedly emphasizes that desire is the desire for recognition by the other as a void of desire, at other moments he boldly asserts that desire, "in the final analysis, always remains the desire of the body, desire of the body of the other and nothing but desire of his body" (*Seminar X*, May 8, 1963). Whether this is a real or seeming contradiction I leave as an open question. Or, to give another example, on the one hand, Lacan claims that the ego is the seat of defenses against the fracturing upsurge of desire, that "in analytic experience, the ego represents the center of all resistances to the treatment of symptoms" (*E*: 96/118), while, on the other hand, he asserts that "the ego is the metonymy of desire" (*E*: 534/640). A final example: Lacan warns against propelling "psychoanalysis down the path of the prejudices of science," since this would let "the entire essence of human reality escape" (*Seminar III*: 296); yet as massively averse to research programs that would reduce the subject to a predicable, manipulable object of knowledge as he is, he claims that the aim of interpretation is "reducing signifiers to their nonmeaning (lack of meaning) so as to find *the determinants of the whole of the subject's behavior*" (*Seminar XI*: 212; emphasis added).

274. For example, consider the unmarked tension between the following two claims by Freud: (1) Though a series of dreams is "distorted according to rule and couched in the usual dream-language, [it] could nevertheless be translated with certainty" (*SE XVIII*: 164). (2) "There is often a passage in even the most thoroughly interpreted dream which

has to be left obscure; this is because we become aware during the work of interpretation that at that point there is a tangle of dream-thoughts which cannot be unraveled and which moreover adds nothing to our knowledge of the content of the dream. This is the dream's navel, the spot where it reaches down into the unknown" (*SE V*: 525).

275. But even to admit an identification with the aggressor and side with Klein would be to take some distance from her. For identification with the aggressor is a concept developed by Klein's great adversary, Anna Freud. To admit to an identification with the aggressor would be to make a crucial concession to Klein's adversary, to admit the relevance of a concept and the work constellated around it that, at the very least, calls into question the exclusive privileging of the Kleinian apparatus. The Klein with whom one would identify would be a "compromised" Klein.

276. Strikingly, Lacan says elsewhere, "In order to know how to respond to the subject in analysis, the procedure is to determine *first of all* the place where his *ego* is . . . in other words, to know through whom and for whom the subject pose*s his question*. As long as this is not known, there will be risk of misunderstanding concerning the desire that is there to be recognized and concerning the object to whom this desire is addressed" (*E*: 250/303; initial emphasis added and trans. modified).

277. Or perversely manipulative of his analytic prowess? To anticipate, Klein will be figured as (1) a paragon of masculine violence, the bearer of the paternal function, the representative of the Law, and so, perhaps, as a viable target for (unconscious) Oedipal revolt against the Law and/or (unconscious) Oedipal rivalry, (2) an inept woman who feels rather than thinks, who has experience but no real theoretical competence, thus, perhaps, as an unconscious target for the displacement of and subsequent aggression against bodily life, dependency, vulnerability, etc. (*Seminar I*: 68), and (3) a terrorizing, over-intrusive, micromanaging mother, or maybe an infantilizing, paternalistic stage director or obtuse analyst who "only feed[s] him these kind of lines," (*Seminar I*: 85)—e.g., "*The station is mummy. Dick is going into mummy*" (Klein 1975: 225). If the figurations implied by these several assaults are combined, is Klein not figured as an inept yet brutal bearer of the Law, a self-complete synthesis of masculine and feminine who has no need of us and before whose might we cannot but tremble, and yet a weakling who cannot withstand our Oedipal revolt and rivalry? Would this not prompt unconscious fear of her world-annihilating reaction consequent upon the assaults against her to which she is all too susceptible? Is this not all the "reason" in the world to turn against her?

278. Cf. "Intervention on Transference," op cit.

279. Cf. Fink 1999: 163.

280. *Seminar IV*: 182, 188.

281. Insofar as it sets on display the limited scope of his theoretical claims and the limited propriety of his therapeutic orientation, Lacan's engagement with this particular case may function as a preemptive, global autocriticism. Taking up *this* case, this case for which his conceptual apparatus is so manifestly inadequate, this case that forces him to concede the value of therapeutic orientations he otherwise condemns, may be a way of insisting in advance of an anticipated rise to intellectual stardom on the provisionality and partiality of the perspective he is forging. Perhaps taking up this case was simply a mistake, an oversight. Or perhaps Lacan is the first, and maybe the best, anti-Lacanian.

282. "[T]here is never a subject without an ego" (*Seminar II*: 246). Though already in *Seminar II* (as if as a reparatory gesture) Lacan attributes psychosis to a want of Imaginary mediation between the Real and the Symbolic (cf. especially "Response to Jean Hyppolite's Commentary on Freud's *Verneinung*"), later, from *Seminar XX* on, he will be more frequently explicit about the proximity of *desire* and psychotic collapse.

283. Though this is often discussed in terms of breaking out of maternal-infant symbiosis and into language, this example of reorientation is highly overwrought, more a sensational dramatization than an original and controlling model. As an indication of the fabulous character of this overworked example, consider that, according to Lacan, the infant's cry is addressed to the mother and already "inserted in a synchronic world of cries organized in a symbolic system" (*Seminar IV*: 182, 188).

284. "Psychoanalysis is neither a Weltanschuung, nor a philosophy that claims to provide the key to the universe. It is governed by a particular aim, which is historically defined by the elaboration of the notion of the subject. It poses this notion in a new way, by leading the subject back to its signifying dependence" (*Seminar XI*: 77/90).

285. In the following pages, strictly as a matter of convenience, I will sometimes use the language of conceptuality as shorthand for all manners of discursive elaboration.

286. Cf. *Seminar XVII*: 110/127.

287. To put it in Hegelese, neither the "in-self" nor the "for us" can be sacrificed, and this refusal of sacrifice is, in an Adornoian idiom, what sustains dialectics as negative dialectics.

288. Cf. Robert Pippin, *Hegel's Idealism: The Satisfactions of Self-Consciousness* (Cambridge: Cambridge University Press, 1989).

289. At least she had plenty of acolytes on the British scene. A widespread, positive reception for Klein in France was, at the time of *Seminar I*, long forthcoming; and she still is much less well-known and respected there than she is in the United Kingdom and South America. And even though Kleinians now have a much stronger presence on the American analytic scene, her work did not gain popularity in the States until discussions of borderline disorders motivated a turn to her work.

290. Later in *Seminar VII* when Lacan describes "the bad object that Kleinian theory is concerned with" as "a capricious and arbitrary law, the law of the oracle, the law of signs in which the subject receives no guarantee from anywhere, the law in relation to which he has no *Sicherung*," is it not entirely clear that he is by no means attempting to understand Kleinian theory (73)? Is not Lacan's transcription of the Kleinian mother as *Das Ding* throughout *Seminar VII* (and especially on 106–107) further evidence that he is trying to shift the terms of the conversion, not to understand what Klein has to say?

291. "I only attack causes that are victorious; I may even wait until they become victorious" (Friedrich Nietzsche, *Ecce Homo*, sec. 7., trans. and ed. Walter Kaufmann [New York: Vintage: 1989]).

292. Is it then surprising that in September of 1953, very shortly before *Seminar I*, Lacan had subdued his virulent assaults on those forms of psychoanalysis that focus on the ego to the point of claiming that "[i]n order to know how to respond to the subject in analysis, the procedure is to determine first of all the place where his *ego* is . . . in other words, to know through whom and for whom the subject poses *his question*" (*E*: 250/303)?

293. "[F]ull speech is defined by the fact that it is identical to what it speaks about" (*E*: 319/381).

294. Compare Nietzsche: "For one may doubt, first, whether these are opposites at all, and secondly, whether these popular valuations and opposite values on which metaphysicians put their seal, are not maybe merely foreground estimates, only provisional perspectives, maybe even from some nook, maybe from below, frog perspectives, as it were, to borrow an expression painters use" (in "On the Prejudice of the Philosophers", *Beyond Good and Evil*, sec. 2, trans. Walter Kaufmann [New York: Vintage Books, 1966]).

295. Lacan's later turn to Borromean knots and various topographical figures may be read as a continuation of this mimetic strategy, that is, as an explication of the interlocked character of what had been, initially, "analytically" separated. Notice the parallel between Lacan's theoretical itinerary and his clinical procedure: just as the isolation of signifiers, punctuation, directing attention to the enigmatic, etc. often gives way to genetic reconstruction in late stages of Lacanian therapy, Lacan's late theoretical work allows the complex interconnections of what had been shaken up and isolated to slowly emerge.

296. In *Seminar XXII* and the few seminars that follow, which is to say in his waning years, Lacan explicitly enjoins his audience to interrogate the complex interrelations between the Imaginary, Symbolic, and Real rather than just turn away from the Imaginary or seek its dissipation.

297. Is it not also a sign of bemused, if also genuinely troubled, friendship that Lacan calls Klein "*la tripera*"—literally, "she who handles tripe or guts," often translated into English as "gut butcher"? Is this not a term of endearment as much as it is a ruthless flaying (thus mirroring?), even a term of praise? When Lacan calls Klein "*la tripera*," is he not surreptitiously praising her for digging into the deep and messy entrails of aggressive phantasies rather than forming an alliance with the client's ego in order to help him better adjust to social norms?

298. When Lacan later says that "the father is he who acknowledges us," does he not corroborate the link between symbolic recognition and the violence associated with the father/paternal metaphor (*Seminar VII*: 309)?

299. Though Lacan is highly cautious about attending to affect due to four interrelated risks—(1) obstructing comprehension of signifying forms of fantasy, (2) interpretive overconfidence on the side of the analyst, (3) resistance to interpretation and other forms of intervention on the side of the analysand, (4) forgetting that affect may be a consequence of other affects, e.g., a defense; generally, it's hard to argue with affect—the sorts of questions about affect raised above are fully consonant with his concerns here. Cf. *E*: 66–67/83, 206/248, 221/267.

300. Jacques Lacan, "Les complexes familiaux dans la formation de l'individu," in *Autres écrits* (Paris: Seuil, 2001), 34.

301. It is worth mentioning here that one of the major differences between Klein and contemporary Kleinians is that, for the latter, dependency and its incumbent anxieties are major concerns in the analysis of aggression and envy. While Klein claimed that constitutional aggression is the ineradicable source of primitive destructiveness and envy, contemporary Kleinians tend to claim that aggression and envy are flights from dependency and the anxieties pertaining to it. This brings them closer to Lacan, as does their practice of abstaining from countertransference disclosures and from responding to

requests, though not the reasoning behind it, i.e., fear that anything but neutrality and interpretation will be manipulated by the analysand's envy, specifically by an urge to spoil in order to get out of a situation of anxious dependency.

302. Notice in passing that by displaying intimacy with Klein, specifically a mutual penchant for violence, and thereby raising the prospect of an unavoidable complicity in violence, Lacan at once qualifies and sustains his criticisms of Klein. For recall that the violence of the social bond is, on Lacan's reading, manifestly on display in Klein's treatment of Dick but unaddressed by her and our psychic metabolism of this violence is what Lacan considers one of the biggest blind spots in Klein's treatment of Dick.

303. Betty Joseph, "Transference: The Total Situation," in *Melanie Klein Today: Theory and Practice, Volume 2; Mainly Practice*, ed. Elizabeth Bott Spillius (London: Routledge, 1988), 63. Originally published in the *International Journal of Psychoanalysis* 66 (1985): 447–54.

304. On this point Lacan is allied with someone who takes himself to be one of Lacan's most vehement critics: Gilles Deleuze. Cf. the discussion of "problematicity" in *The Logic of Sense*, ed. Constantin Boundas, trans. Mark Lester and Charles Stivale (New York: Columbia University Press, 1990).

305. In this light, might we discern a surreptitiously self-referential dimension of the following claim? "In order to know how to reply to the subject in analysis [recall Lacan's self-positioning as an analysand in his seminars], the procedure is to recognize first of all the place where his *ego* is . . . in other words, to know through whom and for whom the subject poses *his question*. So long as this is not known, there will be risk of misunderstanding concerning the desire that is there to be recognized and concerning the object to whom this desire is addressed" (*E*: 250/303). Might this be an instance of Lacan giving *his question*—the question of *desire*, basically, what is most central to his perspective—over to a Kleinian reading?

306. "War is another matter. I am warlike by nature. Attacking is one of my instincts. Being *able* to be an enemy, *being* an enemy—perhaps that presupposes a strong nature. It needs objects of resistance; hence it *looks for* what resists: the *aggressive* pathos belongs just as necessarily to strength as vengefulness and rancor belong to weakness. . . . The strength of those who attack can be measured in a way by the opposition they require: every growth is indicated by the search for a mighty opponent—or problem. . . . The task is *not* simply to master what happens to resist, but what requires us to stake all our strength, suppleness, and fighting skill—opponents that are our *equals*" (*Ecce Homo*, sec. 7).

307. Likewise, we might ask, Is the exaggerated primacy of the paternal in Lacan responsive to the exaggerated primacy of the maternal in Klein? Might the primacy of Oedipal relations in Lacan, especially the Lacan of the '50s, respond to primacy of the pre-Oedipal in Klein? Broadly, can one *read* Lacan without Klein in view?

308. Perhaps, to risk a hypothesis that has been hinted at throughout, Lacan's concern with cultivating continual critical scrupulousness, i.e., generating effective resistance to authority, is responsive to the memory of fascism. Recall that we are dealing with the seminar of 1953–1954.

Index

About the Author

Adam Rosen-Carole is visiting assistant professor of philosophy at Bard College.

www.ingramcontent.com/pod-product-compliance
Lightning Source LLC
Chambersburg PA
CBHW051253200926
51612CB00001B/27
9780739164563